ELIZABETH BARRETT BROWNING

Aurora Leigh and other Poems

Edited by JOHN ROBERT GLORNEY BOLTON
and JULIA BOLTON HOLLOWAY

PENGUIN BOOKS

PENGUIN BOOKS

Published by the Penguin Group
Penguin Books Ltd, 80 Strand, London WC2R 0RL, England
Penguin Putnam Inc., 375 Hudson Street, New York, New York 10014, USA
Penguin Books Australia Ltd, Ringwood, Victoria, Australia
Penguin Books Canada Ltd, 10 Alcorn Avenue, Toronto, Ontario, Canada M4V 3B2
Penguin Books India (P) Ltd, 11 Community Centre, Panchsheel Park, New Delhi – 110 017, India
Penguin Books (NZ) Ltd, Cnr Rosedale and Airborne Roads, Albany, Auckland, New Zealand
Penguin Books (South Africa) (Pty) Ltd, 24 Sturdee Avenue, Rosebank 2196 South Africa

Penguin Books Ltd, Registered Offices: 80 Strand, London WC2R 0RL, England

www.penguin.com

First published 1995
7

Selection, Preface and Notes copyright © Julia Bolton Holloway, 1995
All rights reserved

Set in 10/11.5 pt Monotype Ehrhardt
Typeset by Datix International Limited, Bungay, Suffolk
Printed in England by Clays Ltd, St Ives plc

ELIZABETH BARRETT BROWNING
AURORA LEIGH AND OTHER POEMS

ELIZABETH BARRETT BROWNING was born in County Durham in 1806. As a child she studied Italian, Greek and Hebrew and read Lord Byron's poetry and Madame de Staël's novels in her father's mansion, Hope End, in Herefordshire, built with Jamaican slave wealth. Crippled in childhood, she also lost her favourite brother, Edward, when he drowned in Torbay. With the freeing of the slaves the Barretts had to sell Hope End and came to live in Wimpole Street in London. Elizabeth Barrett was encouraged by the leading writers of her day in her essay writing and in her poetry; her poem *The Cry of the Children* (1843) was read in the House of Lords and influenced legislation to protect working children. At the age of forty, in September 1846, she eloped from Wimpole Street with Robert Browning following their epistolary courtship. The couple came to Italy with her maid, Elizabeth Wilson, and her dog, Flush, where Elizabeth recovered enough from her invalidism and dependency upon laudanum to bear the child Pen, and where she wrote: *The Runaway Slave at Pilgrim's Point* (1848), against slavery in the United States; *Casa Guidi Windows* (1851), against the oppression of Italy by foreign nations; and *Aurora Leigh* (1856), against the oppression of women and children. Her publications and money from her family supported her husband and child, but gradually Robert and Elizabeth grew apart. She died in 1861, in Casa Guidi, worn out by illness, addiction and arguments with Robert. She keenly wanted her son to study modern languages, the Arts and diplomacy while Robert wanted him to study the Classics and be an English gentleman. At her death Robert took Pen to England but when he grew up, after failing Classics at Balliol, he became an artist and returned to live in his parents' beloved Italy. Robert Browning died in old age in Venice and is buried in Westminster Abbey. His wife lies apart from him in Florence's Protestant Cemetery.

JOHN ROBERT GLORNEY BOLTON was born in Warwick, attended Ardingly, then worked at the Bodleian Library during the First World War. He matriculated to St Catherine's Society of Oxford University, leaving there to write for the *Yorkshire Post*, then the *Times of India*. He covered the Salt March and was Gandhi's friend and biographer, writing *The Tragedy of Gandhi*. He also wrote *Peasant and Prince*, *The Dome of Devotion*, *Christopher Wren*, *Czech Tragedy*, *Pétain* and (with his wife) a dual autobiography, *Two Lives Converge*. He lived in Italy from 1954 until his death, working for the United Nations in Rome, writing a biography of Pope John XXIII, *Roman Century* and an unfinished biography of Elizabeth Barrett Browning.

His daughter, JULIA BOLTON HOLLOWAY, was born in Devonshire Place, London, educated at St Mary's School, Sussex, and received her PhD in Medieval Studies from the University of California at Berkeley. She taught at Princeton University and the University of Colorado, Boulder, and has published *Twice-Told Tales: Brunetto Latino and Dante Alighieri*, *The Pilgrim and the Book: A Study of Dante, Langland and Chaucer*, *Equally in God's Image: Women in the Middle Ages* and *Saint Bride and Her Book: Birgitta of Sweden's Revelations*. She was Acting Curator of Casa Guidi in Florence, 1987–8. After raising her three sons, Richard, Colin and Jonathan, she retired as Professor Emerita to enter an Anglican convent.

CONTENTS

PREFACE

This edition of Elizabeth Barrett Browning's selected poetry, apart from *Aurora Leigh* and 'Sonnets from the Portuguese', presents texts from the earliest printed versions, compared with their manuscripts at Baylor University's Armstrong Browning Library and London's British Library.

Aurora Leigh was dedicated on 17 October 1856 to John Kenyon and published by Chapman and Hall in that year (though it bears the publication date of 1857). *Aurora Leigh*'s text is given from the final revises for the first English edition, which were prepared by Robert Browning, Elizabeth Barrett Browning's literary agent, the corrections being in his handwriting, and then autographed (London, 20 October 1856) by Elizabeth for 'Mr. Francis of New York', to be used in turn for the first American edition. This text, now in the Robert Taylor Collection, Princeton University Library, is chosen because it is closest to the spontaneity of the first English published *Aurora Leigh*, while also being the text used for the nineteenth-century American editions of the poem. Later corrections supplied by Robert Browning and Elizabeth Barrett Browning (and which are adopted in twentieth-century critical editions) make the text more laboured.

The 'Sonnets from the Portuguese' text does not follow the earliest printed edition of 1850, but is given from Elizabeth's manuscript notebook, now in the British Library, which was written by her at 50 Wimpole Street secretly during her courtship in 1846, then brought with her to Italy and only shyly presented to Robert at Bagni di Lucca where they, their child and his nurse, had gone to stay in the mountains away from the heat of Florence in 1849.

Elizabeth Barrett Browning herself never received a copy of the Boston *Liberty Bell* in which *The Runaway Slave at Pilgrim's Point* was thought to have appeared. Nor does the Baylor University Armstrong Browning Library own a copy. The text given

here is that from the manuscript at Baylor and from the 1849 and
1850 London editions.

Elizabeth Barrett Browning tended, though not always, to use
two rather than three ellipses (. .), ampersands (&s) for ands, her
exclamation marks lack the point (which cannot be reproduced
typographically), and she often employed equal signs (=) for
dashes in manuscript; her publishers regularized these to varying
degrees. Her printer for *Aurora Leigh* chose to use single quotation
marks within single quotation marks, and we present a diplomatic
text of that first edition. For the selected poems we use the
punctuation practices of the *Aurora Leigh* 1856 edition, except for
the 1846 manuscript text of the 'Sonnets from the Portuguese'.
Her footnotes are usually supplied as such, her endnotes being
given in the Notes followed by her initials: [EBB].

Elizabeth Barrett Browning wrote of Michelangelo's Medici Tomb
sculpture of Aurora, Dawn, in *Casa Guidi Windows* (1851) and
Aurora Leigh (1856) to convey her love of Florence, her anguish
for Italy, and her loyalty to the Risorgimento. Her poetry worked
for the liberation of the oppressed, whether they were nations or
slaves, women or children. The Notes give the bibliographical,
biographical, political and intertextual contexts of the poems and
discuss Elizabeth Barrett Browning's allusions.

The poems of this edition ideally should be read with her
sprightly and uncomplaining, learned yet joyous letters, especially
those written between herself and Robert during their Wimpole
Street courtship. Better yet, this edition should be read with the
entire Regency period library at Hope End of biblical and classical
texts in their original languages, as Elizabeth Barrett Browning
knew them, or in translation, as in the Penguin Classics, including
volumes of Homer, Aeschylus, Sophocles, Plato, Apuleius, Virgil
and Dante, to be joined by the works of Chaucer, Langland,
Milton, Shakespeare, Fielding, Byron and Dickens, and of
women's books, which she also read avidly though Robert Brown-
ing despised them, such as Mary Wollstonecraft's *A Vindication
of the Rights of Woman* (1792) and Madame de Staël's *Corinne, ou
Italie* (1807), George Sand's *Consuelo* (1842) and Charlotte
Brontë's *Jane Eyre* (1847). To these one could add men's contex-
tual books, such as Robert Browning's *The Ring and the Book*

(1868–9), Nathaniel Hawthorne's *The Marble Faun* (1860) and *The Blithedale Romance* (1852), Henry James's *Princess Casamassima* (1886) and *William Wetmore Story and his Friends* (1903), which fed upon the lives and works of women associated with the Italian Risorgimento, such as Elizabeth Barrett Browning, Margaret Fuller Ossoli, Jesse White Mario, Harriet Beecher Stowe, Anna Brownell Jameson, Isa Blagden, Harriet Hosmer, Cristina Trivulzio, Princess Belgioioso, Theodosia Garrow Trollope and Anita Garibaldi.

ACKNOWLEDGEMENTS

The editors acknowledge their gratitude to the British Council, Rome, the British Institute, Florence, the Library of the University of California at Berkeley, the Robert Taylor Collection at Princeton University, Quincy University's Library, London's British Library, Baylor University's Armstrong Browning Library, the Browning Institute of New York and Florence and the Friends of Casa Guidi.

The text of *Aurora Leigh* is published with permission from the Department of Rare Books and Special Collections (Robert Taylor Collection), Princeton University Libraries; John Murray granted permission for the study and use of Elizabeth Barrett Browning manuscript and copyright materials.

TABLE OF DATES

includes unsigned essays by EBB and RB. EBB meets Anna Jameson, the art critic and author of *The Loves of the Poets*. EBB publishes *Poems*, which include 'Lady Geraldine's Courtship'. Flush again stolen, ransomed.

1845 *10 January*: Courtship by letter with RB begins, prompted by her reference to him in 'Lady Geraldine's Courtship', her *Poems* being given to his family by Kenyon.

1846 EBB writes still untitled 'Sonnets from the Portuguese'. *31 July*: She visits Westminster Abbey and makes other expeditions towards recovery. *5 September*: EBB goes personally to negotiate ransom with dog-robbers for Flush. *12 September*: Marriage to RB, EBB's maid, Elizabeth Wilson, her witness. *19 September*: EBB, RB, Wilson and Flush leave for the Continent, meeting Anna Jameson and her niece Gerardine in Paris, on 21 September, who travel on with them to Italy, visiting Petrarch and Laura's Vaucluse, near Avignon, on the way to Pisa.

1847 *4 April*: Easter, Margaret Fuller meets Marchese Angelo Ossoli in St Peter's, Rome. *17 April*: Brownings come to Florence. EBB and RB meet the American sculptor, William Wetmore Story. *14 July*: Brownings visit Vallombrosa, lease Casa Guidi.

1848 *10 May*: Hugh Stuart Boyd's death. *5 September*: Angelo Eugenio Filippo Ossoli born to Margaret Fuller. EBB sends *The Runaway Slave at Pilgrim's Point* to be published, Boston, the *Liberty Bell*; writes *Casa Guidi Windows*, Part One; reads *Jane Eyre*.

1849 *9 March*: Robert Weidemann ('Pen') Browning born, EBB's maid, Elizabeth Wilson, having urged EBB to stop taking opium long enough to have successful pregnancy. Austrians arrive in Florence at the Grand Duke's invitation to take over control of Tuscany. *30 June*: Brownings go to stay at Bagni di Lucca, EBB gives RB the untitled manuscript of 'Sonnets from the Portuguese' written secretly during their courtship; RB urges their publication, EBB suggests title of 'Sonnets from the Bosnian', RB choosing 'Sonnets from the Portuguese'. Margaret Fuller works under Princess Belgioioso (James's *Princess Casamassima*) in Roman hospitals during French siege against Risorgimento's Roman

Republic. *29 June*: Rome falls to French, Anita Garibaldi dies in childbirth during flight.

1850 *April*: EBB's friendship with Margaret Fuller. *1 June*: The *Athenaeum* proposes EBB for Poet Laureate at death of William Wordsworth. *19 July*: Margaret Fuller's death at sea. *28 July*: EBB's fourth miscarriage. EBB publishes *Poems*; reads *Shirley*.

1851 Brownings visit England and see the Great Exhibition at Crystal Palace with Hiram Powers's *Greek Slave*. EBB publishes *Casa Guidi Windows*, Parts One and Two.

1852 *14 February*: EBB meets George Sand. American sculptor Hiram Powers in Florence when the Brownings return; later, they meet Harriet Hosmer in Rome. Hawthorne publishes *The Blithedale Romance*.

1854 RB and EBB publish *Two Poems*, which includes 'A Plea for the Ragged Schools of London'. Flush dies and is buried in cellar at Casa Guidi.

1855 *27 September*: Tennyson reads *Maud* to Brownings and Dante Gabriel Rossetti. RB publishes *Men and Women*.

1856 EBB publishes *Aurora Leigh*, dedicates poem to Kenyon. *3 December*: Kenyon's death, leaves Brownings £11,000 in his will. EBB's *Poems* reissued in three volumes.

1857 *17 April*: Death of EBB's father following eleven years of bitter estrangement from his daughter.

1859 *March*: RB, by command of the Queen, dines with the Prince of Wales in Rome.

1860 EBB publishes *Poems before Congress*. *June*: RB finds 'The Old Yellow Book', of 1698 Roman trial of Guido Franceschini for the murder of his wife, Pompilia, in the San Lorenzo market, from which RB composes *The Ring and the Book*. Hawthorne publishes *The Marble Faun*, Donatello being modelled on RB.

1861 *18 February*: Italy, except for Papal States, accepts government by Victor Emmanuel II, King of Sardinia and Piedmont. *20 May*: Hans Christian Andersen and RB recite 'The Ugly Duckling' and 'The Pied Piper of Hamelin' at children's party. *6 June*: Death of Risorgimento's Camille Cavour. *29 June*: EBB's death, Casa Guidi. *1 July*: Funeral in Florence. *27 July*: RB and Pen leave Florence, RB never to return there.

1862 EBB's *Last Poems*, edited by RB, published.

1863 EBB's *The Greek Christian Poets and the English Poets*, edited by RB, published; George Eliot publishes *Romola*, which she had researched in Florence in 1861.

1868–9 RB publishes *The Ring and the Book*.

1870 Italy, including Papal States, a free and unified nation.

1889 RB dies in his son's Palazzo Rezzonico, Venice; buried in Westminster Abbey.

1912 EBB and RB's son, Pen, dies in Asolo, the Venetian town celebrated by RB in *Pippa Passes*. Pen had hoped to make Casa Guidi a shrine to his parents; Balliol College, Oxford, to have the manuscript of *Aurora Leigh* (he had given Balliol his portrait of RB; EBB's Castellani ring was presented to Balliol by Mrs Orr).

1913 The Brownings' manuscripts and art treasures, which Pen had intended for Casa Guidi and Balliol, sold at auction by Sotheby's.

FURTHER READING

Editions

The Battle of Marathon, London: Printed for W. Lindsell, 1820.

Essay on Mind, with Other Poems, London: James Duncan, 1826.

Sir Uvedale Price, *An Essay on the Modern Pronunciation of the Greek and Latin Languages*, 1827. [EBB anonymously co-authored work.]

Prometheus Bound, Translated from the Greek of Aeschylus, and Miscellaneous Poems, by the Translator, Author of 'An Essay on Mind', with Other Poems, London: A. J. Valpy, 1833.

The Seraphim, and Other Poems, by Elizabeth B. Barrett, Author of a Translation of the 'Prometheus Bound', Etc., London: Saunders and Otley, 1838.

Richard Hengist Horne, ed., *The Poems of Chaucer Modernized*, London: Whittaker, 1841.

Poems, by Elizabeth B. Barrett, Author of 'The Seraphim', Etc., 1st edn., 2 vols., London: Edward Moxon, 1844.

Richard Hengist Horne, ed., *A New Spirit of the Age*, London: Smith, Elder, 1844; repr. New York: Garland, 1986. [Includes EBB's unsigned essays.]

The Runaway Slave at Pilgrim's Point, Boston: *Liberty Bell*, 1848; London: Edward Moxon, 1849; London: Chapman and Hall, 1850.

Poems, 2nd edn., 2 vols., London: Chapman and Hall, 1850.

Casa Guidi Windows: A Poem, London: Chapman and Hall, 1851.

Poems, by Elizabeth Barrett Browning, 2 vols., London: Chapman and Hall, 1853.

Two Poems, by Elizabeth Barrett and Robert Browning, London: Chapman and Hall, 1854.

Poems, 3rd edn., 3 vols., London: Chapman and Hall, 1856.

Aurora Leigh, London: Chapman and Hall, 1856, 1857.

Poems before Congress, London: Chapman and Hall, 1860.

Last Poems, London: Chapman and Hall, 1862. [Dedicated by Robert Browning to 'Grateful Florence'.]

The Greek Christian Poets and the English Poets, London: Chapman and Hall, 1863.

Psyche Apocalypté and 'Queen Annelida and False Arcite' from *Chaucer Modernized*, see Townshend Mayer, ed., *Letters*, 1877.

Charlotte Porter and Helen A. Clarke, eds., *The Complete Works of Elizabeth Barrett Browning*, 6 vols., New York: T. Y. Crowell, 1900; repr., New York: AMS Press, 1973.

Julia Markus, ed., *Casa Guidi Windows*, New York: Browning Institute, 1977.

Cora Kaplan, ed., *Aurora Leigh, and Other Poems*, The Women's Press, 1978. [Repr. facsimile, 1900 edn.]

Gardner Blake Taplin, ed., *Aurora Leigh*, Chicago, 1979. [Repr. facsimile, 1856 edn.]

Miroslava Wien Dow, ed., *A Variorum Edition of Elizabeth Barrett Browning's Sonnets from the Portuguese*, Troy, New York: Whitston Publishing Company, 1980.

Margaret Forster, ed., *Elizabeth Barrett Browning: Selected Poems*, Baltimore: Johns Hopkins University Press, 1988. [Excludes *Aurora Leigh*.]

Margaret Reynolds, ed., *Aurora Leigh*, Athens: Ohio University Press, 1992.

Letters

Townshend Mayer, ed., *Letters of Elizabeth Barrett Browning Addressed to Richard Hengist Horne, Author of 'Orion', Etc.*, 2 vols., London, 1877.

Frederic Kenyon, ed., *The Letters of Elizabeth Barrett Browning*, 2 vols., London: Smith, Elder, 1897.

Robert Wiedemann Barrett Browning, ed., *The Letters of Robert Browning and Elizabeth Barrett Barrett, 1845–1846*, 2 vols., London, 1899.

Leonard Huxley, ed., *Elizabeth Barrett Browning: Letters to her Sister, 1846–1859*, London, 1929.

Martha Hale Shackford, ed., *Letters from Elizabeth Barrett to B. R. Haydon*, London, 1939.

Edward C. McAleer, ed., *Dearest Isa: Robert Browning's Letters to Isabella Blagden*, Austin, Texas, 1951.

Betty Miller, ed., *Elizabeth Barrett Browning to Miss Mitford*, London, 1954.

Barbara P. McCarthy, ed., *Elizabeth Barrett to Mr Boyd*, New Haven, 1955.

Paul Landis and Ronald B. Freeman, eds., *Letters of the Brownings to George Barrett*, Urbana, 1958.

Gertrude Reese Hudson, ed., *Browning to his American Friends: Letters between the Brownings, the Storys and James Russell Lowell, 1841–1890*, London, 1965.

Elvan Kintner, ed., *The Letters of Robert Browning and Elizabeth Barrett Barrett 1845–1846*, 2 vols., Harvard, 1969.

Willard Bissell Pope, ed., *Invisible Friends: The Correspondence of Elizabeth Barrett Browning and Benjamin Robert Haydon, 1842–1845*, Cambridge, Massachusetts, 1972.

Peter N. Heydon and Philip Kelley, eds., *Elizabeth Barrett Browning's Letters to Mrs David Ogilvy 1849–1861*, New York, 1973.

Meredith B. Raymond and Mary Rose Sullivan, eds., *The Letters of Elizabeth Barrett Browning and Mary Russell Mitford 1836–1854*, 3 vols., Winfield, Kansas, 1983.

Philip Kelley and Ronald Hudson, eds., *The Brownings' Correspondence, 1809–?*, Winfield, Kansas: Wedgestone Press, 1984–?.

Daniel Karlin, ed., *The Courtship of Robert Browning and Elizabeth Barrett*, Oxford, 1985.

Michael Meredith, ed., *More than Friend: The Letters of Robert Browning to Katherine de Kay Bronson*, Winfield, Kansas, 1985.

Biography

Giuliana Artom Treves, *The Golden Ring: The Anglo-Florentines 1847–1862*, trans. Sylvia Sprigge, London, 1956.

Elizabeth Berridge, *The Barretts at Hope End: The Early Diary of Elizabeth Barrett Browning*, London, 1974.

The Browning Collections: A Reconstruction, with Other Memora-

bilia, Philip Kelley and Betty A. Coley, eds., Winfield, Kansas, 1984.

Helen Cooper, *Elizabeth Barrett Browning, Woman and Artist*, Chapel Hill, 1988.

Joseph Jay Deiss, *The Roman Years of Margaret Fuller*, New York, 1969.

Kate Field, 'English Authors in Florence', *Atlantic Monthly* (December, 1865), p. 139.

'Elizabeth Barrett Browning', *Atlantic Monthly* (September, 1861), pp. 368–76.

'Last Days of Walter Savage Landor', *Atlantic Monthly* (April, 1886), pp. 387–8.

Margaret Forster, *Elizabeth Barrett Browning: A Biography*, London, 1988.

Alethea Hayter, *Mrs Browning: A Poet's Work and Its Setting*, Yale University Press, 1962.

Dorothy Hewlett, *Elizabeth Barrett Browning: A Life*, New York, 1953, 1972.

Henry James, *William Wetmore Story and His Friends from Letters, Diaries, and Recollections*, 2 vols., Boston, 1903.

Angela Leighton, *Elizabeth Barrett Browning*, Bloomington, 1986.

Edward McAleer, *The Brownings of Casa Guidi*, New York, 1979.

Jeanette Marks, *The Family of the Barrett: A Colonial Romance*, New York, 1938.

Michael Meredith, *Meeting the Brownings*, New York, 1986.

Betty Miller, *Robert Browning: A Portrait*, London, 1952.

Sotheby, Wilkinson and Hodge, *The Browning Collections: Catalogue of Oil Paintings, Drawings & Prints; Autograph Letters and Manuscripts; Books; Statuary, Furniture, Tapestries, and Works of Art, the Property of R. W. Barrett Browning, Esq. (Deceased), of Asolo, Veneto and La Torre all' Antella, near Florence, Italy, Including Many Relics of His Parents, Robert and Elizabeth Barrett Browning*, London, 1913.

Sotheby and Co., *Catalogue of the Papers of Lt. Col. Harry Peyton Moulton-Barrett, Decd., of High Park, Bideford, Devon, Nephew of Elizabeth Barrett Browning*, London, 1937.

Gardner Blake Taplin, *The Life of Elizabeth Barrett Browning*, New Haven, 1957; New York, 1970.

Maisie Ward, *Robert Browning and His World: The Private Face,*
    1812–1861, London, 1967.
    The Tragi-Comedy of Pen Browning, New York, 1972.
Lilian Whiting, *The Brownings: Their Life and Art*, London,
    1911.
    A Study of Elizabeth Barrett Browning, London, 1899.
    Women Who Have Ennobled Life, Philadelphia, 1915.
Virginia Woolf, *Flush: A Biography*, London: Hogarth Press, 1933.

Criticism and Scholarship

Browning Institute Studies, 1971–90. [Includes Annotated Bibliography on Robert and Elizabeth Barrett Browning.]
Deirdre David, *Intellectual Women and Victorian Patriarchy: Harriet Martineau, Elizabeth Barrett Browning, George Eliot*,
    Ithaca, New York: Cornell University Press, 1987.
George Eliot, 'Belles Lettres', *The Westminster Review* (January,
    1857), pp. 306–10. [Reviewing EBB.]
Sandra Gilbert, 'From *Patria* to *Matria*: EBB's Risorgimento',
    PMLA, 99 (1984), pp. 194–211.
Julia Bolton Holloway, '*Aurora Leigh and Jane Eyre*', *Brontë
    Society Transactions*, 17 (1977), pp. 126–32.
    'Death and the Emperor in Dante, Browning, Dickinson and
    Stevens', *Studies in Medievalism*, 2 (1983), pp. 67–72.
Dorothy Mermin, *Elizabeth Barrett Browning: The Origins of a
    New Poetry*, Chicago, 1989.
    Godiva's Ride: Women of Letters in England, 1830–1880, Bloomington, 1993.
Ellen Moers, *Literary Women: The Great Writers*, Garden City,
    1977.
Coventry Patmore, 'Mrs Browning's *Poems* and *Aurora Leigh*',
    The North British Review, 26 (1857), pp. 443–62.
J. M. S. Tompkins, '*Aurora Leigh*: The Fawcett Lecture, 1961',
    Bedford College, 1962.
Thomas J. Wise, *A Bibliography of Elizabeth Barrett Browning*,
    London, 1918.
Virginia Woolf, 'Aurora Leigh', *The Common Reader*, 2nd series,
    London, 1932.

AURORA LEIGH (1856)

First Book

Of writing many books there is no end;
And I who have written much in prose and verse
For others' uses, will write now for mine,—
Will write my story for my better self,
As when you paint your portrait for a friend,   5
Who keeps it in a drawer and looks at it
Long after he has ceased to love you, just
To hold together what he was and is.

I, writing thus, am still what men call young;
I have not so far left the coasts of life   10
To travel inland, that I cannot hear
That murmur of the outer Infinite
Which unweaned babies smile at in their sleep
When wondered at for smiling; not so far,
But still I catch my mother at her post   15
Beside the nursery-door, with finger up,
'Hush, hush—here's too much noise!' while her sweet eyes
Leap forward, taking part against her word
In the child's riot. Still I sit and feel
My father's slow hand, when she had left us both,   20
Stroke out my childish curls across his knee;
And hear Assunta's daily jest (she knew
He liked it better than a better jest)
Inquire how many golden scudi went
To make such ringlets. O my father's hand,   25
Stroke the poor hair down, stroke it heavily,—
Draw, press the child's head closer to thy knee!
I'm still too young, too young to sit alone.

*

I write. My mother was a Florentine,
30   Whose rare blue eyes were shut from seeing me
When scarcely I was four years old; my life,
A poor spark snatched up from a failing lamp,
Which went out therefore. She was weak and frail;
She could not bear the joy of giving life—
35   The mother's rapture slew her. If her kiss
Had left a longer weight upon my lips,
It might have steadied the uneasy breath,
And reconciled and fraternised my soul
With the new order. As it was, indeed,
40   I felt a mother-want about the world,
And still went seeking, like a bleating lamb
Left out at night, in shutting up the fold,—
As restless as a nest-deserted bird
Grown chill through something being away, though what
45   It knows not. I, Aurora Leigh, was born
To make my father sadder, and myself
Not overjoyous, truly. Women know
The way to rear up children, (to be just,)
They know a simple, merry, tender knack
50   Of tying sashes, fitting baby-shoes,
And stringing pretty words that make no sense,
And kissing full sense into empty words;
Which things are corals to cut life upon,
Although such trifles: children learn by such,
55   Love's holy earnest in a pretty play,
And get not over-early solemnised,—
But seeing, as in a rose-bush, Love's Divine,
Which burns and hurts not,—not a single bloom,—
Become aware and unafraid of Love.
60   Such good do mothers. Fathers love as well
—Mine did, I know,—but still with heavier brains,
And wills more consciously responsible,
And not as wisely, since less foolishly;
So mothers have God's licence to be missed.

*

65 My father was an austere Englishman,
    Who, after a dry life-time spent at home
    In college-learning, law, and parish talk,
    Was flooded with a passion unaware,
    His whole provisioned and complacent past
70 Drowned out from him that moment. As he stood
    In Florence, where he had come to spend a month
    And note the secret of Da Vinci's drains,
    He musing somewhat absently perhaps
    Some English question . . whether men should pay
75 The unpopular but necessary tax
    With left or right hand—in the alien sun
    In that great square of the Santissima,
    There drifted past him (scarcely marked enough
    To move his comfortable island-scorn,)
80 A train of priestly banners, cross and psalm,—
    The white-veiled rose-crowned maidens holding up
    Tall tapers, weighty for such wrists, aslant
    To the blue luminous tremor of the air,
    And letting drop the white wax as they went
85 To eat the bishop's wafer at the church;
    From which long trail of chanting priests and girls,
    A face flashed like a cymbal on his face
    And shook with silent clangour brain and heart,
    Transfiguring him to music. Thus, even thus,
90 He too received his sacramental gift
    With eucharistic meanings; for he loved.

    And thus beloved, she died. I've heard it said
    That but to see him in the first surprise
    Of widower and father, nursing me,
95 Unmothered little child of four years old,
    His large man's hands afraid to touch my curls,
    As if the gold would tarnish,—his grave lips
    Contriving such a miserable smile,
    As if he knew needs must, or I should die,
100 And yet 'twas hard,—would almost make the stones
    Cry out for pity. There's a verse he set
    In Santa Croce to her memory,

'Weep for an infant too young to weep much
When death removed this mother'—stops the mirth
105 To-day on women's face when they walk
With rosy children hanging on their gowns,
Under the cloister, to escape the sun
That scorches in the piazza. After which,
He left our Florence, and made haste to hide
110 Himself, his prattling child, and silent grief,
Among the mountains above Pelago;
Because unmothered babes, he thought, had need
Of mother nature more than others use,
And Pan's white goats, with udders warm and full
115 Of mystic contemplations, come to feed
Poor milkless lips of orphans like his own—
Such scholar-scraps he talked, I've heard from friends,
For even prosaic men, who wear grief long,
Will get to wear it as a hat aside
120 With a flower stuck in't. Father, then, and child,
We lived among the mountains many years,
God's silence on the outside of the house,
And we, who did not speak too loud, within;
And old Assunta to make up the fire,
125 Crossing herself whene'er a sudden flame
Which lightened from the firewood, made alive
That picture of my mother on the wall.
The painter drew it after she was dead;
And when the face was finished, throat and hands,
130 Her cameriera carried him, in hate
Of the English-fashioned shroud, the last brocade
She dressed in at the Pitti. 'He should paint
No sadder thing than that,' she swore, 'to wrong
Her poor signora.' Therefore very strange
135 The effect was. I, a little child, would crouch
For hours upon the floor, with knees drawn up,
And gaze across them, half in terror, half
In adoration, at the picture there,—
That swan-like supernatural white life,
140 Just sailing upward from the red stiff silk
Which seemed to have no part in it, nor power

To keep it from quite breaking out of bounds:
For hours I sate and stared. Assunta's awe
And my poor father's melancholy eyes
145 Still pointed that way. That way, went my thoughts
When wondering beyond sight. And as I grew
In years, I mixed, confusedly, unconsciously,
Whatever I last read or heard or dreamed,
Abhorrent, admirable, beautiful,
150 Pathetical, or ghastly, or grotesque,
With still that face . . . which did not therefore change,
But kept the mystic level of all forms,
And fears and admirations; was by turns
Ghost, fiend, and angel, fairy, witch, and sprite,—
155 A dauntless Muse who eyes a dreadful Fate,
A loving Psyche who loses sight of Love,
A still Medusa, with mild milky brows
All curdled and all clothed upon with snakes
Whose slime falls fast as sweat will; or, anon,
160 Our Lady of the Passion, stabbed with swords
Where the Babe sucked; or, Lamia in her first
Moonlighted pallor, ere she shrunk and blinked,
And, shuddering, wriggled down to the unclean;
Or, my own mother, leaving her last smile
165 In her last kiss, upon the baby-mouth
My father pushed down on the bed for that,—
Or my dead mother, without smile or kiss,
Buried at Florence. All which images,
Concentred on the picture, glassed themselves
170 Before my meditative childhood, . . as
The incoherencies of change and death
Are represented fully, mixed and merged,
In the smooth fair mystery of perpetual Life.

And while I stared away my childish wits
175 Upon my mother's picture, (ah, poor child!)
My father, who through love had suddenly
Thrown off the old conventions, broken loose
From chin-bands of the soul, like Lazarus,
Yet had no time to learn to talk and walk

180   Or grow anew familiar with the sun,—
      Who had reached to freedom, not to action, lived,
      But lived as one entranced, with thoughts, not aims,—
      Whom love had unmade from a common man
      But not completed to an uncommon man,—
185   My father taught me what he had learnt the best
      Before he died and left me,—grief and love.
      And, seeing we had books among the hills,
      Strong words of counselling souls, confederate
      With vocal pines and waters,—out of books
190   He taught me all the ignorance of men,
      And how God laughs in heaven when any man
      Says 'Here I'm learned; this, I understand;
      In that, I am never caught at fault or doubt.'
      He sent the schools to school, demonstrating
195   A fool will pass for such through one mistake,
      While a philosopher will pass for such,
      Through said mistakes being ventured in the gross
      And heaped up to a system.
                                 I am like,
      They tell me, my dear father. Broader brows
200   Howbeit, upon a slenderer undergrowth
      Of delicate features,—paler, near as grave;
      But then my mother's smile breaks up the whole,
      And makes it better sometimes than itself.

      So, nine full years, our days were hid with God
205   Among his mountains. I was just thirteen,
      Still growing like the plants from unseen roots
      In tongue-tied Springs,—and suddenly awoke
      To full life and its needs and agonies,
      With an intense, strong, struggling heart beside
210   A stone-dead father. Life, struck sharp on death,
      Makes awful lightning. His last word was 'Love—'
      'Love, my child, love, love!'—(then he had done with
            grief)
      'Love, my child.' Ere I answered he was gone,
      And none was left to love in all the world.

                          *

215 There, ended childhood: what succeeded next
I recollect as, after fevers, men
Thread back the passage of delirium,
Missing the turn still, baffled by the door;
Smooth endless days, notched here and there with knives;
220 A weary, wormy darkness, spurred i' the flank
With flame, that it should eat and end itself
Like some tormented scorpion. Then, at last,
I do remember clearly how there came
A stranger with authority, not right,
225 (I thought not) who commanded, caught me up
From old Assunta's neck; how, with a shriek,
She let me go,—while I, with ears too full
Of my father's silence, to shriek back a word,
In all a child's astonishment at grief
230 Stared at the wharfage where she stood and moaned,
My poor Assunta, where she stood and moaned!
The white walls, the blue hills, my Italy,
Drawn backward from the shuddering steamer-deck,
Like one in anger drawing back her skirts
235 Which suppliants catch at. Then the bitter sea
Inexorably pushed between us both
And sweeping up the ship with my despair
Threw us out as a pasture to the stars.

Ten nights and days we voyaged on the deep;
240 Ten nights and days without the common face
Of any day or night; the moon and sun
Cut off from the green reconciling earth,
To starve into a blind ferocity
And glare unnatural; the very sky
245 (Dropping its bell-net down upon the sea
As if no human heart should scape alive,)
Bedraggled with the desolating salt,
Until it seemed no more that holy heaven
To which my father went. All new, and strange—
250 The universe turned stranger, for a child.

*

Then, land!—then, England! oh, the frosty cliffs
Looked cold upon me. Could I find a home
Among those mean red houses through the fog?
And when I heard my father's language first
255　From alien lips which had no kiss for mine,
I wept aloud, then laughed, then wept, then wept,—
And some one near me said the child was mad
Through much sea-sickness. The train swept us on.
Was this my father's England? the great isle?
260　The ground seemed cut up from the fellowship
Of verdure, field from field, as man from man;
The skies themselves looked low and positive,
As almost you could touch them with a hand,
And dared to do it, they were so far off
265　From God's celestial crystals; all things, blurred
And dull and vague. Did Shakspeare and his mates
Absorb the light here?—not a hill or stone
With heart to strike a radiant colour up
Or active outline on the indifferent air.

270　I think I see my father's sister stand
Upon the hall-step of her country-house
To give me welcome. She stood straight and calm,
Her somewhat narrow forehead braided tight
As if for taming accidental thoughts
275　From possible pulses; brown hair pricked with grey
By frigid use of life (she was not old,
Although my father's elder by a year)
A nose drawn sharply, yet in delicate lines;
A close mild mouth, a little soured about
280　The ends, through speaking unrequited loves,
Or peradventure niggardly half-truths;
Eyes of no colour,—once they might have smiled,
But never, never have forgot themselves
In smiling; cheeks, in which was yet a rose
285　Of perished summers, like a rose in a book,
Kept more for ruth than pleasure,—if past bloom,
Past fading also.
　　　　　　　　　　She had lived, we'll say,

A harmless life, she called a virtuous life,
A quiet life, which was not life at all,
290 (But that, she had not lived enough to know)
Between the vicar and the country squires,
The lord-lieutenant looking down sometimes
From the empyreal, to assure their souls
Against chance-vulgarisms, and, in the abyss,
295 The apothecary looked on once a year,
To prove their soundness of humility.
The poor-club exercised her Christian gifts
Of knitting stockings, stitching petticoats,
Because we are of one flesh after all
300 And need one flannel, (with a proper sense
Of difference in the quality)—and still
The book-club, guarded from your modern trick
Of shaking dangerous questions from the crease,
Preserved her intellectual. She had lived
305 A sort of cage-bird life, born in a cage,
Accounting that to leap from perch to perch
Was act and joy enough for any bird.
Dear heaven, how silly are the things that live
In thickets, and eat berries!
                                    I, alas,
310 A wild bird, scarcely fledged, was brought to her cage,
And she was there to meet me. Very kind.
Bring the clean water; give out the fresh seed.

She stood upon the steps to welcome me,
Calm, in black garb. I clung about her neck,—
315 Young babes, who catch at every shred of wool
To draw the new light closer, catch and cling
Less blindly. In my ears, my father's word
Hummed ignorantly, as the sea in shells,
'Love, love, my child.' She, black there with my grief,
320 Might feel my love—she was his sister once—
I clung to her. A moment, she seemed moved,
Kissed me with cold lips, suffered me to cling,
And drew me feebly through the hall, into

The room she sate in.
                            There, with some strange spasm
325 Of pain and passion, she wrung loose my hands
    Imperiously, and held me at arm's length,
    And with two grey-steel naked-bladed eyes
    Searched through my face,—ay stabbed it through and
            through,
    Through brows and cheeks and chin, as if to find
330 A wicked murderer in my innocent face,
    If not here, there perhaps. Then, drawing breath,
    She struggled for her ordinary calm,
    And missed it rather,—told me not to shrink,
    As if she had told me not lie or swear,—
335 'She loved my father and would love me too
    As long as I deserved it.' Very kind.

    I understood her meaning afterward;
    She thought to find my mother in my face,
    And questioned it for that. For she, my aunt,
340 Had loved my father truly, as she could,
    And hated, with the gall of gentle souls,
    My Tuscan mother, who had fooled away
    A wise man from wise courses, a good man
    From obvious duties, and, depriving her,
345 His sister, of the household precedence,
    Had wronged his tenants, robbed his native land,
    And made him mad, alike by life and death,
    In love and sorrow. She had pored for years
    What sort of woman could be suitable
350 To her sort of hate, to entertain it with;
    And so, her very curiosity
    Became hate too, and all the idealism
    She ever used in life, was used for hate,
    Till hate, so nourished, did exceed at last
355 The love from which it grew, in strength and heat,
    And wrinkled her smooth conscience with a sense
    Of disputable virtue (say not, sin)
    When Christian doctrine was enforced at church.

                            *

And thus my father's sister was to me
360 My mother's hater. From that day, she did
Her duty to me, (I appreciate it
In her own words as spoken to herself)
Her duty, in large measure, well-pressed out,
But measured always. She was generous, bland,
365 More courteous than was tender, gave me still
The first place,—as if fearful that God's saints
Would look down suddenly and say, 'Herein
You missed a point, I think, through lack of love.'
Alas, a mother never is afraid
370 Of speaking angerly to any child,
Since love, she knows, is justified of love.

And I, I was a good child on the whole,
A meek and manageable child. Why not?
I did not live, to have the faults of life:
375 There seemed more true life in my father's grave
Than in all England. Since *that* threw me off
Who fain would cleave, (his latest will, they say,
Consigned me to his land) I only thought
Of lying quiet there where I was thrown
380 Like sea-weed on the rocks, and suffer her
To prick me to a pattern with her pin,
Fibre from fibre, delicate leaf from leaf,
And dry out from my drowned anatomy
This last sea-salt left in me.
                                    So it was.
385 I broke the copious curls upon my head
In braids, because she liked smooth-ordered hair.
I left off saying my sweet Tuscan words
Which still at any stirring of the heart
Came up to float across the English phrase
390 As lilies, (*Bene* . . or *che ch'è*) because
She liked my father's child to speak his tongue.
I learnt the collects and the catechism,
The creeds, from Athanasius back to Nice,
The Articles . . the Tracts *against* the times,
395 (By no means Buonaventure's 'Prick of Love,')

And various popular synopses of
Inhuman doctrines never taught by John,
Because she liked instructed piety.
I learnt my complement of classic French
400 (Kept pure of Balzac and neologism,)
And German also, since she liked a range
Of liberal education,—tongues, not books.
I learnt a little algebra, a little
Of the mathematics,—brushed with extreme flounce
405 The circle of the sciences, because
She misliked women who are frivolous.
I learnt the royal genealogies
Of Oviedo, the internal laws
Of the Burmese empire, . . by how many feet
410 Mount Chimborazo outsoars Himmeleh.
What navigable river joins itself
To Lara, and what census of the year five
Was taken at Klagenfurt,—because she liked
A general insight into useful facts.
415 I learnt much music,—such as would have been
As quite impossible in Johnson's day
As still it might be wished—fine sleights of hand
And unimagined fingering, shuffling off
The hearer's soul through hurricanes of notes
420 To a noisy Tophet; and I drew . . costumes
From French engravings, nereids neatly draped
With smirks of simmering godship,—I washed in
From nature, landscapes, (rather say, washed out.)
I danced the polka and Cellarius,
425 Spun glass, stuffed birds, and modelled flowers in wax,
Because she liked accomplishment in girls.
I read a score of books on womanhood
To prove, if women do not think at all,
They may teach thinking, (to a maiden aunt
430 Or else the author)—books demonstrating
Their right of comprehending husband's talk
When not too deep, and even of answering
With pretty 'may it please you,' or 'so it is,'—
Their rapid insight and fine aptitude,

435 Particular worth and general missionariness,
    As long as they keep quiet by the fire
    And never say 'no' when the world says 'ay,'
    For that is fatal,—their angelic reach
    Of virtue, chiefly used to sit and darn,
440 And fatten household sinners,—their, in brief,
    Potential faculty in everything
    Of abdicating power in it: she owned
    She liked a woman to be womanly,
    And English women, she thanked God and sighed,
445 (Some people always sigh in thanking God)
    Were models to the universe. And last
    I learnt cross-stitch, because she did not like
    To see me wear the night with empty hands,
    A-doing nothing. So, my shepherdess
450 Was something after all, (the pastoral saints
    Be praised for't) leaning lovelorn with pink eyes
    To match her shoes, when I mistook the silks;
    Her head uncrushed by that round weight of hat
    So strangely similar to the tortoise-shell
455 Which slew the tragic poet.
                              By the way,
    The works of women are symbolical.
    We sew, sew, prick our fingers, dull our sight,
    Producing what? A pair of slippers, sir,
    To put on when you're weary—or a stool
460 To stumble over and vex you . . 'curse that stool!'
    Or else at best, a cushion, where you lean
    And sleep, and dream of something we are not,
    But would be for your sake. Alas, alas!
    This hurts most, this . . that, after all, we are paid
465 The worth of our work, perhaps.
                                 In looking down
    Those years of education, (to return)
    I wonder if Brinvilliers suffered more
    In the water-torture, . . flood succeeding flood
    To drench the incapable throat and split the veins . .
470 Than I did. Certain of your feebler souls
    Go out in such a process; many pine

To a sick, inodorous light; my own endured:
I had relations in the Unseen, and drew
The elemental nutriment and heat
475   From nature, as earth feels the sun at nights,
Or as a babe sucks surely in the dark.
I kept the life, thrust on me, on the outside
Of the inner life, with all its ample room
For heart and lungs, for will and intellect,
480   Inviolable by conventions. God,
I thank thee for that grace of thine!

                                At first
I felt no life which was not patience,—did
The thing she bade me, without heed to a thing
Beyond it, sate in just the chair she placed,
485   With back against the window, to exclude
The sight of the great lime-tree on the lawn,
Which seemed to have come on purpose from the woods
To bring the house a message,—ay, and walked
Demurely in her carpeted low rooms,
490   As if I should not, harkening my own steps,
Misdoubt I was alive. I read her books,
Was civil to her cousin, Romney Leigh,
Gave ear to her vicar, tea to her visitors,
And heard them whisper, when I changed a cup,
495   (I blushed for joy at that)—'The Italian child,
For all her blue eyes and her quiet ways,
Thrives ill in England: she is paler yet
Than when we came the last time; she will die.'

'Will die.' My cousin, Romney Leigh, blushed too,
500   With sudden anger, and approaching me
Said low between his teeth—'You're wicked now?
You wish to die and leave the world a-dusk
For others, with your naughty light blown out?'
I looked into his face defyingly.
505   He might have known, that, being what I was,
'Twas natural to like to get away
As far as dead folk can; and then indeed
Some people make no trouble when they die.

He turned and went abruptly, slammed the door,
510   And shut his dog out.
                              Romney, Romney Leigh.
I have not named my cousin hitherto,
And yet I used him as a sort of friend;
My elder by few years, but cold and shy
And absent . . tender, when he thought of it,—
515   Which scarcely was imperative, grave betimes,
As well as early master of Leigh Hall,
Whereof the nightmare sate upon his youth,
Repressing all its seasonable delights,
And agonising with a ghastly sense
520   Of universal hideous want and wrong
To incriminate possession. When he came
From college to the country, very oft
He crossed the hill on visits to my aunt,
With gifts of blue grapes from the hothouses,
525   A book in one hand,—mere statistics, (if
I chanced to lift the cover) count of all
The goats whose beards are sprouting down toward hell,
Against God's separating judgment-hour.
And she, she almost loved him,—even allowed
530   That sometimes he should seem to sigh my way;
It made him easier to be pitiful,
And sighing was his gift. So, undisturbed
At whiles she let him shut my music up
And push my needles down, and lead me out
535   To see in that south angle of the house
The figs grow black as if by a Tuscan rock,
On some light pretext. She would turn her head
At other moments, go to fetch a thing,
And leave me breath enough to speak with him,
540   For his sake; it was simple.
                              Sometimes too
He would have saved me utterly, it seemed,
He stood and looked so.
                              Once, he stood so near
He dropped a sudden hand upon my head
Bent down on woman's work, as soft as rain—

545 But then I rose and shook it off as fire,
    The stranger's touch that took my father's place,
    Yet dared seem soft.
                        I used him for a friend
    Before I ever knew him for a friend.
    'Twas better, 'twas worse also, afterward:
550 We came so close, we saw our differences
    Too intimately. Always Romney Leigh
    Was looking for the worms, I for the gods.
    A godlike nature his; the gods look down,
    Incurious of themselves; and certainly
555 'Tis well I should remember, how, those days,
    I was a worm too, and he looked on me.

    A little by his act perhaps, yet more
    By something in me, surely not my will,
    I did not die. But slowly, as one in swoon,
560 To whom life creeps back in the form of death,
    With a sense of separation, a blind pain
    Of blank obstruction, and a roar i' the ears
    Of visionary chariots which retreat
    As earth grows clearer .. slowly, by degrees,
565 I woke, rose up .. where was I! in the world;
    For uses, therefore, I must count worth while.

    I had a little chamber in the house,
    As green as any privet-hedge a bird
    Might choose to build in, though the nest itself
570 Could show but dead-brown sticks and straws; the walls
    Were green, the carpet was pure green, the straight
    Small bed was curtained greenly, and the folds
    Hung green about the window, which let in
    The out-door world with all its greenery.
575 You could not push your head out and escape
    A dash of dawn-dew from the honeysuckle,
    But so you were baptised into the grace
    And privilege of seeing . . .
                                First, the lime,
    (I had enough, there, of the lime, be sure,—

580 My morning-dream was often hummed away
By the bees in it;) past the lime, the lawn,
Which, after sweeping broadly round the house,
Went trickling through the shrubberies in a stream
Of tender turf, and wore and lost itself
585 Among the acacias, over which, you saw
The irregular line of elms by the deep lane
Which stopped the grounds and dammed the overflow
Of arbutus and laurel. Out of sight
The lane was; sunk so deep, no foreign tramp
590 Nor drover of wild ponies out of Wales
Could guess if lady's hall or tenant's lodge
Dispensed such odours,—though his stick well-crooked
Might reach the lowest trail of blossoming briar
Which dipped upon the wall. Behind the elms,
595 And through their tops, you saw the folded hills
Striped up and down with hedges, (burly oaks
Projecting from the line to show themselves)
Through which my cousin Romney's chimneys smoked
As still as when a silent mouth in frost
600 Breathes—showing where the woodlands hid Leigh Hall;
While, far above, a jut of table-land,
A promontory without water, stretched,—
You could not catch it if the days were thick,
Or took it for a cloud; but, otherwise
605 The vigorous sun would catch it up at eve
And use it for an anvil till he had filled
The shelves of heaven with burning thunderbolts,
And proved he need not rest so early:—then,
When all his setting trouble was resolved
610 To a trance of passive glory, you might see
In apparition on the golden sky
(Alas, my Giotto's background!) the sheep run
Along the fine clear outline, small as mice
That run along a witch's scarlet thread.

615 Not a grand nature. Not my chestnut woods
Of Vallombrosa, cleaving by the spurs
To the precipices. Not my headlong leaps

Of waters, that cry out for joy or fear
In leaping through the palpitating pines,
620   Like a white soul tossed out to eternity
With thrills of time upon it. Not indeed
My multitudinous mountains, sitting in
The magic circle, with the mutual touch
Electric, panting from their full deep hearts
625   Beneath the influent heavens, and waiting for
Communion and commission. Italy
Is one thing, England one.
                    On English ground
You understand the letter . . ere the fall,
How Adam lived in a garden. All the fields
630   Are tied up fast with hedges, nosegay-like;
The hills are crumpled plains,—the plains, parterres,—
The trees, round, woolly, ready to be clipped;
And if you seek for any wilderness
You find, at best, a park. A nature tamed
635   And grown domestic like a barn-door fowl,
Which does not awe you with its claws and beak,
Nor tempt you to an eyrie too high up,
But which, in cackling, sets you thinking of
Your eggs tomorrow at breakfast, in the pause
640   Of finer meditation.
                    Rather say,
A sweet familiar nature, stealing in
As a dog might, or child, to touch your hand
Or pluck your gown, and humbly mind you so
Of presence and affection, excellent
645   For inner uses, from the things without.

I could not be unthankful, I who was
Entreated thus and holpen. In the room
I speak of, ere the house was well awake,
And also after it was well asleep,
650   I sate alone, and drew the blessing in
Of all that nature. With a gradual step,
A stir among the leaves, a breath, a ray,
It came in softly, while the angels made

A place for it beside me. The moon came,
655   And swept my chamber clean of foolish thoughts.
The sun came, saying, 'Shall I lift this light
Against the lime-tree, and you will not look?
I make the birds sing—listen! . . but, for you,
God never hears your voice, excepting when
660   You lie upon the bed at nights and weep.'

Then, something moved me. Then, I wakened up
More slowly than I verily write now,
But wholly, at last, I wakened, opened wide
The window and my soul, and let the airs
665   And out-door sights sweep gradual gospels in,
Regenerating what I was. O Life,
How oft we throw it off and think,—'Enough,
Enough of life in so much!—here's a cause
For rupture;—herein we must break with Life,
670   Or be ourselves unworthy; here we are wronged,
Maimed, spoiled for aspiration: farewell Life!'
—And so, as froward babes, we hide our eyes
And think all ended.—Then, Life calls to us
In some transformed, apocryphal, new voice,
675   Above us, or below us, or around . .
Perhaps we name it Nature's voice, or Love's,
Tricking ourselves, because we are more ashamed
To own our compensations than our griefs:
Still, Life's voice!—still, we make our peace with Life.

680   And I, so young then, was not sullen. Soon
I used to get up early, just to sit
And watch the morning quicken in the grey,
And hear the silence open like a flower,
Leaf after leaf,—and stroke with listless hand
685   The woodbine through the window, till at last
I came to do it with a sort of love,
At foolish unaware: whereat I smiled,—
A melancholy smile, to catch myself
Smiling for joy.
                        Capacity for joy

690   Admits temptation. It seemed, next, worth while
       To dodge the sharp sword set against my life;
       To slip down stairs through all the sleepy house,
       As mute as any dream there, and escape
       As a soul from the body, out of doors,—
695   Glide through the shrubberies, drop into the lane,
       And wander on the hills an hour or two,
       Then back again before the house should stir.

       Or else I sate on in my chamber green,
       And lived my life, and thought my thoughts, and prayed
700   My prayers without the vicar; read my books,
       Without considering whether they were fit
       To do me good. Mark, there. We get no good
       By being ungenerous, even to a book,
       And calculating profits . . so much help
705   By so much reading. It is rather when
       We gloriously forget ourselves, and plunge
       Soul-forward, headlong, into a book's profound,
       Impassioned for its beauty and salt of truth—
       'Tis then we get the right good from a book.

710   I read much. What my father taught before
       From many a volume, Love re-emphasised
       Upon the self-same pages: Theophrast
       Grew tender with the memory of his eyes,
       And Ælian made mine wet. The trick of Greek
715   And Latin, he had taught me, as he would
       Have taught me wrestling or the game of fives
       If such he had known,—most like a shipwrecked man
       Who heaps his single platter with goats' cheese
       And scarlet berries; or like any man
720   Who loves but one, and so gives all at once,
       Because he has it, rather than because
       He counts it worthy. Thus, my father gave;
       And thus, as did the women formerly
       By young Achilles, when they pinned the veil
725   Across the boy's audacious front, and swept
       With tuneful laughs the silver-fretted rocks,

He wrapt his little daughter in his large
Man's doublet, careless did it fit or no.

But, after I had read for memory,
730   I read for hope. The path my father's foot
Had trod me out, which suddenly broke off,
(What time he dropped the wallet of the flesh
And passed) alone I carried on, and set
My child-heart 'gainst the thorny underwood,
735   To reach the grassy shelter of the trees.
Ah, babe i' the wood, without a brother-babe!
My own self-pity, like the red-breast bird,
Flies back to cover all that past with leaves.

Sublimest danger, over which none weeps,
740   When any young wayfaring soul goes forth
Alone, unconscious of the perilous road,
The day-sun dazzling in his limpid eyes,
To thrust his own way, he an alien, through
The world of books! Ah, you!—you think it fine,
745   You clap hands—'A fair day!'—you cheer him on,
As if the worst, could happen, were to rest
Too long beside a fountain. Yet, behold,
Behold!—the world of books is still the world;
And worldlings in it are less merciful
750   And more puissant. For the wicked there
Are winged like angels. Every knife that strikes,
Is edged from elemental fire to assail
A spiritual life. The beautiful seems right
By force of beauty, and the feeble wrong
755   Because of weakness. Power is justified,
Though armed against St. Michael. Many a crown
Covers bald foreheads. In the book-world, true,
There's no lack, neither, of God's saints and kings,
That shake the ashes of the grave aside
760   From their calm locks, and undiscomfited
Look stedfast truths against Time's changing mask.
True, many a prophet teaches in the roads;
True, many a seer pulls down the flaming heavens

Upon his own head in strong martyrdom,
765   In order to light men a moment's space.
But stay!—who judges?—who distinguishes
'Twixt Saul and Nahash justly, at first sight,
And leaves king Saul precisely at the sin,
To serve king David? who discerns at once
770   The sound of the trumpets, when the trumpets blow
For Alaric as well as Charlemagne?
Who judges prophets, and can tell true seers
From conjurers? The child, there? Would you leave
That child to wander in a battle-field
775   And push his innocent smile against the guns?
Or even in a catacomb, . . his torch
Grown ragged in the fluttering air, and all
The dark a-mutter round him? not a child!

I read books bad and good—some bad and good
780   At once: good aims not always make good books:
Well-tempered spades turn up ill-smelling soils
In digging vineyards, even: books, that prove
God's being so definitely, that man's doubt
Grows self-defined the other side the line,
785   Made atheist by suggestion; moral books,
Exasperating to license; genial books,
Discounting from the human dignity;
And merry books, which set you weeping when
The sun shines,—ay, and melancholy books,
790   Which make you laugh that any one should weep
In this disjointed life, for one wrong more.

The world of books is still the world, I write,
And both worlds have God's providence, thank God,
To keep and hearten: with some struggle, indeed,
795   Among the breakers, some hard swimming through
The deeps—I lost breath in my soul sometimes
And cried 'God save me if there's any God,'
But, even so, God saved me; and, being dashed
From error on to error, every turn
800   Still brought me nearer to the central truth.

*

I thought so. All this anguish in the thick
Of men's opinions . . press and counterpress,
Now up, now down, now underfoot, and now
Emergent . . all the best of it, perhaps,
805 But throws you back upon a noble trust
And use of your own instinct,—merely proves
Pure reason stronger than bare inference
At strongest. Try it,—fix against heaven's wall
Your scaling-ladders of high logic—mount
810 Step by step!—Sight goes faster; that still ray
Which strikes out from you, how, you cannot tell,
And why, you know not—(did you eliminate,
That such as you, indeed, should analyse?)
Goes straight and fast as light, and high as God.

815 The cygnet finds the water; but the man
Is born in ignorance of his element,
And feels out blind at first, disorganised
By sin i' the blood,—his spirit-insight dulled
And crossed by his sensations. Presently
820 We feel it quicken in the dark sometimes;
Then, mark, be reverent, be obedient,—
For those dumb motions of imperfect life
Are oracles of vital Deity
Attesting the Hereafter. Let who says
825 'The soul's a clean white paper,' rather say,
A palimpsest, a prophet's holograph
Defiled, erased and covered by a monk's,—
The apocalypse, by a Longus! poring on
Which obscene text, we may discern perhaps
830 Some fair, fine trace of what was written once,
Some upstroke of an alpha and omega
Expressing the old scripture.
                                        Books, books, books!
I had found the secret of a garret-room
Piled high with cases in my father's name;
835 Piled high, packed large,—where, creeping in and out
Among the giant fossils of my past,
Like some nimble mouse between the ribs

Of a mastodon, I nibbled here and there
At this or that box, pulling through the gap,
840   In heats of terror, haste, victorious joy,
The first book first. And how I felt it beat
Under my pillow, in the morning's dark,
An hour before the sun would let me read!
My books!

       At last because the time was ripe,
845   I chanced upon the poets.

           As the earth
Plunges in fury, when the internal fires
Have reached and pricked her heart, and, throwing flat
The marts and temples, the triumphal gates
And towers of observation, clears herself
850   To elemental freedom—thus, my soul,
At poetry's divine first finger-touch,
Let go conventions and sprang up surprised,
Convicted of the great eternities
Before two worlds.

       What's this, Aurora Leigh,
855   You write so of the poets, and not laugh?
Those virtuous liars, dreamers after dark,
Exaggerators of the sun and moon,
And soothsayers in a tea-cup?

          I write so
Of the only truth-tellers, now left to God,—
860   The only speakers of essential truth,
Opposed to relative, comparative,
And temporal truths; the only holders by
His sun-skirts, through conventional grey glooms;
The only teachers who instruct mankind,
865   From just a shadow on a charnel-wall,
To find man's veritable stature out,
Erect, sublime,—the measure of a man,
And that's the measure of an angel, says
The apostle. Ay, and while your common men
870   Build pyramids, gauge railroads, reign, reap, dine,
And dust the flaunty carpets of the world
For kings to walk on, or our senators,

The poet suddenly will catch them up
With his voice like a thunder, . . 'This is soul,
875 This is life, this word is being said in heaven,
Here's God down on us! what are you about?'
How all those workers start amid their work,
Look round, look up, and feel, a moment's space,
That carpet-dusting, though a pretty trade,
880 Is not the imperative labour after all.

My own best poets, am I one with you,
That thus I love you,—or but one through love?
Does all this smell of thyme about my feet
Conclude my visit to your holy hill
885 In personal presence, or but testify
The rustling of your vesture through my dreams
With influent odours? When my joy and pain,
My thought and aspiration, like the stops
Of pipe and flute, are absolutely dumb
890 If not melodious, do you play on me
My pipers,—and if, sooth, you did not blow,
Would no sound come? or is the music mine,
As a man's voice or breath is called his own,
Inbreathed by the Life-breather? There's a doubt
895 For cloudy seasons!
                          But the sun was high
When first I felt my pulses set themselves
For concords; when the rhythmic turbulence
Of blood and brain swept outward upon words,
As wind upon the alders, blanching them
900 By turning up their under-natures till
They trembled in dilation. O delight
And triumph of the poet,—who would say
A man's mere 'yes,' a woman's common 'no,'
A little human hope of that or this,
905 And says the word so that it burns you through
With a special revelation, shakes the heart
Of all the men and women in the world,
As if one came back from the dead and spoke,
With eyes too happy, a familiar thing

910 Become divine i' the utterance! while for him
     The poet, the speaker, he expands with joy;
     The palpitating angel in his flesh
     Thrills inly with consenting fellowship
     To those innumerous spirits who sun themselves
915 Outside of time.
                    O life, O poetry,
     —Which means life in life! cognisant of life
     Beyond this blood-beat,—passionate for truth
     Beyond these senses,—poetry, my life,—
     My eagle, with both grappling feet still hot
920 From Zeus' thunder, who has ravished me
     Away from all the shepherds, sheep, and dogs,
     And set me in the Olympian roar and round
     Of luminous faces, for a cup-bearer,
     To keep the mouths of all the godheads moist
925 For everlasting laughters,—I, myself,
     Half drunk across the beaker, with their eyes!
     How those gods look!
                          Enough so, Ganymede.
     We shall not bear above a round or two—
     We drop the golden cup at Heré's foot
930 And swoon back to the earth,—and find ourselves
     Face-down among the pine-cones, cold with dew,
     While the dogs bark, and many a shepherd scoffs,
     'What's come now to the youth?' Such ups and downs
     Have poets.
                 Am I such indeed? The name
935 Is royal, and to sign it like a queen,
     Is what I dare not,—though some royal blood
     Would seem to tingle in me now and then,
     With sense of power and ache,—with imposthumes
     And manias usual to the race. Howbeit
940 I dare not: 'tis too easy to go mad
     And ape a Bourbon in a crown of straws;
     The thing's too common.
                             Many fervent souls
     Strike rhyme on rhyme, who would strike steel on steel
     If steel had offered, in a restless heat

945   Of doing something. Many tender souls
       Have strung their losses on a rhyming thread,
       As children, cowslips:—the more pains they take,
       The work more withers. Young men, ay, and maids,
       Too often sow their wild oats in tame verse,
950   Before they sit down under their own vine
       And live for use. Alas, near all the birds
       Will sing at dawn,—and yet we do not take
       The chaffering swallow for the holy lark.

       In those days, though, I never analysed,
955   Myself even. All analysis comes late.
       You catch a sight of Nature, earliest,
       In full front sun-face, and your eyelids wink
       And drop before the wonder of 't; you miss
       The form, through seeing the light. I lived, those days,
960   And wrote because I lived—unlicensed else:
       My heart beat in my brain. Life's violent flood
       Abolished bounds,—and, which my neighbour's field,
       Which mine, what mattered? It is so in youth!
       We play at leap-frog over the god Term;
965   The love within us and the love without
       Are mixed, confounded; if we are loved or love,
       We scarce distinguish. So, with other power.
       Being acted on and acting seem the same:
       In that first onrush of life's chariot-wheels,
970   We know not if the forests move or we.

       And so, like most young poets, in a flush
       Of individual life, I poured myself
       Along the veins of others, and achieved
       Mere lifeless imitations of live verse,
975   And made the living answer for the dead,
       Profaning nature. 'Touch not, do not taste,
       Nor handle,'—we're too legal, who write young:
       We beat the phorminx till we hurt our thumbs,
       As if still ignorant of counterpoint;
980   We call the Muse . . 'O Muse, benignant Muse,'—
       As if we had seen her purple-braided head,

With the eyes in it, start between the boughs
As often as a stag's. What make-believe,
With so much earnest! What effete results,
985   From virile efforts! what cold wire-drawn odes,
From such white heats!—bucolics, where the cows
Would scare the writer if they splashed the mud
In lashing off the flies,—didactics, driven
Against the heels of what the master said;
990   And counterfeiting epics, shrill with trumps
A babe might blow between two straining cheeks
Of bubbled rose, to make his mother laugh;
And elegiac griefs, and songs of love,
Like cast-off nosegays picked up on the road,
995   The worse for being warm: all these things, writ
On happy mornings, with a morning heart,
That leaps for love, is active for resolve,
Weak for art only. Oft, the ancient forms
Will thrill, indeed, in carrying the young blood.
1000   The wine-skins, now and then, a little warped,
Will crack even, as the new wine gurgles in.
Spare the old bottles!—spill not the new wine.

By Keats' soul, the man who never stepped
In gradual progress like another man,
1005   But, turning grandly on his central self,
Ensphered himself in twenty perfect years
And died, not young,—(the life of a long life,
Distilled to a mere drop, falling like a tear
Upon the world's cold cheek to make it burn
1010   For ever;) by that strong excepted soul,
I count it strange and hard to understand,
That nearly all young poets should write old;
That Pope was sexagenarian at sixteen,
And beardless Byron academical,
1015   And so with others. It may be, perhaps,
Such have not settled long and deep enough
In trance, to attain to clairvoyance,—and still
The memory mixes with the vision, spoils,
And works it turbid.
                    Or perhaps, again,

1020   In order to discover the Muse-Sphinx,
  The melancholy desert must sweep round,
  Behind you as before.—
         For me, I wrote
  False poems, like the rest, and thought them true,
  Because myself was true in writing them.
1025   I, peradventure, have writ true ones since
  With less complacence.
         But I could not hide
  My quickening inner life from those at watch.
  They saw a light at a window now and then,
  They had not set there. Who had set it there?
1030   My father's sister started when she caught
  My soul agaze in my eyes. She could not say
  I had no business with a sort of soul,
  But plainly she objected,—and demurred
  That souls were dangerous things to carry straight
1035   Through all the spilt saltpetre of the world.

  She said sometimes 'Aurora, have you done
  Your task this morning?—have you read that book?
  And are you ready for the crochet here?'—
  As if she said, 'I know there's something wrong;
1040   I know I have not ground you down enough
  To flatten and bake you to a wholesome crust
  For household uses and proprieties,
  Before the rain has got into my barn
  And set the grains a-sprouting. What, you're green
1045   With out-door impudence? you almost grow?'
  To which I answered, 'Would she hear my task,
  And verify my abstract of the book?
  Or should I sit down to the crochet work?
  Was such her pleasure?' . . Then I sate and teased
1050   The patient needle till it split the thread,
  Which oozed off from it in meandering lace
  From hour to hour. I was not, therefore, sad;
  My soul was singing at a work apart
  Behind the wall of sense, as safe from harm

1055 As sings the lark when sucked up out of sight,
     In vortices of glory and blue air.

     And so, through forced work and spontaneous work,
     The inner life informed the outer life,
     Reduced the irregular blood to settled rhythms,
1060 Made cool the forehead with fresh-sprinkling dreams,
     And, rounding to the spheric soul the thin
     Pined body, struck a colour up the cheeks,
     Though somewhat faint. I clenched my brows across
     My blue eyes greatening in the looking-glass,
1065 And said, 'We'll live, Aurora! we'll be strong.
     The dogs are on us—but we will not die.'

     Whoever lives true life, will love true love.
     I learnt to love that England. Very oft,
     Before the day was born, or otherwise
1070 Through secret windings of the afternoons,
     I threw my hunters off and plunged myself
     Among the deep hills, as a hunted stag
     Will take the waters, shivering with the fear
     And passion of the course. And when, at last
1075 Escaped,—so many a green slope built on slope
     Betwixt me and the enemy's house behind,
     I dared to rest, or wander,—like a rest
     Made sweeter for the step upon the grass,—
     And view the ground's most gentle dimplement,
1080 (As if God's finger touched but did not press
     In making England!) such an up and down
     Of verdure,—nothing too much up or down,
     A ripple of land; such little hills, the sky
     Can stoop to tenderly and the wheatfields climb;
1085 Such nooks of valleys, lined with orchises,
     Fed full of noises by invisible streams;
     And open pastures, where you scarcely tell
     White daisies from white dew,—at intervals
     The mythic oaks and elm-trees standing out
1090 Self-poised upon their prodigy of shade,—
     I thought my father's land was worthy too

Of being my Shakspeare's.
                              Very oft alone,
Unlicensed; not infrequently with leave
To walk the third with Romney and his friend
1095   The rising painter, Vincent Carrington,
Whom men judge hardly, as bee-bonnetted,
Because he holds that, paint a body well,
You paint a soul by implication, like
The grand first Master. Pleasant walks! for if
1100   He said . . 'When I was last in Italy' . .
It sounded as an instrument that's played
Too far off for the tune—and yet it's fine
To listen.
              Often we walked only two,
If cousin Romney pleased to walk with me.
1105   We read, or talked, or quarrelled, as it chanced:
We were not lovers, nor even friends well-matched—
Say rather, scholars upon different tracks,
And thinkers disagreed; he, overfull
Of what is, and I, haply, overbold
1110   For what might be.
                        But then the thrushes sang,
And shook my pulses and the elms' new leaves,—
At which I turned, and held my fingers up,
And bade him mark that, howsoe'er the world
Went ill, as he related, certainly
1115   The thrushes still sang in it.—At which word
His brow would soften,—and he bore with me
In melancholy patience, not unkind,
While breaking into voluble ecstasy,
I flattered all the beauteous country round,
1120   As poets use . . the skies, the clouds, the fields,
The happy violets hiding from the roads
The primroses run down to, carrying gold,—
The tangled hedgerows, where the cows push out
Impatient horns and tolerant churning mouths
1125   'Twixt dripping ash-boughs,—hedgerows all alive
With birds and gnats and large white butterflies
Which look as if the May-flower had caught life

And palpitated forth upon the wind,—
Hills, vales, woods, netted in a silver mist,
1130 Farms, granges, doubled up among the hills,
And cattle grazing in the watered vales,
And cottage-chimneys smoking from the woods,
And cottage-gardens smelling everywhere,
Confused with smell of orchards. 'See,' I said,
1135 'And see! is God not with us on the earth?
And shall we put Him down by aught we do?
Who says there's nothing for the poor and vile
Save poverty and wickedness? behold!'
And ankle-deep in English grass I leaped,
1140 And clapped my hands, and called all very fair.

In the beginning when God called all good,
Even then, was evil near us, it is writ.
But we, indeed, who call things good and fair,
The evil is upon us while we speak;
1145 Deliver us from evil, let us pray.

Second Book

TIMES followed one another. Came a morn
I stood upon the brink of twenty years,
And looked before and after, as I stood
Woman and artist,—either incomplete,
5   Both credulous of completion. There I held
The whole creation in my little cup,
And smiled with thirsty lips before I drank,
'Good health to you and me, sweet neighbour mine,
And all these peoples.'
                  I was glad, that day;
10   The June was in me, with its multitudes
Of nightingales all singing in the dark,
And rosebuds reddening where the calyx split.
I felt so young, so strong, so sure of God!
So glad, I could not choose be very wise!
15   And, old at twenty, was inclined to pull
My childhood backward in a childish jest
To see the face of't once more, and farewell!
In which fantastic mood I bounded forth
At early morning,—would not wait so long
20   As even to snatch my bonnet by the strings,
But, brushing a green trail across the lawn
With my gown in the dew, took will and way
Among the acacias of the shrubberies,
To fly my fancies in the open air
25   And keep my birthday, till my aunt awoke
To stop good dreams. Meanwhile I murmured on,
As honeyed bees keep humming to themselves;
'The worthiest poets have remained uncrowned
Till death has bleached their foreheads to the bone,
30   And so with me it must be, unless I prove
Unworthy of the grand adversity,—
And certainly I would not fail so much.
What, therefore, if I crown myself to-day
In sport, not pride, to learn the feel of it,

35 Before my brows be numb as Dante's own
   To all the tender pricking of such leaves?
   Such leaves! what leaves?'
                          I pulled the branches down,
   To choose from.
                     'Not the bay! I choose no bay;
   The fates deny us if we are overbold:
40 Nor myrtle—which means chiefly love; and love
   Is something awful which one dares not touch
   So early o' mornings. This verbena strains
   The point of passionate fragrance; and hard by,
   This guelder-rose, at far too slight a beck
45 Of the wind, will toss about her flower-apples.
   Ah—there's my choice,—that ivy on the wall,
   That headlong ivy! not a leaf will grow
   But thinking of a wreath. Large leaves, smooth leaves,
   Serrated like my vines, and half as green.
50 I like such ivy; bold to leap a height
   'Twas strong to climb! as good to grow on graves
   As twist about a thyrsus; pretty too,
   (And that's not ill) when twisted round a comb.'

   Thus speaking to myself, half singing it,
55 Because some thoughts are fashioned like a bell
   To ring with once being touched, I drew a wreath
   Drenched, blinding me with dew, across my brow,
   And fastening it behind so, . . turning faced
   . . My public!—cousin Romney—with a mouth
60 Twice graver than his eyes.
                           I stood there fixed—
   My arms up, like the caryatid, sole
   Of some abolished temple, helplessly
   Persistent in a gesture which derides
   A former purpose. Yet my blush was flame,
65 As if from flax, not stone.
                           'Aurora Leigh,
   The earliest of Auroras!'
                           Hand stretched out
   I clasped, as shipwrecked men will clasp a hand,

Indifferent to the sort of palm. The tide
Had caught me at my pastime, writing down
70 My foolish name too near upon the sea
Which drowned me with a blush as foolish. 'You,
My cousin!'
           The smile died out in his eyes
And dropped upon his lips, a cold dead weight,
For just a moment . . 'Here's a book, I found!
75 No name writ on it—poems by the form;
Some Greek upon the margin,—lady's Greek
Without the accents. Read it? Not a word.
I saw at once the thing had witchcraft in't,
Whereof the reading calls up dangerous spirits;
80 I rather bring it to the witch.'
                'My book!
You found it' . .
           'In the hollow by the stream,
That beech leans down into—of which you said,
The Oread in it has a Naiad's heart
And pines for waters.'
               'Thank you.'
                    'Rather *you*,
85 My cousin! that I have seen you not too much
A witch, a poet, scholar, and the rest,
To be a woman also.'
             With a glance
The smile rose in his eyes again and touched
The ivy on my forehead, light as air.
90 I answered gravely, 'Poets needs must be
Or men or women—more's the pity.'
                   'Ah,
But men, and still less women, happily,
Scarce need be poets. Keep to the green wreath,
Since even dreaming of the stone and bronze
95 Brings headaches, pretty cousin, and defiles
The clean white morning dresses.'
               'So you judge!
Because I love the beautiful, I must
Love pleasure chiefly, and be overcharged

For ease and whiteness! Well—you know the world,
100 And only miss your cousin; 'tis not much!—
But learn this: I would rather take my part
With God's Dead, who afford to walk in white
Yet spread His glory, than keep quiet here,
And gather up my feet from even a step,
105 For fear to soil my gown in so much dust.
I choose to walk at all risks.—Here, if heads
That hold a rhythmic thought, must ache perforce,
For my part, I choose headaches,—and today's
My birthday.'
                    'Dear Aurora, choose instead
110 To cure such. You have balsams.'
                                        'I perceive!—
The headache is too noble for my sex.
You think the heartache would sound decenter,
Since that's the woman's special, proper ache,
And altogether tolerable, except
115 To a woman.'
                    Saying which, I loosed my wreath
And, swinging it beside me as I walked,
Half petulant, half playful, as we walked,
I sent a sidelong look to find his thought,—
As falcon set on falconer's finger may,
120 With sidelong head, and startled, braving eye,
Which means, 'You'll see—you'll see! I'll soon take flight—
You shall not hinder.' He, as shaking out
His hand and answering 'Fly then,' did not speak,
Except by such a gesture. Silently
125 We paced, until, just coming into sight
Of the house-windows, he abruptly caught
At one end of the swinging wreath, and said
'Aurora!' There I stopped short, breath and all.

'Aurora, let's be serious, and throw by
130 This game of head and heart. Life means, be sure,
Both heart and head,—both active, both complete,
And both in earnest. Men and women make
The world, as head and heart make human life.

Work man, work woman, since there's work to do
135 In this beleaguered earth, for head and heart,
And thought can never do the work of love!
But work for ends, I mean for uses; not
For such sleek fringes (do you call them ends?
Still less God's glory) as we sew ourselves
140 Upon the velvet of those baldaquins
Held 'twixt us and the sun. That book of yours,
I have not read a page of; but I toss
A rose up—it falls calyx down, you see! . .
The chances are that, being a woman, young,
145 And pure, with such a pair of large, calm eyes, . .
You write as well . . and ill . . upon the whole,
As other women. If as well, what then?
If even a little better, . . still, what then?
We want the Best in art now, or no art.
150 The time is done for facile settings up
Of minnow gods, nymphs here and tritons there;
The polytheists have gone out in God,
That unity of Bests. No best, no God!—
And so with art, we say. Give art's divine,
155 Direct, indubitable, real as grief,—
Or leave us to the grief we grow ourselves
Divine by overcoming with mere hope
And most prosaic patience. You, you are young
As Eve with nature's daybreak on her face;
160 But this same world you are come to, dearest coz,
Has done with keeping birthdays, saves her wreaths
To hang upon her ruins,—and forgets
To rhyme the cry with which she still beats back
Those savage, hungry dogs that hunt her down
165 To the empty grave of Christ. The world's hard pressed;
The sweat of labour in the early curse
Has (turning acrid in six thousand years)
Become the sweat of torture. Who has time
An hour's time . . think! . . to sit upon a bank
170 And hear the cymbal tinkle in white hands?
When Egypt's slain, I say, let Miriam sing!—
Before . . where's Moses?'

                    'Ah—exactly that!

Where's Moses?—is a Moses to be found?—
You'll seek him vainly in the bulrushes,
175 While I in vain touch cymbals. Yet, concede,
Such sounding brass has done some actual good
(The application in a woman's hand,
If that were credible, being scarcely spoilt,)
In colonising beehives.'
                    'There it is!—
180 You play beside a death-bed like a child,
Yet measure to yourself a prophet's place
To teach the living. None of all these things,
Can women understand. You generalise
Oh, nothing!—not even grief! Your quick-breathed hearts,
185 So sympathetic to the personal pang,
Close on each separate knife-stroke, yielding up
A whole life at each wound; incapable
Of deepening, widening a large lap of life
To hold the world-full woe. The human race
190 To you means, such a child, or such a man,
You saw one morning waiting in the cold,
Beside that gate, perhaps. You gather up
A few such cases, and, when strong, sometimes
Will write of factories and of slaves, as if
195 Your father were a negro, and your son
A spinner in the mills. All's yours and you,—
All, coloured with your blood, or otherwise
Just nothing to you. Why, I call you hard
To general suffering. Here's the world half blind
200 With intellectual light, half brutalised
With civilisation, having caught the plague
In silks from Tarsus, shrieking east and west
Along a thousand railroads, mad with pain
And sin too! . . does one woman of you all,
205 (You who weep easily) grow pale to see
This tiger shake his cage?—does one of you
Stand still from dancing, stop from stringing pearls,
And pine and die because of the great sum
Of universal anguish?—Show me a tear
210 Wet as Cordelia's, in eyes bright as yours,

Because the world is mad! You cannot count,
That you should weep for this account, not you!
You weep for what you know. A red-haired child
Sick in a fever, if you touch him once,
215   Though but so little as with a finger-tip,
Will set you weeping; but a million sick . .
You could as soon weep for the rule of three,
Or compound fractions. Therefore, this same world,
Uncomprehended by you, must remain
220   Uninfluenced by you.—Women as you are,
Mere women, personal and passionate,
You give us doating mothers, and chaste wives,
Sublime Madonnas, and enduring saints!
We get no Christ from you,—and verily
225   We shall not get a poet, in my mind.'

'With which conclusion you conclude!' . .
                                        'But this—
That you, Aurora, with the large live brow
And steady eyelids, cannot condescend
To play at art, as children play at swords,
230   To show a pretty spirit, chiefly admired
Because true action is impossible.
You never can be satisfied with praise
Which men give women when they judge a book
Not as mere work, but as mere woman's work,
235   Expressing the comparative respect
Which means the absolute scorn. 'Oh, excellent,
'What grace! what facile turns! what fluent sweeps!
'What delicate discernment . . almost thought!
'The book does honour to the sex, we hold.
240   'Among our female authors we make room
'For this fair writer, and congratulate
'The country that produces in these times
'Such women, competent to . . spell.''
                                        'Stop there!'
I answered—burning through his thread of talk
245   With a quick flame of emotion,—'You have read
My soul, if not my book, and argue well

I would not condescend . . we will not say
To such a kind of praise, (a worthless end
Is praise of all kinds), but to such a use
250 Of holy art and golden life. I am young,
And peradventure weak—you tell me so—
Through being a woman. And, for all the rest,
Take thanks for justice. I would rather dance
At fairs on tight-rope, till the babies dropped
255 Their gingerbread for joy,—than shift the types
For tolerable verse, intolerable
To men who act and suffer. Better far,
Pursue a frivolous trade by serious means,
Than a sublime art frivolously.'

                                          'You,
260 Choose nobler work than either, O moist eyes,
And hurrying lips and heaving heart! We are young
Aurora, you and I. The world . . look round . .
The world, we're come to late, is swollen hard
With perished generations and their sins:
265 The civiliser's spade grinds horribly
On dead men's bones, and cannot turn up soil
That's otherwise than fetid. All success
Proves partial failure; all advance implies
What's left behind; all triumph, something crushed
270 At the chariot-wheels; all government, some wrong:
And rich men make the poor, who curse the rich,
Who agonise together, rich and poor,
Under and over, in the social spasm
And crisis of the ages. Here's an age,
275 That makes its own vocation! here, we have stepped
Across the bounds of time! here's nought to see,
But just the rich man and just Lazarus,
And both in torments; with a mediate gulph,
Though not a hint of Abraham's bosom. Who,
280 Being man and human, can stand calmly by
And view these things, and never tease his soul
For some great cure? No physic for this grief,
In all the earth and heavens too?'

                                    'You believe

In God, for your part?—ay? that He who makes
285   Can make good things from ill things, best from worst,
As men plant tulips upon dunghills when
They wish them finest?'
                                    'True. A death-heat is
The same as life-heat, to be accurate;
And in all nature is no death at all,
290   As men account of death, so long as God
Stands witnessing for life perpetually
By being just God. That's abstract truth, I know,
Philosophy, or sympathy with God:
But I, I sympathise with man, not God,
295   I think I was a man for chiefly this;
And when I stand beside a dying bed,
'Tis death to me. Observe,—it had not much
Consoled the race of mastodons to know,
Before they went to fossil, that anon
300   Their place would quicken with the elephant;
They were not elephants but mastodons:
And I, a man, as men are now, and not
As men may be hereafter, feel with men
In the agonising present.'
                                    'Is it so,'
305   I said, 'my cousin? is the world so bad,
While I hear nothing of it through the trees?
The world was always evil,—but so bad?'

'So bad, Aurora. Dear, my soul is grey
With poring over the long sum of ill;
310   So much for vice, so much for discontent,
So much for the necessities of power,
So much for the connivances of fear,—
Coherent in statistical despairs
With such a total of distracted life, . .
315   To see it down in figures on a page,
Plain, silent, clear . . as God sees through the earth
The sense of all the graves! . . . that's terrible
For one who is not God, and cannot right
The wrong he looks on. May I choose indeed,

320 But vow away my years, my means, my aims,
Among the helpers, if there's any help
In such a social strait? The common blood
That swings along my veins, is strong enough
To draw me to this duty.'
                              Then I spoke
325 'I have not stood long on the strand of life,
And these salt waters have had scarcely time
To creep so high up as to wet my feet.
I cannot judge these tides—I shall, perhaps.
A woman's always younger than a man
330 At equal years, because she is disallowed
Maturing by the outdoor sun and air,
And kept in long-clothes past the age to walk.
Ah well, I know you men judge otherwise!
You think a woman ripens as a peach,—
335 In the cheeks, chiefly. Pass it to me now;
I'm young in age, and younger still, I think,
As a woman. But a child may say amen
To a bishop's prayer and see the way it goes;
And I, incapable to loose the knot
340 Of social questions, can approve, applaud
August compassion, christian thoughts that shoot
Beyond the vulgar white of personal aims.
Accept my reverence.'
                          There he glowed on me
With all his face and eyes. 'No other help?'
345 Said he—'no more than so?'
                                  'What help?' I asked.
'You'd scorn my help,—as Nature's self, you say,
Has scorned to put her music in my mouth,
Because a woman's. Do you now turn round
And ask for what a woman cannot give?'

350 'For what she only can, I turn and ask,'
He answered, catching up my hands in his,
And dropping on me from his high-eaved brow
The full weight of his soul,—'I ask for love,
And that, she can; for life in fellowship

355 Through bitter duties—that, I know she can;
For wifehood . . will she?'
        'Now,' I said, 'may God
Be witness 'twixt us two!' and with the word,
Meseemed I floated into a sudden light
Above his stature,—'am I proved too weak
360 To stand alone, yet strong enough to bear
Such leaners on my shoulder? poor to think,
Yet rich enough to sympathise with thought?
Incompetent to sing, as blackbirds can,
Yet competent to love, like HIM?'
          I paused:
365 Perhaps I darkened, as the light-house will
That turns upon the sea. 'It's always so!
Anything does for a wife.'
         'Aurora, dear,
And dearly honoured' . . he pressed in at once
With eager utterance,—'you translate me ill.
370 I do not contradict my thought of you
Which is most reverent, with another thought
Found less so. If your sex is weak for art,
(And I, who said so, did but honour you
By using truth in courtship) it is strong
375 For life and duty. Place your fecund heart
In mine, and let us blossom for the world
That wants love's colour in the grey of time.
With all my talk I can but set you where
You look down coldly on the arena-heaps
380 Of headless bodies, shapeless, indistinct!
The Judgment-Angel scarce would find his way
Through such a heap of generalised distress
To the individual man with lips and eyes—
Much less Aurora. Ah, my sweet, come down
385 And, hand in hand, we'll go where yours shall touch
These victims, one by one! till, one by one,
The formless, nameless trunk of every man
Shall seem to wear a head, with hair you know,
And every woman catch your mother's face
390 To melt you into passion.'
         'I am a girl,'

I answered slowly; 'you do well to name
My mother's face. Though far too early, alas,
God's hand did interpose 'twixt it and me,
I know so much of love, as used to shine
395   In that face and another. Just so much;
No more indeed at all. I have not seen
So much love since, I pray you pardon me,
As answers even to make a marriage with,
In this cold land of England. What you love,
400   Is not a woman, Romney, but a cause:
You want a helpmate, not a mistress, sir,—
A wife to help your ends . . in her no end.
Your cause is noble, your ends excellent,
But I, being most unworthy of these and that,
405   Do otherwise conceive of love. Farewell.'

'Farewell, Aurora? you reject me thus?'
He said.
            'Why, sir, you are married long ago.
You have a wife already whom you love,
Your social theory. Bless you both, I say.
410   For my part, I am scarcely meek enough
To be the handmaid of a lawful spouse.
Do I look a Hagar, think you?'
                            'So, you jest!'

'Nay so, I speak in earnest,' I replied.
'You treat of marriage too much like, at least,
415   A chief apostle; you would bear with you
A wife . . a sister . . shall we speak it out?
A sister of charity.'
                        'Then, must it be
Indeed farewell? And was I so far wrong
In hope and in illusion, when I took
420   The woman to be nobler than the man,
Yourself the noblest woman,—in the use
And comprehension of what love is,—love,
That generates the likeness of itself
Through all heroic duties? so far wrong,

425 In saying bluntly, venturing truth on love,
'Come, human creature, love and work with me,'—
Instead of 'Lady, thou art wondrous fair,
'And, where the Graces walk before, the Muse
'Will follow at the lighting of their eyes,
430 'And where the Muse walks, lovers need to creep:
'Turn round and love me, or I die of love.''

With quiet indignation I broke in.
'You misconceive the question like a man,
Who sees a woman as the complement
435 Of his sex merely. You forget too much
That every creature, female as the male,
Stands single in responsible act and thought,
As also in birth and death. Whoever says
To a loyal woman, 'Love and work with me,'
440 Will get fair answers, if the work and love,
Being good themselves, are good for her—the best
She was born for. Woman of a softer mood,
Surprised by men when scarcely awake to life,
Will sometimes only hear the first word, love,
445 And catch up with it any kind of work,
Indifferent, so that dear love go with it:
I do not blame such women, though, for love,
They pick much oakum; earth's fanatics make
Too frequently heaven's saints. But *me*, your work
450 Is not the best for,—nor your love the best,
Nor able to commend the kind of work
For love's sake merely. Ah, you force me, sir,
To be over-bold in speaking of myself,—
I, too, have my vocation,—work to do,
455 The heavens and earth have set me, since I changed
My father's face for theirs,—and, though your world
Were twice as wretched as you represent,
Most serious work, most necessary work,
As any of the economists'. Reform,
460 Make trade a Christian possibility,
And individual right no general wrong;
Wipe out earth's furrows of the Thine and Mine,

And leave one green, for men to play at bowls,
With innings for them all! . . what then, indeed,
465 If mortals were not greater by the head
Than any of their prosperities? what then,
Unless the artist keep up open roads
Betwixt the seen and unseen,—bursting through
The best of your conventions with his best,
470 The speakable, imaginable best
God bids him speak, to prove what lies beyond
Both speech and imagination? A starved man
Exceeds a fat beast: we'll not barter, sir,
The beautiful for barley.—And, even so,
475 I hold you will not compass your poor ends
Of barley-feeding and material ease,
Without a poet's individualism
To work your universal. It takes a soul,
To move a body: it takes a high-souled man,
480 To move the masses . . even to a cleaner stye:
It takes the ideal, to blow a hair's-breadth off
The dust of the actual.—Ah, your Fouriers failed,
Because not poets enough to understand
That life develops from within.—For me,
485 Perhaps I am not worthy, as you say,
Of work like this! . . perhaps a woman's soul
Aspires, and not creates! yet we aspire,
And yet I'll try out your perhapses, sir;
And if I fail . . why, burn me up my straw
490 Like other false works—I'll not ask for grace,
Your scorn is better, cousin Romney. I
Who love my art, would never wish it lower
To suit my stature. I may love my art.
You'll grant that even a woman may love art,
495 Seeing that to waste true love on anything,
Is womanly, past question.'
                                        I retain
The very last word which I said, that day,
As you the creaking of the door, years past,
Which let upon you such disabling news
500 You ever after have been graver. He,

His eyes, the motions in his silent mouth,
Were fiery points on which my words were caught,
Transfixed for ever in my memory
For his sake, not their own. And yet I know
505   I did not love him . . nor he me . . that's sure . .
And what I said, is unrepented of,
As truth is always. Yet . . a princely man!—
If hard to me, heroic for himself!
He bears down on me through the slanting years,
510   The stronger for the distance. If he had loved,
Ay, loved me, with that retributive face, . .
I might have been a common woman now,
And happier, less known and less left alone;
Perhaps a better woman after all,—
515   With chubby children hanging on my neck
To keep me low and wise. Ah me, the vines
That bear such fruit are proud to stoop with it.
The palm stands upright in a realm of sand.

And I, who spoke the truth then, stand upright,
520   Still worthy of having spoken out the truth,
By being content I spoke it, though it set
Him there, me here.—O woman's vile remorse,
To hanker after a mere name, a show,
A supposition, a potential love!
525   Does every man who names love in our lives,
Become a power for that? is love's true thing
So much best to us, that what personates love
Is next best? A potential love, forsooth!
We are not so vile. No, no—he cleaves, I think,
530   This man, this image, . . chiefly for the wrong
And shock he gave my life, in finding me
Precisely where the devil of my youth
Had set me, on those mountain-peaks of hope
All glittering with the dawn-dew, all erect
535   And famished for the morning,—saying, while
I looked for empire and much tribute, 'Come,
I have some worthy work for thee below.
Come, sweep my barns and keep my hospitals,—

And I will pay thee with a current coin
540 Which men give women.'
                              As we spoke, the grass
Was trod in haste beside us, and my aunt,
With smile distorted by the sun,—face, voice,
As much at issue with the summer-day
As if you brought a candle out of doors,—
545 Broke in with 'Romney, here!—My child, entreat
Your cousin to the house, and have your talk,
If girls must talk upon their birthdays. Come.'

He answered for me calmly, with pale lips
That seemed to motion for a smile in vain,
550 'The talk is ended, madam, where we stand.
Your brother's daughter has dismissed me here;
And all my answer can be better said
Beneath the trees, than wrong by such a word
Your house's hospitalities. Farewell.'

555 With that he vanished. I could hear his heel
Ring bluntly in the lane, as down he leapt
The short way from us.—Then, a measured speech
Withdrew me. 'What means this, Aurora Leigh?
My brother's daughter has dismissed my guests?'

560 The lion in me felt the keeper's voice,
Through all its quivering dewlaps: I was quelled
Before her,—meekened to the child she knew:
I prayed her pardon, said, 'I had little thought
To give dismissal to a guest of hers,
565 In letting go a friend of mine, who came
To take me into service as a wife,—
No more than that, indeed.'
                              'No more, no more?
Pray Heaven,' she answered, 'that I was not mad.
I could not mean to tell her to her face
570 That Romney Leigh had asked me for a wife,
And I refused him?'
                       'Did he ask?' I said;

'I think he rather stooped to take me up
For certain uses which he found to do
For something called a wife. He never asked.'

575 'What stuff!' she answered; 'are they queens, these girls?
They must have mantles, stitched with twenty silks,
Spread out upon the ground, before they'll step
One footstep for the noblest lover born.'

'But I am born,' I said with firmness, 'I,
580 To walk another way than his, dear aunt.'

'You walk, you walk! A babe at thirteen months
Will walk as well as you,' she cried in haste,
'Without a steadying finger. Why, you child,
God help you, you are groping in the dark,
585 For all the sunlight. You suppose, perhaps,
That you, sole offspring of an opulent man,
Are rich and free to choose a way to walk?
You think, and it's a reasonable thought,
That I besides, being well to do in life,
590 Will leave my handful in my niece's hand
When death shall paralyse these fingers? Pray,
Pray, child,—albeit I know you love me not,—
As if you loved me, that I may not die!
For when I die and leave you, out you go,
595 (Unless I make room for you in my grave)
Unhoused, unfed, my dear, poor brother's lamb,
(Ah heaven,—that pains!)—without a right to crop
A single blade of grass beneath these trees,
Or cast a lamb's small shadow on the lawn,
600 Unfed, unfolded! Ah, my brother, here's
The fruit you planted in your foreign loves!—
Ay, there's the fruit he planted! never look
Astonished at me with your mother's eyes,
For it was they, who set you where you are,
605 An undowered orphan. Child, your father's choice
Of that same mother, disinherited
His daughter, his and hers. Men do not think

Of sons and daughters, when they fall in love,
So much more than of sisters; otherwise,
610 He would have paused to ponder what he did,
And shrunk before that clause in the entail
Excluding offspring by a foreign wife
(The clause set up a hundred years ago
By a Leigh who wedded a French dancing-girl
615 And had his heart danced over in return)
But this man shrunk at nothing, never thought
Of you, Aurora, any more than me—
Your mother must have been a pretty thing,
For all the coarse Italian blacks and browns,
620 To make a good man, which my brother was,
Unchary of the duties to his house;
But so it fell indeed. Our cousin Vane,
Vane Leigh, the father of this Romney, wrote
Directly on your birth, to Italy,
625 'I ask your baby daughter for my son
In whom the entail now merges by the law.
Betroth her to us out of love, instead
Of colder reasons, and she shall not lose
By love or law from henceforth'—so he wrote;
630 A generous cousin, was my cousin Vane.
Remember how he drew you to his knee
The year you came here, just before he died,
And hollowed out his hands to hold your cheeks,
And wished them redder,—you remember Vane?
635 And now his son who represents our house,
And holds the fiefs and manors in his place,
To whom reverts my pittance when I die,
(Except a few books and a pair of shawls),
The boy is generous like him, and prepared
640 To carry out his kindest word and thought
To you, Aurora. Yes, a fine young man
Is Romney Leigh; although the sun of youth
Has shone too straight upon his brain, I know,
And fevered him with dreams of doing good
645 To good-for-nothing people. But a wife

Will put all right, and stroke his temples cool
With healthy touches' . .
                              I broke in at that.
I could not lift my heavy heart to breathe
Till then, but then I raised it, and it fell
650 In broken words like these—'No need to wait.
The dream of doing good to . . me, at least,
Is ended, without waiting for a wife
To cool the fever for him. We've escaped
That danger . . thank Heaven for it.'
                                    'You,' she cried,
655 'Have got a fever. What, I talk and talk
An hour long to you,—I instruct you how
You cannot eat or drink or stand or sit,
Or even die, like any decent wretch
In all this unroofed and unfurnished world,
660 Without your cousin,—and you still maintain
There's room 'twixt him and you, for flirting fans
And running knots in eyebrows? You must have
A pattern lover sighing on his knee:
You do not count enough a noble heart
665 Above book-patterns, which this very morn
Unclosed itself, in two dear father's names
To embrace your orphaned life? fie, fie! But stay,
I write a word, and counteract this sin.'

She would have turned to leave me, but I clung.
670 'O sweet my father's sister, hear my word
Before you write yours. Cousin Vane did well,
And cousin Romney well,—and I well too,
In casting back with all my strength and will
The good they meant me. O my God, my God!
675 God meant me good, too, when he hindered me
From saying 'yes' this morning. If you write
A word, it shall be 'no.' I say no, no!
I tie up 'no' upon His altar-horns,
Quite out of reach of perjury! At least
680 My soul is not a pauper; I can live
At least my soul's life, without alms from men;

And if it must be in heaven instead of earth,
Let heaven look to it,—I am not afraid.'

She seized my hands with both hers, strained them fast,
685 And drew her probing and unscrupulous eyes
Right through me, body and heart. 'Yet, foolish Sweet,
You love this man. I have watched you when he came,
And when he went, and when we've talked of him:
I am not old for nothing; I can tell
690 The weather-signs of love—you love this man.'

Girls blush, sometimes, because they are alive,
Half wishing they were dead to save the shame.
The sudden blush devours them, neck and brow;
They have drawn too near the fire of life, like gnats,
695 And flare up bodily, wings and all. What then?
Who's sorry for a gnat . . or girl?
                                        I blushed.
I feel the brand upon my forehead now
Strike hot, sear deep, as guiltless men may feel
The felon's iron, say, and scorn the mark
700 Of what they are not. Most illogical
Irrational nature of our womanhood,
That blushes one way, feels another way,
And prays, perhaps, another! After all,
We cannot be the equal of the male,
705 Who rules his blood a little.
                                        For although
I blushed indeed, as if I loved the man,
And her incisive smile, accrediting
That treason of false witness in my blush,
Did bow me downward like a swathe of grass
710 Below its level that struck me,—I attest
The conscious skies and all their daily suns,
I think I loved him not . . nor then, nor since . .
Nor ever. Do we love the schoolmaster,
Being busy in the woods? much less, being poor,
715 The overseer of the parish? Do we keep
Our love to pay our debts with?
                                        White and cold

I grew next moment. As my blood recoiled
From that imputed ignominy, I made
My heart great with it. Then, at last, I spoke,—
720 Spoke veritable words, but passionate,
Too passionate perhaps .. ground up with sobs
To shapeless endings. She let fall my hands,
And took her smile off, in sedate disgust,
As peradventure she had touched a snake,—
725 A dead snake, mind!—and turning round, replied,
'We'll leave Italian manners, if you please.
I think you had an English father, child,
And ought to find it possible to speak
A quiet 'yes' or 'no,' like English girls,
730 Without convulsions. In another month
We'll take another answer .. no, or yes.'
With that, she left me in the garden-walk.

I had a father! yes, but long ago—
How long it seemed that moment. Oh, how far,
735 How far and safe, God, dost thou keep thy saints
When once gone from us! We may call against
The lighted windows of thy fair June-heaven
Where all the souls are happy,—and not one,
Not even my father, look from work or play
740 To ask, 'Who is it that cries after us,
Below there, in the dusk?' Yet formerly
He turned his face upon me quick enough,
If I said 'father.' Now I might cry loud;
The little lark reached higher with his song
745 Than I with crying. Oh, alone, alone,—
Not troubling any in heaven, nor any on earth,
I stood there in the garden, and looked up
The deaf blue sky that brings the roses out
On such June mornings.
                                    You who keep account
750 Of crisis and transition in this life,
Set down the first time Nature says plain 'no'
To some 'yes' in you, and walks over you
In gorgeous sweeps of scorn. We all begin

By singing with the birds, and running fast
755 With June-days, hand in hand: but once, for all,
The birds must sing against us, and the sun
Strike down upon us like a friend's sword caught
By an enemy to slay us, while we read
The dear name on the blade which bites at us!—
760 That's bitter and convincing: after that,
We seldom doubt that something in the large
Smooth order of creation, though no more
Than haply a man's footstep, has gone wrong.

Some tears fell down my cheeks, and then I smiled,
765 As those smile who have no face in the world
To smile back to them. I had lost a friend
In Romney Leigh; the thing was sure—a friend,
Who had looked at me most gently now and then,
And spoke of my favourite books . . 'our books' . .
770 With such a voice! Well, voice and look were now
More utterly shut out from me, I felt,
Than even my father's. Romney now was turned
To a benefactor, to a generous man,
Who had tied himself to marry . . me, instead
775 Of such a woman, with low timorous lids
He lifted with a sudden word one day,
And left, perhaps, for my sake.—Ah, self-tied
By a contract,—male Iphigenia, bound
At a fatal Aulis for the winds to change,
780 (But loose him—they'll not change); he well might seem
A little cold and dominant in love!
He had a right to be dogmatical,
This poor, good Romney. Love, to him, was made
A simple law-clause. If I married him,
785 I would not dare to call my soul my own,
Which he had bought and paid for: every thought
And every heart-beat down there in the bill,—
Not one found honestly deductible
From any use that pleased him! He might cut
790 My body into coins to give away

Among his other paupers; change my sons,
While I stood dumb as Griseld, for black babes
Or piteous foundlings; might unquestioned set
My right hand teaching in the Ragged Schools,
795   My left hand washing in the Public Baths,
What time my angel of the Ideal stretched
Both his to me in vain. I could not claim
The poor right of a mouse in a trap, to squeal,
And take so much as pity, from myself.

800   Farewell, good Romney! if I loved you even,
I could but ill afford to let you be
So generous to me. Farewell, friend, since friend
Betwixt us two, forsooth, must be a word
So heavily overladen. And, since help
805   Must come to me from those who love me not,
Farewell, all helpers—I must help myself,
And am alone from henceforth.—Then I stooped
And lifted the soiled garland from the ground,
And set it on my head as bitterly
810   As when the Spanish king did crown the bones
Of his dead love. So be it. I preserve
That crown still,—in the drawer there! 'twas the first;
The rest are like it;—those Olympian crowns,
We run for, till we lose sight of the sun
815   In the dust of the racing chariots!

                                    After that,
Before the evening fell, I had a note
Which ran,—'Aurora, sweet Chaldean, you read
My meaning backward like your eastern books,
While I am from the west, dear. Read me now
820   A little plainer. Did you hate me quite
But yesterday? I loved you for my part;
I love you. If I spoke untenderly
This morning, my beloved, pardon it;
And comprehend me that I loved you so,
825   I set you on the level of my soul,
And overwashed you with the bitter brine
Of some habitual thoughts. Henceforth, my flower,

Be planted out of reach of any such,
And lean the side you please, with all your leaves!
830   Write woman's verses and dream woman's dreams;
But let me feel your perfume in my home
To make my sabbath after working-days;
Bloom out your youth beside me,—be my wife.'

I wrote in answer—'We, Chaldeans, discern
835   Still farther than we read. I know your heart,
And shut it like the holy book it is,
Reserved for mild-eyed saints to pore upon
Betwixt their prayers at vespers. Well, you're right,
I did not surely hate you yesterday;
840   And yet I do not love you enough to-day
To wed you, cousin Romney. Take this word,
And let it stop you as a generous man
From speaking farther. You may tease, indeed,
And blow about my feelings, or my leaves,—
845   And here's my aunt will help you with east winds,
And break a stalk, perhaps, tormenting me;
But certain flowers grow near as deep as trees,
And, cousin, you'll not move my root, not you,
With all your confluent storms. Then let me grow
850   Within my wayside hedge, and pass your way!
This flower has never as much to say to you
As the antique tomb which said to travellers, 'Pause,
Siste, viator.'' Ending thus, I signed.

The next week passed in silence, so the next,
855   And several after: Romney did not come,
Nor my aunt chide me. I lived on and on,
As if my heart were kept beneath a glass,
And everybody stood, all eyes and ears,
To see and hear it tick. I could not sit,
860   Nor walk, nor take a book, nor lay it down,
Not sew on steadily, nor drop a stitch
And a sigh with it, but I felt her looks
Still cleaving to me, like the sucking asp
To Cleopatra's breast, persistently

865 Through the intermittent pantings. Being observed,
    When observation is not sympathy,
    Is just being tortured. If she said a word,
    A 'thank you' or an 'if it please you, dear,'
    She meant a commination, or, at best,
870 An exorcism against the devildom
    Which plainly held me. So with all the house.
    Susannah could not stand and twist my hair,
    Without such glancing at the looking-glass
    To see my face there, that she missed the plait:
875 And John,—I never sent my plate for soup,
    Or did not send it, but the foolish John
    Resolved the problem, 'twixt his napkined thumbs,
    Of what was signified by taking soup
    Or choosing mackerel. Neighbours, who dropped in
880 On morning visits, feeling a joint wrong,
    Smiled admonition, sate uneasily,
    And talked with measured, emphasised reserve,
    Of parish news, like doctors to the sick,
    When not called in,—as if, with leave to speak,
885 They might say something. Nay, the very dog
    Would watch me from his sun-patch on the floor,
    In alternation with the large black fly
    Not yet in reach of snapping. So I lived.

    A Roman died so; smeared with honey, teased
890 By insects, stared to torture by the noon:
    And many patient souls 'neath English roofs
    Have died like Romans. I, in looking back,
    Wish only, now, I had borne the plague of all
    With meeker spirits than were rife in Rome.

895 For, on the sixth week, the dead sea broke up,
    Dashed suddenly through beneath the heel of Him
    Who stands upon the sea and earth and swears
    Time shall be nevermore. The clock struck nine
    That morning, too,—no lark was out of tune;
900 The hidden farms among the hills, breathed straight
    Their smoke toward heaven; the lime-tree scarcely stirred

Beneath the blue weight of the cloudless sky.
Though still the July air came floating through
The woodbine at my window, in and out,
905 With touches of the out-door country-news
For a bending forehead. There I sate, and wished
That morning-truce of God would last till eve,
Or longer. 'Sleep,' I thought, 'late sleepers,—sleep,
And spare me yet the burden of your eyes.'

910 Then, suddenly, a single ghastly shriek
Tore upward from the bottom of the house.
Like one who wakens in a grave and shrieks,
The still house seemed to shriek itself alive,
And shudder through its passages and stairs
915 With slam of doors and clash of bells.—I sprang,
I stood up in the middle of the room,
And there confronted at my chamber-door,
A white face,—shivering, ineffectual lips.

'Come, come,' they tried to utter, and I went;
920 As if a ghost had drawn me at the point
Of a fiery finger through the uneven dark,
I went with reeling footsteps down the stair,
Nor asked a question.
                    There she sate, my aunt,—
Bolt upright in the chair beside her bed,
925 Whose pillow had no dint! she had used no bed
For that night's sleeping . . yet slept well. My God;
The dumb derision of that grey, peaked face
Concluded something grave against the sun,
Which filled the chamber with its July burst
930 When Susan drew the curtains, ignorant
Of who sat open-eyed behind her. There,
She sate . . it sate . . we said 'she' yesterday . .
And held a letter with unbroken seal,
As Susan gave it to her hand last night:
935 All night she had held it. If its news referred
To duchies or to dunghills, not an inch
She'd budge, 'twas obvious, for such worthless odds:

Nor, though the stars were suns, and overburned
Their spheric limitations, swallowing up
940 Like wax the azure spaces, could they force
Those open eyes to wink once. What last sight
Had left them blank and flat so,—drawing out
The faculty of vision from the roots,
As nothing more, worth seeing, remained behind?

945 Were those the eyes that watched me, worried me?
That dogged me up and down the hours and days,
A beaten, breathless, miserable soul?
And did I pray, a half-hour back, but so,
To escape the burden of those eyes . . those eyes?
950 'Sleep late' I said.—

               Why, now, indeed, they sleep.
God answers sharp and sudden on some prayers,
And thrusts the thing we have prayed for in our face,
A gauntlet with a gift in't. Every wish
Is like a prayer . . with God.

                  I had my wish,—
955 To read and meditate the thing I would,
To fashion all my life upon my thought,
And marry, or not marry. Henceforth, none
Could disapprove me, vex me, hamper me.
Full ground-room, in this desert newly-made,
960 For Babylon or Balbec,—when the breath,
Just choked with sand, returns, for building towns!

The heir came over on the funeral day,
And we two cousins met before the dead,
With two pale faces. Was it death or life
965 That moved us? When the will was read and done,
The official guest and witnesses withdrawn,
We rose up in a silence almost hard,
And looked at one another. Then I said,
'Farewell, my cousin.'

                 But he touched, just touched
970 My hatstrings tied for going, (at the door
The carriage stood to take me) and said low,

His voice a little unsteady through his smile,
'Siste, viator.'
                              'Is there time,' I asked,
'In these last days of railroads, to stop short ·
975   Like Cæsar's chariot (weighing half a ton)
On the Appian road, for morals?'
                                    'There is time,'
He answered grave, 'for necessary words,
Inclusive, trust me, of no epitaph
On man or act, my cousin. We have read
980   A will, which gives you all the personal goods
And funded monies of your aunt.'
                                    'I thank
Her memory for it. With three hundred pounds
We buy, in England even, clear standing-room
To stand and work in. Only two hours since,
985   I fancied I was poor.'
                              'And, cousin, still
You're richer than you fancy. The will says,
Three hundred pounds, and any other sum
Of which the said testatrix dies possessed.
I say she died possessed of other sums.'

990   'Dear Romney, need we chronicle the pence?
I'm richer than I thought—that's evident.
Enough so.'
                  'Listen rather. You've to do
With business and a cousin,' he resumed,
'And both, I fear, need patience. Here's the fact.
995   The other sum (there *is* another sum,
Unspecified in any will which dates
After possession, yet bequeathed as much
And clearly as those said three hundred pounds)
Is thirty thousand. You will have it paid
1000 When? . . where? My duty troubles you with words.'

He struck the iron when the bar was hot;
No wonder if my eyes sent out some sparks.
'Pause there! I thank you. You are delicate

In glosing gifts;—but I, who share your blood,
1005　Am rather made for giving, like yourself,
Than taking, like your pensioners. Farewell.'

He stopped me with a gesture of calm pride.
'A Leigh,' he said, 'gives largesse and gives love,
But gloses neither: if a Leigh could glose,
1010　He would not do it, moreover, to a Leigh,
With blood trained up along nine centuries
To hound and hate a lie from eyes like yours.
And now we'll make the rest as clear; your aunt
Possessed these monies.'
　　　　　　　　　　　　'You will make it clear,
1015　My cousin, as the honour of us both,
Or one of us speaks vainly—that's not I.
My aunt possessed this sum,—inherited
From whom, and when? bring documents, prove dates.'

'Why now indeed you throw your bonnet off,
1020　As if you had time left for a logarithm!
The faith's the want. Dear cousin, give me faith,
And you shall walk this road with silken shoes,
As clean as any lady of our house
Supposed the proudest. Oh, I comprehend
1025　The whole position from your point of sight.
I oust you from your father's halls and lands,
And make you poor by getting rich—that's law;
Considering which, in common circumstance,
You would not scruple to accept from me
1030　Some compensation, some sufficiency
Of income—that were justice; but, alas,
I love you . . that's mere nature!—you reject
My love . . that's nature also;—and at once,
You cannot, from a suitor disallowed,
1035　A hand thrown back as mine is, into yours
Receive a doit, a farthing, . . not for the world!
That's etiquette with women, obviously
Exceeding the claim of nature, law, and right,
Unanswerable to all. I grant, you see,

1040   The case as you conceive it,—leave you room
To sweep your ample skirts of womanhood,
While, standing humbly squeezed against the wall,
I own myself excluded from being just,
Restrained from paying indubitable debts,
1045   Because denied from giving you my soul—
That's my misfortune!—I submit to it
As if, in some more reasonable age,
'Twould not be less inevitable. Enough.
You'll trust me, cousin, as a gentleman,
1050   To keep your honour, as you count it, pure,—
Your scruples (just as if I thought them wise)
Safe and inviolate from gifts of mine.'

I answered mild but earnest. 'I believe
In no one's honour which another keeps,
1055   Nor man's nor woman's. As I keep, myself,
My truth and my religion, I depute
No father, though I had one this side death,
Nor brother, though I had twenty, much less you,
Though twice my cousin, and once Romney Leigh,
1060   To keep my honour pure. You face, to-day,
A man who wants instruction, mark me, not
A woman who wants protection. As to a man,
Show manhood, speak out plainly, be precise
With facts and dates. My aunt inherited
1065   This sum, you say—'
                              'I said she died possessed
Of this, dear cousin.'
                              'Not by heritage.
Thank you: we're getting to the facts at last.
Perhaps she played at commerce with a ship
Which came in heavy with Australian gold?
1070   Or touched a lottery with her finger-end,
Which tumbled on a sudden into her lap
Some old Rhine tower or principality?
Perhaps she had to do with a marine
Sub-transatlantic railroad, which pre-pays
1075   As well as pre-supposes? or perhaps

Some stale ancestral debt was after-paid
By a hundred years, and took her by surprise?—
You shake your head, my cousin; I guess ill.'

'You need not guess, Aurora, nor deride;—
1080   The truth is not afraid of hurting you.
You'll find no cause, in all your scruples, why
Your aunt should cavil at a deed of gift
'Twixt her and me.'
                        'I thought so—ah! a gift.'

'You naturally thought so,' he resumed.
1085   A very natural gift.'
                        'A gift, a gift!
Her individual life being stranded high
Above all want, approaching opulence,
Too haughty was she to accept a gift
Without some ultimate aim: ah, ah, I see,—
1090   A gift intended plainly for her heirs,
And so accepted . . if accepted . . ah,
Indeed that might be; I am snared perhaps,
Just so. But, cousin, shall I pardon you,
If thus you have caught me with a cruel springe?'

1095   He answered gently, 'Need you tremble and pant
Like a netted lioness? is't my fault, mine,
That you're a grand wild creature of the woods,
And hate the stall built for you? Any way,
Though triply netted, need you glare at me?
1100   I do not hold the cords of such a net;
You're free from me, Aurora!'
                        'Now may God
Deliver me from this strait! This gift of yours
Was tendered . . when? accepted . . when?' I asked.
'A month . . a fortnight since? Six weeks ago
1105   It was not tendered. By a word she dropped,
I know it was not tendered nor received.
When was it? bring your dates.'
                        'What matters when?

A half-hour ere she died, or a half-year,
Secured the gift, maintains the heritage
1110 Inviolable with law. As easy pluck
The golden stars from heaven's embroidered stole
To pin them on the grey side of this earth,
As make you poor again, thank God.'
                                        'Not poor
Nor clean again from henceforth, you thank God?
1115 Well, sir—I ask you . . I insist at need, . .
Vouchsafe the special date, the special date.'

'The day before her death-day,' he replied,
'The gift was in her hands. We'll find that deed,
And certify that date to you.'
                                        As one
1120 Who has climbed a mountain-height and carried up
His own heart climbing, panting in his throat
With the toil of the ascent, takes breath at last,
Looks back in triumph—so I stood and looked:
'Dear cousin Romney, we have reached the top
1125 Of this steep question, and may rest, I think.
But first,—I pray you pardon, that the shock
And surge of natural feeling and event
Has made me oblivious of acquainting you
That this, this letter . . unread, mark,—still sealed,
1130 Was found enfolded in the poor dead hand:
That spirit of hers had gone beyond the address,
Which could not find her though you wrote it clear,—
I know your writing, Romney,—recognize
The open-hearted *A*, the liberal sweep
1135 Of the *G*. Now listen,—let us understand;
You will not find that famous deed of gift,
Unless you find it in the letter here,
Which, not being mine, I give you back.—Refuse
To take the letter? well then—you and I,
1140 As writer and as heiress, open it
Together, by your leave.—Exactly so:
The words in which the noble offering's made
Are nobler still, my cousin; and, I own,

The proudest and most delicate heart alive,
1145 Distracted from the measure of the gift
By such a grace in giving, might accept
Your largesse without thinking any more
Of the burthen of it, than King Solomon
Considered, when he wore his holy ring
1150 Charactered over with the ineffable spell,
How many carats of fine gold made up
Its money-value. So, Leigh gives to Leigh—
Or rather, might have given, observe!—for that's
The point we come to. Here's a proof of gift,
1155 But here's no proof, sir, of acceptancy,
But, rather disproof. Death's black dust, being blown,
Infiltrated through ever secret fold
Of this sealed letter by a puff of fate,
Dried up for ever the fresh-written ink,
1160 Annulled the gift, disutilised the grace,
And left these fragments.'
                              As I spoke, I tore
The paper up and down, and down and up
And crosswide, till it fluttered from my hands,
As forest-leaves, stripped suddenly and rapt
1165 By a whirlwind on Valdarno, drop again,
Drop slow, and strew the melancholy ground
Before the amazèd hills . . . why, so, indeed,
I'm writing like a poet, somewhat large
In the type of the image,—and exaggerate
1170 A small thing with a great thing, topping it!—
But then I'm thinking how his eyes looked . . his,
With what despondent and surprised reproach!
I think the tears were in them, as he looked—
I think the manly mouth just trembled. Then
1175 He broke the silence.
                      'I may ask, perhaps,
Although no stranger . . only Romney Leigh,
Which means still less . . than Vincent Carrington . .
Your plans in going hence, and where you go.
This cannot be a secret.'
                              'All my life

1180 Is open to you, cousin. I go hence
     To London, to the gathering-place of souls,
     To live mine straight out, vocally, in books;
     Harmoniously for others, if indeed
     A woman's soul, like man's, be wide enough
1185 To carry the whole octave (that's to prove),
     Or, if I fail, still, purely for myself.
     Pray God be with me, Romney.'
                                    'Ah, poor child,
     Who fight against the mother's 'tiring hand,
     And choose the headsman's! May God change his world
1190 For your sake, sweet, and make it mild as heaven,
     And juster than I have found you.'
                                    But I paused.
     'And you, my cousin?'—
                              'I,' he said,—'you ask?
     You care to ask? Well, girls have curious minds,
     And fain would know the end of everything,
1195 Of cousins, therefore, with the rest. For me,
     Aurora, I've my work; you know my work;
     And, having missed this year some personal hope,
     I must beware the rather that I miss
     No reasonable duty. While you sing
1200 Your happy pastorals of the meads and trees,
     Bethink you that I go to impress and prove
     On stifled brains and deafened ears, stunned deaf,
     Crushed dull with grief, that nature sings itself,
     And needs no mediate poet, lute or voice,
1205 To make it vocal. While you ask of men
     Your audience, I may get their leave perhaps
     For hungry orphans to say audibly
     'We're hungry, see,'—for beaten and bullied wives
     To hold their unweaned babies up in sight,
1210 Whom orphanage would better; and for all
     To speak and claim their portion . . by no means
     Of the soil, . . but of the sweat in tilling it,—
     Since this is now-a-days turned privilege,
     To have only God's curse on us, and not man's.
1215 Such work I have for doing, elbow-deep

In social problems,—as you tie your rhymes,
To draw my uses to cohere with needs,
And bring the uneven world back to its round;
Or, failing so much, fill up, bridge at least
1220 To smoother issues some abysmal cracks
And feuds of earth, intestine heats have made
To keep men separate,—using sorry shifts
Of hospitals, almshouses, infant schools,
And other practical stuff of partial good,
1225 You lovers of the beautiful and whole,
Despise by system.'

                '*I* despise? The scorn
Is yours, my cousin. Poets become such,
Through scorning nothing. You decry them for
The good of beauty, sung and taught by them,
1230 While they respect your practical partial good
As being a part of beauty's self. Adieu!
When God helps all the workers of his world,
The singers shall have help of Him, not last.'

He smiled as men smile when they will not speak
1235 Because of something bitter in the thought;
And still I feel his melancholy eyes
Look judgment on me. It is seven years since:
I know not if 'twas pity or 'twas scorn
Has made them so far-reaching: judge it ye
1240 Who have had to do with pity more than love,
And scorn than hatred. I am used, since then,
To other ways, from equal men. But so,
Even so, we let go hands, my cousin and I,
And, in between us, rushed the torrent-world
1245 To blanch our faces like divided rocks,
And bar for ever mutual sight and touch
Except through swirl of spray and all that roar.

Third Book

'TO-DAY thou girdest up thy loins thyself,
And goest where thou wouldest: presently
Others shall gird thee,' said the Lord, 'to go
Where thou would'st not.' He spoke to Peter thus,
5   To signify the death which he should die
When crucified head downwards.

                If He spoke
To Peter then, He speaks to us the same;
The word suits many different martyrdoms,
And signifies a multiform of death,
10 Although we scarcely die apostles, we,
And have mislaid the keys of heaven and earth.

For 'tis not in mere death that men die most;
And, after our first girding of the loins
In youth's fine linen and fair broidery,
15 To run up hill and meet the rising sun,
We are apt to sit tired, patient as a fool,
While others gird us with the violent bands
Of social figments, feints, and formalisms,
Reversing our straight nature, lifting up
20 Our base needs, keeping down our lofty thoughts,
Head downward on the cross-sticks of the world.

Yet He can pluck us from that shameful cross.
God, set our feet low and our forehead high,
And show us how a man was made to walk!

25 Leave the lamp, Susan, and go up to bed.
The room does very well; I have to write
Beyond the stroke of midnight. Get away;
Your steps, for ever buzzing in the room,
Tease me like gnats. Ah, letters! throw them down
30 At once, as I must have them, to be sure,
Whether I bid you never bring me such

At such an hour, or bid you. No excuse.
You choose to bring them, as I choose perhaps
To throw them in the fire. Now, get to bed,
35 And dream, if possible, I am not cross.

Why what a pettish, petty thing I grow,—
A mere, mere woman,—a mere flaccid nerve,—
A kerchief left out all night in the rain,
Turned soft so,—overtasked and overstrained
40 And overlived in this close London life!
And yet I should be stronger.
                                        Never burn
Your letters, poor Aurora! for they stare
With red seals from the table, saying each,
'Here's something that you know not.' Out alas,
45 'Tis scarcely that the world's more good and wise
Or even straighter and more consequent
Since yesterday at this time—yet, again,
If but one angel spoke from Ararat
I should be very sorry not to hear:
50 So open all the letters! let me read.
Blanche Ord, the writer in the 'Lady's Fan,'
Requests my judgment on . . that, afterwards.
Kate Ward desires the model of my cloak,
And signs 'Elisha to you.' Pringle Sharpe
55 Presents his work on 'Social Conduct,' . . craves
A little money for his pressing debts . .
From me, who scarce have money for my needs,—
Art's fiery chariot which we journey in
Being apt to singe our singing-robes to holes,
60 Although you ask me for my cloak, Kate Ward!
Here's Rudgely knows it,—editor and scribe,—
He's 'forced to marry where his heart is not,
Because the purse lacks where he lost his heart.'
Ah,—lost it because no one picked it up!
65 That's really loss! (and passable impudence.)
My critic Hammond flatters prettily,
And wants another volume like the last.
My critic Belfair wants another book

Entirely different, which will sell, (and live?)
70   A striking book, yet not a startling book,
The public blames originalities,
(You must not pump spring-water unawares
Upon a gracious public, full of nerves—)
Good things, not subtle, new yet orthodox,
75   As easy reading as the dog-eared page
That's fingered by said public, fifty years,
Since first taught spelling by its grandmother,
And yet a revelation in some sort:
That's hard, my critic Belfair! So—what next?
80   My critic Stokes objects to abstract thoughts;
'Call a man, John, a woman Joan,' says he,
'And do not prate so of humanities:'
Whereat I call my critic, simply Stokes.
My critic Jobson recommends more mirth,
85   Because a cheerful genius suits the times,
And all true poets laugh unquenchably
Like Shakspeare and the gods. That's very hard.
The gods may laugh, and Shakspeare; Dante smiled
With such a needy heart on two pale lips,
90   We cry 'Weep rather, Dante.' Poems are
Men, if true poems: and who dares exclaim
At any man's door, 'Here, 'tis probable
The thunder fell last week, and killed a wife,
And scared a sickly husband—what of that?
95   Get up, be merry, shout, and clap your hands,
Because a cheerful genius suits the times—'?
None says so to the man,—and why indeed
Should any to the poem? A ninth seal;
The apocalypse is drawing to a close.
100   Ha,—this from Vincent Carrington,—'Dear friend,
I want good counsel. Will you lend me wings
To raise me to the subject, in a sketch
I'll bring tomorrow—may I? at eleven?
A poet's only born to turn to use;
105   So save you! for the world . . and Carrington.'
'(Writ after.) Have you heard of Romney Leigh,
Beyond what's said of him in newspapers,

His phalansteries there, his speeches here,
His pamphlets, pleas, and statements, everywhere?
110   He dropped *me* long ago; but no one drops
A golden apple—though, indeed, one day,
You hinted that, but jested. Well, at least,
You know Lord Howe, who sees him . . whom he sees,
And *you* see and I hate to see,—for Howe
115   Stands high upon the brink of theories,
Observes the swimmers and cries 'Very fine,'
But keeps dry linen equally,—unlike
That gallant breaster, Romney. Strange it is,
Such sudden madness seizing a young man,
120   To make the earth over again,—while I'm content
To make the pictures. Let me bring the sketch.
A tiptoe Danae, overbold and hot;
Both arms a-flame to meet her wishing Jove
Halfway, and burn him faster down; the face
125   And breasts upturned and straining, the loose locks
All glowing with the anticipated gold.
Or here's another on the self-same theme.
She lies here—flat upon her prison-floor
The long hair swathed about her to the heel,
130   Like wet sea-weed. You dimly see her through
The glittering haze of that prodigious rain,
Half blotted out of nature by a love
As heavy as fate. I'll bring you either sketch.
I think, myself, the second indicates
135   More passion.'
                              Surely. Self is put away,
And calm with abdication. She is Jove,
And no more Danae—greater thus. Perhaps
The painter symbolises unawares
Two states of the recipient artist-soul;
140   One, forward, personal, wanting reverence,
Because aspiring only. We'll be calm,
And know that, when indeed our Joves come down,
We all turn stiller than we have ever been.

*

Kind Vincent Carrington. I'll let him come.
145 He talks of Florence,—and may say a word
Of something as it chanced seven years ago,—
A hedgehog in the path, or a lame bird,
In those green country walks, in that good time,
When certainly I was so miserable . .
150 I seemed to have missed a blessing ever since.

The music soars within the little lark,
And the lark soars. It is not thus with men.
We do not make our places with our strains,—
Content, while they rise, to remain behind,
155 Alone on earth instead of so in heaven.
No matter—I bear on my broken tale.

When Romney Leigh and I had parted thus,
I took a chamber up three flights of stairs
Not far from being as steep as some larks climb,
160 And, in a certain house in Kensington,
Three years I lived and worked. Get leave to work
In this world—'tis the best you get at all;
For God, in cursing, gives us better gifts
Than men in benediction. God says, 'Sweat
165 For foreheads,' men say 'crowns,' and so we are
     crowned,—
Ay, gashed by some tormenting circle of steel
Which snaps with a secret spring. Get work, get work;
Be sure 'tis better than what you work to get.

So, happy and unafraid of solitude,
170 I worked the short days out,—and watched the sun
On lurid morns or monstrous afternoons
Like some Druidic idol's fiery brass,
With fixed unflickering outline of dead heat,
In which the blood of wretches pent inside
175 Seemed oozing forth to incarnadine the air,—
Push out through fog with his dilated disk,
And startle the slant roofs and chimney-pots
With splashes of fierce colour. Or I saw

Fog only, the great tawny weltering fog,
180 Involve the passive city, strangle it
Alive, and draw it off into the void,
Spires, bridges, streets, and squares, as if a spunge
Had wiped out London,—or as noon and night
Had clapped together and utterly struck out
185 The intermediate time, undoing themselves
In the act. Your city poets see such things,
Not despicable. Mountains of the south,
When, drunk and mad with elemental wines,
They rend the seamless mist and stand up bare,
190 Make fewer singers, haply. No one sings,
Descending Sinai: on Parnassus mount,
You take a mule to climb, and not a muse,
Except in fable and figure: forests chant
Their anthems to themselves, and leave you dumb.
195 But sit in London, at the day's decline,
And view the city perish in the mist
Like Pharoah's armaments in the deep Red Sea,—
The chariots, horsemen, footmen, all the host,
Sucked down and choked to silence—then, surprised
200 By a sudden sense of vision and of tune,
You feel as conquerors though you did not fight,
And you and Israel's other singing girls,
Ay, Miriam with them, sing the song you choose.

I worked with patience, which means almost power.
205 I did some excellent things indifferently,
Some bad things excellently. Both were praised,
The latter loudest. And by such a time
That I myself had set them down as sins
Scarce worth the price of sackcloth, week by week,
210 Arrived some letter through the sedulous post,
Like these I've read, and yet dissimilar,
With pretty maiden seals,—initials twined
Of lilies, or a heart marked *Emily*,
(Convicting Emily of being all heart);
215 Or rarer tokens from young bachelors,
Who wrote from college (with the same goosequill,

Suppose, they had just been plucked of) and a snatch
From Horace, 'Collegisse juvat,' set
Upon the first page. Many a letter, signed
220 Or unsigned, showing the writers at eighteen
Had lived too long, although every muse should help
The daylight, holding candles,—compliments
To smile or sigh at. Such could pass with me
No more than coins from Moscow circulate
225 At Paris. Would ten roubles buy a tag
Of ribbon on the boulevard, worth a sou?
I smiled that all this youth should love me,—sighed
That such a love could scarcely raise them up
To love what was more worthy than myself;
230 Then sighed again, again, less generously,
To think the very love they lavished so,
Proved me inferior. The strong loved me not,
And he . . my cousin Romney . . did not write.
I felt the silent finger of his scorn
235 Prick every bubble of my frivolous fame
As my breath blew it, and resolve it back
To the air it came from. Oh, I justified
The measure he had taken of my height:
The thing was plain—he was not wrong a line;
240 I played at art, made thrusts with a toy-sword,
Amused the lads and maidens.
                                             Came a sigh
Deep, hoarse with resolution,—I would work
To better ends, or play in earnest. 'Heavens,
I think I should be almost popular
245 If this went on!'—I ripped my verses up,
And found no blood upon the rapier's point;
The heart in them was just an embryo's heart
Which never yet had beat, that it should die;
Just gasps of make-believe galvanic life;
250 Mere tones, inorganised to any tune.

And yet I felt it in me where it burnt,
Like those hot fire-seeds of creation held
In Jove's clenched palm before the worlds were sown,—

But I—I was not Juno even! my hand
255 Was shut in weak convulsion, woman's ill,
And when I yearned to loose a finger—lo,
The nerve revolted. 'Tis the same even now:
This hand may never, haply, open large,
Before the spark is quenched, or the palm charred,
260 To prove the power not else than by the pain.

It burns, it burnt—my whole life burnt with it,
And light, not sunlight and not torchlight, flashed
My steps out through the slow and difficult road.
I had grown distrustful of too forward Springs,
265 The season's books in drear significance
Or morals, dropping round me. Lively books?
The ash has livelier verdure than the yew:
And yet the yew's green longer, and alone
Found worthy of the holy Christmas time:
270 We'll plant more yews if possible, albeit
We plant the graveyards with them.
                    Day and night
I worked my rhythmic thought, and furrowed up
Both watch and slumber with long lines of life
Which did not suit their season. The rose fell
275 From either cheek, my eyes globed luminous
Through orbits of blue shadow, and my pulse
Would shudder along the purple-veined wrist
Like a shot bird. Youth's stern, set face to face
With youth's ideal: and when people came
280 And said 'You work too much, you are looking ill,'
I smiled for pity of them who pitied me,
And thought I should be better soon perhaps
For those ill looks. Observe—'I,' means in youth
Just *I* . . the conscious and eternal soul
285 With all its ends,—and not the outside life,
The parcel-man, the doublet of the flesh,
The so much liver, lung, integument,
Which make the sum of 'I' hereafter, when
World-talkers talk of doing well or ill.
290 *I* prosper, if I gain a step, although

A nail then pierced my foot: although my brain
Embracing any truth, froze paralysed,
I prosper. I but change my instrument;
I break the spade off, digging deep for gold,
295 And catch the mattock up.
                                        I worked on, on.
Through all the bristling fence of nights and days
Which hedges time in from the eternities;
I struggled, . . never stopped to note the stakes
Which hurt me in my course. The midnight oil
300 Would stink sometimes; there came some vulgar needs:
I had to live, that therefore I might work,
And, being but poor, I was constrained, for life
To work with one hand for the booksellers,
While working with the other for myself
305 And art. You swim with feet as well as hands,
Or make small way. I apprehended this,—
In England, no one lives by verse that lives;
And, apprehending, I resolved by prose
To make a space to sphere my living verse.
310 I wrote for cyclopædias, magazines,
And weekly papers, holding up my name
To keep it from the mud. I learnt the use
Of the editorial 'we' in a review,
As courtly ladies the fine trick of trains,
315 And swept it grandly through the open doors
As if one could not pass through doors at all
Save so encumbered. I wrote tales beside,
Carved many an article on cherry-stones
To suit light readers,—something in the lines
320 Revealing, it was said, the mallet-hand,
But that, I'll never vouch for. What you do
For bread, will taste of common grain, not grapes,
Although you have a vineyard in Champagne,—
Much less in Nephelococcygia
325 As mine was, peradventure.
                                        Having bread
For just so many days, just breathing room
For body and verse, I stood up straight and worked

My veritable work. And as the soul
Which grows within a child, makes the child grow,—
330 Or as the fiery sap, the touch from God,
Careering through a tree, dilates the bark,
And roughs with scale and knob, before it strikes
The summer foliage out in a green flame—
So life, in deepening with me, deepened all
335 The course I took, the work I did. Indeed,
The academic law convinced of sin;
The critics cried out on the falling off,
Regretting the first manner. But I felt
My heart's life throbbing in my verse to show
340 It lived, it also—certes incomplete,
Disordered with all Adam in the blood,
But even its very tumours, warts, and wens,
Still organised by, and implying life.

A lady called upon me on such a day.
345 She had the low voice of your English dames,
Unused, it seems, to need rise half a note
To catch attention,—and their quiet mood,
As if they lived too high above the earth
For that to put them out in anything:
350 So gentle, because verily so proud;
So wary and afeared of hurting you,
By no means that you are not really vile,
But that they would not touch you with their foot
To push you to your place; so self-possessed
355 Yet gracious and conciliating, it takes
An effort in their presence to speak truth:
You know the sort of woman,—brilliant stuff,
And out of nature. 'Lady Waldemar.'
She said her name quite simply, as if it meant
360 Not much indeed, but something,—took my hands,
And smiled as if her smile could help my case,
And dropped her eyes on me and let them melt.
'Is this,' she said, 'the Muse?'
                                    'No sybil even,'
I answered, 'since she fails to guess the cause

365 Which taxed you with this visit, madam.'
                                        'Good,'
     She said, 'I like to be sincere at once;
     Perhaps, if I had found a literal Muse,
     The visit might have taxed me. As it is,
     You wear your blue so chiefly in your eyes,
370 My fair Aurora, in a frank good way,
     It comforts me entirely for your fame,
     As well as for the trouble of my ascent
     To this Olympus.'
                        There, a silver laugh
     Ran rippling through her quickened little breaths
375 That steep stair somewhat justified.
                                        'But still
     Your ladyship has left me curious why
     You dared the risk of finding the said Muse?'

     'Ah,—keep me, notwithstanding, to the point,
     Like any pedant. Is the blue in eyes
380 As awful as in stockings, after all,
     I wonder, that you'd have my business out
     Before I breathe—exact the epic plunge
     In spite of gasps? Well, naturally you think
     I've come here, as the lion-hunters go
385 To deserts, to secure you, with a trap,
     For exhibition in my drawing-rooms
     On zoologic soirées? Not in the least.
     Roar softly at me; I am frivolous,
     I dare say; I have played at lions, too,
390 Like other women of my class,—but now
     I meet my lion simply as Androcles
     Met his . . when at his mercy.'
                                   So, she bent
     Her head, as queens may mock,—then lifting up
     Her eyelids with a real grave queenly look,
395 Which ruled, and would not spare, not even herself,—
     'I think you have a cousin:—Romney Leigh.'

                        *

'You bring a word from *him?*'—my eyes leapt up
To the very height of hers,—'a word from *him?*'

'I bring a word about him, actually.
400 But first,'—she pressed me with her urgent eyes—
'You do not love him,—you?'
                                          'You're frank at least
In putting questions, madam,' I replied.
'I love my cousin cousinly—no more.'

'I guessed as much. I'm ready to be frank
405 In answering also, if you'll question me,
Or even with something less. You stand outside,
You artist women, of the common sex;
You share not with us, and exceed us so
Perhaps by what you're mulcted in, your hearts
410 Being starved to make your heads: so run the old
Traditions of you. I can therefore speak,
Without the natural shame which creatures feel
When speaking on their level, to their like.
There's many a papist she, would rather die
415 Than own to her maid she put a ribbon on
To catch the indifferent eye of such a man,—
Who yet would count adulteries on her beads
At holy Mary's shrine, and never blush;
Because the saints are so far off, we lose
420 All modesty before them. Thus, today.
'Tis *I*, love Romney Leigh.'
                                          'Forbear,' I cried.
'If here's no Muse, still less is any saint;
Not even a friend, that Lady Waldemar
Should make confessions' . .
                                          'That's unkindly said:
425 If no friend, what forbids to make a friend
To join to our confession ere we have done?
I love your cousin. If it seems unwise
To say so, it's still foolisher (we're frank)
To feel so. My first husband left me young,
430 And pretty enough, so please you, and rich enough,

To keep my booth in May-fair with the rest
To happy issues. There are marquises
Would serve seven years to call me wife, I know:
And, after seven, I might consider it,
435   For there's some comfort in a marquisate
When all's said,—yes, but after the seven years;
I, now, love Romney. You put up your lip,
So like a Leigh! so like him!—Pardon me,
I'm well aware I do not derogate
440   In loving Romney Leigh. The name is good,
The means are excellent; but the man, the man—
Heaven help us both,—I am near as mad as he,
In loving such an one.'
                                        She slowly swung
Her heavy ringlets till they touched her smile,
445   As reasonably sorry for herself;
And thus continued,—
                                        'Of a truth, Miss Leigh,
I have not, without struggle, come to this.
I took a master in the German tongue,
I gamed a little, went to Paris twice;
450   But, after all, this love! . . you eat of love,
And do as vile a thing as if you ate
Of garlic—which, whatever else you eat,
Tastes uniformly acrid, till your peach
Reminds you of your onion. Am I coarse?
455   Well, love's coarse, nature's coarse—ah, there's the rub!
We fair fine ladies, who park out our lives,
From common sheep-paths, cannot help the crows
From flying over,—we're as natural still
As Blowsalinda. Drape us perfectly
460   In Lyons' velvet,—we are not, for that,
Lay-figures, look you! we have hearts within,
Warm, live, improvident, indecent hearts,
As ready for distracted ends and acts
As any distressed sempstress of them all
465   That Romney groans and toils for. We catch love
And other fevers, in the vulgar way.
Love will not be outwitted by our wit,

Nor outrun by our equipages:—mine
Persisted, spite of efforts. All my cards
470 Turned up but Romney Leigh; my German stopped
At germane Wertherism; my Paris rounds
Returned me from the Champs Elysées just
A ghost, and sighing like Dido's. I came home
Uncured,—convicted rather to myself
475 Of being in love . . . in love! That's coarse, you'll say.
I'm talking garlic.'
               Coldly I replied:
'Apologise for atheism, not love!
For me, I do believe in love, and God.
I know my cousin: Lady Waldemar
480 I know not: yet I say as much as this—
Whoever loves him, let her not excuse
But cleanse herself, that, loving such a man,
She may not do it with such unworthy love
He cannot stoop and take it.'
                      'That is said
485 Austerely, like a youthful prophetess,
Who knits her brows across her pretty eyes
To keep them back from following the grey flight
Of doves between the temple-columns. Dear,
Be kinder with me. Let us two be friends.
490 I'm a mere woman,—the more weak perhaps
Through being so proud; you're better; as for him,
He's best. Indeed he builds his goodness up
So high, it topples down to the other side,
And makes a sort of badness; there's the worst
495 I have to say against your cousin's best!
And so be mild, Aurora, with my worst
For his sake, if not mine.'
                    'I own myself
Incredulous of confidence like this
Availing him or you.'
                      'I, worthy of him?
500 In your sense I am not so—let it pass.
And yet I save him if I marry him;
Let that pass too.'
               'Pass, pass! we play police

Upon my cousin's life, to indicate
What may or may not pass?' I cried. 'He knows
505   What's worthy of him; the choice remains with *him;*
And what he chooses, act or wife, I think
I shall not call unworthy, I, for one.'

''Tis somewhat rashly said,' she answered slow.
'Now let's talk reason, though we talk of love.
510   Your cousin Romney Leigh's a monster! there,
The word's out fairly, let me prove the fact.
We'll take, say, that most perfect of antiques,
They call the Genius of the Vatican,
Which seems too beauteous to endure itself
515   In this mixed world, and fasten it for once
Upon the torso of the Drunken Fawn
(Who might limp surely, if he did not dance,)
Instead of Buonarroti's mask: what then?
We show the sort of monster Romney is,
520   With god-like virtues and heroic aims
Subjoined to limping possibilities
Of mismade human nature. Grant the man
Twice godlike, twice heroic—still he limps,
And here's the point we come to.'

                       'Pardon me,
525   But, Lady Waldemar, the point's the thing
We never come to.'

               'Caustic, insolent
At need. I like you'—(there, she took my hands)
'And now my lioness, help Androcles,
For all your roaring. Help me! for myself
530   I would not say so—but for him. He limps
So certainly, he'll fall into the pit
A week hence,—so I lose him—so he is lost
For when he's fairly married, he a Leigh,
To a girl of doubtful life, undoubtful birth,
535   Starved out in London, till her coarse-grained hands
Are whiter than her morals,—you, for one,
May call his choice most worthy.'

                       'Married! Lost!

He, . . Romney!'
                              'Ah, you're moved at last,' she said.
'These monsters, set out in the open sun,
540 Of course throw monstrous shadows: those who think
Awry, will scarce act straightly. Who but he?
And who but you can wonder? He has been mad,
The whole world knows, since first, a nominal man,
He soured the proctors, tried the gownsmen's wits,
545 With equal scorn of triangles and wine,
And took no honours, yet was honourable.
They'll tell you he lost count of Homer's ships
In Melbourne's poor-bills, Ashley's factory bills,—
Ignored the Aspasia we all dare to praise,
550 For other women, dear, we could not name
Because we're decent. Well, he had some right
On his side probably; men always have,
Who go absurdly wrong. The living boor
Who brews your ale, exceeds in vital worth
555 Dead Cæsar who 'stops bungholes' in the cask;
And also, to do good is excellent.
For persons of his income, even to boors:
I sympathise with all such things. But he
Went mad upon them . . madder and more mad,
560 From college times to these,—as, going down hill,
The faster still, the farther! you must know
Your Leigh by heart: he has sown his black young curls
With bleaching cares of half a million men
Already. If you do not starve, or sin,
565 You're nothing to him. Pay the income-tax,
And break your heart upon't . . he'll scarce be touched;
But come upon the parish, qualified
For the parish stocks, and Romney will be there
To call you brother, sister, or perhaps
570 A tenderer name still. Had I any chance
With Mister Leigh, who am Lady Waldemar
And never committed felony?'
                              'You speak
Too bitterly,' I said, 'for the literal truth.'

                              *

'The truth is bitter. Here's a man who looks
575 For ever on the ground! you must be low;
Or else a pictured ceiling overhead,
Good painting thrown away. For me, I've done
What women may, (we're somewhat limited,
We modest women) but I've done my best.
580 —How men are perjured when they swear our eyes
Have meaning in them! they're just blue or brown,—
They just can drop their lids a little. In fact,
Mine did more, for I read half Fourier through,
Proudhon, Considerant, and Louis Blanc,
585 With various others of his socialists;
And if I had been a fathom less in love,
Had cured myself with gaping. As it was,
I quoted from them prettily enough,
Perhaps, to make them sound half rational
590 To a saner man than he, whene'er we talked
(For which I dodged occasion)—learnt by heart
His speeches in the Commons and elsewhere
Upon the social question; heaped reports
Of wicked women and penitentiaries,
595 On all my tables, with a place for Sue;
And gave my name to swell subscription lists
Toward keeping up the sun at nights in heaven,
And other possible ends. All things I did,
Except the impossible . . such as wearing gowns
600 Provided by the Ten Hours' movement! there,
I stopped—we must stop somewhere. He, meanwhile,
Unmoved as the Indian tortoise 'neath the world,
Let all that noise go on upon his back:
He would not disconcert or throw me out,
605 'Twas well to see a woman of my class
With such a dawn of conscience. For the heart,
Made firewood for his sake, and flaming up
To his very face . . he warmed his feet at it;
But deigned to let my carriage stop him short
610 In park or street,—he leaning on the door,
With news of the committee which sate last
On pickpockets at suck.'

*

'You jest—you jest.'

'As martyrs jest, dear (if you've read their lives)
Upon the axe which kills them. When all's done
615   By me, . . for him—you'll ask him presently
The colour of my hair—he cannot tell,
Or answers 'dark' at random,—while, be sure,
He's absolute on the figure, five or ten,
Of my last subscription. Is it bearable,
620   And I a woman?'
                    'Is it reparable,
Though *I* were a man?'
                        'I know not. That's to prove.
But, first, this shameful marriage?'
                                    'Ay?' I cried.
'Then really there's a marriage?'
                                'Yesterday
I held him fast upon it. 'Mister Leigh,'
625   Said I, 'shut up a thing, it makes more noise.
'The boiling town keeps secrets ill; I've known
'Yours since last week. Forgive my knowledge so:
'You feel I'm not the woman of the world
'The world thinks; you have borne with me before
630   'And used me in your noble work, our work,
'And now you shall not cast me off because
'You're at the difficult point, the *join*. 'Tis true
'Even I can scarce admit the cogency
'Of such a marriage . . where you do not love,
635   '(Except the class) yet marry and throw your name
'Down to the gutter, for a fire-escape
'To future generations! it's sublime,
'A great example,—a true Genesis
'Of the opening social era. But take heed;
640   'This virtuous act must have a patent weight,
'Or lose half its virtue. Make it tell,
'Interpret it, and set it in the light,
'And do not muffle it in a winter-cloak
'As a vulgar bit of shame,—as if, at best,
645   'A Leigh had made a misalliance and blushed

'A Howard should know it.' Then, I pressed him more—
'He would not choose,' I said, 'that even his kin, . .
'Aurora Leigh, even . . should conceive his act
'Less sacrifice, more appetite.' At which
650   He grew so pale, dear, . . to the lips, I knew
I had touched him. 'Do you know her,' he enquired,
'My cousin Aurora?' 'Yes,' I said, and lied,
(But truly we all know you by your books)
And so I offered to come straight to you,
655   Explain the subject, justify the cause,
And take you with me to St. Margaret's Court
To see this miracle, this Marian Erle,
This drover's daughter (she's not pretty, he swears)
Upon whose finger, exquisitely pricked
660   By a hundred needles, we're to hang the tie
'Twixt class and class in England,—thus, indeed,
By such a presence, yours and mine, to lift
The match up from the doubtful place. At once
He thanked me, sighing . . murmured to himself,
665   'She'll do it perhaps; she's noble,'—thanked me twice,
And promised, as my guerdon, to put off
His marriage for a month.'
                                        I answered then.
'I understand your drift imperfectly.
You wish to lead me to my cousin's betrothed,
670   To touch her hand if worthy, and hold her hand
If feeble, thus to justify his match.
So be it then. But how this serves your ends,
And how the strange confession of your love
Serves this, I have to learn—I cannot see.'

675   She knit her restless forehead. 'Then, despite,
Aurora, that most radiant morning name,
You're dull as any London afternoon.
I wanted time,—and gained it,—wanted *you*,
And gain you! You will come and see the girl,
680   In whose most prodigal eyes, the lineal pearl
And pride of all your lofty race of Leighs
Is destined to solution. Authorised

By sight and knowledge, then, you'll speak your mind,
And prove to Romney, in your brilliant way,
685 He'll wrong the people and posterity
(Say such a thing is bad for you and me,
And you fail utterly,) by concluding thus
An execrable marriage. Break it up,
Disroot it—peradventure, presently,
690 We'll plant a better fortune in its place.
Be good to me, Aurora, scorn me less
For saying the thing I should not. Well I know
I should not. I have kept, as others have,
The iron rule of womanly reserve
695 In lip and life, till now: I wept a week
Before I came here.'—Ending, she was pale;
The last words, haughtily said, were tremulous.
This palfrey pranced in harness, arched her neck,
And, only by the foam upon the bit,
700 You saw she champed against it.
                                                    Then I rose.
'I love love: truth's no cleaner thing than love.
I comprehend a love so fiery hot
It burns its natural veil of august shame,
And stands sublimely in the nude, as chaste
705 As Medicean Venus. But I know,
A love that burns through veils, will burn through masks,
And shrivel up treachery. What, love and lie!
Nay—go to the opera! your love's curable.'

'I love and lie?' she said—'I lie, forsooth?'
710 And beat her taper foot upon the floor,
And smiled against the shoe,—'You're hard, Miss Leigh,
Unversed in current phrases.—Bowling greens
Of poets are fresher than the world's highways:
Forgive me that I rashly blew the dust
715 Which dims our hedges even, in your eyes,
And vexed you so much. You find, probably,
No evil in this marriage,—rather good
Of innocence, to pastoralise in song:
You'll give the bond your signature, perhaps,

720 Beneath the lady's mark,—indifferent
That Romney chose a wife, could write her name,
In witnessing he loved her.'
                              'Loved!' I cried;
'Who tells you that he wants a wife to love?
He gets a horse to use, not love, I think:
725 There's work for wives as well,—and after, straw,
When men are liberal. For myself, you err
Supposing power in me to break this match.
I could not do it, to save Romney's life;
And would not, to save mine.'
                              'You take it so,'
730 She said, 'farewell then. Write your books in peace,
As far as may be for some secret stir
Now obvious to me,—for, most obviously,
In coming hither I mistook the way.'
Whereat she touched my hand, and bent her head,
735 And floated from me like a silent cloud
That leaves the sense of thunder.
                              I drew a breath,
As hard as in a sick room. After all
This woman breaks her social system up
For love, so counted—the love possible
740 To such,—and lilies are still lilies, pulled
By smutty hands, though spotted from their white;
And thus she is better, haply, of her kind,
Than Romney Leigh, who lives by diagrams,
And crosses out the spontaneities
745 Of all his individual, personal life,
With formal universals. As if man
Were set upon a high stool at a desk,
To keep God's books for Him, in red and black,
And feel by millions! What, if even God
750 Were chiefly God by living out Himself
To an individualism of the Infinite,
Eterne, intense, profuse,—still throwing up
The golden spray of multitudinous worlds
In measure to the proclive weight and rush
755 Of His inner nature,—the spontaneous love

Still proof and outflow of spontaneous life?
Then live, Aurora!
                              Two hours afterward,
Within St. Margaret's Court I stood alone,
Close-veiled. A sick child, from an ague-fit,
760   Whose wasted right hand gambled 'gainst his left
With an old brass button; in a blot of sun,
Jeered weakly at me as I passed across
The uneven pavement; while a woman, rouged
Upon the angular cheek-bones, kerchief torn,
765   Thin dangling locks, and flat lascivious mouth,
Cursed at a window, both ways, in and out,
By turns some bed-rid creature and myself,—
'Lie still there, mother! liker the dead dog
You'll be to-morrow. What, we pick our way,
770   Fine madam, with those damnable small feet!
We cover up our face from doing good
As if it were our purse! What brings you here,
My lady? is't to find my gentleman
Who visits his tame pigeon in the eaves?
775   Our cholera catch you with its cramps and spasms,
And tumble up your good clothes, veil and all,
And turn your whiteness dead-blue.' I looked up;
I think I could have walked through hell that day,
And never flinched. 'The dear Christ comfort you,'
780   I said, 'you must have been most miserable
To be so cruel,'—and I emptied out
My purse upon the stones: when, as I had cast
The last charm in the cauldron, the whole court
Went boiling, bubbling up, from all its doors
785   And windows, with a hideous wail of laughs
And roar of oaths, and blows perhaps . . I passed.
Too quickly for distinguishing . . and pushed
A little side-door hanging on a hinge,
And plunged into the dark, and groped and climbed
790   The long, steep, narrow stair 'twixt broken rail
And mildewed wall that let the plaster drop
To startle me in the blackness. Still, up, up!
So high lived Romney's bride. I paused at last

Before a low door in the roof, and knocked;
795 There came an answer like a hurried dove—
'So soon? can that be Master Leigh? so soon?'
And, as I entered, an ineffable face
Met mine upon the threshold. 'Oh, not you,
Not you!' . . the dropping of the voice implied;
800 'Then, if not you, for me not any one.'
I looked her in the eyes, and held her hands,
And said 'I am his cousin,—Romney Leigh's;
And here I'm come to see my cousin too.'
She touched me with her face and with her voice,
805 This daughter of the people. Such soft flowers
From such rough roots? the people, under there,
Can sin so, curse so, look so, smell so . . faugh!
Yet have such daughters?

                              No wise beautiful
Was Marian Erle. She was not white nor brown,
810 But could look either, like a mist that changed
According to being shone on more or less.
The hair, too, ran its opulence of curls
In doubt 'twixt dark and bright, nor left you clear
To name the colour. Too much hair perhaps
815 (I'll name a fault here) for so small a head,
Which seemed to droop on that side and on this,
As a full-blown rose uneasy with its weight,
Though not a breath should trouble it. Again,
The dimple in the cheek had better gone
820 With redder, fuller rounds: and somewhat large
The mouth was, though the milky little teeth
Dissolved it to so infantine a smile!
For soon it smiled at me; the eyes smiled too,
But 'twas as if remembering they had wept,
825 And knowing they should, some day, weep again.

We talked. She told me all her story out,
Which I'll re-tell with fuller utterance,
As coloured and confirmed in aftertimes
By others, and herself too. Marian Erle
830 Was born upon the ledge of Malvern Hill,

To eastward, in a hut, built up at night,
To evade the landlord's eye, of mud and turf,
Still liable, if once he looked that way,
To being straight levelled, scattered by his foot,
835   Like any other anthill. Born, I say;
God sent her to his world, commissioned right,
Her human testimonials fully signed,
Not scant in soul—complete in lineaments;
But others had to swindle her a place
840   To wail in when she had come. No place for her,
By man's law! born an outlaw, was this babe.
Her first cry in our strange and strangling air,
When cast in spasms out by the shuddering womb,
Was wrong against the social code,—forced wrong.
845   What business had the baby to cry there?

I tell her story and grow passionate.
She, Marian, did not tell it so, but used
Meek words that made no wonder of herself
For being so sad a creature. 'Mister Leigh
850   Considered truly that such things should change.
They *will*, in heaven—but meantime, on the earth,
There's none can like a nettle as a pink,
Except himself. We're nettles, some of us,
And give offence by the act of springing up;
855   And, if we leave the damp side of the wall,
The hoes, of course, are on us.' So she said.

Her father earned his life by random jobs
Despised by steadier workmen—keeping swine
On commons, picking hops, or hurrying on
860   The harvest at wet seasons,—or, at need,
Assisting the Welsh drovers, when a drove
Of startled horses plunged into the mist
Below the mountain-road, and sowed the wind
With wandering neighings. In between the gaps
865   Of such irregular work, he drank and slept,
And cursed his wife because, the pence being out,
She could not buy more drink. At which she turned

(The worm) and beat her baby in revenge
For her own broken heart. There's not a crime
870 But takes its proper change out still in crime,
If once rung on the counter of this world;
Let sinners look to it.
                              Yet the outcast child,
For whom the very mother's face forewent
The mother's special patience, lived and grew;
875 Learnt early to cry low, and walk alone,
With that pathetic vacillating roll
Of the infant body on the uncertain feet,
(The earth being felt unstable ground so soon)
At which most women's arms unclose at once
880 With irrepressive instinct. Thus, at three,
This poor weaned kid would run off from the fold,
This babe would steal off from the mother's chair,
And, creeping through the golden walls of gorse,
Would find some keyhole toward the secrecy
885 Of Heaven's high blue, and, nestling down, peer out—
Oh, not to catch the angels at their games,
She had never heard of angels,—but to gaze
She knew not why, to see she knew not what,
A-hungering outward from the barren earth
890 For something like a joy. She liked, she said,
To dazzle black her sight against the sky,
For then, it seemed, some grand blind Love came down,
And groped her out, and clasped her with a kiss;
She learnt God that way, and was beat for it
895 Whenever she went home,—yet came again,
As surely as the trapped hare, getting free,
Returns to his form. This grand blind Love, she said,
This skyey father and mother both in one,
Instructed her and civilised her more
900 Than even the Sunday-school did afterward,
To which a lady sent her to learn books
And sit upon a long bench in a row
With other children. Well, she laughed sometimes
To see them laugh and laugh, and moil their texts;
905 But ofter she was sorrowful with noise,

And wondered if their mothers beat them hard,
That ever they should laugh so. There was one
She loved indeed,—Rose Bell, a seven years' child,
So pretty and clever, who read syllables
910 When Marian was at letters; *she* would laugh
At nothing—hold your finger up, she laughed,
Then shook her curls down on her eyes and mouth
To hide her make-mirth from the schoolmaster.
And Rose's pelting glee, as frank as rain
915 On cherry-blossoms, brightened Marian too,
To see another merry whom she loved.
She whispered once (the children side by side,
With mutual arms entwined about their necks)
'Your mother lets you laugh so?' 'Ay,' said Rose,
920 'She lets me. She was dug into the ground
Six years since, I being but a yearling wean.
Such mothers let us play and lose our time,
And never scold nor beat us! don't you wish
You had one like that?' There, Marian breaking off
925 Looked suddenly in my face. 'Poor Rose,' said she,
'I heard her laugh last night in Oxford Street.
I'd pour out half my blood to stop that laugh,—
Poor Rose, poor Rose!' said Marian.
                                        She resumed.
It tried her, when she had learnt at Sunday-school
930 What God was, what he wanted from us all,
And how in choosing sin, we vexed the Christ,
To go straight home and hear her father pull
The Name down on us from the thunder-shelf,
Then drink away his soul into the dark
935 From seeing judgment. Father, mother, home,
Were God and heaven reversed to her: the more
She knew of Right, the more she guessed their wrong;
Her price paid down for knowledge, was to know
The vileness of her kindred: through her heart,
940 Her filial and tormented heart, henceforth,
They struck their blows at virtue. Oh, 'tis hard
To learn you have a father up in heaven
By a gathering certain sense of being, on earth,

Still worse than orphaned: 'tis too heavy a grief,
945   The having to thank God for such a joy!

And so passed Marian's life from year to year.
Her parents took her with them when they tramped,
Dodged lanes and heaths, frequented towns and fairs,
And once went farther and saw Manchester,
950   And once the sea, that blue end of the world,
That fair scroll-finis of a wicked book,—
And twice a prison,—back at intervals,
Returning to the hills. Hills draw like heaven,
And stronger sometimes, holding out their hands
955   To pull you from the vile flats up to them;
And though, perhaps, these strollers still strolled back,
As sheep do, simply that they knew the way,
They certainly felt bettered unaware
Emerging from the social smut of towns
960   To wipe their feet clean on the mountain turf.

In which long wanderings, Marian lived and learned,
Endured and learned. The people on the roads
Would stop and ask her how her eyes outgrew
Her cheeks, and if she meant to lodge the birds
965   In all that hair; and then they lifted her,
The miller in his cart, a mile or twain,
The butcher's boy on horseback. Often, too,
The pedlar stopped, and tapped her on the head
With absolute forefinger, brown and ringed,
970   And asked if peradventure she could read;
And when she answered 'ay,' would toss her down
Some stray odd volume from his heavy pack,
A Thomson's Seasons, mulcted of the Spring,
Or half a play of Shakspeare's, torn across:
975   (She had to guess the bottom of a page
But just the top sometimes,—as difficult,
As, sitting on the moon, to guess the earth!)
Or else a sheaf of leaves (for that small Ruth's
Small gleanings) torn out from the heart of books,
980   From Churchyard Elegies and Edens Lost,

From Burns, and Bunyan, Selkirk, and Tom Jones.
'Twas somewhat hard to keep the things distinct,
And oft the jangling influence jarred the child
Like looking at a sunset full of grace
985   Through a pothouse window while the drunken oaths
Went on behind her; but she weeded out
Her book-leaves, threw away the leaves that hurt,
(First tore them small, that none should find a word)
And made a nosegay of the sweet and good
990   To fold within her breast, and pore upon
At broken moments of the noontide glare,
When leave was given her to untie her cloak
And rest upon the dusty roadside bank
From the highway's dust. Or oft, the journey done,
995   Some city friend would lead her by the hand
To hear a lecture at an institute:
And thus she had grown, this Marian Erle of ours,
To no book-learning,—she was ignorant
Of authors,—not in earshot of the things
1000   Out-spoken o'er the heads of common men,
By men who are uncommon,—but within
The cadenced hum of such, and capable
Of catching from the fringes of the wind
Some fragmentary phrases, here and there,
1005   Of that fine music,—which, being carried in
To her soul, had reproduced itself afresh
In finer motions of the lips and lids.

She said, in speaking of it, 'If a flower
Were thrown you out of heaven at intervals,
1010   You'd soon attain to a trick of looking up,—
And so with her.' She counted me her years,
Till *I* felt old; and then she counted me
Her sorrowful pleasures, till I felt ashamed.
She told me she was almost glad and calm
1015   On such and such a season; sate and sewed,
With no one to break up her crystal thoughts;
While rhymes from lovely poems span around
Their ringing circles of ecstatic tune,

Beneath the moistened finger of the Hour.
1020 Her parents called her a strange, sickly child,
Not good for much, and given to sulk and stare,
And smile into the hedges and the clouds,
And tremble if one shook her from her fit
By any blow, or word even. Out-door jobs
1025 Went ill with her; and household quiet work
She was not born to. Had they kept the north,
They might have had their pennyworth out of her,
Like other parents, in the factories;
(Your children work for you, not you for them,
1030 Or else they better had been choked with air
The first breath drawn;) but, in this tramping life,
Was nothing to be done with such a child,
But tramp and tramp. And yet she knitted hose
Not ill, and was not dull at needlework;
1035 And all the country people gave her pence
For darning stockings past their natural age,
And patching petticoats from old to new,
And other light work done for thrifty wives.

One day, said Marian,—the sun shone that day—
1040 Her mother had been badly beat, and felt
The bruises sore about her wretched soul,
(That must have been): she came in suddenly,
And snatching, in a sort of breathless rage,
Her daughter's headgear comb, let down the hair
1045 Upon her, like a sudden waterfall,
Then drew her drenched and passive, by the arm,
Outside the hut they lived in. When the child
Could clear her blinded face from all that stream
Of tresses . . there, a man stood, with beast's eyes,
1050 That seemed as they would swallow her alive,
Complete in body and spirit, hair and all,—
And burning stertorous breath that hurt her cheek,
He breathed so near. The mother held her tight,
Saying hard between her teeth—'Why wench, why wench,
1055 The squire speaks to you now—the squire's too good;
He means to set you up, and comfort us.

Be mannerly at least.' The child turned round,
And looked up piteous in the mother's face,
(Be sure that mother's death-bed will not want
1060   Another devil to damn, than such a look) . .
'Oh, mother!' then, with desperate glance to heaven,
'God, free me from my mother,' she shrieked out,
'These mothers are too dreadful.' And, with force
As passionate as fear, she tore her hands,
1065   Like lilies from the rocks, from hers and his,
And sprang down, bounded headlong down the steep,
Away from both—away, if possible,
As far as God,—away! They yelled at her,
As famished hounds at a hare. She heard them yell.
1070   She felt her name hiss after her from the hills,
Like shot from guns. On, on. And now she had cast
The voices off with the uplands. On. Mad fear
Was running in her feet and killing the ground;
The white roads curled as if she burnt them up,
1075   The green fields melted, wayside trees fell back
To make room for her. Then, her head grew vexed,
Trees, fields, turned on her and ran after her;
She heard the quick pants of the hills behind,
Their keen air pricked her neck. She had lost her feet,
1080   Could run no more, yet somehow went as fast,—
The horizon, red 'twixt steeples in the east,
So sucked her forward, forward, while her heart
Kept swelling, swelling, till it swelled so big
It seemed to fill her body; then it burst,
1085   And overflowed the world and swamped the light,
'And now I am dead and safe,' thought Marian Erle—
She had dropped, she had fainted.

                                    When the sense returned,
The night had passed—not life's night. She was 'ware
Of heavy tumbling motions, creaking wheels,
1090   The driver shouting to the lazy team
That swung their rankling bells against her brain;
While, through the waggon's coverture and chinks,
The cruel yellow morning pecked at her
Alive or dead, upon the straw inside,—

1095   At which her soul ached back into the dark
      And prayed, 'no more of that.' A waggoner
      Had found her in a ditch beneath the moon,
      As white as moonshine, save for the oozing blood.
      At first he thought her dead; but when he had wiped
1100 The mouth and heard it sigh, he raised her up,
      And laid her in his waggon in the straw,
      And so conveyed her to the distant town
      To which his business called himself, and left
      That heap of misery at the hospital.

1105 She stirred;—the place seemed new and strange as death.
      The white strait bed, with others strait and white,
      Like graves dug side by side, at measured lengths,
      And quiet people walking in and out
      With wonderful low voices and soft steps,
1110 And apparitional equal care for each,
      Astonished her with order, silence, law:
      And when a gentle hand held out a cup,
      She took it, as you do at sacrament,
      Half awed, half melted,—not being used, indeed,
1115 To so much love as makes the form of love
      And courtesy of manners. Delicate drinks
      And rare white bread, to which some dying eyes
      Were turned in observation. O my God,
      How sick we must be, ere we make men just!
1120 I think it frets the saints in heaven to see
      How many desolate creatures on the earth
      Have learnt the simple dues of fellowship
      And social comfort, in a hospital,
      As Marian did. She lay there, stunned, half tranced,
1125 And wished, at intervals of growing sense,
      She might be sicker yet, if sickness made
      The world so marvellous kind, the air so hushed,
      And all her wake-time quiet as a sleep;
      For now she understood, (as such things were)
1130 How sickness ended very oft in heaven,
      Among the unspoken raptures. Yet more sick,
      And surelier happy. Then she dropped her lids,

And, folding up her hands as flowers at night,
Would lose no moment of the blessed time.

1135 She lay and seethed in fever many weeks,
But youth was strong and overcame the test;
Revolted soul and flesh were reconciled
And fetched back to the necessary day
And daylight duties. She could creep about
1140 The long bare rooms, and stare out drearily
From any narrow window on the street,
Till some one, who had nursed her as a friend,
Said coldly to her, as an enemy,
'She had leave to go next week, being well enough,'
1145 While only her heart ached. 'Go next week,' thought she,
'Next week! how would it be with her next week,
Let out into that terrible street alone
Among the pushing people, . . to go . . where?'

One day, the last before the dreaded last,
1150 Among the convalescents, like herself
Prepared to go next morning, she sate dumb,
And heard half absently the women talk,
How one was famished for her baby's cheeks—
'The little wretch would know her! a year old
1155 And lively, like his father!' one was keen
To get to work, and fill some clamorous mouths;
And one was tender for her dear goodman
Who had missed her sorely,—and one, querulous . .
'Would pay those scandalous neighbours who had dared
1160 To talk about her as already dead,'—
And one was proud . . 'and if her sweetheart Luke
Had left her for a ruddier face than hers,
(The gossip would be seen through at a glance)
Sweet riddance of such sweethearts—let him hang!
1165 'Twere good to have been sick for such an end.'

And while they talked, and Marian felt the worse
For having missed the worst of all their wrongs,
A visitor was ushered through the wards

And paused among the talkers. 'When he looked,
1170   It was as if he spoke, and when he spoke
He sang perhaps,' said Marian; 'could she tell?
She only knew' (so much she had chronicled,
As seraphs might, the making of the sun)
'That he who came and spake, was Romney Leigh,
1175   And then, and there, she saw and heard him first.'

And when it was her turn to have the face
Upon her,—all those buzzing pallid lips
Being satisfied with comfort—when he changed
To Marian, saying 'And *you?* you're going, where?'—
1180   She, moveless as a worm beneath a stone
Which some one's stumbling foot has spurned aside,
Writhed suddenly, astonished with the light,
And breaking into sobs cried 'Where I go?
None asked me till this moment. Can I say
1185   Where *I* go? when it has not seemed worth while
To God himself, who thinks of every one,
To think of me, and fix where I shall go?'

'So young,' he gently asked her, 'you have lost
Your father and your mother?'
                        'Both,' she said,
1190   'Both lost! my father was burnt up with gin
Or ever I sucked milk, and so is lost.
My mother sold me to a man last month,
And so my mother's lost, 'tis manifest.
And I, who fled from her for miles and miles,
1195   As if I had caught sight of the fires of hell
Through some wild gap, (she was my mother, sir),
It seems I shall be lost too, presently,
And so we end, all three of us.'
                       'Poor child,'
He said,—with such pity in his voice,
1200   It soothed her more than her own tears,—'poor child!
'Tis simple that betrayal by mother's love
Should bring despair of God's too. Yet be taught;
He's better to us than many mothers are,

And children cannot wander beyond reach
1205 Of the sweep of his white raiment. Touch and hold!
And if you weep still, weep where John was laid
While Jesus loved him.'
                    'She could say the words,'
She told me, 'exactly as he uttered them
A year back, . . since, in any doubt or dark
1210 They came out like the stars, and shone on her
With just their comfort. Common words, perhaps;
The ministers in church might say the same;
But *he*, he made the church with what he spoke,—
The difference was the miracle,' said she.

1215 Then catching up her smile to ravishment,
She added quickly, 'I repeat his words,
But not his tones: can any one repeat
The music of an organ, out of church?
And when he said 'poor child,' I shut my eyes
1220 To feel how tenderly his voice broke through,
As the ointment-box broke on the Holy feet
To let out the rich medicative nard.'

She told me how he had raised and rescued her
With reverent pity, as, in touching grief,
1225 He touched the wounds of Christ,—and made her feel
More self-respecting. Hope, he called, belief
In God,—work, worship . . therefore let us pray!
And thus, to snatch her soul from atheism,
And keep it stainless from her mother's face,
1230 He sent her to a famous sempstress-house
Far off in London, there to work and hope.

With that, they parted. She kept sight of Heaven,
But not of Romney. He had good to do
To others: through the days and through the nights
1235 She sewed and sewed and sewed. She drooped sometimes,
And wondered, while, along the tawny light
She struck the new thread into her needle's eye,
How people, without mothers on the hills,

Could chose the town to live in!—then she drew
1240   The stitch, and mused how Romney's face would look
And if 'twere likely he'd remember her's,
When they two had their meeting after death.

Fourth Book

THEY met still sooner. 'Twas a year from thence
When Lucy Gresham, the sick sempstress girl,
Who sewed by Marian's chair so still and quick,
And leant her head upon the back to cough
5 More freely when, the mistress turning round,
The others took occasion to laugh out,—
Gave up at last. Among the workers, spoke
A bold girl with black eyebrows and red lips,—
'You know the news? Who's dying, do you think?
10 Our Lucy Gresham. I expected it
As little as Nell Hart's wedding. Blush not, Nell,
Thy curls be red enough without thy cheeks;
And, some day, there'll be found a man to dote
On red curls.—Lucy Gresham swooned last night,
15 Dropped sudden in the street while going home;
And now the baker says, who took her up
And laid her by her grandmother in bed,
He'll give her a week to die in. Pass the silk.
Let's hope he gave her a loaf too, within reach,
20 For otherwise they'll starve before they die,
That funny pair of bedfellows! Miss Bell,
I'll thank you for the scissors. The old crone
Is paralytic—that's the reason why
Our Lucy's thread went faster than her breath,
25 Which went too quick, we all know. Marian Erle!
Why, Marian Erle, you're not the fool to cry?
Your tears spoil Lady Waldemar's new dress,
You piece of pity!'
     Marian rose up straight,
And, breaking through the talk and through the work,
30 Went outward, in the face of their surprise,
To Lucy's home, to nurse her back to life
Or down to death. She knew, by such an act,
All place and grace were forfeit in the house,
Whose mistress would supply the missing hand

35   With necessary, not inhuman haste,
      And take no blame. But pity, too, had dues:
      She could not leave a solitary soul
      To founder in the dark, while she sate still
      And lavished stitches on a lady's hem
40   As if no other work were paramount.
      'Why, God,' thought Marian, 'has a missing hand
      This moment; Lucy wants a drink, perhaps.
      Let others miss me! never miss me, God!'

      So Marian sate by Lucy's bed, content
45   With duty, and was strong, for recompense,
      To hold the lamp of human love arm-high,
      To catch the death-strained eyes and comfort them,
      Until the angels, on the luminous side
      Of death, had got theirs ready. And she said,
50   When Lucy thanked her sometimes, called her kind,
      It touched her strangely. 'Marian Erle, called kind!
      What, Marian, beaten and sold, who could not die!
      'Tis verily good fortune to be kind.
      Ah, you,' she said, 'who are born to such a grace,
55   Be sorry for the unlicensed class, the poor,
      Reduced to think the best good fortune means
      That others, simply, should be kind to them.'

      From sleep to sleep while Lucy slid away
      So gently, like the light upon a hill,
60   Of which none names the moment that it goes,
      Though all see when 'tis gone,—a man came in
      And stood beside the bed. The old idiot wretch
      Screamed feebly, like a baby overlain,
      'Sir, sir, you won't mistake me for the corpse?
65   Don't look at me, sir! never bury me!
      Although I lie here, I'm alive as you,
      Except my legs and arms,—I eat and drink,
      And understand,—(that you're the gentleman
      Who fits the funerals up, Heaven speed you, sir,)
70   And certainly I should be livelier still
      If Lucy here .. sir, Lucy is the corpse ..

Had worked more properly to buy me wine:
But Lucy, sir, was always slow at work,
I shan't lose much by Lucy. Marian Erle,
75 Speak up and show the gentleman the corpse.'

And a voice said 'Marian Erle.' She rose;
It was the hour for angels—there, stood hers!
She scarcely marvelled to see Romney Leigh.
As light November snows to empty nests,
80 As grass to graves, as moss to mildewed stones,
As July suns to ruins, through the rents,
As ministering spirits to mourners, through a loss,
As Heaven itself to men, through pangs of death,
He came uncalled wherever grief had come.
85 'And so,' said Marian Erle, 'we met anew,'
And added softly, 'so, we shall not part.'

He was not angry that she had left the house
Wherein he placed her. Well—she had feared it might
Have vexed him. Also, when he found her set
90 On keeping, though the dead was out of sight,
That half-dead, half-alive body left behind
With cankerous heart and flesh,—which took your best
And cursed you for the little good it did,
(Could any leave the bedrid wretch alone,
95 So joyless, she was thankless even to God,
Much more to you?) he did not say 'twas well,
Yet Marian thought he did not take it ill,—
Since day by day he came, and, every day,
She felt within his utterance and his eyes
100 A closer, tenderer presence of the soul,
Until at last he said, 'We shall not part.'

On that same day, was Marian's work complete:
She had smoothed the empty bed, and swept the floor
Of coffin sawdust, set the chairs anew
105 The dead had ended gossip in, and stood
In that poor room so cold and orderly,

The door-key in her hand, prepared to go
As *they* had, howbeit not their way. He spoke.

'Dear Marian, of one clay God made us all,
110 And though men push and poke and paddle in't
(As children play at fashioning dirt-pies)
And call their fancies by the name of facts,
Assuming difference, lordship, privilege,
When all's plain dirt,—they come back to it at last;
115 The first grave-digger proves it with a spade,
And pats all even. Need we wait for this,
You, Marian, and I, Romney?'
                        She, at that,
Looked blindly in his face, as when one looks
Through driving autumn-rains to find the sky.
120 He went on speaking.
                  'Marian, I being born
What men call noble, and you, issued from
The noble people,—though the tyrannous sword,
Which pierced Christ's heart, has cleft the world in twain
'Twixt class and class, opposing rich to poor,—
125 Shall *we* keep parted? Not so. Let us lean
And strain together rather, each to each,
Compress the red lips of this gaping wound,
As far as two souls can,—ay, lean and league,
I, from my superabundance,—from your want,
130 You,—joining in a protest 'gainst the wrong
On both sides!'—
                All the rest, he held her hand
In speaking, which confused the sense of much;
Her heart, against his words, beat out so thick,
They might as well be written on the dust
135 Where some poor bird, escaping from hawk's beak,
Has dropped, and beats its shuddering wings,—the lines
Are rubbed so,—yet 'twas something like to this,
—'That they two, standing at the two extremes
Of social classes, had received one seal,
140 Been dedicate and drawn beyond themselves
To mercy and ministration,—he, indeed,

Through what he knew, and she, through what she felt,
He, by man's conscience, she, by woman's heart,
Relinquishing their several 'vantage posts
145   Of wealthy ease and honourable toil,
To work with God at love. And since God willed
That putting out his hand to touch this ark,
He found a woman's hand there, he'd accept
The sign too, hold the tender fingers fast,
150   And say, 'My fellow-worker, be my wife!''

She told the tale with simple, rustic turns,—
Strong leaps of meaning in her sudden eyes
That took the gaps of any imperfect phrase
Of the unschooled speaker: I have rather writ
155   The thing I understood so, than the thing
I heard so. And I cannot render right
Her quick gesticulation, wild yet soft,
Self-startled from the habitual mood she used,
Half sad, half languid,—like dumb creatures (now
160   A rustling bird, and now a wandering deer,
Or squirrel against the oak-gloom flashing up
His sidelong burnished head, in just her way
Of savage spontaneity,) that stir
Abruptly the green silence of the woods,
165   And make it stranger, holier, more profound;
As Nature's general heart confessed itself
Of life, and then fell backward on repose.

I kissed the lips that ended.—'So indeed
He loves you, Marian?'
                            'Loves me!' She looked up
170   With a child's wonder when you ask him first
Who made the sun—a puzzled blush, that grew,
Then broke off in a rapid radiant smile
Of sure solution. 'Loves me! he loves all,—
And me, of course. He had not asked me else
175   To work with him for ever, and be his wife.'

*

Her words reproved me. This perhaps was love—
To have its hands too full of gifts to give,
For putting out a hand to take a gift;
To love so much, the perfect round of love ·
180   Includes, in strict conclusion, the being loved;
As Eden-dew went up and fell again,
Enough for watering Eden. Obviously
She had not thought about his love at all:
The cataracts of her soul had poured themselves,
185   And risen self-crowned in rainbow: would she ask
Who crowned her?—it sufficed that she was crowned.
With women of my class 'tis otherwise:
We haggle for the small change of our gold,
And so much love, accord, for so much love,
190   Rialto-prices. Are we therefore wrong?
If marriage be a contract, look to it then,
Contracting parties should be equal, just;
But if, a simple fealty on one side,
A mere religion,—right to give, is all,
195   And certain brides of Europe duly ask
To mount the pile, as Indian widows do,
The spices of their tender youth heaped up,
The jewels of their gracious virtues worn,
More gems, more glory,—to consume entire
200   For a living husband! as the man's alive,
Not dead,—the woman's duty, by so much
Advanced in England, beyond Hindostan.

I sate there musing, till she touched my hand
With hers, as softly as a strange white bird
205   She feared to startle in touching. 'You are kind,
But are you, peradventure, vexed at heart
Because your cousin takes me for a wife?
I know I am not worthy—nay, in truth,
I'm glad on't, since, for that, he chooses me.
210   He likes the poor things of the world the best;
I would not therefore, if I could, be rich.
It pleasures him to stoop for buttercups;
I would not be a rose upon the wall

A queen might stop at, near the palace-door,
215 To say to a courtier 'Pluck that rose for me,
'It's prettier than the rest.' O Romney Leigh!
I'd rather far be trodden by his foot,
Than lie in a great queen's bosom.'

                        Out of breath
She paused.
           'Sweet Marian, do you disavow
220 The roses with that face?'
                       She dropt her head,
As if the wind had caught that flower of her,
And bent it in the garden,—then looked up
With grave assurance. 'Well, you think me bold!
But so we all are, when we're praying God.
225 And if I'm bold—yet, lady, credit me,
That, since I know myself for what I am,
Much fitter for his handmaid than his wife,
I'll prove the handmaid and the wife at once,
Serve tenderly, and love obediently,
230 And be a worthier mate, perhaps, than some
Who are wooed in silk among their learned books;
While *I* shall set myself to read his eyes,
Till such grow plainer to me than the French
To wisest ladies. Do you think I'll miss
235 A letter, in the spelling of his mind?
No more than they do, when they sit and write
Their flying words with flickering wild-fowl tails,
Nor ever pause to ask how many *t*s,
Should that be *y* or *i*—they know't so well:
240 I've seen them writing, when I brought a dress
And waited,—floating out their soft white hands
On shining paper. But they're hard sometimes,
For all those hands!—we've used out many nights,
And worn the yellow daylight into shreds
245 Which flapped and shivered down our aching eyes
Till night appeared more tolerable, just
That pretty ladies might look beautiful,
Who said at last . . 'You're lazy in that house!
'You're slow in sending home the work,—I count

250 'I've waited near an hour for't.' Pardon me,—
I do not blame them, madam, nor misprize;
They are fair and gracious; ay, but not like you,
Since none but you has Mister Leigh's own blood,
Both noble and gentle,—and, without it . . well,
255 They are fair, I said; so fair, it scarce seems strange
That, flashing out in any looking-glass
The wonder of their glorious brows and breasts,
They're charmed so, they forget to look behind
And mark how pale we've grown, we pitiful
260 Remainders of the world. And so, perhaps,
If Mister Leigh had chosen a wife from these,
She might . . although he's better than her best,
And dearly she would know it . . steal a thought
Which should be all his, an eye-glance from his face,
265 To plunge into the mirror opposite,
In search of her own beauty's pearl: while *I* . .
Ah, dearest lady, serge will outweigh silk
For winter-wear, when bodies feel a-cold,
And I'll be a true wife to your cousin Leigh.'

270 Before I answered he was there himself.
I think he had been standing in the room
And listened probably to half her talk,
Arrested, turned to stone,—as white as stone.
Will tender sayings make men look so white?
275 He loves her then profoundly.

                              'You are here,
Aurora? Here I meet you!'—We clasped hands.

'Even so, dear Romney. Lady Waldemar
Has sent me in haste to find a cousin of mine
Who shall be.'

                    'Lady Waldemar is good.'

280 'Here's one, at least, who is good,' I sighed, and touched
Poor Marian's happy head, as, doglike, she,
Most passionately patient, waited on,

A-tremble for her turn of greeting words;
'I've sate a full hour with your Marian Erle,
285 And learnt the thing by heart,—and from my heart,
Am therefore competent to give you thanks
For such a cousin.'
                              'You accept at last
A gift from me, Aurora, without scorn?
At last I please you?'—How his voice was changed!

290 'You cannot please a woman against her will,
And once you vexed me. Shall we speak of that?
We'll say, then, you were noble in it all,
And I not ignorant—let it pass. And now,
You please me, Romney, when you please yourself;
295 So, please you, be fanatical in love,
And I'm well pleased. Ah, cousin! at the old hall,
Among the gallery portraits of our Leighs,
We shall not find a sweeter signory
Than this pure forehead's.'
                              Not a word he said.
300 How arrogant men are!—Even philanthropists,
Who try to take a wife up in the way
They put down a subscription-cheque,—if once
She turns and says 'I will not tax you so,
Most charitable sir,'—feel ill at ease
305 As though she had wronged them somehow. I suppose
We women should remember what we are,
And not throw back an obolus inscribed
With Cæsar's image, lightly. I resumed.

'It strikes me, some of those sublime Vandykes
310 Were not too proud, to make good saints in heaven;
And, if so, then they're not too proud to-day,
To bow down (now the ruffs are off their necks)
And own this good, true, noble Marian, . . yours,
And mine, I'll say!—For poets (bear the word),
315 Half-poets even, are still whole democrats,—
Oh, not that we're disloyal to the high,
But loyal to the low, and cognisant

Of the less scrutable majesties. For me,
I comprehend your choice—I justify
320   Your right in choosing.'

                              'No, no, no,' he sighed,
With a sort of melancholy impatient scorn,
As some grown man, who never had a child
Puts by some child who plays at being a man;
—'You did not, do not, cannot comprehend
325   My choice, my ends, my motives, nor myself:
No matter now—we'll let it pass, you say.
I thank you for your generous cousinship
Which helps this present; I accept for her
Your favourable thoughts. We're fallen on days,
330   We two, who are not poets, when to wed
Requires less mutual love than common love,
For two together to bear out at once
Upon the loveless many. Work in pairs,
In galley-couplings or in marriage-rings,
335   The difference lies in the honour, not the work,—
And such we're bound to, I and she. But love,
(You poets are benighted in this age;
The hour's too late for catching even moths,
You've gnats instead,) love!—love's fool-paradise
340   Is out of date, like Adam's. Set a swan
To swim the Trenton, rather than true love
To float its fabulous plumage safely down
The cataracts of this loud transition-time,—
Whose roar, for ever, henceforth, in my ears
345   Must keep me deaf to music.'

                              There, I turned
And kissed poor Marian, out of discontent.
The man had baffled, chafed me, till I flung
For refuge to the woman,—as, sometimes,
Impatient of some crowded room's close smell,
350   You throw a window open, and lean out
To breathe a long breath in the dewy night,
And cool your angry forehead. She, at least,
Was not built up, as walls are, brick by brick;
Each fancy squared, each feeling ranged by line,

355   The very heat of burning youth applied
       To indurate form and systems! excellent bricks,
       A well-built wall,—which stops you on the road,
       And, into which, you cannot see an inch
       Although you beat your head against it—pshaw!

360   'Adieu,' I said, 'for this time, cousins both;
       And, cousin Romney, pardon me the word,
       Be happy!—oh, in some esoteric sense
       Of course!—I mean no harm in wishing well.
       Adieu, my Marian:—may she come to me,
365   Dear Romney, and be married from my house?
       It is not part of your philosophy
       To keep your bird upon the blackthorn?'

                                          'Ay,'
       He answered, 'but it is:—I take my wife
       Directly from the people,—and she comes,
370   As Austria's daughter to imperial France,
       Betwixt her eagles, blinking not her race,
       From Margaret's Court at garret-height, to meet
       And wed me at Saint James's, nor put off
       Her gown of serge for that. The things we do,
375   We do: we'll wear no mask, as if we blushed.'

       'Dear Romney, you're the poet,' I replied,—
       But felt my smile too mournful for my word,
       And turned and went. Ay, masks, I thought,—beware
       Of tragic masks, we tie before the glass,
380   Uplifted on the cothurn half a yard
       Above the natural stature! we would play
       Heroic parts to ourselves,—and end, perhaps,
       As impotently as Athenian wives
       Who shrieked in fits at the Eumenides.

385   His foot pursued me down the stair. 'At least
       You'll suffer me to walk with you beyond
       These hideous streets, these graves, where men alive,
       Packed close with earthworms, burr unconsciously
       About the plague that slew them; let me go.

390   The very women pelt their souls in mud
At any woman who walks here alone.
How came you here alone?—you are ignorant.'

We had a strange and melancholy walk:
The night came drizzling downward in dark rain;
395   And, as we walked, the colour of the time,
The act, the presence, my hand upon his arm,
His voice in my ear, and mine to my own sense,
Appeared unnatural. We talked modern books,
And daily papers; Spanish marriage-schemes
400   And English climate—was't so cold last year?
And will the wind change by to-morrow morn?
Can Guizot stand? is London full? is trade
Competitive? has Dickens turned his hinge
A-pinch upon the fingers of the great?
405   And are potatoes to grow mythical
Like moly? will the apple die out too?
Which way is the wind to-night? south-east? due east?
We talked on fast, while every common word
Seemed tangled with the thunder at one end,
410   And ready to pull down upon our heads
A terror out of sight. And yet to pause
Were surelier mortal: we tore greedily up
All silence, all the innocent breathing-points,
As if, like pale conspirators in haste,
415   We tore up papers where our signatures
Imperilled us to an ugly shame or death.

I cannot tell you why it was. 'Tis plain
We had not loved nor hated: wherefore dread
To spill gunpowder on ground safe from fire?
420   Perhaps we had lived too closely, to diverge
So absolutely: leave two clocks, they say,
Wound up to different hours, upon one shelf,
And slowly, through the interior wheels of each,
The blind mechanic motion sets itself
425   A-throb, to feel out for the mutual time.
It was not so with us, indeed. While he

Struck midnight, I kept striking six at dawn;
While he marked judgment, I, redemption-day;
And such exception to the general law,
430   Imperious upon inert matter even,
Might make us, each to either, insecure,
A beckoning mystery, or a troubling fear.

I mind me, when we parted at the door,
How strange his good-night sounded,—like good-night
435   Beside a deathbed, where the morrow's sun
Is sure to come too late for more good-days:—
And all that night I thought . . 'Good-night,' said he.

And so, a month passed. Let me set it down
At once,—I have been wrong, I have been wrong.
440   We are wrong always, when we think too much
Of what we think or are; albeit our thoughts
Be verily bitter as self-sacrifice,
We're no less selfish. If we sleep on rocks
Or roses, sleeping past the hour of noon
445   We're lazy. This I write against myself.
I had done a duty in the visit paid
To Marian, and was ready otherwise
To give the witness of my presence and name
Whenever she should marry.—Which, I thought,
450   Sufficed. I even had cast into the scale
An overweight of justice toward the match;
The Lady Waldemar had missed her tool,
Had broken it in the lock as being too straight
For a crooked purpose, while poor Marian Erle
455   Missed nothing in my accents or my acts:
I had not been ungenerous on the whole,
Nor yet untender; so, enough. I felt
Tired, overworked: this marriage somewhat jarred;
Or, if it did not, all the bridal noise . .
460   The pricking of the map of life with pins,
In schemes of . . 'Here we'll go,' and 'There we'll stay,'
And 'Everywhere we'll prosper in our love,'
Was scarce my business. Let them order it;

Who else should care? I threw myself aside,
465 As one who had done her work and shuts her eyes
To rest the better.
                              I, who should have known,
Forereckoned mischief! Where we disavow
Being keeper to our brother, we're his Cain.

I might have held that poor child to my heart
470 A little longer! 'twould have hurt me much
To have hastened by its beats the marriage day,
And kept her safe meantime from tampering hands
Or, peradventure, traps? What drew me back
From telling Romney plainly, the designs
475 Of Lady Waldemar, as spoken out
To me . . me? had I any right, ay, right,
With womanly compassion and reserve
To break the fall of woman's impudence?—
To stand by calmly, knowing what I knew,
480 And hear him call her *good!*
                              Distrust that word.
'There is none good save God,' said Jesus Christ.
If He once, in the first creation-week,
Called creatures good,—for ever, afterward,
The Devil only has done it, and his heirs,
485 The knaves who win so, and the fools who lose;
The world's grown dangerous. In the middle age,
I think they called malignant fays and imps
Good people. A good neighbour, even in this,
Is fatal sometimes,—cuts your mornings up
490 To mincemeat of the very smallest talk,
Then helps to sugar her bohea at night
With your reputation. I have known good wives,
As chaste, or nearly so, as Potiphar's;
And good, good mothers, who would use a child
495 To better an intrigue; good friends, beside,
(Very good) who hung succinctly round your neck
And sucked your breath, as cats are fabled to do
By sleeping infants. And we all have known
Good critics, who have stamped out poet's hopes;

500 Good statesmen, who pulled ruin on the state;
Good patriots, who, for a theory, risked a cause;
Good kings, who disembowelled for a tax;
Good popes, who brought all good to jeopardy;
Good Christians, who sate still in easy chairs,
505 And damned the general world for standing up.—
Now may the good God pardon all good men!

How bitterly I speak,—how certainly
The innocent white milk in us is turned,
By much persistent shining of the sun!—
510 Shake up the sweetest in us long enough
With men, it drops to foolish curd, too sour
To feed the most untender of Christ's lambs.

I should have thought . . a woman of the world
Like her I'm meaning,—centre to herself,
515 Who has wheeled on her own pivot half a life
In isolated self-love and self-will,
As a windmill seen at distance radiating
Its delicate white vans against the sky,
So soft and soundless, simply beautiful,—
520 Seen nearer . . what a roar and tear it makes,
How it grinds and bruises! . . if she loves at last,
Her love's a re-adjustment of self-love,
No more; a need felt of another's use
To her one advantage,—as the mill wants grain,
525 The fire wants fuel, the very wolf wants prey;
And none of these is more unscrupulous
Than such a charming woman when she loves.
She'll not be thwarted by an obstacle
So trifling as . . her soul is, . . much less yours!—
530 Is God a consideration?—she loves *you*,
Not God; she will not flinch for Him indeed:
She did not for the Marchioness of Perth,
When wanting tickets for the birthnight-ball.
She loves you, sir, with passion, to lunacy;
535 She loves you like her diamonds . . almost.

                                        Well,

A month passed so, and then the notice came;
On such a day the marriage at the church.
I was not backward.
           Half St. Giles in frieze
Was bidden to meet St. James in cloth of gold,
540 And after contract at the altar, pass
To eat a marriage-feast on Hampstead Heath.
Of course the people came in uncompelled,
Lame, blind, and worse—sick, sorrowful, and worse,
The humours of the peccant social wound
545 All pressed out, poured out upon Pimlico,
Exasperating the unaccustomed air
With a hideous interfusion: you'd suppose
A finished generation, dead of plague,
Swept outward from their graves into the sun,
550 The moil of death upon them. What a sight!
A holiday of miserable men
Is sadder than a burial-day of kings.

They clogged the streets, they oozed into the church
In a dark slow stream, like blood. To see that sight,
555 The noble ladies stood up in their pews,
Some pale for fear, a few as red for hate,
Some simply curious, some just insolent,
And some in wondering scorn,—'What next? what next?'
These crushed their delicate rose-lips from the smile
560 That misbecame them in a holy place,
With broidered hems of perfumed handkerchiefs;
Those passed the salts with confidence of eyes
And simultaneous shiver of moiré silk;
While all the aisles, alive and black with heads,
565 Crawled slowly toward the altar from the street,
As bruised snakes drawl and hiss out of a hole
With shuddering involutions, swaying slow
From right to left, and then from left to right,
In pants and pauses. What an ugly crest
570 Of faces, rose upon you everywhere,
From that crammed mass! you did not usually
See faces like them in the open day:

They hide in cellars, not to make you mad
As Romney Leigh is.—Faces!—O my God,

575 We call those, faces? men's and women's . . ay,
And children's;—babies, hanging like a rag
Forgotten on their mother's neck,—poor mouths,
Wiped clean of mother's milk by mother's blow,
Before they are taught her cursing. Faces! . . phew,
580 We'll call them vices festering to despairs,
Or sorrows petrifying to vices: not
A finger-touch of God left whole on them;
All ruined, lost—the countenance worn out
As the garments, the will dissolute as the acts,
585 The passions loose and draggling in the dirt
To trip a foot up at the first free step!—
Those, faces! 'twas as if you had stirred up hell
To heave its lowest dreg-fiends uppermost
In fiery swirls of slime,—such strangled fronts,
590 Such obdurate jaws were thrown up constantly,
To twit you with your race, corrupt your blood,
And grind to devilish colours all your dreams
Henceforth, . . though, haply, you should drop asleep
By clink of silver waters, in a muse
595 On Raffael's mild Madonna of the Bird.

I've waked and slept through many nights and days
Since then,—but still that day will catch my breath
Like a nightmare. There are fatal days, indeed,
In which the fibrous years have taken root
600 So deeply, that they quiver to their tops
Whene'er you stir the dust of such a day.

My cousin met me with his eyes and hand,
And then, with just a word, . . that 'Marian Erle
Was coming with her bridesmaids presently,'
605 Made haste to place me by the altar-stair,
Where he and other noble gentlemen
And high-born ladies, waited for the bride.

We waited. It was early: there was time
For greeting, and the morning's compliment;
610 And gradually a ripple of women's talk
Arose and fell and tossed about a spray
Of English *ss*, soft as a silent hush,
And, notwithstanding, quite as audible
As louder phrases thrown out by the men.
615 —'Yes, really, if we've need to wait in church,
We've need to talk there.'—'She? 'Tis Lady Ayr,
In blue—not purple! that's the dowager.'
—'She looks as young'—'She flirts as young, you mean!
Why, if you had seen her upon Thursday night,
620 You'd call Miss Norris modest.'—'*You* again!
I waltzed with you three hours back. Up at six,
Up still at ten; scarce time to change one's shoes.
I feel as white and sulky as a ghost,
So pray don't speak to me, Lord Belcher.'—'No,
625 I'll look at you instead, and it's enough
While you have that face.' 'In church, my lord! fie, fie!'
—'Adair, you stayed for the Division?'—'Lost
By one.' 'The devil it is! I'm sorry for't
And if I had not promised Mistress Grove' . .
630 'You might have kept your word to Liverpool.'
'Constituents must remember, after all,
We're mortal.'—'We remind them of it.'—'Hark,
The bride comes! Here she comes, in a stream of milk!'
—'There? Dear, you are asleep still; don't you know
635 The five Miss Granvilles? always dressed in white
To show they're ready to be married.'—'Lower!
The aunt is at your elbow.'—'Lady Maud,
Did Lady Waldemar tell you she had seen
This girl of Leigh's?' 'No,—wait! 'twas Mrs. Brookes,
640 Who told me Lady Waldemar told her—
No, 'twasn't Mrs. Brookes.'—'She's pretty?'—'Who?
Mrs. Brookes? Lady Waldemar?'—'How hot!
Pray is't the law to-day we're not to breathe?
You're treading on my shawl—I thank you, sir.'
645 —'They say the bride's a mere child, who can't read,
But knows the things she shouldn't, with wide-awake

Great eyes. I'd go through fire to look at her.'
—'You do, I think.'—'And Lady Waldemar
(You see her; sitting close to Romney Leigh;
650 How beautiful she looks, a little flushed!)
Has taken up the girl, and organised
Leigh's folly. Should I have come here, you suppose,
Except she'd asked me?'—'She'd have served him more
By marrying him herself.'

     'Ah—there she comes,
655 The bride, at last!'

     'Indeed, no. Past eleven.
She puts off her patched petticoat to-day
And puts on Mayfair manners, so begins
By setting us to wait.'—'Yes, yes, this Leigh
Was always odd; it's in the blood, I think;
660 His father's uncle's cousin's second son
Was, was . . you understand me—and for him,
He's stark!—has turned quite lunatic upon
This modern question of the poor—the poor:
An excellent subject when you're moderate;
665 You've seen Prince Albert's model lodging-house?
Does honour to his Royal Highness. Good!
But would he stop his carriage in Cheapside
To shake a common fellow by the fist
Whose name was . . Shakspeare? No. We draw a line,
670 And if we stand not by our order, we
In England, we fall headlong. Here's a sight,—
A hideous sight, a most indecent sight!
My wife would come, sir, or I had kept her back.
By heaven, sir, when poor Damiens' trunk and limbs
675 Were torn by horses, women of the court
Stood by and stared, exactly as to-day
On this dismembering of society,
With pretty troubled faces.'

     'Now, at last.
She comes now.'

     'Where? who sees? you push me, sir,
680 Beyond the point of what is mannerly.
You're standing, madam, on my second flounce—

I do beseech you.'
                    'No—it's not the bride.
Half-past eleven. How late. The bridegroom, mark,
Gets anxious and goes out.'
                            'And as I said . .
685 These Leighs! our best blood running in the rut!
It's something awful. We had pardoned him
A simple misalliance, got up aside
For a pair of sky-blue eyes; our House of Lords
Has winked at such things, and we've all been young.
690 But here's an inter-marriage reasoned out,
A contract (carried boldly to the light,
To challenge observation, pioneer
Good acts by a great example) 'twixt the extremes
Of martyrised society,—on the left,
695 The well-born,—on the right, the merest mob,
To treat as equals!—'tis anarchical!
It means more than it says—'tis damnable!
Why, sir, we can't have even our coffee good,
Unless we strain it.'
                        'Here, Miss Leigh!'
                                            'Lord Howe,
700 You're Romney's friend. What's all this waiting for?'

'I cannot tell. The bride has lost her head
(And way, perhaps!) to prove her sympathy
With the bridegroom.'
                        What,—you also, disapprove!'

'Oh, *I* approve of nothing in the world,'
705 He answered, 'not of you, still less of me,
Nor even of Romney—though he's worth us both.
We've all gone wrong. The tune in us is lost;
And whistling in back alleys to the moon,
Will never catch it.'
                        Let me draw Lord Howe.
710 A born aristocrat, bred radical,
And educated socialist, who still
Goes floating, on traditions of his kind,

Across the theoretic flood from France,—
Though, like a drenched Noah on a rotten deck,
715   Scarce safer for his place there. He, at least,
Will never land on Ararat, he knows,
To recommence the world on the old plan:
Indeed, he thinks, said world had better end;
He sympathises rather with the fish
720   Outside, than with the drowned paired beasts within
Who cannot couple again or multiply:
And that's the sort of Noah he is, Lord Howe.
He never could be anything complete,
Except a loyal, upright gentleman,
725   A liberal landlord, graceful diner-out,
And entertainer more than hospitable,
Whom authors dine with and forget the port.
Whatever he believes, and it is much,
But no-wise certain . . now here and now there, . .
730   He still has sympathies beyond his creed;
Diverting him from action. In the House,
No party counts upon him, and all praise:
All like his books too, (for he has written books)
Which, good to lie beside a bishop's chair,
735   So oft outreach themselves with jets of fire
At which the foremost of the progressists
May warm audacious hands in passing by.
—Of stature over-tall, lounging for ease;
Light hair, that seems to carry a wind in it,
740   And eyes that, when they look on you, will lean
Their whole weight half in indolence, and half
In wishing you unmitigated good,
Until you know not if to flinch from him
Or thank him.—'Tis Lord Howe.
                                         'We're all gone wrong,'
745   Said he; 'and Romney, that dear friend of ours,
Is no-wise right. There's one true thing on earth,
That's love! He takes it up, and dresses it,
And acts a play with it, as Hamlet did,
To show what cruel uncles we have been,
750   And how we should be uneasy in our minds,

While he, Prince Hamlet, weds a pretty maid
(Who keeps us too long waiting, we'll confess)
By symbol, to instruct us formally
To fill the ditches up 'twixt class and class,
755   And live together in phalansteries.
       What then?—he's mad, our Hamlet! clap his play,
And bind him.'
                    'Ah, Lord Howe, this spectacle
Pulls stronger at us than the Dane's. See there!
The crammed aisles heave and strain and steam with life—
760   Dear Heaven, what life!'
                              'Why, yes,—a poet sees;
Which makes him different from a common man.
I, too, see somewhat, though I cannot sing;
I should have been a poet, only that
My mother took fright at the ugly world,
765   And bore me tongue-tied. If you'll grant me now
That Romney gives us a fine actor-piece
To make us merry on his marriage-morn,—
The fable's worse than Hamlet's, I'll concede.
The terrible people, old and poor and blind,
770   Their eyes eat out with plague and poverty
From seeing beautiful and cheerful sights,
We'll liken to a brutalised King Lear,
Led out,—by no means to clear scores with wrongs—
His wrongs are so far back, . . he has forgot;
775   All's past like youth; but just to witness here
A simple contract,—he, upon his side,
And Regan with her sister Goneril
And all the dappled courtiers and court-fools,
On their side. Not that any of these would say
780   They're sorry, neither. What is done, is done,
And violence is now turned privilege,
As cream turns cheese, if buried long enough.
What could such lovely ladies have to do
With the old man there, in those ill-odorous rags,
785   Except to keep the wind-side of him? Lear
Is flat and quiet, as a decent grave;
He does not curse his daughters in the least.

Be these his daughters? Lear is thinking of
His porridge chiefly . . is it getting cold
790   At Hampstead? will the ale be served in pots?
Poor Lear, poor daughters! Bravo, Romney's play!'

A murmur and a movement drew around;
A naked whisper touched us. Something wrong!
What's wrong? The black crowd, as an overstrained
795   Cord, quivered in vibration, and I saw . .
Was that *his* face I saw? . . his . . Romney Leigh's . .
Which tossed a sudden horror like a sponge
Into all eyes,—while himself stood white upon
The topmost altar-stair, and tried to speak,
800   And failed, and lifted higher above his head
A letter, . . as a man who drowns and gasps.

'My brothers, bear with me! I am very weak.
I meant but only good. Perhaps I meant
Too proudly,—and God snatched the circumstance
805   And changed it therefore. There's no marriage—none.
She leaves me,—she departs,—she disappears,—
I lose her. Yet I never forced her 'ay,'
To have her 'no' so cast into my teeth,
In manner of an accusation, thus.
810   My friends, you are all dismissed. Go, eat and drink
According to the programme,—and farewell!'

He ended. There was silence in the church;
We heard a baby sucking in its sleep
At the farthest end of the aisle. Then spoke a man,
815   'Now, look to it, coves, that all the beef and drink
Be not filched from us like the other fun;
For beer's spilt easier than a woman is!
This gentry is not honest with the poor;
They bring us up, to trick us.'—'Go it, Jim,'
820   A woman screamed back,—'I'm a tender soul;
I never banged a child at two years old
And drew blood from him, but I sobbed for it
Next moment,—and I've had a plague of seven.

I'm tender; I've no stomach even for beef,
825   Until I know about the girl that's lost,
That's killed, mayhap. I did misdoubt, at first,
The fine lord meant no good by her, or us.
He, maybe, got the upper hand of her
By holding up a wedding-ring, and then . .
830   A choking finger on her throat, last night,
And just a clever tale to keep us still,
As she is, poor lost innocent. 'Disappear!'
Who ever disappears except a ghost?
And who believes a story of a ghost?
835   I ask you,—would a girl go off, instead
Of staying to be married? a fine tale!
A wicked man, I say, a wicked man!
For my part, I would rather starve on gin
Than make my dinner on his beef and beer.'—
840   At which a cry rose up—'We'll have our rights.
We'll have the girl, the girl! Your ladies there
Are married safely and smoothly every day,
And *she* shall not drop through into a trap
Because she's poor and of the people: shame!
845   We'll have no tricks played off by gentlefolks;
We'll see her righted.'
                                    Through the rage and roar
I heard the broken words which Romney flung
Among the turbulent masses, from the ground
He held still, with his masterful pale face—
850   As huntsmen throw the ration to the pack,
Who, falling on it headlong, dog on dog
In heaps of fury, rend it, swallow it up
With yelling hound-jaws,—his indignant words,
His suppliant words, his most pathetic words,
855   Whereof I caught the meaning here and there
By his gesture . . torn in morsels, yelled across,
And so devoured. From end to end, the church
Rocked round us like the sea in storm, and then
Broke up like the earth in earthquake. Men cried out
860   'Police'—and women stood and shrieked for God,
Or dropt and swooned; or, like a herd of deer,

(For whom the black woods suddenly grow alive,
Unleashing their wild shadows down the wind
To hunt the creatures into corners, back
865   And forward) madly fled, or blindly fell,
Trod screeching underneath the feet of those
Who fled and screeched.
                              The last sight left to me
Was Romney's terrible calm face above
The tumult!—the last sound was 'Pull him down!
870   Strike—kill him!' Stretching my unreasoning arms,
As men in dreams, who vainly interpose
'Twixt gods and their undoing, with a cry
I struggled to precipitate myself
Head-foremost to the rescue of my soul
875   In that white face, . . till some one caught me back,
And so the world went out,—I felt no more.

What followed, was told after by Lord Howe,
Who bore me senseless from the strangling crowd
In church and street, and then returned alone
880   To see the tumult quelled. The men of law
Had fallen as thunder on a roaring fire,
And made all silent,—while the people's smoke
Passed eddying slowly from the emptied aisles.

Here's Marian's letter, which a ragged child
885   Brought running, just as Romney at the porch
Looked out expectant of the bride. He sent
The letter to me by his friend Lord Howe
Some two hours after, folded in a sheet
On which his well-known hand had left a word.
890   Here's Marian's letter.
                              'Noble friend, dear saint,
Be patient with me. Never think me vile
Who might to-morrow morning be your wife
But that I loved you more than such a name.
Farewell, my Romney. Let me write it once,—
895   My Romney.
                  ''Tis so pretty a coupled word,

I have no heart to pluck it with a blot.
We say 'my God' sometimes, upon our knees,
Who is not therefore vexed: so bear with it . .
And me. I know I'm foolish, weak, and vain;
900 Yet most of all I'm angry with myself
For losing your last footsteps on the stair,
The last time of your coming,—yesterday!
The very first time I lost step of yours
(Its sweetness comes the next to what you speak),
905 But yesterday sobs took me by the throat
And cut me off from music.

               'Mister Leigh,
You'll set me down as wrong in many things.
You've praised me, sir, for truth,—and now you'll learn
I had not courage to be rightly true.
910 I once began to tell you how she came,
The woman . . and you stared upon the floor
In one of your fixed thoughts . . which put me out
For that day. After, some one spoke of me,
So wisely, and of you, so tenderly,
915 Persuading me to silence for your sake . . .
Well, well! it seems this moment I was wrong
In keeping back from telling you the truth:
There might be truth betwixt us two, at least,
If nothing else. And yet 'twas dangerous.
920 Suppose a real angel came from heaven
To live with men and women! he'd go mad,
If no considerate hand should tie a blind
Across his piercing eyes. 'Tis thus with you:
You see us too much in your heavenly light;
925 I always thought so, angel,—and indeed
There's danger that you beat yourself to death
Against the edges of this alien world,
In some divine and fluttering pity.

                       'Yes,
It would be dreadful for a friend of yours,
930 To see all England thrust you out of doors
And mock you from the windows. You might say,

Or think (that's worse) 'There's some one in the house
I miss and love still.' Dreadful!

                           'Very kind,
I pray you mark, was Lady Waldemar.

935 She came to see me nine times, rather ten—
So beautiful, she hurts me like the day
Let suddenly on sick eyes.

                         'Most kind of all,
Your cousin!—ah, most like you! Ere you came
She kissed me mouth to mouth: I felt her soul

940 Dip through her serious lips in holy fire.
God help me, but it made me arrogant;
I almost told her that you would not lose
By taking me to wife: though, ever since
I've pondered much a certain thing she asked . .

945 'He loves you, Marian?' . . in a sort of mild
Derisive sadness . . as a mother asks
Her babe, 'You'll touch that star, you think?'

                                 'Farewell!
I know I never touched it.

                       'This is worst:
Babes grow, and lose the hope of things above;

950 A silver threepence sets them leaping high—
But no more stars! mark that.

                      'I've writ all night
And told you nothing. God, if I could die,
And let this letter break off innocent
Just here! But no—for your sake . .

                         'Here's the last:

955 I never could be happy as your wife,
I never could be harmless as your friend,
I never will look more into your face,
Till God says 'Look!' I charge you, seek me not,
Nor vex yourself with lamentable thoughts

960 That peradventure I have come to grief;
Be sure I'm well, I'm merry, I'm at ease,
But such a long way, long way, long way off,
I think you'll find me sooner in my grave;
And that's my choice, observe. For what remains,

965   An over-generous friend will care for me,
       And keep me happy . . happier . .
                                   'There's a blot!
       This ink runs thick . . we light girls lightly weep . .
       And keep me happier . . was the thing to say, . .
       Than as your wife I could be!—O, my star,
970   My saint, my soul! for surely you're my soul,
       Through whom God touched me! I am not so lost
       I cannot thank you for the good you did,
       The tears you stopped, which fell down bitterly,
       Like these—the times you made me weep for joy
975   At hoping I should learn to write your notes
       And save the tiring of your eyes, at night;
       And most for that sweet thrice you kissed my lips
       And said 'Dear Marian.'
                              ''Twould be hard to read,
       This letter, for a reader half as learn'd,
980   But you'll be sure to master it, in spite
       Of ups and downs. My hand shakes, I am blind,
       I'm poor at writing, at the best,—and yet
       I tried to make my gs the way you showed.
       Farewell—Christ love you.—Say 'poor Marian' now.'

985   Poor Marian!—wanton Marian!—was it so,
       Or so? For days, her touching, foolish lines
       We mused on with conjectural fantasy,
       As if some riddle of a summer-cloud
       On which one tries unlike similitudes
990   Of now a spotted Hydra-skin cast off,
       And now a screen of carven ivory
       That shuts the heavens' conventual secrets up
       From mortals over-bold. We sought the sense:
       She loved him so perhaps, (such words mean love,)
995   That, worked on by some shrewd perfidious tongue,
       (And then I thought of Lady Waldemar)
       She left him, not to hurt him; or perhaps
       She loved one in her class,—or did not love,
       But mused upon her wild bad tramping life
1000 Until the free blood fluttered at her heart,

And black bread eaten by the road-side hedge
Seemed sweeter than being put to Romney's school
Of philanthropical self-sacrifice,
Irrevocably.—Girls are girls, beside,
1005 Thought I, and like a wedding by one rule.
You seldom catch these birds, except with chaff:
They feel it almost an immoral thing
To go out and be married in broad day,
Unless some winning special flattery should
1010 Excuse them to themselves for't, . . 'No one parts
Her hair with such a silver line as you,
One moonbeam from the forehead to the crown!'
Or else . . 'You bite your lip in such a way,
It spoils me for the smiling of the rest,'—
1015 And so on. Then a worthless gaud or two,
To keep for love,—a ribbon for the neck,
Or some glass pin,—they have their weight with girls.

And Romney sought her many days and weeks:
He sifted all the refuse of the town,
1020 Explored the trains, enquired among the ships,
And felt the country through from end to end;
No Marian!—Though I hinted what I knew,—
A friend of his had reasons of her own
For throwing back the match—he would not hear:
1025 The lady had been ailing ever since,
The shock had harmed her. Something in his tone
Repressed me; something in me shamed my doubt
To a sigh, repressed too. He went on to say
That, putting questions where his Marian lodged,
1030 He found she had received for visitors,
Besides himself and Lady Waldemar
And, that once, me—a dubious woman dressed
Beyond us both. The rings upon her hands
Had dazed the children when she threw them pence;
1035 'She wore her bonnet as the queen might hers,
To show the crown,' they said,—'a scarlet crown
Of roses that had never been in bud.'

*

When Romney told me that,—for now and then
He came to tell me how the search advanced,
1040 His voice dropped: I bent forward for the rest:
The woman had been with her, it appeared,·
At first from week to week, then day by day,
And last, 'twas sure . .
                              I looked upon the ground
To escape the anguish of his eyes, and asked
1045 As low as when you speak to mourners new
Of those they cannot bear yet to call dead,
'If Marian had as much as named to him
A certain Rose, an early friend of hers,
A ruined creature.'
                              'Never.'—Starting up
1050 He strode from side to side about the room,
Most like some prisoned lion sprung awake,
Who has felt the desert sting through his dreams.
'What was I to her, that she should tell me aught?
A friend! was *I* a friend? I see all clear.
1055 Such devils would pull angels out of heaven,
Provided they could reach them; 'tis their pride;
And that's the odds 'twixt soul and body-plague!
The veriest slave who drops in Cairo's street
Cries 'Stand off from me,' to the passengers;
1060 While these blotched souls are eager to infect,
And blow their bad breath in a sister's face
As if they got some ease by it.'
                              I broke through.
'Some natures catch no plagues. I've read of babes
Found whole and sleeping by the spotted breast
1065 Of one a full day dead. I hold it true,
As I'm a woman and know womanhood,
That Marian Erle, however lured from place,
Deceived in way, keeps pure in aim and heart,
As snow that's drifted from the garden-bank
1070 To the open road.'
                              'Twas hard to hear him laugh.
'The figure's happy. Well—a dozen carts
And trampers will secure you presently

A fine white snow-drift. Leave it there, your snow!
'Twill pass for soot ere sunset. Pure in aim?
1075 She's pure in aim, I grant you,—like myself,
Who thought to take the world upon my back
To carry it o'er a chasm of social ill,
And end by letting slip through impotence
A single soul, a child's weight in a soul,
1080 Straight down the pit of hell! yes, I and she
Have reason to be proud of our pure aims.'
Then softly, as the last repenting drops
Of a thunder-shower, he added, 'The poor child;
Poor Marian! 'twas a luckless day for her
1085 When first she chanced on my philanthropy.'

He drew a chair beside me, and sate down;
And I, instinctively, as women use
Before a sweet friend's grief,—when, in his ear,
They hum the tune of comfort, though themselves
1090 Most ignorant of the special words of such,
And quiet so and fortify his brain
And give it time and strength for feeling out
To reach the availing sense beyond that sound,—
Went murmuring to him, what, if written here,
1095 Would seem not much, yet fetched him better help
Than, peradventure, if it had been more.

I've known the pregnant thinkers of this time,
And stood by breathless, hanging on their lips,
When some chromatic sequence of fine thought
1100 In learned modulation phrased itself
To an unconjectured harmony of truth.
And yet I've been more moved, more raised, I say,
By a simple word . . a broken easy thing
A three-years infant might say after you,—
1105 A look, a sigh, a touch upon the palm,
Which meant less than 'I love you' . . than by all
The full-voiced rhetoric of those master-mouths.

*

'Ah dear Aurora,' he began at last,
His pale lips fumbling for a sort of smile,
1110 'Your printer's devils have not spoilt your heart:
That's well. And who knows but, long years ago
When you and I talked, you were somewhat right
In being so peevish with me? You, at least,
Have ruined no one through your dreams! Instead,
1115 You've helped the facile youth to live youth's day
With innocent distraction, still perhaps
Suggestive of things better than your rhymes.
The little shepherd-maiden, eight years old
I've seen upon the mountains of Vaucluse,
1120 Asleep i' the sun, her head upon her knees,
The flocks all scattered,—is more laudable
Than any sheep-dog, trained imperfectly,
Who bites the kids through too much zeal.'

                                      'I look
As if I had slept, then!'

                        He was touched at once
1125 By something in my face. Indeed 'twas sure
That he and I,—despite a year or two
Of younger life on my side, and on his,
The heaping of the years' work on the days,—
The three-hour speeches from the member's seat,
1130 The hot committees in and out the House,
The pamphlets, 'Arguments,' 'Collective Views,'
Tossed out as straw before sick houses, just
To show one's sick and so be trod to dirt,
And no more use,—through this world's underground
1135 The burrowing, groping effort, whence the arm
And heart come bleeding,—sure, that he and I
Were, after all, unequally fatigued!
That he, in his developed manhood, stood
A little sunburnt by the glare of life;
1140 While I .. it seemed no sun had shone on me,
So many seasons I had forgot my Springs;
My cheeks had pined and perished from their orbs,
And all the youth-blood in them had grown white

As dew on autumn cyclamens: alone
1145 My eyes and forehead answered for my face.

He said, 'Aurora, you are changed—are ill!'

'Not so, my cousin,—only not asleep!'
I answered, smiling gently. 'Let it be.
You scarcely found the poet of Vaucluse
1150 As drowsy as the shepherds. What is art,
But life upon the larger scale, the higher,
When, graduating up in a spiral line
Of still expanding and ascending gyres,
It pushes toward the intense significance
1155 Of all things, hungry for the Infinite?
Art's life,—and where we live, we suffer and toil.'

He seemed to sift me with his painful eyes.
'Alas! you take it gravely; you refuse
Your dreamland, right of common, and green rest.
1160 You break the mythic turf where danced the nymphs,
With crooked ploughs of actual life,—let in
The axes to the legendary woods,
To pay the head-tax. You are fallen indeed
On evil days, you poets, if yourselves
1165 Can praise that art of yours no otherwise;
And, if you cannot, . . better take a trade
And be of use! 'twere cheaper for your youth.'

'Of use!' I softly echoed, 'there's the point
We sweep about for ever in argument,
1170 Like swallows, which the exasperate, dying year
Sets spinning in black circles, round and round,
Preparing for far flights o'er unknown seas.
And we . . where tend we?'

                                 'Where?' he said, and sighed.
'The whole creation, from the hour we are born,
1175 Perplexes us with questions. Not a stone
But cries behind us, every weary step,
'Where, where?' I leave stones to reply to stones.

Enough for me and for my fleshy heart
To harken the invocations of my kind,
1180 When men catch hold upon my shuddering nerves
And shriek 'What help? what hope? what bread i' the
house,
'What fire i' the frost?' There must be some response,
Though mine fail utterly. This social Sphinx,
Who sits between the sepulchres and stews,
1185 Makes mock and mow against the crystal heavens,
And bullies God,—exacts a word at least
From each man standing on the side of God,
However paying a sphinx-price for it.
We pay it also if we hold our peace,
1190 In pangs and pity. Let me speak and die.
Alas, you'll say, I speak and kill, instead.'

I pressed in there. 'The best men, doing their best,
Know peradventure least of what they do:
Men usefullest i' the world, are simply used;
1195 The nail that holds the wood, must pierce it first,
And He alone who wields the hammer, sees
The work advanced by the earliest blow. Take heart.'

'Ah, if I could have taken yours!' he said,
'But that's past now.' Then rising . . 'I will take
1200 At least your kindness and encouragement.
I thank you. Dear, be happy. Sing your songs,
If that's your way! but sometimes slumber too,
Nor tire too much with following, out of breath,
The rhymes upon your mountains of Delight.
1205 Reflect, if Art be, in truth, the higher life,
You need the lower life to stand upon,
In order to reach up unto that higher;
And none can stand a-tiptoe in the place
He cannot stand in with two stable feet.
1210 Remember then!—for art's sake, hold your life.'

We parted so. I held him in respect.
I comprehended what he was in heart

And sacrificial greatness. Ay, but *he*
Supposed me a thing too small to deign to know:
1215 He blew me, plainly, from the crucible,
As some intruding, interrupting fly
Not worth the pains of his analysis
Absorbed on nobler subjects. Hurt a fly!
He would not for the world: he's pitiful
1220 To flies even. 'Sing,' says he, 'and teaze me still,
If that's your way, poor insect.' That's your way!

Fifth Book

AURORA LEIGH, be humble. Shall I hope
To speak my poems in mysterious tune
With man and nature,—with the lava-lymph
That trickles from successive galaxies
5 Still drop by drop adown the finger of God,
In still new worlds?—with summer-days in this
That scarce dare breathe, they are so beautiful?—
With spring's delicious trouble in the ground,
Tormented by the quickened blood of roots,
10 And softly pricked by golden crocus-sheaves
In token of the harvest-time of flowers?—
With winters and with autumns,—and beyond,
With the human heart's large seasons,—when it hopes
And fears, joys, grieves, and loves?—with all that strain
15 Of sexual passion, which devours the flesh
In a sacrament of souls? with mother's breasts
Which, round the new-made creatures hanging there,
Throb luminous and harmonious like pure spheres?—
With multitudinous life, and finally
20 With the great out-goings of ecstatic souls,
Who, in a rush of too long prisoned flame,
Their radiant faces upward, burn away
This dark of the body, issuing on a world
Beyond our mortal?—can I speak my verse
25 So plainly in tune to these things and the rest,
That men shall feel it catch them on the quick,
As having the same warrant over them
To hold and move them, if they will or no,
Alike imperious as the primal rhythm
30 Of that theurgic nature?—I must fail,
Who fail at the beginning to hold and move
One man,—and he my cousin, and he my friend,
And he born tender, made intelligent,
Inclined to ponder the precipitous sides
35 Of difficult questions; yet, obtuse to *me*,—

Of *me*, incurious! likes me very well,
And wishes me a paradise of good,
Good looks, good means, and good digestion!—ay,
But otherwise evades me, puts me off
40 With kindness, with a tolerant gentleness,—
Too light a book for a grave man's reading! Go,
Aurora Leigh: be humble.
                                        There it is;
We women are too apt to look to one,
Which proves a certain impotence in art.
45 We strain our natures at doing something great,
Far less because it's something great to do,
Than, haply, that we, so, commend ourselves
As being not small, and more appreciable
To some one friend. We must have mediators
50 Betwixt our highest conscience and the judge;
Some sweet saint's blood must quicken in our palms,
Or all the life in heaven seems slow and cold:
Good only, being perceived as the end of good,
And God alone pleased,—that's too poor, we think,
55 And not enough for us, by any means.
Ay—Romney, I remember, told me once
We miss the abstract, when we comprehend!
We miss it most when we aspire, . . and fail.

Yet, so, I will not.—This vile woman's way
60 Of trailing garments, shall not trip me up:
I'll have no traffic with the personal thought
In art's pure temple. Must I work in vain,
Without the approbation of a man?
It cannot be; it shall not. Fame itself,
65 That approbation of the general race,
Presents a poor end, (though the arrow speed
Shot straight with vigorous finger to the white,)
And the highest fame was never reached except
By what was aimed above it. Art for art,
70 And good for God Himself, the essential Good!
We'll keep our aims sublime, our eyes erect,
Although our woman-hands should shake and fail;

And if we fail . . But must we?—
                              Shall I fail?
The Greeks said grandly in their tragic phrase,
75 'Let no one be called happy till his death.'
To which I add,—Let no one till his death
Be called unhappy. Measure not the work
Until the day's out and the labour done;
Then bring your gauges. If the day's work's scant,
80 Why, call it scant; affect no compromise;
And, in that we have nobly striven at least,
Deal with us nobly, women though we be,
And honour us with truth, if not with praise.

My ballads prospered; but the ballad's race
85 Is rapid for a poet who bears weights
Of thought and golden image. He can stand
Like Atlas, in the sonnet,—and support
His own heavens pregnant with dynastic stars;
But then he must stand still, nor take a step.

90 In that descriptive poem called 'The Hills,'
The prospects were too far and indistinct.
'Tis true my critics said 'A fine view, that!'
The public scarcely cared to climb the book
For even the finest; and the public's right,
95 A tree's mere firewood, unless humanised;
Which well the Greeks knew when they stirred the bark
With close-pressed bosoms of subsiding nymphs,
And made the forest-rivers garrulous
With babble of gods. For us, we are called to mark
100 A still more intimate humanity
In this inferior nature,—or, ourselves
Must fall like dead leaves trodden underfoot
By veritabler artists. Earth, shut up
By Adam, like a fakir in a box
105 Left too long buried, remained stiff and dry,
A mere dumb corpse, till Christ the Lord came down,
Unlocked the doors, forced open the blank eyes,
And used his kingly chrisms to straighten out

The leathery tongue turned back into the throat:
110 Since when, she lives, remembers, palpitates
In every limb, aspires in every breath,
Embraces infinite relations. Now,
We want no half-gods, Panomphæan Joves,
Fauns, Naiads, Tritons, Oreads and the rest,
115 To take possession of a senseless world
To unnatural vampire-uses. See the earth,
The body of our body, the green earth,
Indubitably human, like this flesh
And these articulated veins through which
120 Our heart drives blood! there's not a flower of spring
That dies ere June, but vaunts itself allied
By issue and symbol, by significance
And correspondence, to that spirit-world
Outside the limits of our space and time,
125 Whereto we are bound. Let poets give it voice
With human meanings; else they miss the thought,
And henceforth step down lower, stand confessed
Instructed poorly for interpreters,—
Thrown out by an easy cowslip in the text.

130 Even so my pastoral failed: it was a book
Of surface-pictures—pretty, cold, and false
With literal transcript,—the worse done, I think,
For being not ill-done. Let me set my mark
Against such doings, and do otherwise.
135 This strikes me.—If the public whom we know
Could catch me at such admissions, I should pass
For being right modest. Yet how proud we are,
In daring to look down upon ourselves!

The critics say that epics have died out
140 With Agamemnon and the goat-nursed gods—
I'll not believe it. I could never dream,
As Payne Knight did, (the mythic mountaineer
Who travelled higher than he was born to live,
And showed sometimes the goitre in his throat
145 Discoursing of an image seen through fog,)

That Homer's heroes measured twelve feet high.
They were but men!—his Helen's hair turned grey
Like any plain Miss Smith's, who wears a front;
And Hector's infant blubbered at a plume
150   As yours last Friday at a turkey-cock.
All men are possible heroes: every age,
Heroic in proportions, double-faced,
Looks backward and before, expects a morn
And claims an epos.

           Ay, but every age
155   Appears to souls who live in it, (ask Carlyle)
Most unheroic. Ours, for instance, ours!
The thinkers scout it, and the poets abound
Who scorn to touch it with a finger-tip:
A pewter age,—mixed metal, silver-washed;
160   An age of scum, spooned off the richer past;
An age of patches for old gaberdines;
An age of mere transition, meaning nought,
Except that what succeeds must shame it quite,
If God please. That's wrong thinking, to my mind,
165   And wrong thoughts make poor poems.

           Every age,
Through being beheld too close, is ill-discerned
By those who have not lived past it. We'll suppose
Mount Athos carved, as Persian Xerxes schemed,
To some colossal statue of a man:
170   The peasants, gathering brushwood in his ear,
Had guessed as little of any human form
Up there, as would a flock of browsing goats,
They'd have, in fact, to travel ten miles off
Or ere the giant image broke on them,
175   Full human profile, nose and chin distinct,
Mouth, muttering rhythms of silence up the sky,
And fed at evening with the blood of suns;
Grand torso,—hand, that flung perpetually
The largesse of a silver river down
180   To all the country pastures. 'Tis even thus
With times we live in,—evermore too great
To be apprehended near.

           But poets should

Exert a double vision; should have eyes
To see near things as comprehensively
185   As if afar they took their point of sight,
And distant things, as intimately deep
As if they touched them. Let us strive for this.
I do distrust the poet who discerns
No character or glory in his times,
190   And trundles back his soul five hundred years,
Past moat and drawbridge, into a castle-court,
Oh not to sing of lizards or of toads
Alive i' the ditch there,—'twere excusable;
But of some black chief, half knight, half sheep-lifter,
195   Some beauteous dame, half chattel and half queen,
As dead as must be, for the greater part,
The poems made on their chivalric bones;
And that's no wonder: death inherits death.

Nay, if there's room for poets in the world
200   A little overgrown, (I think there is),
Their sole work is to represent the age,
Their age, not Charlemagne's,—this live, throbbing age,
That brawls, cheats, maddens, calculates, aspires,
And spends more passion, more heroic heat,
205   Betwixt the mirrors of its drawing-rooms,
Than Roland with his knights, at Roncesvalles.
To flinch from modern varnish, coat or flounce,
Cry out for togas and the picturesque
Is fatal,—foolish too. King Arthur's self
210   Was commonplace to Lady Guenever;
And Camelot to minstrels seemed as flat,
As Regent Street to poets.
                                          Never flinch,
But still, unscrupulously epic, catch
Upon the burning lava of a song
215   The full-veined, heaving, double-breasted Age:
That, when the next shall come, the men of that
May touch the impress with reverent hand, and say
'Behold,—behold the paps we all have sucked!
That bosom seems to beat still, or at least

220 It sets ours beating. This is living art,
Which thus presents, and thus records true life.'

What form is best for poems? Let me think ·
Of forms less, and the external. Trust the spirit,
As sovran nature does, to make the form;
225 For otherwise we only imprison spirit,
And not embody. Inward evermore
To outward,—so in life, and so in art,
Which still is life.
                    Five acts to make a play.
And why not fifteen? why not ten? or seven?
230 What matter for the number of the leaves,
Supposing the tree lives and grows? exact
The literal unities of time and place,
When 'tis the essence of passion to ignore
Both time and place? Absurd. Keep up the fire,
235 And leave the generous flames to shape themselves.

'Tis true the stage requires obsequiousness
To this or that convention; 'exit' here
And 'enter' there; the points for clapping, fixed,
Like Jacob's white-peeled rods before the rams;
240 And all the close-curled imagery clipped
In manner of their fleece at shearing time.
Forget to prick the galleries to the heart
Precisely at the fourth act,—culminate
Our five pyramidal acts with one act more,—
245 We're lost so! Shakspeare's ghost could scarcely plead
Against our just damnation. Stand aside;
We'll muse for comfort that, last century,
On this same tragic stage on which we have failed,
A wigless Hamlet would have failed the same.

250 And whosoever writes good poetry,
Looks just to art. He does not write for you
Or me,—for London or for Edinburgh;
He will not suffer the best critic known

To step into his sunshine of free thought
255   And self-absorbed conception, and exact
An inch-long swerving of the holy lines.
If virtue done for popularity
Defiles like vice, can art for praise or hire,
Still keep its splendour, and remain pure art?
260   Eschew such serfdom. What the poet writes,
He writes: mankind accepts it, if it suits,
And that's success: if not, the poem's passed
From hand to hand, and yet from hand to hand,
Until the unborn snatch it, crying out
265   In pity on their fathers' being so dull,
And that's success too.
                                    I will write no plays.
Because the drama, less sublime in this,
Makes lower appeals, defends more menially,
Adopts the standard of the public taste
270   To chalk its height on, wears a dog-chain round
Its regal neck, and learns to carry and fetch
The fashions of the day to please the day;
Fawns close on pit and boxes, who clap hands,
Commending chiefly its docility
275   And humour in stage-tricks; or else indeed
Gets hissed at, howled at, stamped at like a dog,
Or worse, we'll say. For dogs, unjustly kicked,
Yell, bite at need; but if your dramatist
(Being wronged by some five hundred nobodies
280   Because their grosser brains most naturally
Misjudge the fineness of his subtle wit)
Shows teeth an almond's breadth, protests the length
Of a modest phrase,—'My gentle countrymen,
'There's something in it, haply, of your fault,'—
285   Why then, besides five hundred nobodies,
He'll have five thousand and five thousand more,
Against him,—the whole public,—Call the hoofs
Of King Saul's father's asses, in full drove,—
And obviously deserve it. He appealed
290   To these,—and why say more if they condemn,
Than if they praised him?—Weep, my Æschylus,

But low and far, upon Sicilian shores!
For since 'twas Athens (so I read the myth)
Who gave commission to that fatal weight,
295   The tortoise, cold and hard, to drop on thee
And crush thee,—better cover thy bald head;
She'll hear the softest hum of Hyblan bee
Before thy loud'st protestation.—For the rest,
The risk's still worse upon the modern stage:
300   I could not, in so little, accept success,
Nor would I risk so much, in ease and calm,
For manifester gains: let those who prize,
Pursue them: *I* stand off.
      And yet, forbid,
That any irreverent fancy or conceit
305   Should litter in the Drama's throne-room, where
The rulers of our art, in whose full veins
Dynastic glories mingle, sit in strength
And do their kingly work,—conceive, command,
And, from the imagination's crucial heat,
310   Catch up their men and women all a-flame
For action, all alive, and forced to prove
Their life by living out heart, brain, and nerve,
Until mankind makes witness, 'These be men
As we are,' and vouchsafe the kiss that's due
315   To Imogen and Juliet—sweetest kin
On art's side.
     'Tis that, honouring to its worth
The drama, I would fear to keep it down
To the level of the footlights. Dies no more
The sacrificial goat, for Bacchus slain,—
320   His filmed eyes fluttered by the whirling white
Of choral vestures,—troubled in his blood,
While tragic voices that clanged keen as swords,
Leapt high together with the altar-flame,
And made the blue air wink. The waxen mask,
325   Which set the grand still front of Themis' son
Upon the puckered visage of a player;—
The buskin, which he rose upon and moved,
As some tall ship, first conscious of the wind,

Sweeps slowly past the piers;—the mouthpiece, where
330 The mere man's voice with all its breaths and breaks
Went sheathed in brass, and clashed on even heights
Its phrasèd thunders;—these things are no more,
Which once were. And concluding, which is clear,
The growing drama has outgrown such toys
335 Of simulated stature, face, and speech,
It also, peradventure, may outgrow
The simulation of the painted scene,
Boards, actors, prompters, gaslight, and costume;
And take for a worthier stage the soul itself,
340 Its shifting fancies and celestial lights,
With all its grand orchestral silences
To keep the pauses of the rhythmic sounds.

Alas, I still see something to be done,
And what I do falls short of what I see
345 Though I waste myself on doing. Long green days,
Worn bare of grass and sunshine,—long calm nights,
From which the silken sleeps were fretted out,—
Be witness for me, with no amateur's
Irreverent haste and busy idleness
350 I've set myself to art! What then? what's done?
What's done, at last?
                        Behold, at last, a book.
If life-blood's necessary,—which it is,
(By that blue vein athrob on Mahomet's brow,
Each prophet-poet's book must show man's blood!)
355 If life-blood's fertilising, I wrung mine
On every leaf of this,—unless the drops
Slid heavily on one side and left it dry.
That chances often: many a fervid man
Writes books as cold and flat as grave-yard stones
360 From which the lichen's scraped; and if St. Preux
Had written his own letters, as he might,
We had never wept to think of the little mole
'Neath Julie's drooping eyelid. Passion is
But something suffered, after all.
                                While Art

365 Sets action on the top of suffering:
    The artist's part is both to be and do,
    Transfixing with a special, central power
    The flat experience of the common man,
    And turning outward, with a sudden wrench,
370 Half agony, half ecstasy, the thing
    He feels the inmost: never felt the less
    Because he sings it. Does a torch less burn
    For burning next reflectors of blue steel,
    That *he* should be the colder for his place
375 'Twixt two incessant fires,—his personal life's
    And that intense refraction which burns back
    Perpetually against him from the round
    Of crystal conscience he was born into
    If artist-born? O sorrowful great gift
380 Conferred on poets, of a twofold life,
    When one life has been found enough for pain!
    We, staggering 'neath our burden as mere men,
    Being called to stand up straight as demi-gods,
    Support the intolerable strain and stress
385 Of the universal, and send clearly up,
    With voices broken by the human sob,
    Our poems to find rhymes among the stars!
    But soft!—a 'poet' is a word soon said;
    A book's a thing soon written. Nay, indeed,
390 The more the poet shall be questionable,
    The more unquestionably comes his book!
    And this of mine—well, granting to myself
    Some passion in it, furrowing up the flats,
    Mere passion will not prove a volume worth
395 Its gall and rags even. Bubbles round a keel
    Mean nought, excepting that the vessel moves.
    There's more than passion goes to make a man,
    Or book, which is a man too.
                                    I am sad.
    I wonder if Pygmalion had these doubts,
400 And, feeling the hard marble first relent,
    Grow supple to the straining of his arms,
    And tingle through its cold to his burning lip,

Supposed his senses mocked, and that the toil
Of stretching past the known and seen, to reach
405 The archetypal Beauty out of sight,
Had made his heart beat fast enough for two,
And with his own life dazed and blinded him!
Not so; Pygmalion loved,—and whoso loves
Believes the impossible.
                              And I am sad:
410 I cannot thoroughly love a work of mine,
Since none seems worthy of my thought and hope
More highly mated. He has shot them down,
My Phœbus Apollo, soul within my soul,
Who judges, by the attempted, what's attained,
415 And with the silver arrow from his height,
Has struck down all my works before my face
While *I* said nothing. Is there aught to say?
I called the artist but a greatened man:
He may be childless also, like a man.

420 I laboured on alone. The wind and dust
And sun of the world beat blistering in my face;
And hope, now for me, now against me, dragged
My spirits onward,—as some fallen balloon,
Which, whether caught by blossoming tree or bare,
425 Is torn alike. I sometimes touched my aim,
Or seemed,—and generous souls cried out, 'Be strong,
Take courage; now you're on our level,—now!
The next step saves you!' I was flushed with praise,
But, pausing just a moment to draw breath,
430 I could not choose but murmur to myself
'Is this all? all that's done? and all that's gained?
If this then be success, 'tis dismaller
Than any failure.'
                    O my God, my God,
O supreme Artist, who as sole return
435 For all the cosmic wonder of Thy work,
Demandest of us just a word . . a name,
'My Father!'—thou hast knowledge, only thou,
How dreary 'tis for women to sit still

On winter nights by solitary fires,
440   And hear the nations praising them far off,
Too far! ay, praising our quick sense of love,
Our very heart of passionate womanhood,
Which could not beat so in the verse without
Being present also in the unkissed lips,
445   And eyes undried because there's none to ask
The reason they grew moist.
                To sit alone
And think, for comfort, how, that very night,
Affianced lovers, leaning face to face
With sweet half-listenings for each other's breath,
450   Are reading haply from some page of ours,
To pause with a thrill, as if their cheeks had touched,
When such a stanza, level to their mood,
Seems floating their own thought out—'So I feel
For thee,'—'And I, for thee: this poet knows
455   What everlasting love is!'—how, that night,
Some father, issuing from the misty roads
Upon the luminous round of lamp and hearth
And happy children, having caught up first
The youngest there until it shrunk and shrieked
460   To feel the cold chin prick its dimples through
With winter from the hills, may throw i' the lap
Of the eldest, (who has learnt to drop her lids
To hide some sweetness newer than last year's)
Our book and cry, . . 'Ah you, you care for rhymes;
465   So here be rhymes to pore on under trees,
When April comes to let you! I've been told
They are not idle as so many are,
But set hearts beating pure as well as fast:
It's yours, the book; I'll write your name in it,—
470   That so you may not lose, however lost
In poet's lore and charming reverie,
The thought of how your father thought of *you*
In riding from the town.'
                    To have our books
Appraised by love, associated with love,
475   While *we* sit loveless! is it hard, you think?

At least 'tis mournful. Fame, indeed, 'twas said,
Means simply love. It was a man said that.
And then, there's love and love: the love of all
(To risk, in turn, a woman's paradox,)
480   Is but a small thing to the love of one.
You bid a hungry child be satisfied
With a heritage of many corn-fields: nay,
He says he's hungry,—he would rather have
That little barley-cake you keep from him
485   While reckoning up his harvests. So with us;
(Here, Romney, too, we fail to generalise!)
We're hungry.
                    Hungry! but it's pitiful
To wail like unweaned babes and suck our thumbs
Because we're hungry. Who, in all this world,
490   (Wherein we are haply set to pray and fast,
And learn what good is by its opposite),
Has never hungered? Woe to him who has found
The meal enough! if Ugolino's full,
His teeth have crunched some foul unnatural thing:
495   For here satiety proves penury
More utterly irremediable. And since
We needs must hunger,—better, for man's love,
Than God's truth! better, for companions sweet,
Than great convictions! let us bear our weights,
500   Preferring dreary hearths to desert souls.
Well, well! they say we're envious, we who rhyme;
But I, because I am a woman perhaps,
And so rhyme ill, am ill at envying.
I never envied Graham his breadth of style,
505   Which gives you, with a random smutch or two
(Near-sighted critics analyse to smutch)
Such delicate perspectives of full life:
Nor Belmore, for the unity of aim
To which he cuts his cedarn poems, fine
510   As sketchers do their pencils; nor Mark Gage,
For that caressing colour and trancing tone
Whereby you're swept away and melted in
The sensual element, which, with a back wave

Restores you to the level of pure souls
515 And leaves you with Plotinus. None of these,
For native gifts or popular applause,
I've envied; but for this,—that when, by chance
Says some one,—'There goes Belmore, a great man!
He leaves clean work behind him, and requires
520 No sweeper up of the chips,' . . a girl I know,
Who answers nothing, save with her brown eyes,
Smiles unaware, as if a guardian saint
Smiled in her:—for this, too,—that Gage comes home
And lays his last book's prodigal review
525 Upon his mother's knees, where, years ago,
He laid his childish spelling-book and learned
To chirp and peck the letters from her mouth,
As young birds must. 'Well done,' she murmured then,
She will not say it now more wonderingly;
530 And yet the last 'Well done' will touch him more,
As catching up to-day and yesterday
In a perfect chord of love; and so, Mark Gage,
I envy you your mother!—and you, Graham,
Because you have a wife who loves you so,
535 She half forgets, at moments, to be proud
Of being Graham's wife, until a friend observes,
'The boy here has his father's massive brow,
Done small in wax . . if we push back the curls.'

Who loves *me*? Dearest father,—mother sweet,—
540 I speak the names out sometimes by myself,
And make the silence shiver: they sound strange,
As Hindostanee to an Ind-born man
Accustomed many years to English speech;
Or lovely poet-words grown obsolete,
545 Which will not leave off singing. Up in heaven
I have my father,—with my mother's face
Beside him in a blotch of heavenly light;
No more for earth's familiar, household use,
No more. The best verse written by this hand,
550 Can never reach them where they sit, to seem
Well done to *them*. Death quite unfellows us,

Sets dreadful odds betwixt the live and dead,
And makes us part as those at Babel did,
Through sudden ignorance of a common tongue.
555 A living Cæsar would not dare to play
At bowls, with such as my dead father is.

And yet, this may be less so than appears,
This change and separation. Sparrows five
For just two farthings, and God cares for each.
560 If God is not too great for little cares,
Is any creature, because gone to God?
I've seen some men, veracious, nowise mad,
Who have thought or dreamed, declared and testified,
They've heard the Dead a-ticking like a clock
565 Which strikes the hours of the eternities,
Beside them, with their natural ears,—and known
That human spirits feel the human way
And hate the unreasoning awe which waves them off
From possible communion. It may be.

570 At least, earth separates as well as heaven.
For instance, I have not seen Romney Leigh
Full eighteen months . . add six, you get two years.
They say he's very busy with good works,—
Has parted Leigh Hall into almshouses.
575 He made an almshouse of his heart one day,
Which ever since is loose upon the latch
For those who pull the string.—I never did.

It always makes me sad to go abroad;
And now I'm sadder that I went to-night,
580 Among the lights and talkers at Lord Howe's.
His wife is gracious, with her glossy braids,
And even voice, and gorgeous eyeballs, calm
As her other jewels. If she's somewhat cold,
Who wonders, when her blood has stood so long
585 In the ducal reservoir she calls her line
By no means arrogantly? she's not proud;
Not prouder than the swan is of the lake

He has always swum in;—'tis her element;
And so she takes it with a natural grace,
590 Ignoring tadpoles. She just knows, perhaps
There *are* men, move on without outriders,
Which isn't her fault. Ah, to watch her face,
When good Lord Howe expounds his theories
Of social justice and equality—
595 'Tis curious, what a tender, tolerant bend
Her neck takes: for she loves him, likes his talk,
'Such clever talk—that dear, odd Algernon!'
She listens on, exactly as if he talked
Some Scandinavian myth of Lemures,
600 Too pretty to dispute, and too absurd.

She's gracious to me as her husband's friend,
And would be gracious, were I not a Leigh,
Being used to smile just so, without her eyes,
On Joseph Strangways, the Leeds mesmerist,
605 And Delia Dobbs, the lecturer from 'the States'
Upon the 'Woman's question.' Then, for him,
I like him . . he's my friend. And all the rooms
Were full of crinkling silks that swept about
The fine dust of most subtle courtesies.
610 What then?—why then, we come home to be sad.

How lovely One I love not looked to-night!
She's very pretty, Lady Waldemar.
Her maid must use both hands to twist that coil
Of tresses, then be careful lest the rich
615 Bronze rounds should slip:—she missed, though, a grey
        hair,
A single one,—I saw it; otherwise
The woman looked immortal. How they told,
Those alabaster shoulders and bare breasts,
On which the pearls, drowned out of sight in milk,
620 Were lost, excepting for the ruby clasp!
They split the amaranth velvet-boddice down
To the waist, or nearly, with the audacious press
Of full-breathed beauty. If the heart within

Were half as white!—but, if it were, perhaps
625 The breast were closer covered and the sight
Less aspectable, by half, too.
      I heard
The young man with the German student's look—
A sharp face, like a knife in a cleft stick,
Which shot up straight against the parting line
630 So equally dividing the long hair,—
Say softly to his neighbour, (thirty-five
And mediæval), 'Look that way, Sir Blaise.
She's Lady Waldemar—to the left—in red—
Whom Romney Leigh, our ablest man just now,
635 Is soon about to marry.'
      Then replied
Sir Blaise Delorme, with quiet, priestlike voice,
Too used to syllable damnations round
To make a natural emphasis worth while:
'Is Leigh your ablest man? the same, I think,
640 Once jilted by a recreant pretty maid
Adopted from the people? Now, in change,
He seems to have plucked a flower from the other side
Of the social hedge.'
     'A flower, a flower,' exclaimed
My German student,—his own eyes full-blown
645 Bent on her. He was twenty, certainly.

Sir Blaise resumed with gentle arrogance
As if he had dropped his alms into a hat,
And gained the right to counsel,—'My young friend,
I doubt your ablest man's ability
650 To get the least good or help meet for him,
For pagan phalanstery or Christian home,
From such a flowery creature.'
      'Beautiful!'
My student murmured, rapt,—'Mark how she stirs!
Just waves her head, as if a flower indeed,
655 Touched far off by the vain breath of our talk.'
     *

At which that bilious Grimwald, (he who writes
For the Renovator) who had seemed absorbed
Upon the table-book of autographs,
(I dare say mentally he crunched the bones ·
660 Of all those writers, wishing them alive
To feel his tooth in earnest) turned short round
With low carniverous laugh,—'A flower, of course!
She neither sews nor spins,—and takes no thought
Of her garments . . falling off.'
                              The student flinched;
665 Sir Blaise, the same; then both, drawing back their chairs
As if they spied black-beetles on the floor,
Pursued their talk, without a word being thrown
To the critic.
                   Good Sir Blaise's brow is high
And noticeably narrow: a strong wind,
670 You fancy, might unroof him suddenly,
And blow that great top attic off his head
So piled with feudal relics. You admire
His nose in profile, though you miss his chin;
But, though you miss his chin, you seldom miss
675 His golden cross worn innermostly, (carved
For penance, by a saintly Styrian monk
Whose flesh was too much with him,) slipping through
Some unaware unbuttoned casualty
Of the under-waistcoat. With an absent air
680 Sir Blaise sate fingering it and speaking low,
While I, upon the sofa, heard it all.

'My dear young friend, if we could bear our eyes,
Like blessedest St. Lucy, on a plate,
They would not trick us into choosing wives,
685 As doublets, by the colour. Otherwise
Our fathers chose,—and therefore, when they had hung
Their household keys about a lady's waist,
The sense of duty gave her dignity:
She kept her bosom holy to her babes;
690 And, if a moralist reproved her dress,
'Twas 'Too much starch!'—and not 'Too little lawn!''

*

'Now, pshaw!' returned the other in a heat,
A little fretted by being called 'young friend,'
Or so I took it,—'for St. Lucy's sake,
695 If she's the saint to curse by, let us leave
Our fathers,—plagued enough about our sons!'
(He stroked his beardless chin) 'yes, plagued, sir, plagued:
The future generations lie on us
As heavy as the nightmare of a seer;
700 Our meat and drink grow painful prophecy:
I ask you,—have we leisure, if we liked,
To hollow out our weary hands to keep
Your intermittent rushlight of the past
From draughts in lobbies? Prejudice of sex
705 And marriage-law . . the socket drops them through
While we two speak,—however may protest
Some over-delicate nostrils, like your own,
'Gainst odours thence arising.
                                        'You are young,'
Sir Blaise objected.
                            'If I am,' he said
710 With fire,—'though somewhat less so than I seem,
The young run on before, and see the thing
That's coming. Reverence for the young, I cry.
In that new church for which the world's near ripe,
You'll have the younger in the Elder's chair,
715 Presiding with his ivory front of hope
O'er foreheads clawed by cruel carrion-birds
Of life's experience.'
                            'Pray your blessing, sir,'
Sir Blaise replied good-humouredly,—'I plucked
A silver hair this morning from my beard,
720 Which left me your inferior. Would I were
Eighteen and worthy to admonish you!
If young men of your order run before
To see such sights as sexual prejudice
And marriage-law dissolved,—in plainer words,
725 A general concubinage expressed
In a universal pruriency,—the thing
Is scarce worth running fast for, and you'd gain

By loitering with your elders.'

                                 'Ah,' he said,
'Who, getting to the top of Pisgah-hill,
730 Can talk with one at bottom of the view,
To make it comprehensible? Why, Leigh
Himself, although our ablest man, I said,
Is scarce advanced to see as far as this,
Which some are: he takes up imperfectly
735 The social question—by one handle—leaves
The rest to trail. A Christian socialist
Is Romney Leigh, you understand.'

                                    'Not I.
I disbelieve in Christian-pagans, much
As you in women-fishes. If we mix
740 Two colours, we lose both, and make a third
Distinct from either. Mark you! to mistake
A colour is the sign of a sick brain,
And mine, I thank the saints, is clear and cool:
A neutral tint is here impossible.
745 The church,—and by the church I mean, of course,
The catholic, apostolic, mother-church,—
Draws lines as plain and straight as her own wall;
Inside of which are Christians, obviously,
And outside . . dogs.'

                           'We thank you. Well I know
750 The ancient mother-church would fain still bite,
For all her toothless gums,—as Leigh himself
Would fain be a Christian still, for all his wit;
Pass that; you two may settle it, for me.
You're slow in England. In a month I learnt
755 At Göttingen, enough philosophy
To stock your English schools for fifty years;
Pass that, too. Here, alone, I stop you short,
—Supposing a true man like Leigh could stand
Unequal in the stature of his life
760 To the height of his opinions. Choose a wife
Because of a smooth skin?—not he, not he!
He'd rail at Venus' self for creaking shoes,
Unless she walked his way of righteousness:

And if he takes a Venus Meretrix
765 (No imputation on the lady there)
Be sure that, by some sleight of Christian art,
He has metamorphosed and converted her
To a Blessed Virgin.'
                              'Soft!' Sir Blaise drew breath
As if it hurt him,—'Soft! no blasphemy,
770 I pray you!'
                         'The first Christians did the thing;
Why not the last?' asked he of Göttingen,
With just that shade of sneering on the lip,
Compensates for the lagging of the beard,—
'And so the case is. If that fairest fair
775 Is talked of as the future wife of Leigh,
She's talked of too, at least as certainly,
As Leigh's disciple. You may find her name
On all his missions and commissions, schools,
Asylums, hospitals,—he has had her down,
780 With other ladies whom her starry lead
Persuaded from their spheres, to his country-place
In Shropshire, to the famed phalanstery
At Leigh Hall, christianised from Fourier's own,
(In which he has planted out his sapling stocks
785 Of knowledge into social nurseries)
And there, they say, she has tarried half a week,
And milked the cows, and churned, and pressed the curd,
And said 'my sister' to the lowest drab
Of all the assembled castaways; such girls!
790 Ay, sided with them at the washing-tub—
Conceive, Sir Blaise, those naked perfect arms,
Round glittering arms, plunged elbow-deep in suds,
Like wild swans hid in lilies all a-shake.'

Lord Howe came up. 'What, talking poetry
795 So near the image of the unfavouring Muse?
That's you, Miss Leigh: I've watched you half an hour,
Precisely as I watched the statue called
A Pallas in the Vatican;—you mind
The face, Sir Blaise?—intensely calm and sad,

800   As wisdom cut it off from fellowship,—
       But *that* spoke louder. Not a word from *you!*
       And these two gentlemen were bold, I marked,
       And unabashed by even your silence.'
                                              'Ah,'
       Said I, 'my dear Lord Howe, you shall not speak
805   To a printing woman who has lost her place,
       (The sweet safe corner of the household fire
       Behind the heads of children) compliments,
       As if she were a woman. We who have clipt
       The curls before our eyes, may see at least
810   As plain as men do. Speak out, man to man;
       No compliments, beseech you.'
                                     'Friend to friend,
       Let that be. We are sad to-night, I saw,
       (—Good night, Sir Blaise! Ah, Smith—he has slipped
            away),
       I saw you across the room, and stayed, Miss Leigh,
815   To keep a crowd of lion-hunters off,
       With faces toward your jungle. There were three;
       A spacious lady, five feet ten and fat,
       Who has the devil in her (and there's room)
       For walking to and fro upon the earth,
820   From Chipewa to China; she requires
       Your autograph upon a tinted leaf
       'Twixt Queen Pomare's and Emperor Soulouque's;
       Pray give it; she has energies, though fat:
       For me, I'd rather see a rick on fire
825   Than such a woman angry. Then a youth
       Fresh from the backwoods, green as the underboughs,
       Asks modestly, Miss Leigh, to kiss your shoe,
       And adds, he has an epic, in twelve parts,
       Which when you've read, you'll do it for his boot.—
830   All which I saved you, and absorb next week
       Both manuscript and man,—because a lord
       Is still more potent than a poetess
       With any extreme republican. Ah, ah,
       You smile, at last, then.'
                                  'Thank you.'
                                              'Leave the smile.

835   I'll lose the thanks for't,—ay, and throw you in
     My transatlantic girl, with golden eyes,
     That draw you to her splendid whiteness, as
     The pistil of a water-lily draws,
     Adust with gold. Those girls across the sea
840   Are tyrannously pretty,—and I swore
     (She seemed to me an innocent, frank girl)
     To bring her to you for a woman's kiss,
     Not now, but on some other day or week:
     —We'll call it perjury; I give her up.'

845   'No, bring her.'
                 'Now,' said he, 'you make it hard
     To touch such goodness with a grimy palm.
     I thought to tease you well, and fret you cross,
     And steel myself, when rightly vexed with you,
     For telling you a thing to tease you more.'

850   'Of Romney?'
             'No, no; nothing worse,' he cried,
     'Of Romney Leigh, than what is buzzed about,—
     That *he* is taken in an eye-trap too,
     Like many half as wise. The thing I mean
     Refers to you, not him.'
                 'Refers to me.'
855   He echoed,—'Me! You sound it like a stone
     Dropped down a dry well very listlessly
     By one who never thinks about the toad
     Alive at the bottom. Presently perhaps
     You'll sound your 'me' more proudly—till I shrink.'

860   'Lord Howe's the toad, then, in this question?'
                                   'Brief,
     We'll take it graver. Give me sofa-room,
     And quiet hearing. You know Eglinton,
     John Eglinton, of Eglinton in Kent?'

     'Is *he* the toad?—he's rather like the snail;
865   Known chiefly for the house upon his back:

Divide the man and house—you kill the man;
That's Eglinton of Eglinton, Lord Howe.'

He answered grave. 'A reputable man,
An excellent landlord of the olden stamp,
870 If somewhat slack in new philanthropies,
Who keeps his birthdays with a tenants' dance,
Is hard upon them when they miss the church
Or keep their children back from catechism,
But not ungentle when the aged poor
875 Pick sticks at hedge-sides; nay, I've heard him say
'The old dame has a twinge because she stoops;
'That's punishment enough for felony.''

'O tender-hearted landlord! May I take
My long lease with him, when the time arrives
880 For gathering winter-faggots!'
                 'He likes art,
Buys books and pictures . . of a certain kind;
Neglects no patent duty; a good son' . .

'To a most obedient mother. Born to wear
His father's shoes, he wears her husband's too:
885 Indeed I've heard it's touching. Dear Lord Howe,
You shall not praise *me* so against your heart,
When I'm at worst for praise and faggots.'
                    'Be
Less bitter with me, for . . in short,' he said
'I have a letter, which he urged me so
890 To bring you . . I could scarcely choose but yield;
Insisting that a new love passing through
The hand of an old friendship, caught from it
Some reconciling perfume.'
                   'Love, you say?
My lord, I cannot love. I only find
895 The rhymes for love,—and that's not love, my lord.
Take back your letter.'
               'Pause: you'll read it first?'

*

'I will not read it: it is stereotyped;
The same he wrote to,—anybody's name,—
Anne Blythe the actress, when she had died so true,
900 A duchess fainted in a private box:
Pauline, the dancer, after the great *pas*
In which her little feet winked overhead
Like other fire-flies, and amazed the pit:
Or Baldinacci, when her F in alt
905 Had touched the silver tops of heaven itself
With such a pungent soul-dart, even the Queen
Laid softly, each to each, her white-gloved palms,
And sighed for joy: or else (I thank your friend)
Aurora Leigh,—when some indifferent rhymes,
910 Like those the boys sang round the holy ox
On Memphis-highway, have chanced perhaps, to set
Our Apis-public lowing. Oh, he wants,
Instead of any worthy wife at home,
A star upon his stage of Eglinton!
915 Advise him that he is not overshrewd
In being so little modest: a dropped star
Makes bitter waters, says a Book I've read,—
And there's his unread letter.'

       'My dear friend,'
Lord Howe began . .
      In haste I tore the phrase.
920 'You mean your friend of Eglinton, or me?'

'I mean you, you,' he answered with some fire.
'A happy life means prudent compromise;
The tare runs through the farmer's garnered sheaves;
And though the gleaner's apron holds pure wheat,
925 We count her poorer. Tare with wheat, we cry,
And good with drawbacks. You, you love your art,
And, certain of vocation, set your soul
On utterance. Only, . . in this world we have made
(They say God made it first, but, if He did,
930 'Twas so long since, . . and, since, we have spoiled it so,
He scarce would know it, if He looked this way,
From hells we preach of, with the flames blown out,)

      —In this bad, twisted, topsy-turvy world,
      Where all the heaviest wrongs get uppermost,—
935   In this uneven, unfostering England here,
      Where ledger-strokes and sword-strokes count indeed,
      But soul-strokes merely tell upon the flesh
      They strike from,—it is hard to stand for art,
      Unless some golden tripod from the sea
940   Be fished up, by Apollo's divine chance,
      To throne such feet as yours, my prophetess,
      At Delphi. Think,—the god comes down as fierce
      As twenty bloodhounds! shakes you, strangles you,
      Until the oracular shriek shall ooze in froth!
945   At best it's not all ease,—at worst too hard:
      A place to stand on is a 'vantage gained,
      And here's your tripod. To be plain, dear friend,
      You're poor, except in what you richly give;
      You labour for your own bread painfully,
950   Or ere you pour our wine. For art's sake, pause.'

      I answered slow,—as some wayfaring man,
      Who feels himself at night too far from home,
      Makes stedfast face against the bitter wind.
      'Is art so less a thing than virtue is,
955   That artists first must cater for their ease
      Or ever they make issue past themselves
      To generous use? alas, and is it so
      That we, who would be somewhat clean, must sweep
      Our ways as well as walk them, and no friend
960   Confirm us nobly,—'Leave results to God,
      But you, be clean?' What! 'prudent compromise
      Makes acceptable life,' you say instead,
      You, you, Lord Howe?—in things indifferent, well.
      For instance, compromise the wheaten bread
965   For rye, the meat for lentils, silk for serge,
      And sleep on down, if needs, for sleep on straw;
      But there, end compromise. I will not bate
      One artist-dream, on straw or down, my lord,
      Nor pinch my liberal soul, though I be poor,
970   Nor cease to love high, though I live thus low.'

                              *

So speaking, with less anger in my voice
Than sorrow, I rose quickly to depart;
While he, thrown back upon the noble shame
Of such high-stumbling natures, murmured words,
975   The right words after wrong ones. Ah, the man
Is worthy, but so given to entertain
Impossible plans of superhuman life,—
He sets his virtues on so raised a shelf,
To keep them at the grand millennial height,
980   He has to mount a stool to get at them;
And, meantime, lives on quite the common way,
With everybody's morals.
                                    As we passed,
Lord Howe insisting that his friendly arm
Should oar me across the sparkling brawling stream
985   Which swept from room to room,—we fell at once
On Lady Waldemar. 'Miss Leigh,' she said,
And gave me such a smile, so cold and bright,
As if she tried it in a 'tiring glass
And liked it, 'all to-night I've strained at you
990   As babes at baubles held up out of reach
By spiteful nurses, ('Never snatch,' they say,)
And there you sate, most perfectly shut in
By good Sir Blaise and clever Mister Smith
And then our dear Lord Howe! at last, indeed,
995   I almost snatched. I have a world to speak
About your cousin's place in Shropshire, where
I've been to see his work . . our work,—you heard
I went? . . and of a letter, yesterday,
In which, if I should read a page or two,
1000   You might feel interest, though you're locked of course
In literary toil.—You'll like to hear
Your last book lies at the phalanstery,
As judged innocuous for the elder girls
And younger women who still care for books.
1005   We all must read, you see, before we live:
But slowly the ineffable light comes up,
And, as it deepens, drowns the written word,—
So said your cousin, while we stood and felt

A sunset from his favourite beech-tree seat.
1010 He might have been a poet if he would,
But then he saw the higher thing at once,
And climbed to it. I think he looks well now,
Has quite got over that unfortunate . .
Ah, ah . . I know it moved you. Tender-heart!
1015 You took a liking to the wretched girl.
Perhaps you thought the marriage suitable,
Who knows? a poet hankers for romance,
And so on. As for Romney Leigh, 'tis sure
He never loved her,—never. By the way,
1020 You have not heard of *her* . . ? quite out of sight,
And out of saving? lost in every sense?'

She might have gone on talking half-an-hour,
And I stood still, and cold, and pale, I think,
As a garden-statue a child pelts with snow
1025 For pretty pastime. Every now and then
I put in 'yes' or 'no,' I scarce knew why;
The blind man walks wherever the dog pulls,
And so I answered. Till Lord Howe broke in;
'What penance takes the wretch who interrupts
1030 The talk of charming women? I, at last,
Must brave it. Pardon, Lady Waldemar,
The lady on my arm is tired, unwell,
And loyally I've promised she shall say
No harder word this evening than . . good-night;
1035 The rest her face speaks for her.'—Then we went.

And I breathe large at home. I drop my cloak,
Unclasp my girdle, loose the band that ties
My hair . . now could I but unloose my soul!
We are sepulchred alive in this close world,
1040 And want more room.
                    The charming woman there—
This reckoning up and writing down her talk
Affects me singularly. How she talked
To pain me! women's spite.—You wear steel-mail;

A woman takes a housewife from her breast
1045 And plucks the delicatest needle out
As 'twere a rose, and pricks you carefully
'Neath nails, 'neath eyelids, in your nostrils,—say,
A beast would roar so tortured,—but a man,
A human creature, must not, shall not flinch,
1050 No, not for shame.
                              What vexes, after all,
Is just that such as she, with such as I,
Knows how to vex. Sweet heaven, she takes me up
As if she had fingered me and dog-eared me
And spelled me by the fireside, half a life!
1055 She knows my turns, my feeble points.—What then?
The knowledge of a thing implies the thing;
Of course, she found *that* in me, she saw *that*,
Her pencil underscored *this* for a fault,
And I, still ignorant. Shut the book up! close!
1060 And crush that beetle in the leaves.
                                                    O heart,
At last we shall grow hard too, like the rest,
And call it self-defence because we are soft.

And after all, now . . why should I be pained,
That Romney Leigh, my cousin, should espouse
1065 This Lady Waldemar? And, say, she held
Her newly-blossomed gladness in my face, . .
'Twas natural surely, if not generous,
Considering how, when winter held her fast,
I helped the frost with mine, and pained her more
1070 Than she pains me. Pains me!—but wherefore pained?
'Tis clear my cousin Romney wants a wife,—
So, good!—The man's need of the woman, here,
Is greater than the woman's of the man,
And easier served; for where the man discerns
1075 A sex, (ah, ah, the man can generalise,
Said he) we see but one, ideally
And really: where we yearn to lose ourselves
And melt like white pearls in another's wine,

He seeks to double himself by what he loves,
1080 And make his drink more costly by our pearls.
At board, at bed, at work, and holiday,
It is not good for man to be alone,—
And that's his way of thinking, first and last;
And thus my cousin Romney wants a wife.

1085 But then my cousin sets his dignity
On personal virtue. If he understands
By love, like others, self-aggrandisement,
It is that he may verily be great
By doing rightly and kindly. Once he thought,
1090 For charitable ends set duly forth
In Heaven's white judgment-book, to marry . . ah,
We'll call her name Aurora Leigh, although
She's changed since then!—and once, for social ends,
Poor Marian Erle, my sister Marian Erle,
1095 My woodland sister, sweet maid Marian,
Whose memory moans on in me like the wind
Through ill-shut casements, making me more sad
Than ever I find reasons for. Alas,
Poor pretty plaintive face, embodied ghost,
1100 He finds it easy then, to clap thee off
From pulling at his sleeve and book and pen,—
He locks thee out at night into the cold
Away from butting with thy horny eyes
Against his crystal dreams,—that, now, he's strong
1105 To love anew? that Lady Waldemar
Succeeds my Marian?
                           After all, why not?
He loved not Marian, more than once he loved
Aurora. If he loves, at last, that Third,
Albeit she prove as slippery as spilt oil
1110 On marble floors, I will not augur him
Ill-luck for that. Good love, howe'er ill-placed,
Is better for a man's soul in the end,
Than if he loved ill what deserves love well.
A pagan, kissing, for a step of Pan,

1115 The wild-goat's hoof-print on the loamy down,
Exceeds our modern thinker who turns back
The strata . . granite, limestone, coal, and clay,
Concluding coldly with, 'Here's law! where's God?'

And then at worst,—if Romney loves her not,—
1120 At worst,—if he's incapable of love,
Which may be—then indeed, for such a man
Incapable of love, she's good enough;
For she, at worst too, is a woman still
And loves him . . as the sort of woman can.

1125 My loose long hair began to burn and creep,
Alive to the very ends, about my knees:
I swept it backward as the wind sweeps flame,
With the passion of my hands. Ah, Romney laughed
One day . . (how full the memories come up!)
1130 '—Your Florence fire-flies live on in your hair,'
He said, 'it gleams so.' Well, I wrung them out,
My fire-flies; made a knot as hard as life,
Of those loose, soft, impracticable curls,
And then sat down and thought . . 'She shall not think
1135 Her thought of me,'—and drew my desk and wrote.

'Dear Lady Waldemar, I could not speak
With people round me, nor can sleep to-night
And not speak, after the great news I heard
Of you and of my cousin. May you be
1140 Most happy; and the good he meant the world,
Replenish his own life. Say what I say,
And let my word be sweeter for your mouth,
As you are *you* . . I only Aurora Leigh.'

That's quiet, guarded! though she hold it up
1145 Against the light, she'll not see through it more
Than lies there to be seen. So much for pride;
And now for peace, a little. Let me stop
All writing back . . 'Sweet thanks, my sweetest friend,
You've made more joyful my great joy itself.'

1150 —No, that's too simple! she would twist it thus,
'My joy would still be as sweet as thyme in drawers,
However shut up in the dark and dry;
But violets aired and dewed by love like yours,
Out-smell all thyme: we keep that in our clothes,
1155 But drop the other down our bosoms till
They smell like—' . . ah, I see her writing back
Just so. She'll make a nosegay of her words,
And tie it with blue ribbons at the end
To suit a poet;—pshaw!
                                        And then we'll have
1160 The call to church, the broken sad, bad dream
Dreamed out at last, the marriage-vow complete
With the marriage breakfast; praying in white gloves,
Drawn off in haste for drinking pagan toasts
In somewhat stronger wine than any sipped
1165 By gods since Bacchus had his way with grapes.

A postscript stops all that and rescues me.
'You need not write. I have been overworked,
And think of leaving London, England even,
And hastening to get nearer to the sun,
1170 Where men sleep better. So, adieu.'—I fold
And seal,—and now I'm out of all the coil;
I breathe now; I spring upward like a branch,
A ten-years school-boy with a crooked stick
May pull down to his level, in search of nuts,
1175 But cannot hold a moment. How we twang
Back on the blue sky, and assert our height,
While he stares after! Now, the wonder seems
That I could wrong myself by such a doubt.
We poets always have uneasy hearts;
1180 Because our hearts, large-rounded as the globe,
Can turn but one side to the sun at once.
We are used to dip our artist-hands in gall
And potash, trying potentialities
Of alternated colour, till at last
1185 We get confused, and wonder for our skin
How nature tinged it first. Well—here's the true

Good flesh-colour; I recognise my hand,—
Which Romney Leigh may clasp as just a friend's,
And keep his clean.
                              And now, my Italy.
1190 Alas, if we could ride with naked souls
And make no noise and pay no price at all,
I would have seen thee sooner, Italy,—
For still I have heard thee crying through my life,
Thou piercing silence of extatic graves,
1195 Men call that name!

                                   But even a witch, to-day,
Must melt down golden pieces in the nard
Wherewith to anoint her broomstick ere she rides;
And poets evermore are scant of gold,
And if they find a piece behind the door,
1200 It turns by sunset to a withered leaf.
The Devil himself scarce trusts his patented
Gold-making art to any who makes rhymes,
But culls his Faustus from philosophers
And not from poets. 'Leave my Job,' said God;
1205 And so the Devil leaves him without pence,
And poverty proves, plainly, special grace.
In these new, just, administrative times
Men clamour for an order of merit. Why?
Here's black bread on the table, and no wine!

1210 At least I am a poet in being poor,
Thank God. I wonder if the manuscript
Of my long poem, if 'twere sold outright,
Would fetch enough to buy me shoes, to go
A-foot, (thrown in, the necessary patch
1215 For the other side the Alps)? it cannot be.
I fear that I must sell this residue
Of my father's books; although the Elzevirs
Have fly-leaves over-written by his hand,
In faded notes as thick and fine and brown
1220 As cobwebs on a tawny monument
Of the old Greeks—*conferenda hæc cum his*—

Corruptè citat—lege potiùs,
And so on, in the scholar's regal way
Of giving judgment on the parts of speech,
1225 As if he sate on all twelve thrones up-piled,
Arraigning Israel. Ay, but books and notes
Must go together. And this Proclus too,
In quaintly dear contracted Grecian types,
Fantastically crumpled, like his thoughts
1230 Which would not seem too plain; you go round twice
For one step forward, then you take it back,
Because you're somewhat giddy; there's the rule
For Proclus. Ah, I stained this middle leaf
With pressing in't my Florence iris-bell,
1235 Long stalk and all: my father chided me
For that stain of blue blood,—I recollect
The peevish turn his voice took,—'Silly girls,
Who plant their flowers in our philosophy
To make it fine, and only spoil the book!
1240 No more of it, Aurora.' Yes—no more!
Ah, blame of love, that's sweeter than all praise
Of those who love not! 'tis so lost to me,
I cannot, in such beggared life, afford
To lose my Proclus. Not for Florence, even.

1245 The kissing Judas, Wolff, shall go instead,
Who builds us such a royal book as this
To honour a chief-poet, folio-built,
And writes above, 'The house of Nobody:'
Who floats in cream, as rich as any sucked
1250 From Juno's breasts, the broad Homeric lines,
And, while with their spondaic prodigious mouths
They lap the lucent margins as babe-gods,
Proclaims them bastards. Wolff's an atheist;
And if the Iliad fell out, as he says,
1255 By mere fortuitous concourse of old songs,
We'll guess as much, too, for the universe.

That Wolff, those Platos: sweep the upper shelves
As clean as this, and so I am almost rich,

Which means, not forced to think of being poor
1260 In sight of ends. To-morrow: no delay.
I'll wait in Paris till good Carrington
Dispose of such, and, having chaffered for
My book's price with the publisher, direct
All proceeds to me. Just a line to ask
1265 His help.
         And now I come, my Italy,
My own hills! Are you 'ware of me, my hills,
How I burn toward you? do you feel to-night
The urgency and yearning of my soul,
As sleeping mothers feel the sucking babe
1270 And smile?—ay, not so much as when, in heat
Vain lightnings catch at your inviolate tops,
And tremble while ye are stedfast. Still, ye go
Your own determined, calm, indifferent way
Toward sunrise, shade by shade, and light by light,
1275 Of all the grand progression nought left out;
As if God verily made you for yourselves
And would not interrupt your life with ours.

Sixth Book

THE English have a scornful insular way
Of calling the French light. The levity
Is in the judgment only, which yet stands;
For say a foolish thing but oft enough,
5 (And here's the secret of a hundred creeds,—
Men get opinions as boys learn to spell,
By re-iteration chiefly) the same thing
Shall pass at last for absolutely wise,
And not with fools exclusively. And so,
10 We say the French are light, as if we said
The cat mews, or the milch-cow gives us milk:
Say rather, cats are milked and milch-cows mew;
For what is lightness but inconsequence,
Vague fluctuation 'twixt effect and cause,
15 Compelled by neither? Is a bullet light,
That dashes from the gun-mouth, while the eye
Winks, and the heart beats one, to flatten itself
To a wafer on the white speck on a wall
A hundred paces off? Even so direct,
20 So sternly undivertible of aim,
Is this French people.
             All, idealists
Too absolute and earnest, with them all
The idea of a knife cuts real flesh;
And still, devouring the safe interval
25 Which Nature placed between the thought and act
With those too fiery and impatient souls,
They threaten conflagration to the world
And rush with most unscrupulous logic on
Impossible practice. Set your orators
30 To blow upon them with loud windy mouths,
Through watchword phrases, jest or sentiment,
Which drive our burley brutal English mobs
Like so much chaff, whichever way they blow,—
This light French people will not thus be driven.

35 They turn indeed; but then they turn upon
    Some central pivot of their thought and choice,
    And veer out by the force of holding fast.
    —That's hard to understand, for Englishmen
    Unused to abstract questions, and untrained
40 To trace the involutions, valve by valve,
    In each orbed bulb-root of a general truth,
    And mark what subtly fine integument
    Divides opposed compartments. Freedom's self
    Comes concrete to us, to be understood,
45 Fixed in a feudal form incarnately
    To suit our ways of thought and reverence,
    The special form, with us, being still the thing.
    With us, I say, though I'm of Italy
    By mother's birth and grave, by father's grave
50 And memory; let it be,—a poet's heart
    Can swell to a pair of nationalities,
    However ill-lodged in a woman's breast.

    And so I am strong to love this noble France,
    This poet of the nations, who dreams on
55 And wails on (while the household goes to wreck)
    For ever, after some ideal good,—
    Some equal poise of sex, some unvowed love
    Inviolate, some spontaneous brotherhood,
    Some wealth, that leaves none poor and finds none tired,
60 Some freedom of the many, that respects
    The wisdom of the few. Heroic dreams!
    Sublime, to dream so; natural, to wake:
    And sad, to use such lofty scaffoldings,
    Erected for the building of a church,
65 To build instead a brothel .. or a prison—
    May God save France!
                          However she have sighed
    Her great soul up into a great man's face,
    To flush his temples out so gloriously
    That few dare carp at Cæsar for being bald,
70 What then?—this Cæsar represents, not reigns,
    And is no despot, though twice absolute;

This Head has all the people for a heart;
This purple's lined with the democracy,—
Now let him see to it! for a rent within
75 Must leave irreparable rags without.

A serious riddle: find such anywhere
Except in France; and when it's found in France,
Be sure to read it rightly. So, I mused
Up and down, up and down, the terraced streets,
80 The glittering boulevards, the white colonnades
Of fair fantastic Paris who wears boughs
Like plumes, as if man made them,—tossing up
Her fountains in the sunshine from the squares,
As dice i' the game of beauty, sure to win;
85 Or as she blew the down-balls of her dreams,
And only waited for their falling back,
To breathe up more, and count her festive hours.

The city swims in verdure, beautiful
As Venice on the waters, the sea-swan.
90 What bosky gardens, dropped in close-walled courts
As plums in ladies' laps, who start and laugh:
What miles of streets that run on after trees,
Still carrying the necessary shops,
Those open caskets, with the jewels seen!
95 The trade is art, and art's philosophy,
In Paris. There's a silk, for instance, there,
As worth an artist's study for the folds,
As that bronze opposite! nay, the bronze has faults;
Art's here too artful,—conscious as a maid,
100 Who leans to mark her shadow on the wall
Until she lose a 'vantage in her step.
Yet Art walks forward, and knows where to walk:
The artists also, are idealists,
Too absolute for nature, logical
105 To austerity in the application of
The special theory: not a soul content
To paint a crooked pollard and an ass,
As the English will, because they find it so,

And like it somehow.—Ah, the old Tuileries
110 Is pulling its high cap down on its eyes,
Confounded, conscience-stricken, and amazed
By the apparition of a new fair face
In those devouring mirrors. Through the grate,
Within the gardens, what a heap of babes,
115 Swept up like leaves beneath the chesnut-trees,
From every street and alley of the town,
By ghosts perhaps, that blow too bleak this way
A-looking for their heads! Dear pretty babes,
I'll wish them luck to have their ball-play out
120 Before the next change comes.—And, farther on,
What statues, poised upon their columns fine,
As if to stand a moment were a feat,
Against that blue! What squares! what breathing-room
For a nation that runs fast,—ay, runs against
125 The dentist's teeth at the corner, in pale rows,
Which grin at progress in an epigram.

I walked that day out, listening to the chink
Of the first Napoleon's dry bones, as they lay
In his second grave beneath the golden dome
130 That caps all Paris like a bubble. 'Shall
These dry bones live?' thought Louis Philippe once,
And lived to know. Herein is argument
For kings and politicians, but still more
For poets, who bear buckets to the well,
135 Of ampler draught.
           These crowds are very good
For meditation, (when we are very strong)
Though love of beauty makes us timorous,
And draws us backward from the coarse town-sights
To count the daisies upon dappled fields,
140 And hear the streams bleat on among the hills
In innocent and indolent repose;
While still with silken elegiac thoughts
We wind out from us the distracting world,
And die into the chrysalis of a man,
145 And leave the best that may, to come of us,

In some brown moth. Be, rather, bold, and bear
To look into the swarthiest face of things,
For God's sake who has made them.

                              Seven days' work;
The last day shutting 'twixt its dawn and eve,
150 The whole work bettered, of the previous six!
Since God collected and resumed in man
The firmaments, the strata, and the lights,
Fish, fowl, and beast, and insect,—all their trains
Of various life caught back upon His arm,
155 Reorganised, and constituted MAN,
The microcosm, the adding up of works;
Within whose fluttering nostrils, then, at last,
Consummating Himself, the Maker sighed,
As some strong winner at the foot-race sighs
160 Touching the goal.
                         Humanity is great;
And, if I would not rather pore upon
An ounce of common, ugly, human dust,
An artisan's palm, or a peasant's brow,
Unsmooth, ignoble, save to me and God,
165 Than track old Nilus to his silver roots,
And wait on all the changes of the moon
Among the mountain-peaks of Thessaly,
(Until her magic crystal round itself
For many a witch to see in)—set it down
170 As weakness,—strength by no means. How is this,
That men of science, osteologists
And surgeons, beat some poets, in respect
For nature,—count nought common or unclean,
Spend raptures upon perfect specimens
175 Of indurated veins, distorted joints,
Or beautiful new cases of curved spine;
While we, we are shocked at nature's falling off,
We dare to shrink back from her warts and blains,
We will not, when she sneezes, look at her,
180 Not even to say 'God bless her'? That's our wrong;
For that, she will not trust us often with

Her larger sense of beauty and desire,
But tethers us to a lily or a rose
And bids us diet on the dew inside,—
185   Left ignorant that the hungry beggar-boy
(Who stares unseen against our absent eyes,
And wonders at the gods that we must be,
To pass so careless for the oranges!)
Bears yet a breastful of a fellow-world
190   To this world, undisparaged, undespoiled,
And (while we scorn him for a flower or two,
As being, Heaven help us, less poetical)
Contains, himself, both flowers and firmaments
And surging seas and aspectable stars,
195   And all that we would push him out of sight
In order to see nearer. Let us pray
God's grace to keep God's image in repute;
That so, the poet and philanthropist,
(Even I and Romney) may stand side by side,
200   Because we both stand face to face with men,
Contemplating the people in the rough,—
Yet each so follow a vocations,—his
And mine.
          I walked on, musing with myself
On life and art, and whether, after all
205   A larger metaphysics might not help
Our physics, a completer poetry
Adjust our daily life and vulgar wants,
More fully than the special outside plans,
Phalansteries, material institutes,
210   The civil conscriptions and lay monasteries
Preferred by modern thinkers, as they thought
The bread of man indeed made all his life,
And washing seven times in the 'People's Baths'
Were sovereign for a people's leprosy,—
215   Still leaving out the essential prophet's word
That comes in power. On which, we thunder down,
We prophets, poets,—Virtue's in the *word!*
The maker burnt the darkness up with His,
To inaugurate the use of vocal life;

220 And, plant a poet's word even, deep enough
     In any man's breast, looking presently
     For offshoots, you have done more for the man,
     Than if you dressed him in a broad-cloth coat
     And warmed his Sunday potage at your fire.
225 Yet Romney leaves me . .
                              God! what face is that?
     O Romney, O Marian!
                              Walking on the quays
     And pulling thoughts to pieces leisurely,
     As if I caught at grasses in a field,
     And bit them slow between my absent lips,
230 And shred them with my hands . .
                              What face is that?
     What a face, what a look, what a likeness! Full on mine
     The sudden blow of it came down, till all
     My blood swam, my eyes dazzled. Then I sprang—

     It was as if a meditative man
235 Were dreaming out a summer afternoon
     And watching gnats a-prick upon a pond,
     When something floats up suddenly, out there,
     Turns over . . a dead face, known once alive—
     So old, so new! It would be dreadful now
240 To lose the sight and keep the doubt of this.
     He plunges—ha! he has lost it in the splash.

     I plunged—I tore the crowd up, either side,
     And rushed on,—forward, forward . . after her.
     Her? whom?
                    A woman sauntered slow, in front,
245 Munching an apple,—she left off amazed
     As if I had snatched it: that's not she, at least.
     A man walked arm-linked with a lady veiled,
     Both heads dropped closer than the need of talk:
     They started; he forgot her with his face,
250 And she, herself,—and clung to him as if
     My look were fatal. Such a stream of folk,
     And all with cares and business of their own!

I ran the whole quay down against their eyes;
No Marian; nowhere Marian. Almost, now,
255 I could call Marian, Marian, with the shriek
Of desperate creatures calling for the Dead.
Where is she, was she? was she anywhere?
I stood still, breathless, gazing, straining out
In every uncertain distance, till, at last,
260 A gentleman abstracted as myself
Came full against me, then resolved the clash
In voluble excuses,—obviously
Some learned member of the Institute
Upon his way there, walking, for his health,
265 While meditating on the last 'Discourse;'
Pinching the empty air 'twixt finger and thumb,
From which the snuff being ousted by that shock,
Defiled his snow-white waistcoat, duly pricked
At the button-hole with honourable red;
270 'Madame, your pardon,'—there, he swerved from me
A metre, as confounded as he had heard
That Dumas would be chosen to fill up
The next chair vacant, by his 'men *in us.*'
Since when was genius found respectable?
275 It passes in its place, indeed,—which means
The seventh floor back, or else the hospital:
Revolving pistols are ingenious things,
But prudent men (Academicians are)
Scarce keep them in the cupboard, next the prunes.

280 And so, abandoned to a bitter mirth,
I loitered to my inn. O world, O world,
O jurists, rhymers, dreamers, what you please,
We play a weary game of hide and seek!
We shape a figure of our fantasy,
285 Call nothing something, and run after it
And lose it, lose ourselves too in the search;
Till, clash against us, comes a somebody
Who also has lost something and is lost,
Philosopher against philanthropist,
290 Academician against poet, man

Against woman, against the living, the dead,—
Then home, with a bad headache and worse jest!

To change the water for my heliotropes
And yellow roses. Paris has such flowers.
295 But England, also. 'Twas a yellow rose,
By that south window of the little house,
My cousin Romney gathered with his hand
On all my birthdays for me, save the last;
And then I shook the tree too rough, too rough,
300 For roses to stay after.
                                        Now, my maps.
I must not linger here from Italy
Till the last nightingale is tired of song,
And the last fire-fly dies off in the maize.
My soul's in haste to leap into the sun
305 And scorch and seethe itself to a finer mood,
Which here, in this chill north, is apt to stand
Too stiffly in former moulds.
                                        That face persists,
It floats up, it turns over in my mind,
As like to Marian, as one dead is like
310 The same alive. In very deed a face
And not a fancy, though it vanished so;
The small fair face between the darks of hair,
I used to liken, when I saw her first,
To a point of moonlit water down a well:
315 The low brow, the frank space between the eyes,
Which always had the brown pathetic look
Of a dumb creature who had been beaten once,
And never since was easy with the world.
Ah, ah—now I remember perfectly
320 Those eyes, to-day,—how overlarge they seemed,
As if some patient, passionate despair
(Like a coal dropt and forgot on tapestry,
Which slowly burns a widening circle out)
Had burnt them larger, larger. And those eyes,
325 To-day, I do remember, saw me too,
As I saw them, with conscious lids astrain

In recognition. Now, a fantasy,
A simple shade or image of the brain,
Is merely passive, does not retro-act,
330 Is seen, but sees not..
                         'Twas a real face,
Perhaps a real Marian.
                         Which being so,
I ought to write to Romney, 'Marian's here;
Be comforted for Marian.'
                         My pen fell,
My hands struck sharp together, as hands do
335 Which hold at nothing. Can I write to *him*
A half truth? can I keep my own soul blind
To the other half, . . the worse? What are our souls,
If still, to run on straight a sober pace
Nor start at every pebble or dead leaf,
340 They must wear blinkers, ignore facts, suppress
Six tenths of the road? Confront the truth, my soul!
And oh, as truly as that was Marian's face,
The arms of that same Marian clasped a thing
. . Not hid so well beneath the scanty shawl,
345 I cannot name it now for what it was.

A child. Small business has a cast-away
Like Marian, with that crown of prosperous wives
At which the gentlest she grows arrogant
And says 'my child.' Who'll find an emerald ring
350 On a beggar's middle finger, and require
More testimony to convict a thief?
A child's too costly for so mere a wretch;
She filched it somewhere; and it means, with her,
Instead of honour, blessing, . . merely shame.

355 I cannot write to Romney, 'Here she is,
Here's Marian found! I'll set you on her track:
I saw her here, in Paris, . . and her child.
She put away your love two years ago,
But, plainly, not to starve. You suffered then;
360 And, now that you've forgot her utterly

As any last year's annual in whose place
You've planted a thick flowering evergreen,
I choose, being kind, to write and tell you this
To make you wholly easy—she's not dead,
365 But only . . damned.'
                  Stop there: I go too fast;
I'm cruel like the rest,—in haste to take
The first stir in the arras for a rat,
And set my barking, biting thoughts upon't.
—A child! what then? Suppose a neighbour's sick,
370 And asked her, 'Marian, carry out my child
In this Spring air,'—I punish her for that?
Or say, the child should hold her round the neck
For good child-reasons, that he liked it so
And would not leave her—she had winning ways—
375 I brand her therefore, that she took the child?
Not so.
        I will not write to Romney Leigh.
For now he's happy,—and she may indeed
Be guilty,—and the knowledge of her fault
Would draggle his smooth time. But I, whose days
380 Are not so fine they cannot bear the rain,
And who, moreover, having seen her face
Must see it again, . . *will* see it, by my hopes
Of one day seeing heaven too. The police
Shall track her, hound her, ferret their own soil;
385 We'll dig this Paris to its catacombs
But certainly we'll find her, have her out,
And save her, if she will or will not—child
Or no child,—if a child, then one to save!

The long weeks passed on without consequence.
390 As easy find a footstep on the sand
The morning after spring-tide, as the trace
Of Marian's feet between the incessant surfs
Of this live flood. She may have moved this way,—
But so the star-fish does, and crosses out
395 The dent of her small shoe. The foiled police
Renounced me. 'Could they find a girl and child,

No other signalment but girl and child?
No data shown, but noticeable eyes
And hair in masses, low upon the brow,
400　As if it were an iron crown and pressed?
Friends heighten, and suppose they specify:
Why, girls with hair and eyes, are everywhere
In Paris; they had turned me up in vain
No Marian Erle indeed, but certainly
405　Mathildes, Justines, Victoires, . . or, if I sought
The English, Betsis, Saras, by the score.
They might as well go out into the fields
To find a speckled bean, that's somehow specked,
And somewhere in the pod.'—They left me so.
410　Shall *I* leave Marian? have I dreamed a dream?

　　—I thank God I have found her! I must say
'Thank God,' for finding her, although 'tis true
I find the world more sad and wicked for't.
But she—
　　　　I'll write about her, presently.
415　My hand's a-tremble as I had just caught up
My heart to write with, in the place of it.
At least you'd take these letters to be writ
At sea, in storm!—wait now . .
　　　　　　　　A simple chance
Did all. I could not sleep last night, and, tired
420　Of turning on my pillow and harder thoughts,
Went out at early morning, when the air
Is delicate with some last starry touch,
To wander through the Market-place of Flowers
(The prettiest haunt in Paris), and make sure
425　At worst, that there were roses in the world.
So, wandering, musing, with the artist's eye,
That keeps the shade-side of the thing it loves,
Half-absent, whole-observing, while the crowd
Of young vivacious and black-braided heads
430　Dipped, quick as finches in a blossomed tree,
Among the nosegays, cheapening this and that
In such a cheerful twitter of rapid speech,—

My heart leapt in me, startled by a voice
That slowly, faintly, with long breaths that marked
435 The interval between the wish and word,
Inquired in stranger's French, 'Would *that* be much,
That branch of flowering mountain-gorse?'—'So much?
Too much for me, then!' turning the face round
So close upon me that I felt the sigh
440 It turned with.
                         'Marian, Marian!'—face to face—
'Marian! I find you. Shall I let you go?'
I held her two slight wrists with both my hands;
'Ah Marian, Marian, can I let you go?'
—She fluttered from me like a cyclamen,
445 As white, which, taken in a sudden wind,
Beats on against the palisade.—'Let pass,'
She said at last. 'I will not,' I replied;
'I lost my sister Marian many days,
And sought her ever in my walks and prayers,
450 And, now I find her . . . do we throw away
The bread we worked and prayed for,—crumble it
And drop it, . . to do even so by thee
Whom still I've hungered after more than bread,
My sister Marian?—can I hurt thee, dear?
455 Then why distrust me? Never tremble so.
Come with me rather, where we'll talk and live,
And none shall vex us. I've a home for you
And me and no one else' . . .
                                    She shook her head.
'A home for you and me and no one else
460 Ill suits one of us: I prefer to such
A roof of grass on which a flower might spring,
Less costly to me than the cheapest here;
And yet I could not, at this hour, afford
A like home, even. That you offer yours,
465 I thank you. You are good as heaven itself—
As good as one I knew before . . Farewell.'

I loosed her hands:— 'In *his* name, no farewell!'
(She stood as if I held her.) 'For his sake,

For his sake, Romney's! by the good he meant,
470 Ay, always! by the love he pressed for once,—
And by the grief, reproach, abandonment,
He took in change' . .
                            'He?—Romney! who grieved *him*?
Who had the heart for't? what reproach touched *him*?
Be merciful,—speak quickly.'
                            'Therefore come,'
475 I answered with authority.—'I think
We dare to speak such things and name such names,
In the open squares of Paris!'
                            Not a word
She said, but, in a gentle humbled way,
(As one who had forgot herself in grief)
480 Turned round and followed closely where I went,
As if I led her by a narrow plank
Across devouring waters, step by step,—
And so in silence we walked on a mile.

And then she stopped: her face was white as wax
485 'We go much farther?'
                            'You are ill,' I asked,
'Or tired?'
                  She looked the whiter for her smile.
'There's one at home,' she said, 'has need of me
By this time,—and I must not let him wait.'

'Not even,' I asked, 'to hear of Romney Leigh?'

490 'Not even,' she said, 'to hear of Mister Leigh.'

'In that case,' I resumed, 'I go with you,
And we can talk the same thing there as here.
None waits for me: I have my day to spend.'

Her lips moved in a spasm without a sound,—
495 But then she spoke. 'It shall be as you please;
And better so—'tis shorter seen than told.
And though you will not find me worth your pains,

That even, may be worth some pains to know
For one as good as you are.'
                            Then she led
500 The way, and I, as by a narrow plank
Across devouring waters, followed her,
Stepping by her footsteps, breathing by her breath,
And holding her with eyes that would not slip;
And so, without a word, we walked a mile,
505 And so, another mile, without a word.

Until the peopled streets being all dismissed,
House-rows and groups all scattered like a flock,
The market-gardens thickened, and the long
White walls beyond, like spiders' outside threads,
510 Stretched, feeling blindly toward the country-fields,
Through half-built habitations and half-dug
Foundations,—intervals of trenchant chalk
That bit betwixt the grassy uneven turfs
Where goats (vine-tendrils trailing from their mouths)
515 Stood perched on edges of the cellarage
Which should be, staring as about to leap
To find their coming Bacchus. All the place
Seemed less a cultivation than a waste:
Men work here, only,—scarce begin to live:
520 All's sad, the country struggling with the town,
Like an untamed hawk upon a strong man's fist,
That beats its wings and tries to get away,
And cannot choose be satisfied so soon
To hop through court-yards with its right foot tied,
525 The vintage plains and pastoral hills in sight!

We stopped beside a house too high and slim
To stand there by itself, but waiting till
Five others, two on this side, three on that,
Should grow up from the sullen second floor
530 They pause at now, to build it to a row.
The upper windows partly were unglazed
Meantime,—a meagre, unripe house: a line
Of rigid poplars elbowed it behind,

And, just in front, beyond the lime and bricks
535   That wronged the grass between it and the road,
A great acacia, with its slender trunk
And overpoise of multitudinous leaves,
(In which a hundred fields might spill their dew
And intense verdure, yet find room enough)
540   Stood, reconciling all the place with green.

I followed up the stair upon her step.
She hurried upward, shot across a face,
A woman's on the landing,—'How now, now!
Is no one to have holidays but you?
545   You said an hour, and stay three hours, I think,
And Julie waiting for your betters here?
Why if he had waked, he might have waked, for me.'
—Just murmuring an excusing word, she passed
And shut the rest out with the chamber door,
550   Myself shut in beside her.
               'Twas a room
Scarce larger than a grave, and near as bare;
Two stools, a pallet-bed; I saw the room:
A mouse could find no sort of shelter in't,
Much less a greater secret; curtainless—
555   The window fixed you with its torturing eye,
Defying you to take a step apart,
If peradventure you would hide a thing.
I saw the whole room, I and Marian there
Alone.
      Alone? She threw her bonnet off,
560   Then, sighing as 'twere sighing the last time,
Approached the bed, and drew a shawl away:
You could not peel a fruit you fear to bruise
More calmly and more carefully than so,—
Nor would you find within, a rosier flushed
565   Pomegranate—
            There he lay upon his back,
The yearling creature, warm and moist with life
To the bottom of his dimples,—to the ends
Of the lovely tumbled curls about his face;

For since he had been covered over-much
570   To keep him from the light-glare, both his cheeks
Were hot and scarlet as the first live rose
The shepherd's heart-blood ebbed away into,
The faster for his love. And love was here
As instant! in the pretty baby-mouth,
575   Shut close as if for dreaming that it sucked;
The little naked feet drawn up the way
Of nestled birdlings; everything so soft
And tender,—to the little holdfast hands,
Which, closing on a finger into sleep,
580   Had kept the mould of 't.
                                    While we stood there dumb,
For oh, that it should take such innocence
To prove just guilt, I thought, and stood there dumb;
The light upon his eyelids pricked them wide,
And, staring out at us with all their blue,
585   As half perplexed between the angelhood
He had been away to visit in his sleep,
And our most mortal presence,—gradually
He saw his mother's face, accepting it
In change for heaven itself, with such a smile
590   As might have well been learnt there,—never moved,
But smiled on, in a drowse of ecstasy,
So happy (half with her and half with heaven)
He could not have the trouble to be stirred,
But smiled and lay there. Like a rose, I said:
595   As red and still indeed as any rose,
That blows in all the silence of its leaves,
Content in blowing to fulfil its life.

She leaned above him (drinking him as wine)
In that extremity of love, 'twill pass
600   For agony or rapture, seeing that love
Includes the whole of nature, rounding it
To love . . no more,—since more can never be
Than just love. Self-forgot, cast out of self,
And drowning in the transport of the sight,
605   Her whole pale passionate face, mouth, forehead, eyes,

One gaze, she stood! then, slowly as he smiled
She smiled too, slowly, smiling unaware,
And drawing from his countenance to hers
A fainter red, as if she watched a flame
610 And stood in it a-glow. 'How beautiful,'
Said she.
              I answered, trying to be cold.
(Must sin have compensations, was my thought,
As if it were a holy thing like grief?
And is a woman to be fooled aside
615 From putting vice down, with that woman's toy,
A baby?)—'Ay! the child is well enough,'
I answered. 'If his mother's palms are clean
They need be glad, of course, in clasping such;
But if not,—I would rather lay my hand,
620 Were I she,—on God's brazen altar-bars
Red-hot with burning sacrificial lambs,
Than touch the sacred curls of such a child.'

She plunged her fingers in his clustering locks,
As one who would not be afraid of fire;
625 And then, with indrawn steady utterance, said,—
'My lamb, my lamb! although, through such as thou,
The most unclean got courage and approach
To God, once,—now they cannot, even with men,
Find grace enough for pity and gentle words.'

630 'My Marian,' I made answer, grave and sad,
'The priest who stole a lamb to offer him,
Was still a thief. And if a woman steals
(Through God's own barrier-hedges of true love,
Which fence out licence in securing love)
635 A child like this, that smiles so in her face,
She is no mother, but a kidnapper,
And he's a dismal orphan, . . not a son,
Whom all her kisses cannot feed so full
He will not miss hereafter a pure home
640 To live in, a pure heart to lean against,
A pure good mother's name and memory

To hope by, when the world grows thick and bad,
And he feels out for virtue.'
              'Oh,' she smiled
With bitter patience, 'the child takes his chance,—
645 Not much worse off in being fatherless
Than I was, fathered. He will say, belike,
His mother was the saddest creature born;
He'll say his mother lived so contrary
To joy, that even the kindest, seeing her,
650 Grew sometimes almost cruel: he'll not say
She flew contrarious in the face of God
With bat-wings of her vices. Stole my child,—
My flower of earth, my only flower on earth,
My sweet, my beauty!' . . Up she snatched the child,
655 And, breaking on him in a storm of tears,
Drew out her long sobs from their shivering roots,
Until he took it for a game, and stretched
His feet and flapped his eager arms like wings,
And crowed and gurgled through his infant laugh:
660 'Mine, mine,' she said. 'I have as sure a right
As any glad proud mother in the world,
Who sets her darling down to cut his teeth
Upon her church-ring. If she talks of law,
I talk of law! I claim my mother-dues
665 By law,—the law which now is paramount;
The common law, by which the poor and weak
Are trodden underfoot by vicious men,
And loathed for ever after by the good.
Let pass! I did not filch . . I found the child.'

670 'You found him, Marian?'
                    'Ay, I found him where
I found my curse,—in the gutter, with my shame!
What have you, any of you, to say to that,
Who all are happy, and sit safe and high,
And never spoke before to arraign my right
675 To grief itself? What, what, . . being beaten down
By hoofs of maddened oxen into a ditch,
Half-dead, whole mangled . . when a girl, at last

Breathes, sees . . and finds there, bedded in her flesh,
Because of the overcoming shock perhaps,
680   Some coin of price! . . and when a good man comes
(That's God! the best men are not quite as good)
And says 'I dropped the coin there: take it you,
And keep it,—it shall pay you for the loss,'—
You all put up your finger—'See the thief!
685   'Observe that precious thing she has come to filch.
'How bad these girls are!' Oh, my flower, my pet,
I dare forget I have you in my arms
And fly off to be angry with the world,
And fright you, hurt you with my tempers, till
690   You double up your lip. Ah, that indeed
Is bad: a naughty mother!'

                                    'You mistake,'
I interrupted; 'if I loved you not,
I should not, Marian, certainly be here.'

'Alas,' she said, 'you are so very good;
695   And yet I wish, indeed, you had never come
To make me sob until I vex the child.
It is not wholesome for these pleasure-plats
To be so early watered by our brine.
And then, who knows? he may not like me now
700   As well, perhaps, as ere he saw me fret,—
One's ugly fretting! he has eyes the same
As angels, but he cannot see as deep,
And so I've kept for ever in his sight
A sort of smile to please him,—as you place
705   A green thing from the garden in a cup,
To make believe it grows there. Look, my sweet,
My cowslip-ball! We've done with that cross face,
And here's the face come back you used to like.
Ah, ah! he laughs! he likes me. Ah, Miss Leigh,
710   You're great and pure; but were you purer still,—
As if you had walked, we'll say, no otherwhere
Than up and down the new Jerusalem,
And held your trailing lutestring up yourself
From brushing the twelve stones, for fear of some

715   Small speck as little as a needle prick,
    White stitched on white,—the child would keep to *me*,
    Would choose his poor lost Marian, like me best,
    And, though you stretched your arms, cry back and cling,
    As we do, when God says it's time to die
720   And bids us go up higher. Leave us, then;
    We two are happy. Does *he* push me off?
    He's satisfied with me, as I with him.'

    'So soft to one, so hard to others! Nay,'
    I cried, more angry that she melted me,
725   'We make henceforth a cushion of our faults
    To sit and practise easy virtues on?
    I thought a child was given to sanctify
    A woman,—set her in the sight of all
    The clear-eyed Heavens, a chosen minister
730   To do their business and lead spirits up
    The difficult blue heights. A woman lives,
    Not bettered, quickened toward the truth and good
    Through being a mother? . . then she's none! although
    She damps her baby's cheeks by kissing them,
735   As we kill roses.'
               'Kill! O Christ,' she said,
    And turned her wild sad face from side to side
    With most despairing wonder in it, 'What,
    What have you in your souls against me then,
    All of you? am I wicked, do you think?
740   God knows me, trusts me with the child! but you,
    You think me really wicked?'
                     'Complaisant,'
    I answered softly, 'to a wrong you've done,
    Because of certain profits,—which is wrong
    Beyond the first wrong, Marian. When you left
745   The pure place and the noble heart, to take
    The hand of a seducer' . .
                 'Whom? whose hand?
    I took the hand of' . .
                   Springing up erect,
    And lifting the child at full arm's length,

As if to bear him like an oriflamme
750 Unconquerable to armies of reproach,—
'By *him*,' she said, 'my child's head and its curls,
By these blue eyes no woman born could dare
A perjury on, I make my mother's oath,
That if I left that Heart, to lighten it,
755 The blood of mine was still, except for grief!
No cleaner maid than I was, took a step
To a sadder end,—no matron-mother now
Looks backward to her early maidenhood
Through chaster pulses. I speak steadily;
760 And if I lie so, . . if, being fouled in will
And paltered with in soul by devil's lust,
I dared to bid this angel take my part, . .
Would God sit quiet, let us think, in heaven,
Nor strike me dumb with thunder? Yet I speak:
765 He clears me therefore. What, 'seduced''s your word?
Do wolves seduce a wandering fawn in France?
Do eagles, who have pinched a lamb with claws,
Seduce it into carrion? So with me.
I was not ever, as you say, seduced,
770 But simply, murdered.'

              There she paused, and sighed,
With such a sigh as drops from agony
To exhaustion,—sighing while she let the babe
Slide down upon her bosom from her arms.
And all her face's light fell after him,
775 Like a torch quenched in falling. Down she sank,
And sat upon the bedside with the child.

But I, convicted, broken utterly,
With woman's passion clung about her waist,
And kissed her hair and eyes,—'I have been wrong,
780 Sweet Marian' . . (weeping in a tender rage)
'Sweet holy Marian! And now, Marian, now,
I'll use your oath although my lips are hard,
And by the child, my Marian, by the child,
I'll swear his mother shall be innocent

785   Before my conscience, as in the open Book
Of Him who reads for judgment. Innocent,
My sister! let the night be ne'er so dark
The moon is surely somewhere in the sky;
So surely is your whiteness to be found
790   Through all dark facts. But pardon, pardon me,
And smile a little, Marian,—for the child,
If not for me, my sister.'
                The poor lip
Just motioned for the smile and let it go:
And then, with scarce a stirring of the mouth,
795   As if a statue spoke that could not breathe,
But spoke on calm between its marble lips,—
'I'm glad, I'm very glad you clear me so.
I should be sorry that you set me down
With harlots, or with even a better name
800   Which misbecomes his mother. For the rest,
I am not on a level with your love,
Nor ever was, you know,—but now am worse,
Because that world of yours has dealt with me
As when the hard sea bites and chews a stone
805   And changes the first form of it. I've marked
A shore of pebbles bitten to one shape
From all the various life of madrepores;
And so, that little stone, called Marian Erle,
Picked up and dropped by you and another friend,
810   Was ground and tortured by the incessant sea
And bruised from what she was,—changed! death's a
        change,
And she, I said, was murdered; Marian's dead.
What can you do with people when they are dead,
But, if you are pious, sing a hymn and go,
815   Or, if you are tender, heave a sigh and go,
But go by all means,—and permit the grass
To keep its green feud up 'twixt them and you?
Then leave me,—let me rest. I'm dead, I say,
And if, to save the child from death as well,
820   The mother in me has survived the rest,

Why, that God's miracle you must not tax,—
I'm not less dead for that: I'm nothing more
But just a mother. Only for the child,
I'm warm, and cold, and hungry, and afraid,
825 And smell the flowers a little, and see the sun,
And speak still, and am silent,—just for him!
I pray you therefore to mistake me not
And treat me, haply, as I were alive;
For though you ran a pin into my soul,
830 I think it would not hurt nor trouble me.
Here's proof, dear lady,—in the market-place
But now, you promised me to say a word
About . . a friend, who once, long years ago,
Took God's place toward me, when He draws and loves
835 And does not thunder, . . whom at last I left,
As all of us leave God. You thought perhaps,
I seemed to care for hearing of that friend?
Now, judge me! we have sate here half an hour
And talked together of the child and me,
840 And I not asked as much as 'What's the thing
'You had to tell me of the friend . . the friend?'
He's sad, I think you said,—he's sick perhaps?
'Tis nought to Marian if he's sad or sick.
Another would have crawled beside your foot
845 And prayed your words out. Why, a beast, a dog,
A starved cat, if he had fed it once with milk,
Would show less hardness. But I'm dead, you see,
And that explains it.'
      Poor, poor thing, she spoke
And shook her head, as white and calm as frost
850 On days too cold for raining any more,
But still with such a face, so much alive,
I could not choose but take it on my arm
And stroke the placid patience of its cheeks,—
Then told my story out, of Romney Leigh,
855 How, having lost her, sought her, missed her still,
He, broken-hearted for himself and her,
Had drawn the curtain of the world awhile

As if he had done with morning. There I stopped,
For when she gasped, and pressed me with her eyes,
860 'And now . . how is it with him? tell me now,'—
I felt the shame of compensated grief,
And chose my words with scruple—slowly stepped
Upon the slippery stones set here and there
Across the sliding water. 'Certainly,
865 As evening empties morning into night,
Another morning takes the evening up
With healthful, providential interchange;
And, though he thought still of her,'—

                            'Yes, she knew,
She understood: she had supposed, indeed,
870 That, as one stops a hole upon a flute,
At which a new note comes and shapes the tune,
Excluding her would bring a worthier in,
And, long ere this, that Lady Waldemar
He loved so' . .

                  'Loved,' I started,—'loved her so!
875 Now tell me' . .

               'I will tell you,' she replied:
'But, since we're taking oaths, you'll promise first
That he in England, he, shall never learn
In what a dreadful trap his creature here,
Round whose unworthy neck he had meant to tie
880 The honourable ribbon of his name,
Fell unaware, and came to butchery:
Because,—I know him,—as he takes to heart
The grief of every stranger, he's not like
To banish mine as far as I should choose
885 In wishing him most happy. Now he leaves
To think of me, perverse, who went my way
Unkind, and left him,—but if once he knew . .
Ah, then, the sharp nail of my cruel wrong
Would fasten me for ever in his sight,
890 Like some poor curious bird, through each spread wing
Nailed high up over a fierce hunter's fire,
To spoil the dinner of all tenderer folk

Come in by chance. Nay, since your Marian's dead,
You shall not hang her up, but dig a hole
895   And bury her in silence! ring no bells.'

I answered gaily, though my whole voice wept;
'We'll ring the joy-bells, not the funeral-bells,
Because we have her back, dead or alive.'

She never answered that, but shook her head;
900   Then low and calm, as one who, safe in heaven,
Should tell a story of his lower life,
Unmoved by shame or anger,—so she spoke.
She told me she had loved upon her knees,
As others pray, more perfectly absorbed
905   In the act and aspiration. She felt his,
For just his uses, not her own at all,
His stool, to sit on, or put up his foot,
His cup, to fill with wine or vinegar,
Whichever drink might please him at the chance,
910   For that should please her always: let him write
His name upon her . . it seemed natural;
It was most precious, standing on his shelf,
To wait until he chose to lift his hand.
Well, well,—I saw her then, and must have seen
915   How bright her life went, floating on her love,
Like wicks the housewives send afloat on oil,
Which feeds them to a flame that lasts the night.

To do good seemed so much his business,
That, having done it, she was fain to think,
920   Must fill up his capacity for joy.
At first she never mooted with herself
If *he* was happy, since he made her so,
Or if *he* loved her, being so much beloved:
Who thinks of asking if the sun is light,
925   Observing that it lightens? who's so bold
To question God of His felicity?
Still less. And thus she took for granted first,
What first of all she should have put to proof,

And sinned against him so, but only so.
930   'What could you hope,' she said, 'of such as she?
You take a kid you like, and turn it out
In some fair garden: though the creature's fond
And gentle, it will leap upon the beds
And break your tulips, bite your tender trees:
935   The wonder would be if such innocence
Spoiled less. A garden is no place for kids.'

And, by degrees, when he who had chosen her
Brought in his courteous and benignant friends
To spend their goodness on her, which she took
940   So very gladly, as a part of his,—
By slow degrees, it broke on her slow sense
That she, too, in that Eden of delight
Was out of place, and, like the silly kid,
Still did most mischief where she meant most love.
945   And thought enough to make a woman mad,
(No beast in this but she may well go mad),
That, saying 'I am thine to love and use,'
May blow the plague in her protesting breath
To the very man for whom she claims to die,—
950   That, clinging round his neck, she pulls him down
And drowns him,—and that, lavishing her soul,
She hales perdition on him. 'So, being mad,'
Said Marian . .
                    'Ah—who stirred such thoughts, you ask?
Whose fault it was, that she should have such thoughts?
955   None's fault, none's fault. The light comes, and we see:
But if it were not truly for our eyes,
There would be nothing seen, for all the light;
And so with Marian. If she saw at last,
The sense was in her,—Lady Waldemar
960   Had spoken all in vain else.'
                                        'O my heart,
O prophet in my heart,' I cried aloud,
'Then Lady Waldemar spoke!'
                                        '*Did* she speak,'
Mused Marian softly,—'or did she only sign?

Or did she put a word into her face
965 And look, and so impress you with the word?
Or leave it in the foldings of her gown,
Like rosemary smells, a movement will shake out
When no one's conscious? who shall say, or guess?
One thing alone was certain,—from the day
970 The gracious lady paid a visit first,
She, Marian, saw things different,—felt distrust
Of all that sheltering roof of circumstance
Her hopes were building into the clay nests:
Her heart was restless, pacing up and down
975 And fluttering, like dumb creatures before storms,
Not knowing wherefore she was ill at ease.'

'And still the lady came,' said Marian Erle,
'Much oftener than *he* knew it, Mister Leigh.
She bade me never tell him that she had come,
980 She liked to love me better than he knew,
So very kind was Lady Waldemar:
And every time she brought with her more light,
And every light made sorrow clearer . . Well,
Ah, well! we cannot give her blame for that;
985 'Twould be the same thing if an angel came,
Whose right should prove our wrong. And every time
The lady came, she looked more beautiful,
And spoke more like a flute among green trees,
Until at last, as one, whose heart being sad
990 On hearing lovely music, suddenly
Dissolves in weeping, I brake out in tears
Before her . . asked her counsel . . 'had I erred
'In being too happy? would she set me straight?
'For she, being wise and good and born above
995 'The flats I had never climbed from, could perceive
'If such as I, might grow upon the hills;
'And whether such poor herb sufficed to grow,
'For Romney Leigh to break his fast upon t',—
'Or would he pine on such, or haply starve?'
1000 She wrapt me in her generous arms at once,
And let me dream a moment how it feels

To have a real mother, like some girls:
But when I looked, her face was younger .. ay,
Youth's too bright not to be a little hard,
1005 And beauty keeps itself still uppermost,
That's true!—Though Lady Waldemar was kind
She hurt me, hurt, as if the morning-sun
Should smite us on the eyelids when we sleep,
And wake us up with headache. Ay, and soon
1010 Was light enough to make my heart ache too:
She told me truths I asked for .. 'twas my fault ..
'That Romney could not love me, if he would,
'As men call loving; there are bloods that flow
'Together, like some rivers, and not mix,
1015 'Through contraries of nature. He indeed
'Was set to wed me, to espouse my class,
'Act out a rash opinion,—and, once wed,
'So just a man and gentle, could not choose
'But make my life as smooth as marriage-ring,
1020 'Bespeak me mildly, keep me a cheerful house,
'With servants, broaches, all the flowers I liked,
'And pretty dresses, silk the whole year round' ..
At which I stopped her,—'This for me. And now
'For *him*.' She murmured,—truth grew difficult;
1025 She owned, ''Twas plain a man like Romney Leigh
'Required a wife more level to himself.
'If day by day he had to bend his height
'To pick up sympathies, opinions, thoughts,
'And interchange the common talk of life
1030 'Which helps a man to live as well as talk,
'His days were heavily taxed. Who buys a staff
'To fit the hand, that reaches but the knee?
'He'd feel it bitter to be forced to miss
'The perfect joy of married suited pairs,
1035 'Who, bursting through the separating hedge
'Of personal dues with that sweet eglantine
'Of equal love, keep saying, 'So *we* think,
'It strikes *us*,—that's *our* fancy.',—When I asked
'If earnest will, devoted love, employed
1040 In youth like mine, would fail to raise me up,—

As two strong arms will always raise a child
To a fruit hung overhead?' she sighed and sighed . .
'That could not be,' she feared. 'You take a pink,
'You dig about its roots and water it,
1045 'And so improve it to a garden-pink,
'But will not change it to a heliotrope,
'The kind remains. And then, the harder truth—
'This Romney Leigh, so rash to leap a pale,
'So bold for conscience, quick for martyrdom,
1050 'Would suffer steadily and never flinch,
'But suffer surely and keenly, when his class
'Turned shoulder on him for a shameful match,
'And set him up as nine-pin in their talk,
'To bowl him down with jestings.'—There, she paused;
1055 And when I used the pause in doubting that
We wronged him after all in what we feared—
'Suppose such things could never touch him, more
'In his high conscience, (if the things should be,)
'Than, when the queen sits in an upper room,
1060 'The horses in the street can spatter her!'—
A moment, hope came,—but the lady closed
That door and nicked the lock, and shut it out,
Observing wisely that, 'the tender heart
'Which made him over-soft to a lower class,
1065 'Would scarcely fail to make him sensitive
'To a higher,—how they thought and what they felt.'

'Alas, alas!' said Marian, rocking slow
The pretty baby who was near asleep,
The eyelids creeping over the blue balls,—
1070 'She made it clear, too clear—I saw the whole!
And yet who knows if I had seen my way
Straight out of it, by looking, though 'twas clear,
Unless the generous lady, 'ware of this,
Had set her own house all a-fire for me
1075 To light me forwards? Leaning on my face
Her heavy agate eyes which crushed my will,
She told me tenderly, (as when men come
To a bedside to tell people they must die)

'She knew of knowledge,—ay, of knowledge, knew,
1080 'That Romney Leigh had loved *her* formerly;
'And *she* loved *him*, she might say, now the chance
'Was past . . but that, of course, he never guessed,—
'For something came between them . . something thin
'As a cobweb . . catching every fly of doubt
1085 'To hold it buzzing at the window-pane
'And help to dim the daylight. Ah, man's pride
'Or woman's—which is greatest? most averse
'To brushing cobwebs? Well, but she and he
'Remained fast friends; it seemed not more than so,
1090 'Because he had bound his hands and could not stir.
'An honourable man, if somewhat rash;
'And she, not even for Romney, would she spill
'A blot . . as little even as a tear . .
'Upon his marriage-contract,—not to gain
1095 'A better joy for two than came by that!
'For, though I stood between her heart and heaven,
'She loved me wholly.''
                              Did I laugh or curse?
I think I sate there silent, hearing all,
Ay, hearing double,—Marian's tale, at once,
1100 And Romney's marriage vow, '*I'll keep to* THEE,'
Which means that woman-serpent. Is it time
For church now?
                       'Lady Waldemar spoke more,'
Continued Marian, 'but, as when a soul
Will pass out through the sweetness of a song
1105 Beyond it, voyaging the uphill road,—
Even so, mine wandered from the things I heard,
To those I suffered. It was afterward
I shaped the resolution to the act.
For many hours we talked. What need to talk?
1110 The fate was clear and close; it touched my eyes;
But still the generous lady tried to keep
The case afloat, and would not let it go,
And argued, struggled upon Marian's side,
Which was not Romney's! though she little knew
1115 What ugly monster would take up the end,—

What griping death within the drowning death
Was ready to complete my sum of death.'

I thought,—Perhaps he's sliding now the ring
Upon that woman's finger . .
                                    She went on:
1120   'The lady, failing to prevail her way,
Upgathered my torn wishes from the ground,
And pieced them with her strong benevolence;
And, as I thought I could breathe freer air
Away from England, going without pause,
1125   Without farewell,—just breaking with a jerk
The blossomed offshoot from my thorny life,—
She promised kindly to provide the means,
With instant passage to the colonies
And full protection,—'would commit me straight
1130   'To one who once had been her waiting-maid
'And had the customs of the world, intent
'On changing England for Australia
'Herself, to carry out her fortune so.'
For which I thanked the Lady Waldemar,
1135   As men upon their death-beds thank last friends
Who lay the pillow straight: it is not much,
And yet 'tis all of which they are capable,
This lying smoothly in a bed to die.
And so, 'twas fixed;—and so, from day to day,
1140   The woman named, came in to visit me.'

Just then, the girl stopped speaking,—sate erect,
And stared at me as if I had been a ghost
(Perhaps I looked as white as any ghost),
With large-eyed horror. 'Does God make,' she said,
1145   'All sorts of creatures, really, do you think?
Or is it that the Devil slavers them
So excellently, that we come to doubt
Who's strongest, He who makes, or he who mars?
I never liked the woman's face, or voice,
1150   Or ways: it made me blush to look at her;
It made me tremble if she touched my hand;

And when she spoke a fondling word, I shrank,
As if one hated me who had power to hurt;
And, every time she came, my veins ran cold
1155 As somebody were walking on my grave.
At last I spoke to Lady Waldemar:
'Could such an one be good to trust?' I asked.
Whereat the lady stroked my cheek and laughed
Her silver-laugh—(one must be born to laugh,
1160 To put such music in it) 'Foolish girl,
'Your scattered wits are gathering wool beyond
'The sheep-walk reaches!—leave the thing to me.'
And therefore, half in trust, and half in scorn
That I had heart still for another fear
1165 In such a safe despair, I left the thing.

'The rest is short. I was obedient:
I wrote my letter which delivered *him*
From Marian to his own prosperities,
And followed that bad guide. The lady?—hush,—
1170 I never blame the lady. Ladies who
Sit high, however willing to look down,
Will scarce see lower than their dainty feet:
And Lady Waldemar saw less than I,
With what a Devil's daughter I went forth
1175 The swine's road, headlong over a precipice,
In such a curl of hell-foam caught and choked,
No shriek of soul in anguish could pierce through.
To fetch some help. They say there's help in heaven
For all such cries. But if one cries from hell . . .
1180 What then?—the heavens are deaf upon that side.

'A woman . . hear me,—let me make it plain,—
A woman . . not a monster . . both her breasts
Made right to suckle babes . . she took me off,
A woman also, young and ignorant,
1185 And heavy with my grief, my two poor eyes
Near washed away with weeping, till the trees,
The blessed unaccustomed trees and fields,
Ran either side the train like stranger dogs

Unworthy of any notice,—took me off
1190 So dull, so blind, so only half-alive,
Not seeing by what road, nor by what ship,
Nor toward what place, nor to what end of all.—
Men carry a corpse thus,—past the doorway, past
The garden-gate, the children's playground, up
1195 The green lane,—then they leave it in the pit,
To sleep and find corruption, cheek to cheek
With him who stinks since Friday.

                   'But suppose;
To go down with one's soul into the grave,—
To go down half-dead, half-alive, I say,
1200 And wake up with corruption, . . cheek to cheek
With him who stinks since Friday! There it is,
And that's the horror of 't, Miss Leigh.

                     'You feel?
You understand?—no, do not look at me,
But understand. The blank, blind, weary way
1205 Which led . . where'er it led . . away at least;
The shifted ship . . to Sydney or to France . .
Still bound, wherever else, to another land;
The swooning sickness on the dismal sea,
The foreign shore, the shameful house, the night,
1210 The feeble blood, the heavy-headed grief, . .
No need to bring their damnable drugged cup,
And yet they brought it. Hell's so prodigal
Of devil's gifts . . hunts liberally in packs,
Will kill no poor small creature of the wilds
1215 But fifty red wide throats must smoke at it,—
As HIS at me . . when waking up at last . .
I told you that I waked up in the grave.

'Enough so!—it is plain enough so. True,
We wretches cannot tell out all our wrong,
1220 Without offence to decent happy folk.
I know that we must scrupulously hint
With half-words, delicate reserves, the thing
Which no one scrupled we should feel in full.
Let pass the rest, then; only leave my oath

1225 Upon this sleeping child,—man's violence,
  Not man's seduction, made me what I am,
  As lost as . . I told *him* I should be lost.
  When mothers fail us, can we help ourselves?
  That's fatal!—And you call it being lost,
1230 That down came next day's noon and caught me there
  Half gibbering and half raving on the floor,
  And wondering what had happened up in heaven,
  That suns should dare to shine when God Himself
  Was certainly abolished.
        'I was mad,
1235 How many weeks, I know not,—many weeks.
  I think they let me go, when I was mad,
  They feared my eyes and loosed me, as boys might
  A mad dog whom they had tortured. Up and down
  I went, by road and village, over tracts
1240 Of open foreign country, large and strange,
  Crossed everywhere by long thin poplar-lines
  Like fingers of some ghastly skeleton Hand
  Through sunlight and through moonlight evermore
  Pushed out from hell itself to pluck me back,
1245 And resolute to get me, slow and sure;
  While every roadside Christ upon his cross
  Hung reddening through his gory wounds at me,
  And shook his nails in anger, and came down
  To follow a mile after, wading up
1250 The low vines and green wheat, crying 'Take the girl!
  'She's none of mine from henceforth.' Then, I knew,
  (But this is somewhat dimmer than the rest)
  The charitable peasants gave me bread
  And leave to sleep in straw: and twice they tied,
1255 At parting, Mary's image round my neck—
  How heavy it seemed! as heavy as a stone;
  A woman has been strangled with less weight:
  I threw it in a ditch to keep it clean
  And ease my breath a little, when none looked;
1260 I did not need such safeguards:—brutal men
  Stopped short, Miss Leigh, in insult, when they had seen
  My face,—I must have had an awful look.

And so I lived: the weeks passed on,— I lived.
'Twas living my old tramp-life o'er again,
1265   But, this time, in a dream, and hunted round
By some prodigious Dream-fear at my back
Which ended, yet: my brain cleared presently,
And there I sate, one evening, by the road,
I, Marian Erle, myself, alone, undone,
1270   Facing a sunset low upon the flats,
As if it were the finish of all time,—
The great red stone upon my sepulchre,
Which angels were too weak to roll away.

Seventh Book

'THE woman's motive? shall we daub ourselves
With finding roots for nettles? 'tis soft clay
And easily explored. She had the means,
The monies, by the lady's liberal grace,
5   In trust for that Australian scheme and me,
Which so, that she might clutch with both her hands,
And chink to her naughty uses undisturbed,
She served me (after all it was not strange;
'Twas only what my mother would have done)
10 A motherly, unmerciful, good turn.

'Well, after. There are nettles everywhere,
But smooth green grasses are more common still;
The blue of heaven is larger than the cloud;
A miller's wife at Clichy took me in
15 And spent her pity on me,—made me calm
And merely very reasonably sad.
She found me a servant's place in Paris where
I tried to take the cast-off life again,
And stood as quiet as a beaten ass
20 Who, having fallen through overloads, stands up
To let them charge him with another pack.

'A few months, so. My mistress, young and light,
Was easy with me, less for kindness than
Because she led, herself, an easy time
25 Betwixt her lover and her looking-glass,
Scarce knowing which way she was praised the most.
She felt so pretty and so pleased all day
She could not take the trouble to be cross,
But sometimes, as I stooped to tie her shoe,
30 Would tap me softly with her slender foot,
Still restless with the last night's dancing in't,
And say 'Fie, pale-face! are you English girls
'All grave and silent? mass-book still, and Lent?

'And first-communion colours on your cheeks,
35 'Worn past the time for't? little fool, be gay!'
At which she vanished, like a fairy, through
A gap of silver laughter.
       'Came an hour
When all went otherwise. She did not speak,
But clenched her brows, and clipped me with her eyes
40 As if a viper with a pair of tongs,
Too far for any touch, yet near enough
To view the writhing creature,—then at last;
'Stand still there, in the holy Virgin's name,
'Thou Marian; thou'rt no reputable girl,
45 'Although sufficient dull for twenty saints!
'I think thou mock'st me and my house,' she said;
'Confess thou'lt be a mother in a month,
'Thou mask of saintship.'
       'Could I answer her?
The light broke in so: it meant *that* then, *that*?
50 I had not thought of that, in all my thoughts,—
Through all the cold, numb aching of my brow,
Through all the heaving of impatient life
Which threw me on death at intervals,—through all
The upbreak of the fountains of my heart
55 The rains had swelled too large: it could mean *that*?
Did God make mothers out of victims, then,
And set such pure amens to hideous deeds?
Why not? He overblows an ugly grave
With violets which blossom in the spring.
60 And *I* could be a mother in a month?
I hope it was not wicked to be glad.
I lifted up my voice and wept, and laughed,
To heaven, not her, until it tore my throat.
'Confess, confess!'—what was there to confess,
65 Except man's cruelty, except my wrong?
Except this anguish, or this ecstacy?
This shame, or glory? The light woman there
Was small to take it in: an acorn-cup
Would take the sea in sooner.
       ''Good,' she cried;

70   'Unmarried and a mother, and she laughs!
    'These unchaste girls are always impudent.
    'Get out, intriguer! leave my house, and trot:
    'I wonder you should look me in the face,
    'With such a filthy secret.'
                     'Then I rolled
75   My scanty bundle up and went my way,
    Washed white with weeping, shuddering head and foot
    With blind hysteric passion, staggering forth
    Beyond those doors. 'Twas natural, of course,
    She should not ask me where I meant to sleep;
80   I might sleep well beneath the heavy Seine,
    Like others of my sort; the bed was laid
    For us. But any woman, womanly,
    Had thought of him who should be in a month,
    The sinless babe that should be in a month,
85   And if by chance he might be warmer housed
    Than underneath such dreary, dripping eaves.'

    I broke on Marian there. 'Yet she herself,
    A wife, I think, had scandals of her own,
    A lover, not her husband.'
                     'Ay,' she said,
90   'But gold and meal are measured otherwise;
    I learnt so much at school,' said Marian Erle.

    'O crooked world,' I cried, 'ridiculous
    If not so lamentable! It's the way
    With these light women of a thrifty vice,
95   My Marian,—always hard upon the rent
    In any sister's virtue! while they keep
    Their chastity so darned with perfidy,
    That, though a rag itself, it looks as well
    Across a street, in balcony or coach,
100   As any stronger stuff might. For my part,
    I'd rather take the wind-side of the stews
    Than touch such women with my finger-end!
    They top the poor street-walker by their lie,
    And look the better for being so much worse:

105   The devil's most devilish when respectable.
       But you, dear, and your story.'
                                   'All the rest
       Is here,' she said, and signed upon the child.
       'I found a mistress-sempstress who was kind
       And let me sew in peace among her girls;
110   And what was better than to draw the threads
       All day and half the night, for him, and him?
       And so I lived for him, and so he lives,
       And so I know, by this time, God lives too.'

       She smiled beyond the sun, and ended so,
115   And all my soul rose up to take her part
       Against the world's successes, virtues, fames.
       'Come with me, sweetest sister,' I returned,
       'And sit within my house, and do me good
       From henceforth, thou and thine! ye are my own
120   From henceforth. I am lonely in the world,
       And thou art lonely, and the child is half
       An orphan. Come,—and, henceforth, thou and I
       Being still together, will not miss a friend,
       Nor he a father, since two mothers shall
125   Make that up to him. I am journeying south,
       And in my Tuscan home I'll find a niche
       And set thee there, my saint, the child and thee,
       And burn the lights of love before thy face,
       And ever at thy sweet look cross myself
130   From mixing with the world's prosperities;
       That so, in gravity and holy calm,
       We two may live on toward the truer life.'

       She looked me in the face and answered not,
       Nor signed she was unworthy, nor gave thanks,
135   But took the sleeping child and held it out
       To meet my kiss, as if requiting me
       And trusting me at once. And thus, at once,
       I carried him and her to where I lived;
       She's there now, in the little room, asleep,
140   I hear the soft child-breathing through the door;

And all three of us, at to-morrow's break,
Pass onward, homeward, to our Italy.
Oh, Romney Leigh, I have your debts to pay,
And I'll be just and pay them.
                                          But yourself!
145 To pay your debts is scarcely difficult;
To buy your life is nearly impossible,
Being sold away to Lamia. My head aches;
I cannot see my road along this dark;
Nor can I creep and grope, as fits the dark,
150 For these foot-catching robes of womanhood:
A man might walk a little . . but I!—He loves
The Lamia-woman,—and I, write to him
What stops his marriage, and destroys his peace,—
Or what, perhaps, shall simply trouble him,
155 Until she only need to touch his sleeve
With just a finger's tremulous white flame,
Saying 'Ah,—Aurora Leigh! a pretty tale,
'A very pretty poet! I can guess
'The motive.'—then, to catch his eyes in hers,
160 And vow she does not wonder,—and they two
To break in laughter, as the sea along
A melancholy coast, and float up higher,
In such a laugh, their fatal weeds of love!
Ay, fatal, ay. And who shall answer me
165 Fate has not hurried tides; and if to-night
My letter would not be a night too late,—
An arrow shot into a man that's dead,
To prove a vain intention? Would I show
The new wife vile, to make the husband mad?
170 No, Lamia! shut the shutters, bar the doors
From every glimmer on thy serpent-skin!
I will not let thy hideous secret out
To agonise the man I love—I mean
The friend I love . . as friends love.
                                          It is strange,
175 To-day while Marian told her story, like
To absorb most listeners, how I listened chief
To a voice not hers, nor yet that enemy's,

Nor God's in wrath, . . but one that mixed with mine
Long years ago, among the garden-trees,
180   And said to *me*, to *me* too, 'Be my wife,
Aurora!' It is strange, with what a swell
Of yearning passion, as a snow of ghosts
Might beat against the impervious doors of heaven,
I thought, 'Now, if I had been a woman, such
185   As God made women, to save men by love,—
By just my love I might have saved this man,
And made a nobler poem for the world
Than all I have failed in.' But I failed besides
In this; and now he's lost! through me alone!
190   And, by my only fault, his empty house
Sucks in, at this same hour, a wind from hell
To keep his hearth cold, make his casements creak
For ever to the tune of plague and sin—
O Romney, O my Romney, O my friend!
195   My cousin and friend! my helper, when I would,
My love that might be! mine!
                                                Why, how one weeps
When one's too weary! Were a witness by,
He'd say some folly . . that I loved the man,
Who knows? . . and make me laugh again for scorn.
200   At strongest, women are as weak in flesh,
As men, at weakest, vilest, are in soul:
So, hard for women to keep pace with men!
As well give up at once, sit down at once,
And weep as I do. Tears, tears! *why*, we weep?
205   'Tis worth enquiry?—That we've shamed a life,
Or lost a love, or missed a world, perhaps?
By no means. Simply, that we've walked too far,
Or talked too much, or felt the wind i' the east,—
And so we weep, as if both body and soul
210   Broke up in water—this way.
                                                Poor mixed rags
Forsooth we're made of, like those other dolls
That lean with pretty faces into fairs.
It seems as if I had a man in me,
Despising such a woman.

                         Yet indeed,
215 To see a wrong or suffering moves us all
     To undo it, though we should undo ourselves;
     Ay, all the more, that we undo ourselves;   ·
     That's womanly, past doubt, and not ill-moved.
     A natural movement, therefore, on my part,
220 To fill the chair up of my cousin's wife,
     And save him from a devil's company!
     We're all so,—made so—'tis our woman's trade
     To suffer torment for another's ease.
     The world's male chivalry has perished out,
225 But women are knights-errant to the last;
     And, if Cervantes had been greater still,
     He had made his Don a Donna.
                              So it clears,
     And so we rain our skies blue.
                         Put away
     This weakness. If, as I have just now said,
230 A man's within me,—let him act himself,
     Ignoring the poor conscious trouble of blood
     That's called the woman merely. I will write
     Plain words to England,—if too late, too late,—
     If ill-accounted, then accounted ill;
235 We'll trust the heavens with something.
                              'Dear Lord Howe,
     You'll find a story on another leaf
     That's Marian Erle's,—what noble friend of yours
     She trusted once, through what flagitious means
     To what disastrous ends;—the story's true.
240 I found her wandering on the Paris quays,
     A babe upon her breast,—unnatural
     Unseasonable outcast on such snows
     Unthawed to this time. I will tax in this
     Your friendship, friend,—if that convicted She
245 Be not his wife yet, to denounce the facts
     To himself,—but, otherwise, to let them pass
     On tip-toe like escaping murderers,
     And tell my cousin, merely—Marian lives,

Is found, and finds her home with such a friend,
250   Myself, Aurora. Which good news, 'She's found,'
Will help to make him merry in his love:
I send it, tell him, for my marriage gift,
As good as orange water for the nerves,
Or perfumed gloves for headache,—though aware
255   That he, except of love, is scarcely sick;
I mean the new love this time, . . since last year.
Such quick forgetting on the part of men!
Is any shrewder trick upon the cards
To enrich them? pray instruct me how it's done.
260   First, clubs,—and while you look at clubs, it's spades;
That's prodigy. The lightning strikes a man,
And when we think him dead and charred . .
Why, there he is on a sudden, playing pipes
Beneath the splintered elm-tree! Crime and shame
265   And all their hoggery trample your smooth world,
Nor leave more foot-marks than Apollo's kine,
Whose hoofs were muffled by the thieving god
In tamarisk leaves and myrtle. I'm so sad,
So weary and sad to-night, I'm somewhat sour,—
270   Forgive me. To be blue and shrew at once,
Exceeds all toleration except yours;
But yours, I know, is infinite. Farewell.
To-morrow we take train for Italy.
Speak gently of me to your gracious wife,
275   And one, however far, shall yet be near
In loving wishes to your house.'
                                    I sign,
And now I'll loose my heart upon a page,
This—

          'Lady Waldemar, I'm very glad
I never liked you; which you knew so well,
280   You spared me, in your turn, to like me much.
Your liking surely had done worse for me
Than has your loathing, though the last appears
Sufficiently unscrupulous to hurt,
And not afraid of judgment. Now, there's space
285   Between our faces,—I stand off, as if

I judged a stranger's portrait and pronounced
Indifferently the type was good or bad:
What matter to me that the lines are false,
I ask you? Did I ever ink my lips
290 By drawing your name through them as a friend's,
Or touch your hand as lovers do? thank God
I never did: and, since you're proved so vile,
Ay, vile, I say,—we'll show it presently,—
I'm not obliged to nurse my friend in you,
295 Or wash out my own blots, in counting yours,
Or even excuse myself to honest souls
Who seek to touch my lip or clasp my palm,—
'Alas, but Lady Waldemar came first!'

"'Tis true, by this time you may near me so
300 That you're my cousin's wife. You've gambled deep
As Lucifer, and won the morning-star
In that case,—and the noble house of Leigh
Must henceforth with its good roof shelter you:
I cannot speak and burn you up between
305 Those rafters, I who am born a Leigh,—nor speak
And pierce your breast through Romney's, I who live,
His friend and cousin!—so, you're safe. You two
Must grow together like the tares and wheat
Till God's great fire.—But make the best of time.

310 'And hide this letter! let it speak no more
Than I shall, how you tricked poor Marian Erle,
And set her own love digging her own grave
Within her green hope's pretty garden-ground;
Ay, sent her forth with some one of your sort
315 To a wicked house in France,—from which she fled
With curses in her eyes and ears and throat,
Her whole soul choked with curses,—mad, in short,
And madly scouring up and down for weeks
The foreign hedgeless country, lone and lost,—
320 So innocent, male-fiends might slink within
Remote hell-corners, seeing her so defiled!

*

'But you,—you are a woman and more bold.
To do you justice, you'd not shrink to face . .
We'll say, the unfledged life in the other room,
Which, treading down God's corn, you trod in sight
Of all the dogs, in reach of all the guns,—
Ay, Marian's babe, her poor unfathered child,
Her yearling babe!—you'd face him when he wakes
And opens up his wonderful blue eyes:
You'd meet them and not wink perhaps, nor fear
God's triumph in them and supreme revenge,
So, righting His creation's balance-scale
(You pulled as low as Tophet) to the top
Of most celestial innocence! For me,
Who am not as bold, I own those infant eyes
Have set me praying.

              'While they look at heaven,
No need of protestation in my words
Against the place you've made them! let them look!
They'll do your business with the heavens, be sure:
I spare you common curses.

                'Ponder this.
If haply you're the wife of Romney Leigh,
(For which inheritance beyond your birth
You sold that poisonous porridge called your soul)
I charge you, be his faithful and true wife!
Keep warm his hearth and clean his board, and, when
He speaks, be quick with your obedience;
Still grind your paltry wants and low desires
To dust beneath his heel; though, even thus,
The ground must hurt him,—it was writ of old,
'Ye shall not yoke together ox and ass,'
The nobler and ignobler. Ay, but you
Shall do your part as well as such ill things
Can do aught good. You shall not vex him,—mark,
You shall not vex him, . . jar him when he's sad,
Or cross him when he's eager. Understand
To trick him with apparent sympathies,
Nor let him see thee in the face too near
And unlearn thy sweet seeming. Pay the price

Of lies, by being constrained to lie on still;
360   'Tis easy for thy sort: a million more
Will scarcely damn thee deeper.
                                        'Doing which
You are very safe from Marian and myself:
We'll breathe as softly as the infant here,
And stir no dangerous embers. Fail a point,
365   And show our Romney wounded, ill-content,
Tormented in his home, . . we open mouth,
And such a noise will follow, the last trump's
Will scarcely seem more dreadful, even to you;
You'll have no pipers after: Romney will
370   (I know him) push you forth as none of his,
All other men declaring it well done;
While women, even the worst, your like, will draw
Their skirts back, not to brush you in the street;
And so I warn you. I'm . . Aurora Leigh.'

375   The letter written, I felt satisfied.
The ashes, smouldering in me, were thrown out
By handfuls from me: I had writ my heart
And wept my tears, and now was cool and calm;
And, going straightway to the neighbouring room,
380   I lifted up the curtains of the bed
Where Marian Erle, the babe upon her arm,
Both faces leaned together like a pair
Of folded innocences, self-complete,
Each smiling from the other, smiled and slept.
385   There seemed no sin, no shame, no wrath, no grief.
I felt, she too, had spoken words that night,
But softer certainly, and said to God,—
Who laughs in heaven perhaps, that such as I
Should make ado for such as she.—'Defiled'
390   I wrote? 'defiled' I thought her? Stoop,
Stoop lower, Aurora! get the angels' leave
To creep in somewhere, humbly, on your knees,
Within this round of sequestration white
In which they have wrapt earth's foundlings, heaven's
            elect!

*

395 The next day, we took the train to Italy
And fled on southward in the roar of steam.
The marriage-bells of Romney must be loud,
To sound so clear through all! I was not well;
And truly, though the truth is like a jest,

400 I could not choose but fancy, half the way,
I stood alone i' the belfry, fifty bells
Of naked iron, mad with merriment,
(As one who laughs and cannot stop himself)
All clanking at me, in me, over me,

405 Until I shrieked a shriek I could not hear,
And swooned with noise,—but still, along my swoon,
Was 'ware the baffled changes backward rang,
Prepared, at each emerging sense, to beat
And crash it out with clangour. I was weak;

410 I struggled for the posture of my soul
In upright consciousness of place and time,
But evermore, twixt waking and asleep,
Slipped somehow, staggered, caught at Marian's eyes
A moment, (it is very good for strength

415 To know that some one needs you to be strong)
And so recovered what I called myself,
For that time.
                    I just knew it when we swept
Above the old roofs of Dijon. Lyons dropped
A spark into the night, half trodden out

420 Unseen. But presently the winding Rhone
Washed out the moonlight large along his banks,
Which strained their yielding curves out clear and clean
To hold it,—shadow of town and castle just blurred
Upon the hurrying river. Such an air

425 Blew thence upon the forehead,—half an air
And half a water,—that I leaned and looked;
Then, turning back on Marian, smiled to mark
That she looked only on her child, who slept,
His face toward the moon too.
                              So we passed

430 The liberal open country and the close,
And shot through tunnels, like a lightning-wedge

By great Thor-hammers driven through the rock,
Which, quivering through the intestine blackness, splits,
And lets it in at once: the train swept in
435 Athrob with effort, trembling with resolve,
The fierce denouncing whistle wailing on
And dying off smothered in the shuddering dark,
While we, self-awed, drew troubled breath, oppressed
As other Titans, underneath the pile
440 And nightmare of the mountains. Out, at last,
To catch the dawn afloat upon the land!
—Hills, slung forth broadly and gauntly everywhere,
Not crampt in their foundations, pushing wide
Rich outspreads of the vineyards and the corn,
445 (As if they entertained i' the name of France)
While, down their straining sides, streamed manifest
A soil as red as Charlemagne's knightly blood,
To consecrate the verdure. Some one said
'Marseilles!' And lo, the city of Marseilles,
450 With all her ships behind her, and beyond,
The scimitar of ever-shining sea
For right-hand use, bared blue against the sky!

That night we spent between the purple heaven
And purple water: I think Marian slept;
455 But I, as a dog a-watch for his master's foot,
Who cannot sleep or eat before he hears,
I sate upon the deck and watched all night,
And listened through the stars for Italy.
Those marriage-bells I spoke of, sounded far,
460 As some child's go-cart in the street beneath
To a dying man who will not pass the day,
And knows it, holding by a hand he loves.
I, too, sate quiet, satisfied with death,
Sate silent: I could hear my own soul speak,
465 And had my friend,—for Nature comes sometimes
And says, 'I am ambassador for God.'
I felt the wind soft from the land of souls;
The old miraculous mountains heaved in sight,
One straining past another along the shore,

470   The way of grand dull Odyssean ghosts,
       Athirst to drink the cool blue wine of seas
       And stare on voyagers. Peak pushing peak
       They stood; I watched beyond that Tyrian belt
       Of intense sea betwixt them and the ship,
475   Down all their sides the misty olive-woods
       Dissolving in the weak congenial moon,
       And still disclosing some brown convent-tower
       That seems as if it grew from some brown rock,—
       Or many a little lighted village, dropt
480   Like a fallen star, upon so high a point,
       You wonder what can keep it in its place
       From sliding headlong with the waterfalls
       Which drop and powder all the myrtle-groves
       With spray of silver. Thus my Italy
485   Was stealing on us. Genoa broke with day;
       The Doria's long pale palace striking out,
       From green hills in advance of the white town,
       A marble finger dominant to ships,
       Seen glimmering through the uncertain grey of dawn.

490   And then I did not think, 'my Italy,'
       I thought 'my father!' O my father's house,
       Without his presence!—Places are too much
       Or else too little, for immortal man;
       Too little, when love's May o'ergrows the ground,—
495   Too much, when that luxuriant wealth of green
       Is rustling to our ankles in dead leaves.
       'Tis only good to be, or here or there,
       Because we had a dream on such a stone,
       Or this or that,—but, once being wholly waked,
500   And come back to the stone without the dream,
       We trip upon't,—alas! and hurt ourselves;
       Or else it falls on us and grinds us flat,
       The heaviest grave-stone on this burying earth.
       —But while I stood and mused, a quiet touch
505   Fell light upon my arm, and, turning round,
       A pair of moistened eyes convicted mine.
       'What, Marian! is the babe astir so soon?'

'He sleeps,' she answered; 'I have crept up thrice,
And seen you sitting, standing, still at watch.
510 I thought it did you good till now, but now' . . .
'But now,' I said, 'you leave the child alone.'
'And *you're* alone,' she answered,—and she looked
As if I, too, were something. Sweet the help
Of one we have helped! Thanks, Marian, for that help.

515 I found a house, at Florence, on the hill
Of Bellosguardo. 'Tis a tower that keeps
A post of double observation o'er
The valley of Arno (holding as a hand
The outspread city) straight toward Fiesole
520 And Mount Morello and the setting sun,—
The Vallombrosan mountains to the right,
Which sunrise fills as full as crystal cups
Wine-filled, and red to the brim because it's red.
No sun could die, nor yet be born, unseen
525 By dwellers at my villa: morn and eve
Were magnified before us in the pure
Illimitable space and pause of sky,
Intense as angels' garments blanched with God,
Less blue than radiant. From the outer wall
530 Of the garden, dropped the mystic floating grey
Of olive-trees, (with interruptions green
From maize and vine) until 'twas caught and torn
On that abrupt black line of cypresses
Which signed the way to Florence. Beautiful
535 The city lay along the ample vale,
Cathedral, tower and palace, piazza and street;
The river trailing like a silver cord
Through all, and curling loosely, both before
And after, over the whole stretch of land
540 Sown whitely up and down its opposite slopes,
With farms and villas.
                        Many weeks had passed,
No word was granted.—Last, a letter came
From Vincent Carrington:—'My dear Miss Leigh,
You've been as silent as a poet should,

545 When any other man is sure to speak.
    If sick, if vexed, if dumb, a silver piece
    Will split a man's tongue,—straight he speaks and says,
    'Received that cheque.' But you! . . I send you funds
    To Paris, and you make no sign at all.
550 Remember, I'm responsible and wait
    A sign of you, Miss Leigh.
                          'Meantime your book
    Is eloquent as if you were not dumb;
    And common critics, ordinarily deaf
    To such fine meanings, and, like deaf men, loth
555 To seem deaf, answering chance-wise, yes or no,
    'It must be' or 'it must not,' (most pronounced
    When least convinced) pronounce for once aright:
    You'd think they really heard,—and so they do . .
    The burr of three or four who really hear
560 And praise your book aright: Fame's smallest trump
    Is a great ear-trumpet for the deaf as posts,
    No other being effective. Fear not, friend;
    We think, here, you have written a great book,
    And you, a woman! It was in you—yes,
565 I felt 'twas in you: yet I doubted half
    If that od-force of German Reichenbach,
    Which still from female finger-tips burns blue,
    Could strike out, as our masculine white heats,
    To quicken a man. Forgive me. All my heart
570 Is quick with yours, since, just a fortnight since,
    I read your book and loved it.
                          'Will you love
    My wife, too? Here's my secret, I might keep
    A month more from you! but I yield it up
    Because I know you'll write the sooner for't,—
575 Most women (of your height even) counting love
    Life's only serious business. Who's my wife
    That shall be in a month? you ask? nor guess?
    Remember what a pair of topaz eyes
    You once detected, turned against the wall,
580 That morning, in my London painting-room;
    The face half-sketched, and slurred; the eyes alone!

But you . . you caught them up with yours, and said
'Kate Ward's eyes, surely.' Now I own the truth:
I had thrown them there to keep them safe from Jove;
585 They would so naughtily find out their way
To both the heads of both my Danaës,
Where just it made me mad to look at them.
Such eyes! I could not paint or think of eyes
But those,—and so I flung them into paint
590 And turned them to the wall's care. Ay, but now
I've let them out, my Kate's! I've painted her,
(I'll change my style, and leave mythologies)
The whole sweet face; it looks upon my soul
Like a face on water, to beget itself.
595 A half-length portrait, in a hanging cloak
Like one you wore once; 'tis a little frayed;—
I pressed, too, for the nude harmonious arm—
But she . . she'd have her way, and have her cloak;
She said she could be like you only so,
600 And would not miss the fortune. Ah, my friend,
You'll write and say she shall not miss your love
Through meeting mine? in faith, she would not change.
She has your books by heart, more than my words,
And quotes you up against me till I'm pushed
605 Where, three months since, her eyes were! nay, in fact,
Nought satisfied her but to make me paint
Your last book folded in her dimpled hands,
Instead of my brown palette, as I wished,
(And grant me, the presentment had been newer)
610 She'd grant me nothing: I've compounded for
The naming of the wedding-day next month,
And gladly too. 'Tis pretty, to remark
How women can love women of your sort,
And tie their hearts with love-knots to your feet,
615 Grow insolent about you against men,
And put us down by putting up the lip,
As if a man,—there *are* such, let us own,
Who write not ill,—remains a man, poor wretch,
While you—! Write far worse than Aurora Leigh,
620 And there'll be women who believe of you

(Beside my Kate) that if you walked on sand
You would not leave a foot-print.

'Are you put
To wonder at my marriage, like poor Leigh?
'Kate Ward!' he said. 'Kate Ward!' he said anew.
625   'I thought . .' he said, and stopped—'I did not think . .'
And then he dropped to silence.

'Ah, he's changed.
I had not seen him, you're aware, for long,
But went of course. I have not touched on this
Through all this letter,—conscious of your heart,
630   And writing lightlier for the heavy fact,
As clocks are voluble with lead.

'How weak,
To say I'm sorry! Dear Leigh, dearest Leigh.
In those old days of Shropshire,—pardon me,—
When he and you fought many a field of gold
635   On what you should do, or you should not do,
Make bread or verses, (it just came to that)
I thought you'd one day draw a silken peace
Through a golden ring. I thought so. Foolishly,
The event proved, for you went more opposite
640   To each other, month by month, and year by year,
Until this happened. God knows best, we say,
But hoarsely. When the fever took him first,
Just after I had writ to you in France,
They tell me Lady Waldemar mixed drinks
645   And counted grains, like any salaried nurse,
Excepting that she wept too. Then Lord Howe,
You're right about Lord Howe! Lord Howe's a trump;
And yet, with such in his hand, a man like Leigh
May lose, as *he* does. There's an end to all,—
650   Yes, even this letter, though the second sheet
May find you doubtful. Write a word for Kate:
Even now she reads my letters, like a wife,
And, if she sees her name, I'll see her smile,
And share the luck. So, bless you, friend of two!
655   I will not ask you what your feeling is
At Florence, with my pictures. I can hear

Your heart a-flutter over the snow-hills;
And, just to pace the Pitti with you once,
I'd give a half-hour of to-morrow's walk
660 With Kate . . I think so. Vincent Carrington.'

The noon was hot; the air scorched like the sun,
And was shut out. The closed persiani threw
Their long-scored shadows on my villa-floor,
And interlined the golden atmosphere
665 Straight, still,—across the pictures on the wall,
The statuette on the console, (of young Love
And Psyche made one marble by a kiss)
The low couch where I leaned, the table near,
The vase of lilies, Marian pulled last night,
670 (Each green leaf and each white leaf ruled in black
As if for writing some new text of fate)
And the open letter, rested on my knee,—
But there the lines swerved, trembled, though I sate
Untroubled . . plainly . . reading it again
675 And three times. Well, he's married; that is clear.
No wonder that he's married, nor much more
Than Vincent's therefore, 'sorry.' Why, of course,
The lady nursed him when he was not well,
Mixed drinks,—unless nepenthe was the drink,
680 'Twas scarce worth telling. But a man in love
Will see the whole sex in his mistress' hood,
The prettier for its lining of fair rose;
Although he catches back, and says at last,
'I'm sorry.' Sorry. Lady Waldemar
685 At prettiest, under the said hood, preserved
From such a light as I could hold to her face
To flare its ugly wrinkles out to shame,—
Is scarce a wife for Romney, as friends judge,
Aurora Leigh, or Vincent Carrington,—
690 That's plain. And if he's 'conscious of my heart' . .
Perhaps it's natural, though the phrase is strong;
(One's apt to use strong phrases, being in love)
And even that stuff of 'fields of gold,' 'gold rings,'
And what he 'thought,' poor Vincent! what he 'thought,'

695 May never mean enough to ruffle me.
     —Why, this room stifles. Better burn than choke;
     Best have air, air, although it comes with fire,
     Throw open blinds and windows to the noon
     And take a blister on my brow instead
700 Of this dead weight! best, perfectly be stunned
     By those insufferable cicale, sick
     And hoarse with rapture of the summer-heat,
     That sing, like poets, till their hearts break, . . sing
     Till men say, 'It's too tedious.'
                                  Books succeed,
705 And lives fail. Do I feel it so, at last?
     Kate loves a worn-out cloak for being like mine,
     While I live self-despised for being myself,
     And yearn toward some one else, who yearns away
     From what he is, in his turn. Strain a step
710 For ever, yet gain no step? Are we such,
     We cannot, with our admirations even,
     Our tip-toe aspirations, touch a thing
     That's higher than we? is all a dismal flat,
     And God alone above each,—as the sun
715 O'er level lagunes, to make them shine and stink,—
     Laying stress upon us with immediate flame,
     While we respond with our miasmal fog,
     And call it mounting higher, because we grow
     More highly fatal?
                        Tush, Aurora Leigh!
720 You wear your sackcloth looped in Cæsar's way,
     And brag your failings as mankind's. Be still.
     There *is* what's higher, in this very world,
     That you can live, or catch at. Stand aside
     And look at others—instance little Kate!
725 She'll make a perfect wife for Carrington.
     She always has been looking round the earth
     For something good and green to alight upon
     And nestle into, with those soft-winged eyes,
     Subsiding now beneath his manly hand
730 'Twixt trembling lids of inexpressive joy:
     I will not scorn her, after all, too much,

That so much she should love me. A wise man
Can pluck a leaf, and find a lecture in't;
And I, too, . . God has made me,—I've a heart
735 That's capable of worship, love, and loss;
We say the same of Shakspeare's. I'll be meek,
And learn to reverence, even this poor myself.

The book, too—pass it. 'A good book,' says he,
'And you a woman.' I had laughed at that,
740 But long since. I'm a woman,—it is true;
Alas, and woe to us, when we feel it most!
Then, least care have we for the crowns and goals
And compliments on writing our good books.

The book has some truth in it, I believe:
745 And truth outlives pain, as the soul does life.
I know we talk our Phædons to the end
Through all the dismal faces that we make,
O'er-wrinkled with dishonouring agony
From any mortal drug. I have written truth,
750 And I a woman; feebly, partially,
Inaptly in presentation, Romney'll add,
Because a woman. For the truth itself,
That's neither man's nor woman's, but just God's;
None else has reason to be proud of truth:
755 Himself will see it sifted, disenthralled,
And kept upon the height and in the light,
As far as, and no farther, than 'tis truth;
For,—now He has left off calling firmaments
And strata, flowers and creatures, very good,—
760 He says it still of truth, which is His own.

Truth, so far, in my book,—the truth which draws
Through all things upwards; that a twofold world
Must go to a perfect cosmos. Natural things
And spiritual,—who separates those two
765 In art, in morals, or the social drift,
Tears up the bond of nature and brings death,
Paints futile pictures, writes unreal verse,

Leads vulgar days, deals ignorantly with men,
Is wrong, in short, at all points. We divide
770 This apple of life, and cut it through the pips,—
The perfect round which fitted Venus' hand
Has perished as utterly as if we ate
Both halves. Without the spiritual, observe,
The natural's impossible;—no form,
775 No motion! Without sensuous, spiritual
Is inappreciable;—no beauty or power!
And in this twofold sphere the twofold man
(And still the artist is intensely a man)
Holds firmly by the natural, to reach
780 The spiritual beyond it,—fixes still
The type with mortal vision, to pierce through,
With eyes immortal, to the antitype
Some call the ideal,—better called the real,
And certain to be called so presently
785 When things shall have their names. Look long enough
On any peasant's face here, coarse and lined,
You'll catch Antinous somewhere in that clay,
As perfect-featured as he yearns at Rome
From marble pale with beauty; then persist,
790 And, if your apprehension's competent,
You'll find some fairer angel at his back,
As much exceeding him, as he the boor,
And pushing him with empyreal disdain
For ever out of sight. Ay, Carrington
795 Is glad of such a creed! an artist must,
Who paints a tree, a leaf, a common stone,
With just his hand, and finds it suddenly
A-piece with and conterminous to his soul.
Why else do these things move him, leaf or stone?
800 The bird's not moved, that pecks at a spring-shoot;
Nor yet the horse before a quarry, a-graze:
But man, the two-fold creature, apprehends
The twofold manner, in and outwardly,
And nothing in the world comes single to him,
805 A mere itself,—cup, column, or candlestick,
All patterns of what shall be in the Mount;

The whole temporal show related royally,
And built up to eterne significance
Through the open arms of God. 'There's nothing great
810 Nor small,' has said a poet of our day,
(Whose voice will ring beyond the curfew of eve
And not be thrown out by the matin's bell)
And truly, I reiterate, .. nothing's small!
No lily-muffled hum of a summer-bee,
815 But finds some coupling with the spinning stars;
No pebble at your foot, but proves a sphere;
No chaffinch, but implies the cherubim:
And,—glancing at my own thin, veinéd wrist,—
In such a little tremour of the blood
820 The whole strong clamour of a vehement soul
Doth utter itself distinct. Earth's crammed with heaven
And every common bush afire with God:
But only he who sees, takes off his shoes,
The rest sit round it, and pluck blackberries,
825 And daub their natural faces unaware
More and more, from the first similitude.

Truth so far, in my book! a truth which draws
From all things upward. I, Aurora, still
Have felt it hound me through the wastes of life
830 As Jove did Io; and, until that Hand
Shall overtake me wholly, and, on my head,
Lay down its large unfluctuating peace
The feverish gad-fly pricks me up and down,
It must be. Art's the witness of what Is
835 Behind this show. If this world's show were all,
Then imitation would be all in Art;
There, Jove's hand gripes us!—For we stand here, we,
If genuine artists, witnessing for God's
Complete, consummate, undivided work:
840 —That not a natural flower can grow on earth,
Without a flower upon the spiritual side,
Substantial, archetypal, all a-glow
With blossoming causes,—not so far away,
But we, whose spirit-sense is somewhat cleared,

845 May not catch something of the bloom and breath,—
Too vaguely apprehended, though indeed
Still apprehended, consciously or not,
And still transferred to picture, music, verse,
For thrilling audient and beholding souls
850 By sighs and touches which are known to souls,—
How known, they know not,—why, they cannot find,
So straight call out on genius, say 'A man
Produced this,'—when much rather they should say
''Tis insight and he saw this.'

        Thus is Art
855 Self-magnified in magnifying a truth
Which, fully recognised, would change the world
And shift its morals. If a man could feel,
Not one day, in the artist's ecstasy,
But every day, feast, fast, or working-day,
860 The spiritual significance burn through
The hieroglyphic of material shows,
Henceforward he would paint the globe with wings,
And reverence fish and fowl, the bull, the tree,
And even his very body as a man,—
865 Which now he counts so vile, that all the towns
Make offal of their daughters for its use
On summer-nights, when God is sad in heaven
To think what goes on in his recreant world
He made quite other; while that moon He made
870 To shine there, at the first love's covenant,
Shines still, convictive as a marriage-ring
Before adulterous eyes.

        How sure it is,
That, if we say a true word, instantly
We feel 'tis God's, not ours, and pass it on
875 Like bread at sacrament, we taste and pass
Nor handle for a moment, as indeed
We dared to set up any claim to such!
And I—my poem;—let my readers talk;
I'm closer to it—I can speak as well:
880 I'll say, with Romney, that the book is weak,
The range uneven, the points of sight obscure,

The music interrupted.
                            Let us go.
The end of woman (or of man, I think)
Is not a book. Alas, the best of books
885 Is but a word in Art, which soon grows cramped,
Stiff, dubious-statured with the weight of years,
And drops an accent or digamma down
Some cranny of unfathomable time,
Beyond the critic's reaching. Art itself,
890 We've called the larger life, still must feel the soul
Live past it. For more's felt than is perceived,
And more's perceived than can be interpreted,
And Love strikes higher with his lambent flame
Than A   can pile the faggots.
                                   Is it so?
895 When Jove's hand meets us with composing touch,
And when, at last, we are hushed and satisfied,—
Then, Io does not call it truth, but love?
Well, well! my father was an Englishman:
My mother's blood in me is not so strong
900 That I should bear this stress of Tuscan noon
And keep my wits. The town, there, seems to seethe
In this Medæan boil-pot of the sun,
And all the patient hills are bubbling round
As if a prick would leave them flat. Does heaven
905 Keep far off, not to set us in a blaze?
Not so,—let drag your fiery fringes, heaven,
And burn us up to quiet. Ah, we know
Too much here, not to know what's best for peace;
We have too much light here, not to want more fire
910 To purify and end us. We talk, talk,
Conclude upon divine philosophies,
And get the thanks of men for hopeful books,
Whereat we take our own life up, and . . pshaw!
Unless we piece it with another's life,
915 (A yard of silk to carry out our lawn)
As well suppose my little handkerchief
Would cover Samminiato, church and all,
If out I threw it past the cypresses,

As, in this ragged, narrow life of mine,
920   Contain my own conclusions.
                         But at least
We'll shut up the persiani and sit down,
And when my head's done aching, in the cool,
Write just a word to Kate and Carrington.
May joy be with them! she has chosen well,
925   And he not ill.
                    I should be glad, I think,
Except for Romney. Had *he* married Kate,
I surely, surely, should be very glad.
This Florence sits upon me easily,
With native air and tongue. My graves are calm,
930   And do not too much hurt me. Marian's good,
Gentle and loving,—lets me hold the child,
Or drags him up the hills to find me flowers
And fill those vases, ere I'm quite awake,—
The grandiose red tulips, which grow wild,
935   Or else my purple lilies, Dante blew
To a larger bubble with his prophet-breath;
Or one of those tall flowering reeds which stand
In Arno like a sheaf of sceptres, left
By some remote dynasty of dead gods,
940   To suck the stream for ages and get green,
And blossom wheresoe'er a hand divine
Had warmed the place with ichor. Such I've found
At early morning, laid across my bed,
And woke up pelted with a childish laugh
945   Which even Marian's low precipitous 'hush'
Has vainly interposed to put away,—
While I, with shut eyes, smile and motion for
The dewy kiss that's very sure to come
From mouth and cheeks, the whole child's face at once
950   Dissolved on mine,—as if a nosegay burst
Its string with the weight of roses overblown,
And dropt upon me. Surely I should be glad.
The little creature almost loves me now,
And calls my name, 'Alola,' stripping off
955   The *r*'s like thorns, to make it smooth enough

To take between his dainty, milk-fed lips,
God love him! I should certainly be glad,
Except, God help me, that I'm sorrowful
Because of Romney.
            Romney, Romney! Well,
960 This grows absurd!—too like a tune that runs
I' the head, and forces all things in the world,
Wind, rain, the creaking gnat or stuttering fly,
To sing itself and vex you;—yet perhaps
A paltry tune you never fairly liked,
965 Some 'I'd be a butterfly,' or 'C'est l'amour:'
We're made so,—not such tyrants to ourselves
We are not slaves to nature. Some of us
Are turned, too, overmuch like some poor verse
With a trick of ritournelle: that same thing goes
970 And comes back ever.
            Vincent Carrington
Is 'sorry,' and I'm sorry; but *he*'s strong
To mount from sorrow to his heaven of love,
And when he says at moments, 'Poor, poor Leigh,
Who'll never call his own, so true a heart,
975 So fair a face even,'—he must quickly lose
The pain of pity, in the blush he has made
By his very pitying eyes. The snow, for him,
Has fallen in May, and finds the whole earth warm,
And melts at the first touch of the green grass.

980 But Romney,—he has chosen, after all.
I think he had as excellent a sun
To see by, as most others, and perhaps
Has scarce seen really worse than some of us,
When all's said. Let him pass. I'm not too much
985 A woman, not to be a man for once,
And bury my Dead like Alaric,
Depositing the treasures of my soul
In this drained water-course, and, letting flow
The river of life again, with commerce-ships
990 And pleasure-barges, full of silks and songs.
Blow, winds, and help us.
              Ah, we mock ourselves

With talking of the winds! perhaps as much
With other resolutions. How it weighs,
This hot, sick air! and how I covet here
995   The Dead's provision on the river's couch,
With silver curtains drawn on tinkling rings!
Or else their rest in quiet crypts,—laid by
From heat and noise!—from those cicale, say,
And this more vexing heart-beat.
                                        So it is:
1000 We covet for the soul, the body's part,
To die and rot. Even so, Aurora, ends
Our aspiration, who bespoke our place
So far in the east. The occidental flats
Had fed us fatter, therefore? we have climbed
1005 Where herbage ends? we want the beast's part now,
And tire of the angel's?—Men define a man,
The creature who stands front-ward to the stars
The creature who looks inward to himself,
The tool-wright, laughing creature. 'Tis enough:
1010 We'll say instead, the inconsequent creature, man,—
For that's his specialty. What creature else
Conceives the circle, and then walks the square?
Loves things proved bad, and leaves a thing proved good?
You think the bee makes honey half a year,
1015 To loathe the comb in winter, and desire
The little ant's food rather? But a man—
Note men!—they are but women after all,
As women are but Auroras!—there are men
Born tender, apt to pale at a trodden worm,
1020 Who paint for pastime, in their favourite dream,
Spruce auto-vestments flowered with crocus-flames:
There are, too, who believe in hell, and lie:
There are, who waste their souls in working out
Life's problem on these sands betwixt two tides,
1025 And end,—'Now give us the beast's part, in death.'

Alas, long-suffering and most patient God,
Thou need'st be surelier God to bear with us
Than even to have made us! thou aspire, aspire

From henceforth for me! thou who hast, thyself,
1030   Endured this fleshhood, knowing how, as a soaked
And sucking vesture, it would drag us down
And choke us in the melancholy Deep,
Sustain me, that, with thee, I walk these waves,
Resisting!—breathe me upward, thou for me
1035   Aspiring, who art the way, the truth, the life,—
That no truth henceforth seem indifferent,
No way to truth laborious, and no life,
Not even this life I live, intolerable!

The days went by. I took up the old days
1040   With all their Tuscan pleasures, worn and spoiled,—
Like some lost book we dropt in the long grass
On such a happy summer-afternoon
When last we read it with a loving friend,
And find in autumn, when the friend is gone,
1045   The grass cut short, the weather changed, too late,
And stare at, as at something wonderful
For sorrow,—thinking how two hands, before,
Had held up what is left to only one,
And how we smiled when such a vehement nail
1050   Impressed the tiny dint here, which presents
This verse in fire for ever. Tenderly
And mournfully I lived. I knew the birds
And insects,—which looked fathered by the flowers
And emulous of their hues: I recognised
1055   The moths, with that great overpoise of wings
Which make a mystery of them how at all
They can stop flying: butterflies, that bear
Upon their blue wings such red embers round,
They seem to scorch the blue air into holes
1060   Each flight they take: and fire-flies, that suspire
In short soft lapses of transported flame
Across the tingling Dark, while overhead
The constant and inviolable stars
Outburn those lights-of-love: melodious owls,
1065   (If music had but one note and was sad,
'Twould sound just so) and all the silent swirl

Of bats, that seem to follow in the air
Some grand circumference of a shadowy dome
To which we are blind: and then, the nightingales,
1070 Which pluck our heart across a garden-wall
(When walking in the town) and carry it
So high into the bowery almond trees,
We tremble and are afraid, and feel as if
The golden flood of moonlight unaware
1075 Dissolved the pillars of the steady earth
And made it less substantial. And I knew
The harmless opal snakes, and large-mouthed frogs,
(Those noisy vaunters of their shallow streams)
And lizards, the green lightnings of the wall,
1080 Which, if you sit down quiet, nor sigh too loud,
Will flatter you and take you for a stone,
And flash familiarly about your feet
With such prodigious eyes in such small heads!—
I knew them, though they had somewhat dwindled from
1085 My childish imagery,—and kept in mind
How last I sate among them equally,
In fellowship and mateship, as a child
Will bear him still toward insect, beast, and bird,
Before the Adam in him has foregone
1090 All privilege of Eden,—making friends
And talk, with such a bird or such a goat,
And buying many a two-inch-wide rush-cage
To let out the caged cricket on a tree,
Saying 'Oh, my dear grillino, were you cramped?
1095 And are you happy with the ilex-leaves?
And do you love me who have let you go?
Say *yes* in singing, and I'll understand.'

But now the creatures all seemed farther off,
No longer mine, nor like me; only *there*,
1100 A gulph between us. I could yearn indeed,
Like other rich men, for a drop of dew
To cool this heat,—a drop of the early dew,
The irrecoverable child-innocence
(Before the heart took fire and withered life)

1105   When childhood might pair equally with birds;
But now . . the birds were grown too proud for us!
Alas, the very sun forbids the dew.

And I, I had come back to an empty nest,
Which every bird's too wise for. How I heard
1110   My father's step on that deserted ground,
His voice along that silence, as he told
The names of bird and insect, tree and flower,
And all the presentations of the stars
Across Valdarno, interposing still
1115   'My child,' 'my child.' When fathers say 'my child,'
'Tis easier to conceive the universe,
And life's transitions down the steps of law.

I rode once to the little mountain-house
As fast as if to find my father there,
1120   But, when in sight of 't, within fifty yards,
I dropped my horse's bridle on his neck
And paused upon his flank. The house's front
Was cased with lingots of ripe Indian corn
In tessellated order, and device
1125   Of golden patterns; not a stone of wall
Uncovered,—not an inch of room to grow
A vine-leaf. The old porch had disappeared;
And, in the open doorway, sate a girl
At plaiting straws, her black hair strained away
1130   To a scarlet kerchief caught beneath her chin
In Tuscan fashion,—her full ebon eyes,
Which looked too heavy to be lifted so,
Still dropt and lifted toward the mulberry-tree
On which the lads were busy with their staves
1135   In shout and laughter, stripping all the boughs
As bare as winter, of those summer leaves
My father had not changed for all the silk
In which the ugly silkworms hide themselves.
Enough. My horse recoiled before my heart—
1140   I turned the rein abruptly. Back we went
As fast, to Florence.
               That was trial enough

Of graves. I would not visit, if I could,
My father's, or my mother's any more,
To see if stone cutter or lichen beat
1145   So early in the race, or throw my flowers,
Which could not out-smell heaven, or sweeten earth.
They live too far above, that I should look
So far below to find them: let me think
That rather they are visiting my grave
1150   This life here, (undeveloped yet to life)
And that they drop upon me, now and then,
For token or for solace, some small weed
Least odorous of the growths of paradise,
To spare such pungent scents as kill with joy.

1155   My old Assunta, too, was dead, was dead—
O land of all men's past! for me alone,
It would not mix its tenses. I was past,
It seemed, like others,—only not in heaven.
And, many a Tuscan eve, I wandered down
1160   The cypress alley, like a restless ghost
That tries its feeble ineffectual breath
Upon its own charred funeral-brands put out
Too soon,—where black and stiff, stood up the trees
Against the broad vermilion of the skies.
1165   Such skies!—all clouds abolished in a sweep
Of God's skirt, with a dazzle to ghosts and men,
As down I went, saluting on the bridge
The hem of such, before 'twas caught away
Beyond the peaks of Lucca. Underneath,
1170   The river, just escaping from the weight
Of that intolerable glory, ran
In acquiescent shadow murmurously:
And up, beside it, streamed the festa-folk
With fellow-murmurs from their feet and fans,
1175   (With *issimo* and *ino* and sweet poise
Of vowels in their pleasant scandalous talk)
Returning from the grand-duke's dairy farm
Before the trees grew dangerous at eight,
(For 'trust no tree by moonlight,' the Tuscans say)

1180 To eat their ice at Doni's tenderly,—
     Each lovely lady close to a cavalier
     Who holds her dear fan while she feeds her smile
     On meditative spoonfuls of vanille,
     He breathing hot protesting vows of love,
1185 Enough to thaw her cream and scorch his beard.
     'Twas little matter. I could pass them by
     Indifferently, not fearing to be known.
     No danger of being wrecked upon a friend,
     And forced to take an iceberg for an isle!
1190 The very English, here, must wait to learn
     To hang the cobweb of their gossip out
     To catch a fly. I'm happy. It's sublime,
     This perfect solitude of foreign lands!
     To be, as if you had not been till then,
1195 And were then, simply that you chose to be:
     To spring up, not to be brought forth from the ground,
     Like grasshoppers at Athens, and skip thrice
     Before a woman makes a pounce on you
     And plants you in her hair!—possess, yourself,
1200 A new world all alive with creatures new,
     New sun, new moon, new flowers, new people—ah,
     And be possessed by none of them! no right
     In one, to call your name, inquire your where,
     Or what you think of Mister Some-one's book,
1205 Or Mister Other's marriage, or decease,
     Or how's the headache which you had last week,
     Or why you look so pale still, since it's gone?
     —Such most surprising riddance of one's life
     Comes next one's death; it's disembodiment
1210 Without the pang. I marvel, people choose
     To stand stock-still like fakirs, till the moss
     Grows on them and they cry out, self-admired,
     'How verdant and how virtuous!' Well, I'm glad:
     Or should be, if grown foreign to myself
1215 As surely as to others.
                         Musing so,
     I walked the narrow unrecognising streets,
     Where many a palace-front peers gloomily

Through stony vizors iron-barred, (prepared
Alike, should foe or lover pass that way,
1220 For guest or victim) and came wandering out
Upon the churches with mild open doors
And plaintive wail of vespers, where a few,
Those chiefly women, sprinkled round in blots
Upon the dusky pavement, knelt and prayed
1225 Toward the altar's silver glory. Oft a ray
(I liked to sit and watch) would tremble out,
Just touch some face more lifted, more in need,
Of course a woman's—while I dreamed a tale
To fit its fortunes. There was one who looked
1230 As if the earth had suddenly grown too large
For such a little humpbacked thing as she;
The pitiful black kerchief round her neck
Sole proof she had had a mother. One, again,
Looked sick for love,—seemed praying some soft saint
1235 To put more virtue in the fine new scarf
She spent a fortnight's meals on, yesterday,
That cruel Gigi might return his eyes
From Giuliana. There was one, so old,
So old, to kneel grew easier than to stand,—
1240 So solitary, she accepts at last
Our Lady for her gossip, and frets on
Against the sinful world which goes its rounds
In marrying and being married, just the same
As when 'twas almost good and had the right
1245 (Her Gian alive, and she herself eighteen).
'And yet, now even, if Madonna willed,
She'd win a tern in Thursday's lottery,
And better all things. Did she dream for nought,
That, boiling cabbage for the fast day's soup,
1250 It smelt like blessed entrails? such a dream
For nought? would sweetest Mary cheat her so,
And lose that certain candle, straight and white
As any fair grand-duchess in her teens,
Which otherwise should flare here in a week?
1255 *Benigna sis*, thou beauteous Queen of heaven!'

*

I sate there musing, and imagining
Such utterance from such faces: poor blind souls
That writhed toward heaven along the devil's trail,—
Who knows, I thought, but He may stretch his hand
1260 And pick them up? 'tis written in the Book,
He heareth the young ravens when they cry;
And yet they cry for carrion.—O my God,—
And we, who make excuses for the rest,
We do it in our measure. Then I knelt,
1265 And dropped my head upon the pavement too,
And prayed, since I was foolish in desire
Like other creatures, craving offal-food,
That He would stop his ears to what I said,
And only listen to the run and beat
1270 Of this poor, passionate, helpless blood—
                                        And then
I lay, and spoke not: but He heard in heaven.

So many Tuscan evenings passed the same!
I could not lose a sunset on the bridge,
And would not miss a vigil in the church,
1275 And like to mingle with the out-door crowd
So strange and gay and ignorant of my face,
For men you know not, are as good as trees.
And only once, at the Santissima,
I almost chanced upon a man I knew,
1280 Sir Blaise Delorme. He saw me certainly,
And somewhat hurried, as he crossed himself,
The smoothness of the action,—then half bowed,
But only half, and merely to my shade,
I slipped so quick behind the porphyry plinth,
1285 And left him dubious if 'twas really I,
Or peradventure Satan's usual trick
To keep a mounting saint uncanonised.
But I was safe for that time, and he too;
The argent angels in the altar-flare
1290 Absorbed his soul next moment. The good man!
In England we were scarce acquaintances,
That here in Florence he should keep my thought

Beyond the image on his eye, which came
And went: and yet his thought disturbed my life:
1295 For, after that, I oftener sate at home
On evenings, watching how they fined themselves
With gradual conscience to a perfect night,
Until the moon, diminished to a curve,
Lay out there, like a sickle for His hand
1300 Who cometh down at last to reap the earth.
At such times, ended seemed my trade of verse;
I feared to jingle bells upon my robe
Before the four-faced silent cherubim:
With God so near me, could I sing of God?
1305 I did not write, nor read, nor even think,
But sate absorbed amid the quickening glooms,
Most like some passive broken lump of salt
Dropt in by chance to a bowl of œnomel,
To spoil the drink a little, and lose itself,
1310 Dissolving slowly, slowly, until lost.

Eighth Book

ONE eve it happened, when I sate alone,
Alone, upon the terrace of my tower,
A book upon my knees, to counterfeit
The reading that I never read at all,
5   While Marian, in the garden down below,
Knelt by the fountain (I could just hear thrill
The drowsy silence of the exhausted day)
And peeled a new fig from that purple heap
In the grass beside her,—turning out the red
10   To feed her eager child, who sucked at it
With vehement lips across a gap of air
As he stood opposite, face and curls a-flame
With that last sun-ray, crying, 'give me, give,'
And stamping with imperious baby-feet,
15   (We're all born princes)—something startled me,—
The laugh of sad and innocent souls, that breaks
Abruptly, as if frightened at itself;
'Twas Marian laughed. I saw her glance above
In sudden shame that I should hear her laugh,
20   And straightway dropped my eyes upon my book,
And knew, the first time, 'twas Boccaccio's tales,
The Falcon's,—of the lover who for love
Destroyed the best that loved him. Some of us
Do it still, and then we sit and laugh no more.
25   Laugh *you*, sweet Marian! You've the right to laugh,
Since God Himself is for you, and a child!
For me there's somewhat less,—and so, I sigh.

The heavens were making room to hold the night,
The sevenfold heavens unfolding all their gates
30   To let the stars out slowly (prophesied
In close-approaching advent, not discerned),
While still the cue-owls from the cypresses
Of the Poggio called and counted every pulse
Of the skyey palpitation. Gradually

35   The purple and transparent shadows slow
     Had filled up the whole valley to the brim,
     And flooded all the city, which you saw
     As some drowned city in some enchanted sea,
     Cut off from nature,—drawing you who gaze,
40   With passionate desire, to leap and plunge,
     And find a sea-king with a voice of waves,
     And treacherous soft eyes, and slippery locks
     You cannot kiss but you shall bring away
     Their salt upon your lips. The duomo-bell
45   Strikes ten, as if it struck ten fathoms down,
     So deep; and fifty churches answer it
     The same, with fifty various instances.
     Some gaslights tremble along squares and streets;
     The Pitti's palace-front is drawn in fire;
50   And, past the quays, Maria Novella's Place,
     In which the mystic obelisks stand up
     Triangular, pyramidal, each based
     On a single trine of brazen tortoises,
     To guard that fair church, Buonarroti's Bride,
55   That stares out from her large blind dial-eyes,
     Her quadrant and armillary dials, black
     With rhythms of many suns and moons, in vain
     Enquiry for so rich a soul as his,—
     Methinks I have plunged, I see it all so clear . . .
60   And, O my heart, . . . the sea-king!

                                        In my ears
     The sound of waters. There he stood, my king!

     I felt him, rather than beheld him. Up
     I rose, as if he were my king indeed,
     And then sate down, in trouble at myself,
65   And struggling for my woman's empery.
     'Tis pitiful; but women are so made:
     We'll die for you perhaps,—'tis probable;
     But we'll not spare you an inch of our full height:
     We'll have our whole just stature,—five feet four,

70   Though laid out in our coffins: pitiful!
    —'You, Romney!—Lady Waldemar is here?'

    He answered in a voice which was not his.
    'I have her letter; you shall read it soon:
    But first, I must be heard a little, I,
75   Who have waited long and travelled far for that,
    Although you thought to have shut a tedious book
    And farewell. Ah, you dog-eared such a page,
    And here you find me.'
                Did he touch my hand,
    Or but my sleeve? I trembled, hand and foot,—
80   He must have touched me.—'Will you sit?' I asked,
    And motioned to a chair; but down he sate,
    A little slowly, as a man in doubt,
    Upon the couch beside me,—couch and chair
    Being wheeled upon the terrace.
                      'You are come,
85   My cousin Romney?—this is wonderful.
    But all is wonder on such summer-nights;
    And nothing should surprise us any more,
    Who see that miracle of stars. Behold.'

    I signed above, where all the stars were out,
90   As if an urgent heat had started there
    A secret writing from a sombre page,
    A blank last moment, crowded suddenly
    With hurrying splendours.
                   'Then you do not know'—
    He murmured.
             'Yes, I know,' I said, 'I know.
95   I had the news from Vincent Carrington.
    And yet I did not think you'd leave the work
    In England, for so much even,—though, of course,
    You'll make a work-day of your holiday,
    And turn it to our Tuscan people's use,—
100 Who much need helping since the Austrian boar
    (So bold to cross the Alp by Lombardy
    And dash his brute front unabashed against

The steep snow-bosses of the shield of God
Who soon shall rise in wrath and shake it clear,)
105 Came hither also,—raking up our vines
And olive gardens with his tyrannous tusks,
And rolling on our maize with all his swine.'

'You had the news from Vincent Carrington,'
He echoed,—picking up the phrase beyond,
110 As if he knew the rest was merely talk
To fill a gap and keep out a strong wind,—
'You had, then, Vincent's personal news?'
                                        'His own,'
I answered. 'All that ruined world of yours
Seems crumbling into marriage. Carrington
115 Has chosen wisely.'
                        'Do *you* take it so?'
He cried, 'and is it possible at last' . .
He paused there,—and then, inward to himself,
'Too much at last, too late!—yet certainly' . .
(And there his voice swayed as an Alpine plank
120 That feels a passionate torrent underneath)
'The knowledge, had I known it, first or last,
Had never changed the actual case for *me*.
And best, for *her*, at this time.'
                                Nay, I thought,
He loves Kate Ward, it seems, now, like a man,
125 Because he has married Lady Waldemar!
Ah, Vincent's letter said how Leigh was moved
To hear that Vincent was betrothed to Kate.
With what cracked pitchers go we to deep wells
In this world! Then I spoke,—'I did not think,
130 My cousin, you had ever known Kate Ward.'

'In fact, I never knew her. 'Tis enough
That Vincent did, before he chose his wife
For other reasons than those topaz eyes
I've heard of. Not to undervalue them,
135 For all that. One takes up the world with eyes.'
                        *

—Including Romney Leigh, I thought again,
Albeit he knows them only by repute.
How vile must all men be, since *he*'s a man.

His deep pathetic voice, as if he guessed
140   I did not surely love him, took the word;
'You never got a letter from Lord Howe
A month back, dear Aurora?'

                        'None,' I said.

'I felt it was so,' he replied: 'Yet, strange!
Sir Blaise Delorme has passed through Florence?'
                                   'Ay
145   By chance I saw him in Our Lady's church
(I saw him, mark you, but he saw not me),
Clean-washed in holy water from the count
Of things terrestrial,—letters, and the rest;
He had crossed us out together with his sins.
150   Ay, strange; but only strange that good Lord Howe
Preferred him to the post because of pauls.
For me I'm sworn to never trust a man—
At least with letters.'

                      'There were facts to tell,
To smooth with eye and accent. Howe supposed . .
155   Well, well, no matter! there was dubious need;
You heard the news from Vincent Carrington.
And yet perhaps you had been startled less
To see me, dear Aurora, if you had read
That letter.'
              —Now he sets me down as vexed.
160   I think I've draped myself in woman's pride
To a perfect purpose. Oh, I'm vexed, it seems!
My friend Lord Howe deputes his friend Sir Blaise,
To break as softly as a sparrow's egg
That lets a bird out tenderly, the news
165   Of Romney's marriage to a certain saint;
To *smooth with eye and accent*,—indicate

His possible presence. Excellently well
You've played your part, my Lady Waldemar,—
As I've played mine.
         'Dear Romney,' I began,
170 'You did not use, of old, to be so like
A Greek king coming from a taken Troy,
'Twas needful that precursors spread your path
With three-piled carpets, to receive your foot
And dull the sound of't. For myself, be sure,
175 Although it frankly ground the gravel here,
I still could bear it. Yet I'm sorry, too,
To lose this famous letter, which Sir Blaise
Has twisted to a lighter absently
To fire some holy taper with: Lord Howe
180 Writes letters good for all things but to lose;
And many a flower of London gossipry
Has dropt wherever such a stem broke off,—
Of course I know that, lonely among my vines,
Where nothing's talked of, save the blight again,
185 And no more Chianti! Still the letter's use
As preparation . . . . . Did I start indeed?
Last night I started at a cockchafer,
And shook a half-hour after. Have you learnt
No more of women, 'spite of privilege,
190 Than still to take account too seriously
Of such weak flutterings? Why, we like it, sir,—
We get our powers and our effects that way.
The trees stand stiff and still at time of frost,
If no wind tears them; but, let summer come,
195 When trees are happy,—and a breath avails
To set them trembling through a million leaves
In luxury of emotion. Something less
It takes to move a woman: let her start
And shake at pleasure,—nor conclude at yours,
200 The winter's bitter,—but the summer's green.'

He answered: 'Be the summer ever green
With you, Aurora!—though you sweep your sex
With somewhat bitter gusts from where you live

Above them,—whirling downward from your heights
205 Your very own pine-cones, in a grand disdain
Of the lowland burrs with which you scatter them.
So high and cold to others and yourself,   ·
A little less to Romney, were unjust,
And thus, I would not have you. Let it pass:
210 I feel content so. You can bear indeed
My sudden step beside you: but for me,
'Twould move me sore to hear your softened voice,—
Aurora's voice,—if softened unaware
In pity of what I am.'
                              Ah friend, I thought,
215 As husband of the Lady Waldemar
You're granted very sorely pitiable!
And yet Aurora Leigh must guard her voice
From softening in the pity of your case,
As if from lie or licence. Certainly
220 We'll soak up all the slush and soil of life
With softened voices, ere we come to *you*.

At which I interrupted my own thought
And spoke out calmly. 'Let us ponder, friend,
Whate'er our state we must have made it first;
225 And though the thing displease us, ay, perhaps
Displease us warrantably, never doubt
That other states, though possible once, and then
Rejected by the instinct of our lives,—
If then adopted, had displeased us more
230 Than this, in which the choice, the will, the love,
Has stamped the honour of a patent act
From henceforth. What we choose, may not be good,
But, that we choose it, proves it good for *us*
Potentially, fantastically, now
235 Or last year, rather than a thing we saw,
And saw no need for choosing. Moths will burn
Their wings,—which proves that light is good for moths,
Or else they had flown not, where they agonise.'

*

'Ay, light is good,' he echoed, and there paused.
240 And then abruptly, . . 'Marian. Marian's well?'

I bowed my head but found no word. 'Twas hard
To speak of *her* to Lady Waldemar's
New husband. How much did he know, at last?
How much? how little?—He would take no sign,
245 But straight repeated,—'Marian. Is she well?'

'She's well,' I answered.

                She was there in sight
An hour back, but the night had drawn her home;,
Where still I heard her in an upper room,
Her low voice singing to the child in bed,
250 Who restless with the summer-heat and play
And slumber snatched at noon, was long sometimes
At falling off, and took a score of songs
And mother-hushes, ere saw she him sound.

'She's well,' I answered.

               'Here?' he asked.

                        'Yes, here.'

255 He stopped and sighed. 'That shall be presently,
But now this must be. I have words to say,
And would be alone to say them, I with you,
And no third troubling.'

               'Speak, then,' I returned,
'She will not vex you.'

               At which, suddenly
260 He turned his face upon me with its smile
As if to crush me. 'I have read your book,
Aurora.'
        'You have read it,' I replied,
'And I have writ it,—we have done with it.

And now the rest?'
　　　　　　　'The rest is like the first,'
265　He answered,—'for the book is in my heart,
　　Lives in me, wakes in me, and dreams in me:
　　My daily bread tastes of it,—and my wine
　　Which has no smack of it, I pour it out,
　　It seems unnatural drinking.'
　　　　　　　　　　　Bitterly
270　I took the word up; 'Never waste your wine.
　　The book lived in me ere it lived in you;
　　I know it closer than another does,
　　And that it's foolish, feeble, and afraid,
　　And all unworthy so much compliment.
275　Beseech you, keep your wine,—and, when you drink,
　　Still wish some happier fortune to your friend,
　　Than even to have written a far better book.'

　　He answered gently, 'That is consequent:
　　The poet looks beyond the book he has made,
280　Or else he had not made it. If a man
　　Could make a man, he'd henceforth be a god
　　In feeling what a little thing is man:
　　It is not my case. And this special book,
　　I did not make it, to make light of it:
285　It stands above my knowledge, draws me up;
　　'Tis high to me. It may be that the book
　　Is not so high, but I so low, instead;
　　Still high to me. I mean no compliment:
　　I will not say there are not, young or old,
290　Male writers, ay, or female,—let it pass,
　　Who'll write us richer and completer books.
　　A man may love a woman perfectly,
　　And yet by no means ignorantly maintain
　　A thousand women have not larger eyes:
295　Enough that she alone has looked at him
　　With eyes that, large or small, have won his soul.
　　And so, this book, Aurora,—so, your book.'

　　　　　　　　　　　*

'Alas,' I answered, 'is it so indeed?'
And then was silent.

                    'Is it so, indeed.'
300 He echoed, 'that *alas* is all your word.'
    I said,—'I'm thinking of a far-off June,
    When you and I, upon my birthday once,
    Discoursed of life and art, with both untried.
    I'm thinking, Romney, how 'twas morning then,
305 And now 'tis night.'

                    'And now,' he said, ''tis night.'

    'I'm thinking,' I resumed, ''tis somewhat sad,
    That if I had known, that morning in the dew,
    My cousin Romney would have said such words
    On such a night, at close of many years,
310 In speaking of a future book of mine,
    It would have pleased me better as a hope,
    Than as an actual grace it can at all.
    That's sad, I'm thinking.'
                    'Ay,' he said, ''tis night.'

    'And there,' I added lightly, 'are the stars!
315 And here, we'll talk of stars, and not of books.'

    'You have the stars,' he murmured,—'it is well:
    Be like them! shine, Aurora, on my dark,
    Though high and cold and only like a star,
    And for this short night only,—you, who keep
320 The same Aurora of the bright June day
    That withered up the flowers before my face,
    And turned me from the garden evermore
    Because I was not worthy. Oh, deserved,
    Deserved! That I, who verily had not learnt
325 God's lesson half, attaining as a dunce
    To obliterate good words with fractious thumbs
    And cheat myself of the context,—*I* should push
    Aside, with male ferocious impudence,

The world's Aurora who had conned her part
330 On the other side of the leaf! ignore her so,
Because she was a woman and a queen,
And had no beard to bristle through her song,—
My teacher, who has taught me with a book,
My Miriam, whose sweet mouth, when nearly drowned
335 I still heard singing on the shore! Deserved,
That here I should look up into the stars
And miss the glory' . .
                          'Can I understand?'
I broke in. 'You speak wildly, Romney Leigh,
Or I hear wildly. In that morning-time
340 We recollect, the roses were too red,
The trees too green, reproach too natural
If one should see not what the other saw:
And now, it's night, remember; we have shades
In place of colours; we are now grown cold,
345 And old, my cousin Romney. Pardon me,—
I'm very happy that you like my book,
And very sorry that I quoted back
A ten years' birthday; 'twas so mad a thing
In any woman, I scarce marvel much
350 You took it for a venturous piece of spite,
Provoking such excuses, as indeed
I cannot call you slack in.'
                          'Understand,'
He answered sadly, 'something, if but so.
This night is softer than an English day,
355 And men may well come hither when they're sick,
To draw in easier breath from larger air.
'Tis thus with me; I've come to you,—to you,
My Italy of women, just to breathe
My soul out once before you, ere I go,
360 As humble as God makes me at the last,
(I thank Him) quite out of the way of men,
And yours, Aurora,—like a punished child,
His cheeks all blurred with tears and naughtiness,
To silence in a corner. I am come

365 To speak, beloved' . .
                          'Wisely, cousin Leigh,
      And worthily of us both!'
                               'Yes, worthily;
      For this time I must speak out and confess
      That I, so truculent in assumption once,
      So absolute in dogma, proud in aim,
370 And fierce in expectation,—I, who felt
      The whole world tugging at my skirts for help,
      As if no other man than I, could pull,
      Nor woman, but I led her by the hand,
      Nor cloth hold, but I had it in my coat,—
375 Do know myself to-night for what I was
      On that June-day, Aurora. Poor bright day,
      Which meant the best . . a woman and a rose,
      And which I smote upon the cheek with words,
      Until it turned and rent me! Young you were,
380 That birthday, poet, but you talked the right:
      While I, . . I built up follies like a wall
      To intercept the sunshine and your face.
      Your face! that's worse.'
                               'Speak wisely, cousin Leigh.'

      'Yes, wisely, dear Aurora, though too late:
385 But then, not wisely. I was heavy then,
      And stupid, and distracted with the cries
      Of tortured prisoners in the polished brass
      Of that Phalarian bull, society,—
      Which seems to bellow bravely like ten bulls,
390 But, if you listen, moans and cries instead
      Despairingly, like victims tossed and gored
      And trampled by their hoofs. I heard the cries
      Too close: I could not hear the angels lift
      A fold of rustling air, nor what they said
395 To help my pity. I beheld the world
      As one great famishing carniverous mouth,—
      A huge, deserted, callow, black, bird Thing,
      With piteous open beak that hurt my heart,
      Till down upon the filthy ground I dropped,

400 And tore the violets up to get the worms.
Worms, worms, was all my cry: an open mouth,
A gross want, bread to fill it to the lips,
No more! That poor men narrowed their demands
To such an end, was virtue, I supposed,
405 Adjudicating that to see it so
Was reason. Oh, I did not push the case
Up higher, and ponder how it answers, when
The rich take up the same cry for themselves,
Professing equally,—'an open mouth,
410 A gross want, food to fill us, and no more!'
Why that's so far from virtue, only vice
Finds reason for it! That makes libertines:
And slurs our cruel streets from end to end
With eighty thousand women in one smile,
415 Who only smile at night beneath the gas:
The body's satisfaction and no more,
Being used for argument against the soul's,
Here too! the want, here too, implying the right.
—How dark I stood that morning in the sun,
420 My best Aurora, though I saw your eyes,—
When first you told me . . oh, I recollect
The words . . and how you lifted your white hand,
And how your white dress and your burnished curls
Went greatening round you in the still blue air,
425 As if an inspiration from within
Had blown them all out when you spoke the words,
Even these,—'You will not compass your poor ends
'Of barley-feeding and material ease,
'Without the poet's individualism
430 'To work your universal. It takes a soul,
'To move a body,—it takes a high-souled man,
'To move the masses . . even to a cleaner stye:
'It takes the ideal, to blow an inch inside
'The dust of the actual: and your Fouriers failed,
435 'Because not poets enough to understand
'That life develops from within.' I say
Your words,—I could say other words of yours;
For none of all your words has been more lost

Than sweet verbena, which, being brushed against,
440 Will hold you three hours after by the smell,
In spite of long walks on the windy hills.
But these words dealt in sharper perfume,—these
Were ever on me, stinging through my dreams,
And saying themselves for ever o'er my acts
445 Like some unhappy verdict. That I failed,
Is certain. Stye or no stye, to contrive
The swine's propulsion toward the precipice,
Proved easy and plain. I subtly organised
And ordered, built the cards up high and higher,
450 Till, some one breathing, all fell flat again;
In setting right society's wide wrong,
Mere life's so fatal. So I failed indeed
Once, twice, and oftener,—hearing through the rents
Of obstinate purpose, still those words of yours,
455 'You will not compass your poor ends, not you!'
But harder than you said them; every time
Still farther from your voice, until they came
To overcrow me with triumphant scorn
Which vexed me to resistance. Set down this
460 For condemnation,—I was guilty here:
I stood upon my deed and fought my doubt,
As men will,—for I doubted,—till at last
My deed gave way beneath me suddenly,
And left me what I am.—The curtain dropped,
465 My part quite ended, all the footlights quenched,
My own soul hissing at me through the dark,
I, ready for confession,—I was wrong,
I've sorely failed; I've slipped the ends of life,
I yield, you have conquered.'
                              'Stay,' I answered him;
470 'I've something for your hearing, also. I
Have failed too.'
                    'You!' he said, 'you're very great;
The sadness of your greatness fits you well:
As if the plume upon a hero's casque
Should nod a shadow upon his victor face.'

*

475   I took him up austerely,—'You have read
      My book, but not my heart; for recollect,
      'Tis writ in Sanscrit, which you bungle at.
      I've surely failed, I know; if failure means
      To look back sadly on work gladly done,—

480   To wander on my mountains of Delight,
      So called, (I can remember a friend's words
      As well as you, sir,) weary and in want
      Of even a sheep-path, thinking bitterly . .
      Well, well! no matter. I but say so much,

485   To keep you, Romney Leigh, from saying more,
      And let you feel I am not so high indeed,
      That I can bear to have you at my foot,—
      Or safe, that I can help you. That June-day,
      Too deeply sunk in craterous sunsets now

490   For you or me to dig it up alive;
      To pluck it out all bleeding with spent flame
      At the roots, before those moralising stars
      We have got instead,—that poor lost day, you said
      Some words as truthful as the thing of mine

495   You cared to keep in memory; and I hold
      If I, that day, and, being the girl I was,
      Had shown a gentler spirit, less arrogance,
      It had not hurt me. Ah, you'll not mistake
      The point here. I but only think, you see,

500   More justly, that's more humbly, of myself,
      Than when I tried a crown on and supposed . . .
      Nay, laugh, sir,—I'll laugh with you!—pray you, laugh,
      I've had so many birthdays since that day,
      I've learnt to prize mirth's opportunities,

505   Which come too seldom. Was it you who said
      I was not changed! the same Aurora? Ah,
      We could laugh there, too! Why, Ulysses' dog
      Knew *him*, and wagged his tail and died: but if
      I had owned a dog, I too, before my Troy,

510   And, if you brought him here, . . I warrant you
      He'd look into my face, bark lustily,
      And live on stoutly, as the creatures will
      Whose spirits are not troubled by long loves.

A dog would never know me, I'm so changed;
515 Much less a friend . . except that you're misled
By the colour of the hair, the trick of the voice,
Like that Aurora Leigh's.'

       'Sweet trick of voice!
I would be a dog for this, to know it at last,
And die upon the falls of it. O love,
520 O best Aurora! are you then so sad
You scarcely had been sadder as my wife?'

'Your wife, sir! I must certainly be changed,
If I, Aurora, can have said a thing
So light, it catches at the knightly spurs
525 Of a noble gentleman like Romney Leigh,
And trips him from his honourable sense
Of what befits' . .

     'You wholly misconceive,'
He answered.

    I returned,—'I'm glad of it;
But keep from misconception, too, yourself:
530 I am not humbled to so low a point,
Nor so far saddened. If I am sad at all,
Ten layers of birthdays on a woman's head,
Are apt to fossilise her girlish mirth,
Though ne'er so merry: I'm perforce more wise,
535 And that, in truth, means sadder. For the rest,
Look here, sir: I was right upon the whole,
That birthday morning. 'Tis impossible
To get at men excepting through their souls,
However open their carniverous jaws;
540 And poets get directlier at the soul,
Than any of your œconomists:—for which,
You must not overlook the poet's work
When scheming for the world's necessities.
The soul's the way. Not even . . Christ Himself
545 Can save man else than as He holds man's soul;
And therefore did He come into our flesh,
As some wise hunter creeping on his knees,
With a torch, into the blackness of a cave,

To face and quell the beast there,—take the soul,
550 And so possess the whole man, body and soul.
I said, so far, right, yes; not farther, though:
We both were wrong that June-day,—both as wrong
As an east wind had been. I who talked of art,
And you who grieved for all men's griefs . . what then?
555 We surely made too small a part for God
In these things. What we are, imports us more
Than what we eat; and life, you've granted me,
Develops from within. But innermost
Of the inmost, most interior of the interne,
560 God claims His own, Divine humanity
Renewing nature,—of the piercingest verse,
Prest in by subtlest poet, still must keep
As much upon the outside of a man,
As the very bowl, in which he dips his beard.
565 —And then, . . the rest. I cannot surely speak.
Perhaps I doubt more than you doubted then,
If I, the poet's veritable charge,
Have borne upon my forehead. If I have,
It might feel somewhat liker to a crown,
570 The foolish green one even.—Ah, I think,
And chiefly when the sun shines, that I've failed.
But what then, Romney? Though we fail indeed,
You . . I . . a score of such weak workers, . . He
Fails never. If He cannot work by us,
575 He will work over us. Does He want a man,
Much less a woman, think you? Every time
The star winks there, so many souls are born,
Who all shall work too. Let our own be calm:
We should be ashamed to sit beneath those stars,
580 Impatient that we're nothing.'

                              'Could we sit
Just so, for ever, sweetest friend,' he said,
'My failure would seem better than success.
And yet, indeed, your book has dealt with me
More gently, cousin, than you ever will!
585 You book brought down entire the bright June-day,
And set me wandering in the garden-walks,

And let me watch the garland in a place,
You blushed so . . nay, forgive me; do not stir:
I only thank the book for what it taught,
590 And what, permitted. Poet, doubt yourself,
But never doubt that you're a poet to me
From henceforth. You have written poems, sweet,
Which moved me in secret, as the sap is moved
In still March-branches, signless as a stone:
595 But this last book o'ercame me like soft rain
Which falls at midnight, when the tightened bark
Breaks out into unhesitating buds
And sudden protestations of the spring.
In all your other books, I saw but *you*:
600 A man may see the moon so, in a pond,
And not be nearer therefore to the moon,
Nor use the sight . . except to drown himself:
And so I forced my heart back from the sight;
For what had *I*, I thought, to do with *her*,—
605 Aurora . . Romney? But, in this last book,
You showed me something separate from yourself,
Beyond you; and I bore to take it in,
And let it draw me. You have shown me truths,
O June-day friend, that help me now at night,
610 When June is over! truths not yours, indeed,
But set within my reach by means of you:
Presented by your voice and verse the way
To take them clearest. Verily I was wrong;
And verily, many thinkers of this age,
615 Ay, many Christian teachers, half in heaven,
Are wrong in just my sense, who understood
Our natural world too insularly, as if
No spiritual counterpart completed it
Consummating its meaning, rounding all
620 To justice and perfection, line by line,
Form by form, nothing single, nor alone,—
The great below clenching by the great above;
Shade here authenticating substance there;
The body proving spirit, as the effect
625 The cause: we, meantime, being too grossly apt

To hold the natural, as dogs a bone,
(Though reason and nature beat us in the face);
So obstinately, that we'll break our teeth
Or ever we let go. For everywhere
630 We're too materialistic,—eating clay,
(Like men of the west) instead of Adam's corn
And Noah's wine; clay by handfuls, clay by lumps,
Until we're filled up to the throat with clay,
And grow the grimy colour of the ground
635 On which we are feeding. Ay, materialist
The age's name is. God himself, with some,
Is apprehended as the bare result
Of what his hand materially has made,
Expressed in such an algebraic sign,
640 Called God;—that is, to put it otherwise,
They add up nature to a naught of God
And cross the quotient. There are many, even,
Whose names are written in the Christian church
To no dishonour,—diet still on mud
645 And splash the altars with it. You might think
The clay, Christ laid upon their eyelids when,
Still blind, he called them to the use of sight,
Remained there to retard its exercise
With clogging incrustations. Close to heaven,
650 They see, for mysteries, through the open doors,
Vague puffs of smoke from pots of earthernware;
And fain would enter, when their time shall come,
With quite a different body than Saint Paul
Has promised,—husk and chaff, the whole barley-corn
655 Or where's the resurrection?'
                                        'Thus it is,'
I sighed. And he resumed with mournful face,
'Beginning so, and filling up with clay
The wards of this great key, the natural world,
And fumbling vainly therefore at the lock
660 Of the spiritual,—we feel ourselves shut in
With all the wild-beast roar of struggling life,
The terrors and compunctions of our souls,
As saints with lions,—we who are not saints,

And have no heavenly lordship in our stare
665 To awe them backward! Ay, we are forced, so pent,
To judge the whole too partially, . . confound
Conclusions. Is there any common phrase
Significant, with the adverb's heard alone,
The verb being absent, and the pronoun out?
670 But we, distracted in the roar of life,
Still insolently at God's adverb snatch,
And bruit against Him that his thought is void,
His meaning hopeless;—cry, that everywhere
The government is slipping from his hand,
675 Unless some other Christ . . say Romney Leigh . .
Come up and toil and moil, and change the world,
Because the First has proved inadequate,
However we talk bigly of His work
And piously of His person. We blaspheme
680 At last, to finish that doxology,
Despairing on the earth for which He died.'

'So now,' I asked, 'you have more hope of men?'

'I hope,' he answered. 'I am come to think
That God will have His work done, as you said,
685 And that we need not be disturbed too much
For Romney Leigh or others having failed
With this or that quack nostrum,—recipes
For keeping summits by annulling depths,
For learning wrestling with long lounging sleeves,
690 And perfect heroism without a scratch.
We fail,—what then? Aurora, if I smiled
To see you, in your lovely morning-pride,
Try on the poet's wreath which suits the noon,—
(Sweet cousin, walls must get the weather stain
695 Before they grow the ivy!) certainly
I stood myself there worthier of contempt,
Self-rated, in disastrous arrogance,
As competent to sorrow for mankind
And even their odds. A man may well despair,
700 Who counts himself so needful to success.

I failed. I throw the remedy back on God,
And sit down here beside you, in good hope.'

'And yet, take heed,' I answered, 'lest we lean
Too dangerously on the other side,
705 And so fail twice. Be sure, no earnest work
Of any honest creature, howbeit weak,
Imperfect, ill-adapted, fails so much,
It is not gathered as a grain of sand
To enlarge the sum of human action used
710 For carrying out God's end. No creature works
So ill, observe, that therefore he's cashiered.
The honest earnest man must stand and work;
The woman also; otherwise she drops
At once below the dignity of man,
715 Accepting serfdom. Free men freely work.
Whoever fears God, fears to sit at ease.'

He cried: 'True. After Adam, work was curse;
The natural creature labours, sweats and frets.
But, after Christ, work turns to privilege;
720 And henceforth one with our humanity,
The Six-day Worker, working still in us
Has called us freely to work on with Him
In high companionship. So, happiest!
I count that Heaven itself is only work
725 To a surer issue. Let us work, indeed,—
But, no more, work as Adam . . nor as Leigh
Erewhile, as if the only man on earth,
Responsible for all the thistles blown
And tigers couchant,—struggling in amaze
730 Against disease and winter,—snarling on
For ever, that the world's not paradise.
O cousin, let us be content, in work,
To do the thing we can, and not presume
To fret because it's little. 'Twill employ
735 Seven men, they say, to make a perfect pin:
Who makes the head, content to miss the point,—
Who makes the point, agreed to leave the join:

　　　　And if a man should cry, 'I want a pin,
　　　　'And I must make it straightway, head and point,'—
740　　His wisdom is not worth the pin he wants.
　　　　Seven men to a pin,—and not a man too much!
　　　　Seven generations, haply, to this world,
　　　　To right it visibly, a finger's breadth,
　　　　And mend its rents a little. Oh, to storm
745　　And say 'This world here is intolerable;
　　　　'I will not eat this corn, nor drink this wine,
　　　　'Nor love this woman, flinging her my soul
　　　　'Without a bond for't, as a lover should,
　　　　'Nor use the generous leave of happiness
750　　'As not too good for using generously'—
　　　　(Since virtue kindles at the touch of joy,
　　　　Like a man's cheek laid on a woman's hand;
　　　　And God, who knows it, looks for quick returns
　　　　From joys)!—to stand and claim to have a life
755　　Beyond the bounds of the individual man,
　　　　And raze all personal cloisters of the soul
　　　　To build up public stores and magazines,
　　　　As if God's creatures otherwise were lost,
　　　　The builder surely saved by any means!
760　　To think,—I have a pattern on my nail,
　　　　And I will carve the world new after it
　　　　And solve so, these hard social questions,—nay,
　　　　Impossible social questions,—since their roots
　　　　Strike deep in Evil's own existence here,
765　　Which God permits because the question's hard
　　　　To abolish evil nor attaint free-will.
　　　　Ay, hard to God, but not to Romney Leigh!
　　　　For Romney has a pattern on his nail,
　　　　(Whatever might be lacking on the Mount)
770　　And not being over nice to separate
　　　　What's element from what's convention, hastes
　　　　By line on line to draw you out a world,
　　　　Without your help indeed, unless you take
　　　　His yoke upon you, and will learn of him,—
775　　So much he has to teach! so good a world!
　　　　The same, the whole creation's groaning for!

No rich nor poor, no gain nor loss nor stint;
No pottage in it able to exclude
A brother's birthright, and no right of birth,
780 The pottage—both secured to every man;
And perfect virtue dealt out like the rest,
Gratuitously, with the soup at six,
To whoso does not seek it.'
                  'Softly, sir,'
I interrupted,—'I had a cousin once
785 I held in reverence. If he strained too wide,
It was not to take honour, but give help;
The gesture was heroic. If his hand
Accomplished nothing . . (well, it is not proved)
That empty hand thrown impotently out
790 Were sooner caught, I think, by One in heaven,
Than many a hand that reaped a harvest in
And keeps the scythe's glow on it. Pray you, then,
For my sake merely, use less bitterness
In speaking of my cousin.'
                  'Ah,' he said,
795 'Aurora! when the prophet beats the ass,
The angel intercedes.' He shook his head—
'And yet to mean so well, and fail so foul,
Expresses ne'er another beast than man;
The antithesis is human. Harken, dear;
800 There's too much abstract willing, purposing,
In this poor world. We talk by aggregates,
And think by systems; and, being used to face
Our evils in statistics, are inclined
To cap them with unreal remedies
805 Drawn out in haste on the other side the slate.'

'That's true,' I answered, fain to throw up thought
And make a game of 't; 'Oh, we generalise
Enough to please you. If we pray at all,
We pray no longer for our daily bread,
810 But next centenary's harvests. If we give,
Our cup of water is not tendered till
We lay down pipes and found a Company

With Branches. Ass or angel, 'tis the same:
A woman cannot do the thing she ought,
815 Which means whatever perfect thing she can,
In life, in art, in science, but she fears
To let the perfect action take her part
And rest there: she must prove what she can do
Before she does it,—prate of woman's rights,
820 Of woman's mission, woman's function, till
The men (who are prating, too, on their side) cry,
'A woman's function plainly is . . to talk.'
Poor souls, they are very reasonable vexed!
They cannot hear each other speak.'

                'And you,
825 An artist, judge so?'

                'I, an artist,—yes,
Because, precisely, I'm an artist, sir,
And woman,—if another sate in sight,
I'd whisper,—Soft, my sister! not a word!
By speaking we prove only we can speak;
830 Which he, the man here, never doubted. What
He doubts, is whether we can *do* the thing
With decent grace, we've not yet done at all:
Now, do it; bring your statue,—you have room!
He'll see it even by the starlight here;
835 And if 'tis e'er so little like the god
Who looks out from the marble silently
Along the track of his own shining dart
Through the dusk of ages,—there's no need to speak;
The universe shall henceforth speak for you,
840 And witness, 'She who did this thing, was born
To do it,—claims her license in her work.'
—And so with more works. Whoso cures the plague,
Though twice a woman, shall be called a leech:
Who rights a land's finances, is excused
845 For touching coppers, though her hands be white,—
But we, we talk!'

             'It's the age's mood,'
He said; 'we boast, and do not. We put up
Hostelry signs where'er we lodge a day,—

Some red colossal cow, with mighty paps
850 A Cyclops' fingers could not strain to milk;
Then bring out presently our saucer-full
Of curds. We want more quiet in our works,
More knowledge of the bounds in which we work;
More knowledge that each individual man
855 Remains an Adam to the general race,
Constrained to see, like Adam, that he keep
His personal state's condition honestly,
Or vain all thoughts of his to help the world,
Which still must be developed from its *one*
860 If bettered in its many. We, indeed,
Who think to lay it out new like a park,
We take a work on us which is not man's;
For God alone sits far enough above,
To speculate so largely. None of us
865 (Not Romney Leigh) is mad enough to say,
We'll have a grove of oaks upon that slope
And sink the need of acorns. Government,
If veritable and lawful, is not given
By imposition of the foreign hand,—
870 Nor chosen from a pretty pattern-book
Of some domestic idealogue, who sits
And coldly chooses empire, where as well
He might republic. Genuine government
Is but the expression of a nation, good
875 Or less good,—even as all society,
Howe'er unequal, monstrous, crazed, and cursed,
Is but the expression of men's single lives,
The loud sum of the silent units. What,
We'd change the aggregate and yet retain
880 Each separate figure? Whom do we cheat by that?
Now, not even Romney?'
                            'Cousin, you are sad.
Did all your social labour at Leigh Hall,
And elsewhere, come to nought then?'
                                        'It *was* nought,'
He answered mildly. 'There is room indeed,
885 For statues still, in this large world of God's,

But not for vacuums,—so I am not sad:
Not sadder than is good for what I am.
My vain phalanstery dissolved itself;
My men and women of disordered lives,
890   I brought in orderly to dine and sleep,
Broke up those waxen masks I made them wear,
With fierce contortions of the natural face;
And cursed me for my tyrannous constraint
In forcing crooked creatures to live straight;
895   And set the country hounds upon my back
To bite and tear me for my wicked deed
Of trying to do good without the church
Or even the squires, Aurora. Do you mind
Your ancient neighbours? The great book-club teems
900   With 'sketches,' 'summaries,' and 'last tracts' but twelve,
On socialistic troublers of close bonds
Betwixt the generous rich and grateful poor.
The vicar preached from 'Revelations,' (till
The doctor woke), and found me with 'the frogs'
905   On three successive Sundays; ay, and stopped
To weep a little (for he's getting old)
That such perdition should o'ertake a man
Of such fair acres,—in the parish, too!
He printed his discourses 'by request;'
910   And if your book shall sell as his did, then
Your verses are less good than I suppose.
The women of the neighbourhood subscribed
And sent me a copy, bound in scarlet silk,
Tooled edges, blazoned with the arms of Leigh:
915   I own that touched me.'
                'What, the pretty ones?
Poor Romney!'
            'Otherwise the effect was small.
I had my windows broken once or twice
By liberal peasants, naturally incensed
At such a vexer of Arcadian peace,
920   Who would not let men call their wives their own
To kick like Britons,—and made obstacles
When things went smoothly as a baby drugged,

Toward freedom and starvation; bringing down
The wicked London tavern-thieves and drabs,
925 To affront the blessed hillside drabs and thieves
With mended morals, quotha—fine new lives!—
My windows paid for't. I was shot at, once,
By an active poacher who had hit a hare
From the other barrel, tired of springeing game
930 So long upon my acres, undisturbed,
And restless for the country's virtue, (yet
He missed me)—ay, and pelted very oft
In riding through the village. 'There he goes
'Who'd drive away our Christian gentlefolk,
935 'To catch us undefended in the trap
'He baits with poisonous cheese, and lock us up
'In that pernicious prison of Leigh Hall
'With all his murderers! Give another name
'And say Leigh Hell, and burn it up with fire.'
940 And so they did, at last, Aurora.'
                                        'Did?'

'You never heard it, cousin? Vincent's news
Came stinted, then.'
                        'They did? they burnt Leigh Hall.'

'You're sorry, dear Aurora? Yes indeed,
They did it perfectly: a thorough work,
945 And not a failure, this time. Let us grant
'Tis somewhat easier, though, to burn a house
Than build a system:—yet that's easy, too,
In a dream. Books, pictures,—ay, the pictures! what,
You think your dear Vandykes would give them pause?
950 Our proud ancestral Leighs with those peaked beards,
Or bosoms white as foam thrown up on rocks
From the old-spent wave. Such calm defiant looks
They flared up with! now, nevermore they'll twit
The bones in the family-vault with ugly death.
955 Not one was rescued, save the Lady Maud,
Who threw you down, the morning you were born,
The undeniable lineal mouth and chin,

To wear for ever for her gracious sake;
For which good deed I saved her: the rest went:
960 And you, you're sorry, cousin. Well, for me,
With all my phalansterians safely out,
(Poor hearts, they helped the burners, it was said,
And certainly a few clapped hands and yelled),
The ruin did not hurt me as it might,—
965 As when for instance I was hurt one day
A certain letter being destroyed. In fact,
To see the great house flare so . . oaken floors
Our fathers made so fine with rushes once
Before our mothers furbished them with trains,—
970 Carved wainscots, panelled walls, the favourite slide
For draining off a martyr, (or a rogue)
The echoing galleries, half a half-mile long,
And all the various stairs that took you up
And took you down, and took you round about
975 Upon their slippery darkness, recollect,
All helping to keep up one blazing jest;
The flames through all the casements pushing forth,
Like red-hot devils crinkled into snakes,
All signifying,—'Look you, Romney Leigh,
980 'We save the people from your saving, here,
'Yet so as by fire! we make a pretty show
'Besides—and that's the best you've ever done.'—
—To see this, almost moved myself to clap!
The 'vale et plaude' came, too, with effect
985 When, in the roof fell, and the fire, that paused,
Stunned momently beneath the stroke of slates
And tumbling rafters, rose at once and roared,
And wrapping the whole house, (which disappeared
In a mounting whirlwind of dilated flame,)
990 Blew upward, straight, its drift of fiery chaff
In the face of Heaven, . . which blenched, and ran up higher.

'Poor Romney!'
                    'Sometimes when I dream,' he said,
'I hear the silence after; 'twas so still.
For all those wild beasts, yelling, cursing round,

995   Were suddenly silent, while you counted five!
       So silent, that you heard a young bird fall
       From the top nest in the neighbouring rookery,
       Through edging over-rashly toward the light.
       The old rooks had already fled too far,
1000   To hear the screech they fled with, though you saw
       Some flying on still, like scatterings of dead leaves
       In autumn-gusts, seen dark against the sky:
       All flying,—ousted, like the House of Leigh.'

       'Dear Romney!'
                        'Evidently 'twould have been
1005   A fine sight for a poet, sweet, like you,
       To make the verse blaze after. I myself,
       Even I, felt something in the grand old trees,
       Which stood that moment like brute Druid gods
       Amazed upon the rim of ruin, where,
1010   As into a blackened socket, the great fire
       Had dropped,—still throwing up splinters now and then,
       To show them grey with all their centuries,
       Left there to witness that on such a day
       The house went out.'
                            'Ah!'
                                  'While you counted five,
1015   I seemed to feel a little like a Leigh,—
       But then it passed, Aurora. A child cried;
       And I had enough to think of what to do
       With all those houseless wretches in the dark,
       And ponder where they'd dance the next time, they
1020   Who had burnt the viol.'
                                'Did you think of that?
       Who burns his viol will not dance, I know.
       To cymbals, Romney.'
                             'O my sweet, sad voice!'
       He cried,—'O voice that speaks and overcomes!
       The sun is silent, but Aurora speaks.'

1025   'Alas,' I said; 'I speak I know not what:
       I'm back in childhood, thinking as a child,

A foolish fancy—will it make you smile?
I shall not from the window of my room
Catch sight of those old chimneys any more.'

1030 'No more,' he answered. 'If you pushed one day
Through all the green hills to our father's house,
You'd come upon a great charred circle where
The patient earth was singed an acre round;
With one stone-stair, symbolic of my life,
1035 Ascending, winding, leading up to nought!
'Tis worth a poet's seeing. Will you go?'

I made no answer. Had I any right
To weep with this man, that I dared to speak?
A woman stood between his soul and mine,
1040 And waved us off from touching evermore
With those unclean white hands of hers. Enough.
We had burnt our viols, and were silent.
        So,
The silence lengthened till it pressed. I spoke,
To breathe: 'I think you were ill afterward.'

1045 'More ill,' he answered, 'had been scarcely ill.
I hoped this feeble fumbling at life's knot
Might end concisely,—but I failed to die,
As formerly I failed to live,—and thus
Grew willing, having tried all other ways,
1050 To try just God's. Humility's so good,
When pride's impossible. Mark us, how we make
Our virtues, cousin, from our worn-out sins,
Which smack of them from henceforth. Is it right,
For instance, to wed here, while you love there?
1055 And yet because a man sins once, the sin
Cleaves to him, in necessity to sin;
That if he sin not *so*, to damn himself,
He sins *so*, to damn others with himself:
And thus, to wed here, loving there, becomes
1060 A duty. Virtue buds a dubious leaf
Round mortal brows; your ivy's better, dear.

 —Yet she, 'tis certain, is my very wife;
 The very lamb left mangled by the wolves
 Through my own bad shepherding: and could I choose
1065 But take her on my shoulder past this stretch
 Of rough, uneasy wilderness, poor lamb,
 Poor child, poor child?—Aurora, my belov'd,
 I will not vex you any more to-night;
 But, having spoken what I came to say,
1070 The rest shall please you. What she can, in me,—
 Protection, tender liking, freedom, ease,
 She shall have surely, liberally, for her
 And hers, Aurora. Small amends they'll make
 For hideous evils (which she had not known
1075 Except by me) and for this imminent loss,
 This forfeit presence of a gracious friend,
 Which also she must forfeit for my sake,
 Since, ... drop your hand in mine a moment, sweet,
 We're parting!—Ah, my snowdrop, what a touch,
1080 As if the wind had swept it off! you grudge
 Your gelid sweetness on my palm but so,
 A moment? Angry, that I could not bear
 You . . speaking, breathing, living, side by side
 With some one called my wife . . and live, myself?
1085 Nay, be not cruel—you must understand!
 Your lightest footstep on a floor of mine
 Would shake the house, my lintel being uncrossed
 'Gainst angels: henceforth it is night with me,
 And so, henceforth, I put the shutters up:
1090 Auroras must not come to spoil my dark.'

 He smiled so feebly, with an empty hand
 Stretched sideway from me—as indeed he looked
 To any one but me to give him help;—
 And, while the moon came suddenly out full,
1095 The double-rose of our Italian moons,
 Sufficient, plainly, for the heaven and earth,
 (The stars, struck dumb and washed away in dews
 Of golden glory, and the mountains steeped
 In divine languor) he, the man, appeared

1100   So pale and patient, like the marble man
        A sculptor put his personal sadness in
        To join his grandeur of ideal thought,—
        As if his mallet struck me from my height
        Of passionate indignation, I who had risen
1105   Pale,—doubting paused, . . . Was Romney mad indeed?
        Had all this wrong of heart made sick the brain?

        Then quiet, with a sort of tremulous pride,
        'Go, cousin,' I said coldly. 'A farewell
        Was sooner spoken 'twixt a pair of friends
1110   In those old days, than seems to suit you now:
        And if, since then, I've writ a book or two,
        I'm somewhat dull still in the manly art
        Of phrase and metaphrase. Why, any man
        Can carve a score of white Loves out of snow,
1115   As Buonarroti down in Florence there,
        And set them on the wall in some safe shade,
        As safe, sir, as your marriage! very good;
        Though if a woman took one from the ledge
        To put it on the table by her flowers,
1120   And let it mind her of a certain friend,
        'Twould drop at once, (so better) would not bear
        Her nail-mark even, where she took it up
        A little tenderly;—so best, I say:
        For me, I would not touch so light a thing,
1125   And risk to spoil it half an hour before
        The sun shall shine to melt it: leave it there.
        I'm plain at speech, direct in purpose: when
        I speak, you'll take the meaning as it is,
        And not allow for puckerings in the silks
1130   By clever stitches. I'm a woman, sir,
        I use the woman's figures naturally,
        As you the male license. So, I wish you well.
        I'm simply sorry for the griefs you've had—
        And not for your sake only, but mankind's.
1135   This race is never grateful: from the first,
        One fills their cup at supper with pure wine,
        Which back they give at cross-time on a sponge

In bitter vinegar.'
     'If gratefuller,'
He murmured,—'by so much less pitiable!
1140 God's self would never have come down to die,
Could man have thanked him for it.'
        'Happily
'Tis patent that, whatever,' I resumed,
'You suffered from this thanklessness of men,
You sink no more than Moses' bulrush-boat
1145 When once relieved of Moses; for you're light,
You're light, my cousin! which is well for you,
And manly. For myself,—now mark me, sir,
They burnt Leigh Hall; but if, consummated
To devils, heightened beyond Lucifers,
1150 They had burnt instead a star or two, of those
We saw above there just a moment back,
Before the moon abolished them,—destroyed
And riddled them in ashes through a sieve
On the head of the foundering universe,—what then?
1155 If you and I remained still you and I,
It could not shift our places as mere friends,
Nor render decent you should toss a phrase
Beyond the point of actual feeling!—nay,
You shall not interrupt me: as you said,
1160 We're parting. Certainly, not once or twice,
To-night you've mocked me somewhat, or yourself;
And I, at least, have not deserved it so
That I should meet it unsurprised. But now,
Enough: we're parting . . parting. Cousin Leigh,
1165 I wish you well through all the acts of life
And life's relations, wedlock, not the least;
And it shall 'please me,' in your words, to know
You yield your wife, protection, freedom, ease,
And very tender liking. May you live
1170 So happy with her, Romney, that your friends
Shall praise her for it! Meantime, some of us
Are wholly dull in keeping ignorant
Of what she has suffered by you, and what debt
Of sorrow your rich love sits down to pay:

1175 But if 'tis sweet for love to pay its debt,
     'Tis sweeter still for love to give its gift;
     And you, be liberal in the sweeter way,—
     You can, I think. At least, as touches me,
     You owe her, cousin Romney, no amends;
1180 She is not used to hold my gown so fast,
     You need entreat her now to let it go:
     The lady never was a friend of mine,
     Nor capable,—I thought you knew as much,—
     Of losing for your sake so poor a prize
1185 As such a worthless friendship. Be content,
     Good cousin, therefore, both for her and you!
     I'll never spoil your dark, nor dull your noon,
     Nor vex you when you're merry, nor when you rest:
     You shall not need to put a shutter up
1190 To keep out this Aurora,—Ah, your north
     Can make Auroras which vex nobody,
     Scarce known from evenings! also, let me say,
     My larks fly higher than some windows. Right;
     You've read your Leighs. Indeed 'twould shake a house,
1195 If such as I came in with outstretched hand,
     Still warm and thrilling from the clasp of one . .
     Of one we know, . . to acknowledge, palm to palm,
     As mistress there . . the Lady Waldemar.'

     'Now God be with us' . . with a sudden clash
1200 Of voice he interrupted—'what name's that?
     You spoke a name, Aurora.'
                              'Pardon me;
     I would that, Romney, I could name your wife
     Nor wound you, yet be worthy.'
                                   'Are we mad?'
     He echoed—'wife! mine! Lady Waldemar!
1205 I think you said my wife.' He sprang to his feet,
     And threw his noble head back toward the moon
     As one who swims against a stormy sea,
     Then laughed with such a helpless, hopeless scorn,
     I stood and trembled.
                          'May God judge me so,'

1210   He said at last,—'I came convicted here,
        And humbled sorely if not enough. I came,
        Because this woman from her crystal soul
        Had shown me something which a man calls light:
        Because too, formerly, I sinned by her
1215   As, then and ever since, I have, by God,
        Through arrogance of nature,—though I loved . .
        Whom best, I need not say, . . since that is writ
        Too plainly in the book of my misdeeds;
        And thus I came here to abase myself,
1220   And fasten, kneeling, on her regent brows
        A garland which I startled thence one day
        Of her beautiful June-youth. But here again
        I'm baffled!—fail in my abasement as
        My aggrandisement: there's no room left for me,
1225   At any woman's foot, who misconceives
        My nature, purpose, possible actions. What!
        Are you the Aurora who made large my dreams
        To frame your greatness? you conceive so small?
        You stand so less than woman, through being more,
1230   And lose your natural instinct, like a beast,
        Through intellectual culture? since indeed
        I do not think that any common she
        Would dare adopt such fancy-forgeries
        For the legible life-signature of such
1235   As I, with all my blots: with all my blots!
        At last, then, peerless cousin, we are peers—
        At last we're even. Ay, you've left your height;
        And here upon my level we take hands,
        And here I reach you to forgive you, sweet,
1240   And that's a fall, Aurora. Long ago
        You seldom understood me,—but, before,
        I could not blame you. Then, you only seemed
        So high above, you could not see below;
        But now I breathe,—but now I pardon!—nay,
1245   We're parting. Dearest, men have burnt my house,
        Maligned my motives,—but not one, I swear,
        Has wronged my soul as this Aurora has,
        Who called the Lady Waldemar my wife.'

'Not married to her! yet you said' . . .

                    'Again?

1250 Nay, read the lines' (he held a letter out)

'She sent you through me.'

                      By the moonlight there

I tore the meaning out with passionate haste

Much rather than I read it. Thus it ran.

Ninth Book

EVEN thus. I pause to write it out at length,
The letter of the Lady Waldemar.—

'I prayed your cousin Leigh to take you this,
He says he'll do it. After years of love,
5 Or what is called so,—when a woman frets
And fools upon one string of a man's name,
And fingers it for ever till it breaks,—
He may perhaps do for her such a thing,
And she accept it without detriment
10 Although she should not love him any more,
And I, who do not love him, nor love you,
Nor you, Aurora,—choose you shall repent
Your most ungracious letter, and confess,
Constrained by his convictions, (he's convinced)
15 You've wronged me foully. Are you made so ill,
You woman,—to impute such ill to *me?*
We both had mothers,—lay in their bosom once.
Why, after all, I thank you, Aurora Leigh,
For proving to myself that there are things
20 I would not do, . . not for my life . . nor him . .
Though something I have somewhat overdone,—
For instance, when I went to see the gods
One morning on Olympus, with a step
That shook the thunder from a certain cloud,
25 Committing myself vilely. Could I think,
The Muse I pulled my heart out from my breast
To soften, had herself a sort of heart,
And loved my mortal? He, at least, loved her;
I heard him say so; 'twas my recompense,
30 When, watching at his bedside fourteen days,
He broke out ever like a flame at whiles
Between the heats of fever . . . 'Is it thou?
'Breathe closer, sweetest mouth!' and when at last
The fever gone, the wasted face extinct

35   As if it irked him much to know me there,
He said ''Twas kind, 'twas good, 'twas womanly,'
(And fifty praises to excuse one love)
'But was the picture safe he had ventured for?'
And then, half wandering . . 'I have loved her well,
40   'Although she could not love me.'—'Say instead,'
I answered, 'that she loves you.'—'Twas my turn
To rave: (I would have married him so changed,
Although the world had jeered me properly
For taking up with Cupid at his worst,
45   The silver quiver worn off on his hair.)
'No, no,' he murmured; 'no, she loves me not;
'Aurora Leigh does better: bring her book
'And read it softly, Lady Waldemar,
'Until I thank your friendship more for that,
50   'Than even for harder service.' So I read
Your book, Aurora, for an hour, that day:
I kept its pauses, marked its emphasis;
My voice, empaled upon rhyme's golden hooks,
Not once would writhe, nor quiver, nor revolt;
55   I read on calmly,—calmly shut it up,
Observing, 'There's some merit in the book.
'And yet the merit in't is thrown away,
'As chances still with women, if we write
'Or write not: we want string to tie our flowers,
60   'So drop them as we walk, which serves to show
'The way we went. Good morning, Mister Leigh;
'You'll find another reader the next time.
'A woman who does better than to love,
'I hate; she will do nothing very well:
65   'Male poets are preferable, tiring less
'And teaching more.' I triumphed o'er you both,
And left him.
          'When I saw him afterward,
I had read your shameful letter, and my heart.
He came with health recovered, strong though pale,
70   Lord Howe and he, a courteous pair of friends,
To say what men dare say to women, when
Their debtors. But I stopped them with a word;

And proved I had never trodden such a road
To carry so much dirt upon my shoe.
75   Then, putting into it something of disdain,
I asked forsooth his pardon, and my own,
For having done no better than to love,
And that not wisely,—though 'twas long ago,
And though 'twas altered perfectly since then.
80   I told him, as I tell you now, Miss Leigh,
And proved, I took some trouble for his sake
(Because I knew he did not love the girl)
To spoil my hands with working in the stream
Of that poor bubbling nature,—till she went,
85   Consigned to one I trusted, my own maid,
Who once had lived full five months in my house,
(Dressed hair superbly) with a lavish purse,
To carry to Australia where she had left
A husband, said she. If the creature lied,
90   The mission failed, we all do fail and lie
More or less—and I'm sorry—which is all
Expected from us when we fail the most,
And go to church to own it. What I meant,
Was just the best for him, and me, and her . .
95   Best even for Marian!—I am sorry for't,
And very sorry. Yet my creature said
She saw her stop to speak in Oxford Street
To one . . no matter! I had sooner cut
My hand off (though 'twere kissed the hour before,
100   And promised a duke's troth-ring for the next)
Than crush her silly head with so much wrong.
Poor child! I would have mended it with gold,
Until it gleamed like St. Sophia's dome
When all the faithful troop to morning prayer:
105   But he, he nipped the bud of such a thought
With that cold Leigh look which I fancied once,
And broke in, 'Henceforth she was called his wife.
'His wife required no succour: he was bound
'To Florence, to resume this broken bond:
110   'Enough so. Both were happy, he and Howe,
'To acquit me of the heaviest charge of all—'

—At which I shot my tongue against my fly
And struck him; 'Would he carry,—he was just,—
'A letter from me to Aurora Leigh,

115   'And ratify from his authentic mouth
'My answer to her accusation?'—'Yes,
'If such a letter were prepared in time.'
—He's just, your cousin,—ay, abhorrently.
He'd wash his hands in blood, to keep them clean.

120   And so, cold, courteous, a mere gentleman,
He bowed, we parted.
                   'Parted. Face no more,
Voice no more, love no more! wiped wholly out
Like some ill scholar's scrawl from heart and slate,—
Ay, spit on, and so wiped out utterly

125   By some coarse scholar! I have been too coarse,
Too human. Have we business, in our rank,
With blood i' the veins? I will have henceforth none;
Not even to keep the colour at my lip.
A rose is pink and pretty without blood;

130   Why not a woman? What we've played in vain
The game, to adore,—we have resources still,
And can play on at leisure, being adored:
Here's Smith already swearing at my feet
That I'm the typic She. Away with Smith!—

135   Smith smacks of Leigh,—and, henceforth, I'll admit
No socialist within three crinolines,
To live and have his being. But for you,
Though insolent your letter and absurd,
And though I hate you frankly,—take my Smith!

140   For when you have seen this famous marriage tied,
A most unspotted Erle to a noble Leigh
(His love astray on one he should not love),
Howbeit you should not want his love,—beware,
You'll want some comfort. So I leave you Smith;

145   Take Smith!—he talks of Leigh's subjects, somewhat worse;
Adopts a thought of Leigh's, and dwindles it;
Goes leagues beyond, to be no inch behind;
Will mind you of him, as a shoe-string may,
Of a man: and women, when they are made like you,

150 Grow tender to a shoe-string, footprint even,
Adore averted shoulders in a glass,
And memories of what, present once, was loathed.
And yet, you loathed not Romney,—though you've played
At 'fox and goose' about him with your soul:
155 Pass over fox, you rub out fox,—ignore
A feeling, you eradicate it,—the act's
Identical.
            'I wish you joy, Miss Leigh;
You've made a happy marriage for your friend;
And all the honour, well-assorted love,
160 Derives from you who love him, whom he loves!
You need not wish *me* joy to think of it,
I have so much. Observe, Aurora Leigh;
Your droop of eyelid is the same as his,
And, but for you, I might have won his love,
165 And, to you, I have shown my naked heart,—
For which three things, I hate, hate, hate you. Hush,
Suppose a fourth!—I cannot choose but think
That, with him, I were virtuouser than you
Without him: so I hate you from this gulf
170 And hollow of my soul, which opens out
To what, except for you, had been my heaven,
And is, instead, a place to curse by! LOVE.'

An active kind of curse. I stood there cursed—
Confounded. I had seized and caught the sense
175 Of the letter, with its twenty stinging snakes,
In a moment's sweep of eyesight, and I stood
Dazed.—'Ah!—not married.'
                          'You mistake,' he said;
'I'm married. Is not Marian Erle my wife?
As God sees things, I have a wife and child;
180 And I, as I'm a man who honours God,
Am here to claim them as my child and wife.'

I felt it hard to breathe, much less to speak.
Nor word of mine was needed. Some one else
Was there for answering. 'Romney,' she began,

185 'My great good angel, Romney.'
                              Then at first,
     I knew that Marian Erle was beautiful.
     She stood there, still and pallid as a saint,
     Dilated, like a saint in ecstasy,
     As if the floating moonshine interposed
190 Betwixt her foot and the earth, and raised her up
     To float upon it. 'I had left my child,
     Who sleeps,' she said, 'and, having drawn this way,
     I heard you speaking, . . friend!—Confirm me now.
     You take this Marian, such as wicked men
195 Have made her, for your honourable wife?'

     The thrilling, solemn, proud, pathetic voice.
     He stretched his arms out toward that thrilling voice,
     As if to draw it on to his embrace.
     —'I take her as God made her, and as men
200 Must fail to unmake her, for my honoured wife.'

     She never raised her eyes, nor took a step,
     But stood there in her place, and spoke again.
     —'You take this Marian's child, which is her shame
     In sight of men and women, for your child,
205 Of whom you will not ever feel ashamed?'

     The thrilling, tender, proud, pathetic voice.
     He stepped on toward it, still with outstretched arms,
     As if to quench upon his breast that voice.
     —'May God so father me, as I do him,
210 And so forsake me as I let him feel
     He's orphaned haply. Here I take the child
     To share my cup, to slumber on my knee,
     To play his loudest gambol at my foot,
     To hold my finger in the public ways,
215 Till none shall need inquire 'Whose child is this,'
     The gesture saying so tenderly 'My own'.'

     She stood a moment silent in her place;
     Then turning toward me very slow and cold—

'And you,—what say you?—will you blame me much,
220 If, careful for that outcast child of mine,
I catch this hand that's stretched to me and him,
Nor dare to leave him friendless in the world
Where men have stoned me? Have I not the right
To take so mere an aftermath from life,
225 Else found so wholly bare? Or is it wrong
To let your cousin, for a generous bent,
Put out his ungloved fingers among briars
To set a tumbling bird's-nest somewhat straight?
You will not tell him, though we're innocent,
230 We are not harmless? . . and that both our harms
Will stick to his good smooth noble life like burrs,
Never to drop off though you shake the cloak?
You've been my friend: you will not now be his?
You've known him, that he's worthy of a friend,
235 And you're his cousin, lady, after all,
And therefore more than free to take his part,
Explaining, since the nest is surely spoilt,
And Marian what you know her,—though a wife,
The world would hardly understand her case
240 Of being just hurt and honest; while for him,
'Twould ever twit him with his bastard child
And married harlot. Speak, while yet there's time:
You would not stand and let a good man's dog
Turn round and rend him, because his, and reared
245 Of a generous breed,—and will you let his act,
Because it's generous? Speak. I'm bound to you,
And I'll be bound by only you, in this.'

The thrilling, solemn voice, so passionless,
Sustained, yet low, without a rise or fall,
250 As one who had authority to speak,
And not as Marian.
                        I looked up to feel
If God stood near me, and beheld his heaven
As blue as Aaron's priestly robe appeared
To Aaron when he took it off to die.

255 And then I spoke—'Accept the gift, I say,
My sister Marian, and be satisfied.
The hand that gives, has still a soul behind
Which will not let it quail for having given,
Though foolish worldlings talk they know not what,
260 Of what they know not. Romney's strong enough
For this: do you be strong to know he's strong:
He stands on Right's side; never flinch for him,
As if he stood on the other. You'll be bound
By me? I am a woman of repute;
265 No fly-blow gossip has ever specked my life;
My name is clean and open as this hand,
Whose glove there's not a man dares blab about,
As if he had touched it freely:—here's my hand
To clasp your hand, my Marian, owned as pure!
270 As pure,—as I'm a woman and a Leigh!—
And, as I'm both, I'll witness to the world
That Romney Leigh is honoured for his choice,
Who chooses Marian for his honoured wife.'

Her broad wild woodland eyes shot out a light;
275 Her smile was wonderful for rapture. 'Thanks,
My great Aurora.' Forward then she sprang,
And dropping her impassioned spaniel head
With all its brown abandonment of curls
On Romney's feet, we heard the kisses drawn
280 Through sobs upon the foot, upon the ground—
'O Romney! O my angel! O unchanged,
Though, since we've parted, I have past the grave!
But Death itself could only better *thee*,
Not change thee!—*Thee* I do not thank at all:
285 I but thank God who made thee what thou art,
So wholly godlike.'
                              When he tried in vain
To raise her to his embrace, escaping thence
As any leaping fawn from a huntsman's grasp,
She bounded off and 'lighted beyond reach,
290 Before him, with a staglike majesty

Of soft, serene defiance,—as she knew
He could not touch her, so was tolerant
He had cared to try. She stood there with her great
Drowned eyes, and dripping cheeks, and strange sweet
          smile
295   That lived through all, as if one held a light
Across a waste of waters,—shook her head
To keep some thoughts down deeper in her soul,—
Then, white and tranquil as a summer-cloud
Which, having rained itself to a tardy peace,
300   Stands still in heaven as if it ruled the day,
Spoke out again,—'Although, my generous friend,
Since last we met and parted, you're unchanged,
And, having promised faith to Marian Erle,
Maintain it, as she were not changed at all;
305   And though that's worthy, though that's full of balm
To any conscious spirit of a girl
Who once has loved you as I loved you once,—
Yet still it will not make her . . if she's dead,
And gone away where none can give or take
310   In marriage,—able to revive, return
And wed you,—will it, Romney? Here's the point;
O friend, we'll see it plainer: you and I
Must never, never, never join hands so.
Nay, let me say it,—for I said it first
315   To God, and placed it, rounded to an oath,
Far, far above the moon there, at His feet,
As surely as I wept just now at yours,—
We never, never, never join hands so.
And now, be patient with me; do not think
320   I'm speaking from a false humility.
The truth is, I am grown so proud with grief,
And He has said so often through his nights
And through his mornings, 'Weep a little still,
'Thou foolish Marian, because women must,
325   'But do not blush at all except for sin,'—
That I, who felt myself unworthy once
Of virtuous Romney and his high-born race,
Have come to learn, . . a woman, poor or rich,

Despised or honoured, is a human soul;
330 And what her soul is,—that, she is herself,
Although she should be spit upon of men,
As is the pavement of the churches here,
Still good enough to pray in. And, being chaste
And honest, and inclined to do the right,
335 And love the truth, and live my life out green
And smooth beneath his steps, I should not fear
To make him, thus, a less uneasy time
Than many a happier woman. Very proud
You see me. Pardon, that I set a trap
340 To hear a confirmation in your voice . .
Both yours and yours. It is so good to know
'Twas really God who said the same before:
And thus it is in heaven, that first God speaks,
And then his angels. Oh, it does me good,
345 It wipes me clean and sweet from devil's dirt,
That Romney Leigh should think me worthy still
Of being his true and honourable wife!
Henceforth I need not say, on leaving earth,
I had no glory in it. For the rest,
350 The reason's ready (master, angel, friend,
Be patient with me) wherefore you and I
Can never, never, never join hands so.
I know you'll not be angry like a man
(For *you* are none) when I shall tell the truth,—
355 Which is, I do not love you, Romney Leigh,
I do not love you. Ah well! catch my hands,
Miss Leigh, and burn into my eyes with yours,—
I swear I do not love him. Did I once?
'Tis said that women have been bruised to death,
360 And yet, if once they loved, that love of theirs
Could never be drained out with all their blood:
I've heard such things and pondered. Did I indeed
Love once; or did I only worship? Yes,
Perhaps, O friend, I set you up so high
365 Above all actual good or hope of good,
Or fear of evil, all that could be mine,
I haply set you above love itself,

And out of reach of these poor woman's arms,
Angelic Romney. What was in my thought?
370 To be your slave, your help, your toy, your tool..
To be your love . . I never thought of that.
To give you love . . still less. I gave you love?
I think I did not give you anything;
I was but only yours,—upon my knees,
375 All yours, in soul and body, in head and heart,—
A creature you had taken from the ground,
Still crumbling through your fingers to your feet
To join the dust she came from. Did I love,
Or did I worship? judge, Aurora Leigh!
380 But, if indeed I loved, 'twas long ago,—
So long! before the sun and moon were made,
Before the hells were open,—ah, before
I heard my child cry in the desert night,
And knew he had no father. It may be,
385 I'm not as strong as other women are,
Who, torn and crushed, are not undone from love.
It may be, I am colder than the dead,
Who, being dead, love always. But for me,
Once killed, . . this ghost of Marian loves no more,
390 No more . . except the child! . . no more at all.
I told your cousin, sir, that I was dead;
And now, she thinks I'll get up from my grave,
And wear my chin-cloth for a wedding-veil,
And glide along the churchyard like a bride,
395 While all the dead keep whispering through the withes,
'You would be better in your place with us,
'You pitiful corruption!' At the thought,
The damps break out on me like leprosy
Although I'm clean. Ay, clean as Marian Erle:
400 As Marian Leigh, I know, I were not clean:
I have not so much life that I should love,
. . Except the child. Ah God! I could not bear
To see my darling on a good man's knees,
And know by such a look, or such a sigh,
405 Or such a silence, that he thought sometimes,
'This child was fathered by some cursed wretch' . .

For, Romney, angels are less tender-wise
Than God and mothers: even *you* would think
What *we* think never. He is ours, the child;
410 And we would sooner vex a soul in heaven
By coupling with it the dead body's thought,
It left behind it in a last month's grave,
Than, in my child, see other than . . my child.
We only, never call him fatherless
415 Who has God and his mother. O my babe,
My pretty, pretty blossom, an ill-wind
Once blew upon my breast! can any think
I'd have another,—one called happier,
A fathered child, with father's love and race
420 That's worn as bold and open as a smile,
To vex my darling when he's asked his name
And has no answer? What! a happier child
Than mine, my best,—who laughed so loud to-night
He could not sleep for pastime? Nay, I swear,
425 By life and love, that, if I lived like some,
And loved like . . *some* . . ay, loved you, Romney Leigh,
As some love (eyes that have wept so much, see clear),
I've room for no more children in my arms;
My kisses are all melted on one mouth;
430 I would not push my darling to a stool
To dandle babies. Here's a hand, shall keep
For ever clean without a marriage-ring,
To tend my boy, until he cease to need
One steadying finger of it, and desert
435 (Not miss) his mother's lap, to sit with men.
And when I miss him (not he me) I'll come
And say 'Now give me some of Romney's work,
To help your outcast orphans of the world,
And comfort grief with grief.' For you, meantime,
440 Most noble Romney, wed a noble wife,
And open on each other your great souls,—
I need not farther bless you. If I dared
But strain and touch her in her upper sphere,
And say 'Come down to Romney—pay my debt!'
445 I should be joyful with the stream of joy

Sent through me. But the moon is in my face . .
I dare not,—though I guess the name he loves;
I'm learned with my studies of old days,
Remembering how he crushed his under-lip
450 When some one came and spoke, or did not come.
Aurora, I could touch her with my hand,
And fly because I dare not.'
                              She was gone.

He smiled so sternly that I spoke in haste.
'Forgive her—she sees clearly for herself:
455 Her instinct's holy.'
                        '*I* forgive!' he said,
'I only marvel how she sees so sure,
While others' . . there he paused—then hoarse, abrupt,—
'Aurora! you forgive us, her and me?
For her, the thing she sees, poor loyal child,
460 If once corrected by the thing I know,
Had been unspoken; since she loves you well,
Has leave to love you:—while for me, alas,
If once or twice I let my heart escape
This night, . . remember, where hearts slip and fall
465 They break beside: we're parting,—parting,—ah!
You do not love, that you should surely know
What that word means. Forgive, be tolerant;
It had not been, but that I felt myself
So safe in impuissance and despair,
470 I could not hurt you though I tossed my arms
And sighed my soul out. The most utter wretch
Will choose his postures when he comes to die,
However in the presence of a queen;
And you'll forgive me some unseemly spasms
475 Which meant no more than dying. Do you think
I had ever come here in my perfect mind,
Unless I had come here, in my settled mind,
Bound Marian's, bound to keep the bond, and give
My name, my house, my hand, the things I could,
480 To Marian? For even *I* could give as much;
Even I, affronting her exalted soul

By a supposition that she wanted these,
Could act the husband's coat and hat set up
To creak i' the wind and drive the world-crows off
485 From pecking in her garden. Straw can fill
A hole to keep out vermin. Now, at last,
I own heaven's angels round her life suffice
To fight the rats of our society,
Without this Romney: I can see it at last;
490 And here is ended my pretension which
The most pretended. Over-proud of course,
Even so!—but not so stupid . . blind . . that I,
Whom thus the great Taskmaster of the world
Has set to meditate mistaken work,
495 My dreary face against a dim black wall
Throughout man's natural lifetime—could pretend
Or wish . . O love, I have loved you! O my soul,
I have lost you!—but I swear by all yourself,
And all you might have been to me these years,
500 If that June morning had not failed my hope,—
I'm not so bestial, to regret that day
This night,—this night, which still to you is fair;
Nay, not so blind, Aurora. I attest
Those stars above us, which I cannot see' . .

505 'You cannot' . .
                    'That if Heaven itself should stoop,
Re-mix the lots, and give me another chance,
I'd say 'No other!'—I'd record my blank.
Aurora never should be wife of mine.'

'Not see the stars?'
                    ''Tis worse still, not to see
510 To find your hand, although we're parting, dear.
A moment let me hold it, ere we part;
And understand my last words—these, at last!
I would not have you thinking, when I'm gone,
That Romney dared to hanker for your love,
515 In thought or vision, if attainable
(Which certainly for me it never was)

And wished to use it for a dog to-day,
To help the blind man stumbling. God forbid!
And now I know He held you in his palm.
520 And kept you open-eyed to all my faults,
To save you at last from such a dreary end.
Believe me, dear, that, if I had known, like Him
What loss was coming on me, I had done
As well in this as He has.—Farewell, you,
525 Who are still my light,—farewell! How late it is:
I know that, now: you've been too patient, sweet.
I will but blow my whistle toward the lane,
And some one comes . . the same who brought me here.
Get in—Good-night.'
      'A moment. Heavenly Christ!
530 A moment. Speak once, Romney. 'Tis not true.
I hold your hands, I look into your face—
You see me?'
     'No more than the blessed stars.
Be blessed too, Aurora. Ah, my sweet,
You tremble. Tender-hearted! Do you mind
535 Of yore, dear, how you used to cheat old John,
And let the mice out slily from his traps,
Until he marvelled at the soul in mice
Which took the cheese and left the snare? The same
Dear soft heart always! 'Twas for this, I grieved
540 Howe's letter never reached you. Ah, you had heard
Of illness—not the issue . . not the extent:
My life long sick with tossings up and down,
The sudden revulsion in the blazing house,—
The strain and struggle both of body and soul,
545 Which left fire running in my veins, for blood:
Scarce lacked that thunderbolt of the falling beam,
Which nicked me on the forehead as I passed
The gallery-door with a burden. Say heaven's bolt,
Not William Erle's; not Marian's father's; tramp
550 And poacher, whom I found for what he was,
And, eager for her sake to rescue him,
Forth swept from the open highway of the world,
Road-dust and all,—till, like a woodland boar

Most naturally unwilling to be tamed,
555 He notched me with his tooth. But not a word
To Marian! and I do not think, besides,
He turned the tilting of the beam my way,—
And if he laughed, as many swear, poor wretch,
Nor he nor I supposed the hurt so deep.
560 We'll hope his next laugh may be merrier,
In a better cause.'
                          'Blind, Romney?'
                                        'Ah, my friend,
You'll learn to say it in a cheerful voice.
I, too, at first desponded. To be blind,
Turned out of nature, mulcted as a man,
565 Refused the daily largesse of the sun
To humble creatures! When the fever's heat
Dropped from me, as the flame did from my house,
And left me ruined like it, stripped of all
The hues and shapes of aspectable life,
570 A mere bare blind stone in the blaze of day,
A man, upon the outside of the earth,
As dark as ten feet under, in the grave,—
Why, that seemed hard.'
                          'No hope?'
                                        'A tear! you weep,
Divine Aurora? tears upon my hand!
575 I've seen you weeping for a mouse, a bird,—
But, weep for me, Aurora? Yes, there's hope.
Not hope of sight,—I could be learned, dear
And tell you in what Greek and Latin name
The visual nerve is withered to the root,
580 Though the outer eyes appear indifferent,
Unspotted in their crystals. But there's hope.
The spirit, from behind this dethroned sense,
Sees, waits in patience till the walls break up
From which the bas-relief and fresco have dropt:
585 There's hope. The man here, once so arrogant
And restless, so ambitious, for his part,
Of dealing with statistically packed

Disorders, (from a pattern on his nail,)
And packing such things quite another way,—
590 Is now contented. From his personal loss
He has come to hope for others when they lose,
And wear a gladder faith in what we gain . .
Through bitter experience, compensation sweet,
Like that tear, sweetest. I am quiet now,—
595 As tender surely for the suffering world,
But quiet,—sitting at the wall to learn,
Content, henceforth, to do the thing I can:
For, though as powerless, said I, as a stone,
A stone can still give shelter to a worm,
600 And it is worth while being a stone for that:
There's hope, Aurora.'
                              'Is there hope for me?
For me?—and is there room beneath the stone
For such a worm?—And if I came and said . .
What all this weeping scarce will let me say,
605 And yet what women cannot say at all
But weeping bitterly . . (the pride keeps up,
Until the heart breaks under it) . . I love,—
I love you, Romney' . .
                              'Silence!' he exclaimed.
'A woman's pity sometimes makes her mad.
610 A man's distractions must not cheat his soul
To take advantage of it. Yet, 'tis hard—
Farewell, Aurora.'
                              'But I love you, sir;
And when a woman says she loves a man,
The man must hear her, though he love her not,
615 Which . . hush! . . he has leave to answer in his turn;
She will not surely blame him. As for me,
You call it pity,—think I'm generous?
'Twere somewhat easier, for a woman proud
As I am, and I'm very vilely proud,
620 To let it pass as such, and press on you
Love born of pity,—seeing that excellent loves
Are born so, often, nor the quicklier die,—
And this would set me higher by the head

Than now I stand. No matter: let the truth
625 Stand high; Aurora must be humble: no,
My love's not pity merely. Obviously
I'm not a generous woman, never was,
Or else, of old, I had not looked so near
To weights and measures, grudging you the power
630 To give, as first I scorned your power to judge
For me, Aurora: I would have no gifts,
Forsooth, but God's,—and I would use *them*, too,
According to my pleasure and my choice,
As He and I were equals,—you, below,
635 Excluded from that level of interchange
Admitting benefaction. You were wrong
In much? you said so. I was wrong in most.
Oh, most! You only thought to rescue men
By half-means, half-way, seeing half their wants,
640 While thinking nothing of your personal gain.
But I, who saw the human nature broad,
At both sides, comprehending, too, the soul's,
And all the high necessities of Art,
Betrayed the thing I saw, and wronged my own life
645 For which I pleaded. Passioned to exalt
The artist's instinct in me at the cost
Of putting down the woman's,—I forgot
No perfect artist is developed here
From any imperfect woman. Flower from root,
650 And spiritual from natural, grade by grade
In all our life. A handful of the earth
To make God's image! the despised poor earth,
The healthy odorous earth,—I missed, with it,
The divine Breath that blows the nostrils out
655 To ineffable inflatus: ay, the breath
Which love is. Art is much, but love is more.
O Art, my Art, thou'rt much, but Love is more!
Art symbolises heaven, but Love is God
And makes heaven. I, Aurora, fell from mine:
660 I would not be a woman like the rest,
A simple woman who believes in love,
And owns the right of love because she loves,

And, hearing she's beloved, is satisfied
With what contents God: I must analyse,
665   Confront and question; just as if a fly
Refused to warm itself in any sun
Till such was *in leone:* I must fret
Forsooth, because the month was only May;
Be faithless of the kind of proffered love,
670   And captious, lest it miss my dignity,
And scornful, that my lover sought a wife
To use . . to use! O Romney, O my love,
I am changed since then, changed wholly,—for indeed,
If now you'd stoop so low to take my love,
675   And use it roughly, without stint or spare,
As men use common things with more behind,
(And, in this, ever would be more behind)
To any mean and ordinary end,—
The joy would set me like a star, in heaven,
680   So high up, I should shine because of height
And not of virtue. Yet in one respect,
Just one, beloved, I am in no wise changed:
I love you, loved you . . loved you first and last,
And love you on for ever. Now I know
685   I loved you always, Romney. She who died
Knew that, and said so; Lady Waldemar
Knows that; . . and Marian: I had known the same
Except that I was prouder than I knew,
And not so honest. Ay, and, as I live,
690   I should have died so, crushing in my hand
This rose of love, the wasp inside and all,—
Ignoring ever to my soul and you
Both rose and pain,—except for this great loss,
This great despair,—to stand before your face
695   And know I cannot win a look of yours.
You think, perhaps, I am not changed from pride,
And that I chiefly bear to say such words,
Because you cannot shame me with your eyes?
O calm, grand eyes, extinguished in a storm,
700   Blown out like lights o'er melancholy seas,
Though shrieked for by the shipwrecked,—O my Dark,

My Cloud,—to go before me every day
While I go ever toward the wilderness,—
I would that you could see me bare to the soul!—
705   If this be pity, 'tis so for myself,
And not for Romney! *he* can stand alone;
A man like *him* is never overcome:
No woman like me, counts him pitiable
While saints applaud him. He mistook the world:
710   But I mistook my own heart,—and that slip
Was fatal. Romney,—will you leave me here?
So wrong, so proud, so weak, so unconsoled,
So mere a woman!—and I love you so,—
I love you, Romney.'
                              Could I see his face,
715   I wept so? Did I drop against his breast,
Or did his arms constrain me? Were my cheeks
Hot, overflooded, with my tears, or his?
And which of our two large explosive hearts
So shook me? That, I know not. There were words
720   That broke in utterance .. melted, in the fire;
Embrace, that was convulsion, .. then a kiss ..
As long and silent as the ecstatic night,—
And deep, deep, shuddering breaths, which meant beyond
Whatever could be told by word and kiss.

725   But what he said .. I have written day by day,
With somewhat even writing. Did I think
That such a passionate rain would intercept
And dash this last page? What he said, indeed,
I fain would write it down here like the rest,
730   To keep it in my eyes, as in my ears,
The heart's sweet scripture, to be read at night
When weary, or at morning when afraid,
And lean my heaviest oath on when I swear
That, when all's done, all tried, all counted here,
735   All great arts, and all good philosophies,—
This love just puts its hand out in a dream
And straight outreaches all things.
                              What he said,

I fain would write. But if an angel spoke
In thunder, should we, haply, know much more
740   Than that it thundered? If a cloud came down
And wrapped us wholly, could we draw its shape,
As if on the outside, and not overcome?
And so he spake. His breath against my face
Confused his words, yet made them more intense,—
745   As when the sudden finger of the wind
Will wipe a row of single city-lamps
To a pure white line of flame, more luminous
Because of obliteration; more intense,—
The intimate presence carrying in itself
750   Complete communication, as with souls
Who, having put the body off, perceive
Through simply being. Thus, 'twas granted me
To know he loved me to the depth and height
Of such large natures, ever competent
755   With grand horizons by the land or sea,
To love's grand sunrise. Small spheres hold small fires:
· But he loved largely, as a man can love
Who, baffled in his love, dares live his life,
Accept the ends which God loves, for his own,
760   And lift a constant aspect.
                              From the day
I had brought to England my poor searching face,
(An orphan even of my father's grave),
He had loved me, watched me, watched his soul in mine,
Which in me grew and heightened into love.
765   For he, a boy still, had been told the tale
Of how a fairy bride from Italy,
With smells of oleanders in her hair,
Was coming through the vines to touch his hand;
Whereat the blood of boyhood on the palm
770   Made sudden heats. And when at last I came,
And lived before him, lived, and rarely smiled,
He smiled and loved me for the thing I was,
As every child will love the year's first flower,
(Not certainly the fairest of the year,
775   But, in which, the complete year seems to blow)

The poor sad snowdrop,—growing between drifts,
Mysterious medium 'twixt the plant and frost,
So faint with winter while so quick with spring,
And doubtful if to thaw itself away
780 With that snow near it. Not that Romney Leigh
Had loved me coldly. If I thought so once,
It was as if I had held my hand in fire
And shook for cold. But now I understood
For ever, that the very fire and heat
785 Of troubling passion in him, burned him clear,
And shaped to dubious order, word and act:
That, just because he loved me over all,
All wealth, all lands, all social privilege,
To which chance made him unexpected heir,—
790 And, just because on all these lesser gifts,
Constrained by conscience and the sense of wrong
He had stamped with steady hand God's arrow-mark
Of dedication to the human need,
He thought it should be so too, with his love;
795 He, passionately loving, would bring down
His love, his life, his best, (because the best)
His bride of dreams, who walked so still and high
Through flowery poems as through meadow-grass,
The dust of golden lilies on her feet,
800 That *she* should walk beside him on the rocks
In all that clang and hewing out of men,
And help the work of help which was his life,
And prove he kept back nothing,—not his soul.
And when I failed him,—for I failed him, I—
805 And when it seemed he had missed my love,—he thought,
'Aurora makes room for a working-noon;'
And so, self-girded with torn strips of hope,
Took up his life as if it were for death,
(Just capable of one heroic aim,)
810 And threw it in the thickest of the world,—
At which men laughed as if he had drowned a dog:
No wonder,—since Aurora failed him first!
The morning and the evening made his day.

*

But oh, the night! oh, bitter-sweet! oh, sweet!
815 O dark, O moon and stars, O ecstasy
Of darkness! O great mystery of love,—
In which absorbed, loss, anguish, treason's self
Enlarges rapture,—as a pebble dropt
In some full wine-cup, over-brims the wine!
820 While we two sate together, leaned that night
So close, my very garments crept and thrilled
With strange electric life; and both my cheeks
Grew red, then pale, with touches from my hair
In which his breath was; while the golden moon
825 Was hung before our faces as the badge
Of some sublime inherited despair,
Since ever to be seen by only one,—
A voice said, low and rapid as a sigh,
Yet breaking, I felt conscious, from a smile,—
830 'Thank God, who made me blind, to make me see!
Shine on, Aurora, dearest light of souls,
Which rul'st for evermore both day and night!
I am happy.'
            I flung closer to his breast,
As sword that, after battle, flings to sheathe;
835 And, in that hurtle of united souls,
The mystic motions which in common moods
Are shut beyond our sense, broke in on us,
And, as we sate, we felt the old earth spin,
And all the starry turbulence of worlds
840 Swing round us in their audient circles, till
If that same golden moon were overhead
Or if beneath our feet, we did not know.

And then calm, equal, smooth with weights of joy,
His voice rose, as some chief musician's song
845 Amid the old Jewish temple's Selah-pause,
And bade me mark how we two met at last
Upon this moon-bathed promontory of earth,
To give up much on each side, then take all.
'Beloved,' it sang, 'we must be here to work;
850 And men who work, can only work for men,

And, not to work in vain, must comprehend
Humanity and, so, work humanly,
And raise men's bodies still by raising souls,
As God did, first.'
                              'But stand upon the earth,'
855   I said, 'to raise them,—(this is human too;
There's nothing high which has not first been low;
My humbleness, said One, has made me great!)
As God did, last.'
                        'And work all silently
And simply,' he returned, 'as God does all;
860   Distort our nature never, for our work,
Nor count our right hands stronger for being hoofs.
The man most man, with tenderest human hands,
Works best for men,—as God in Nazareth.'

He paused upon the word, and then resumed;
865   'Fewer programmes, we who have no prescience.
Fewer systems; we who are held and do not hold.
Less mapping out of masses, to be saved,
By nations or by sexes. Fourier's void,
And Comte is dwarfed,—and Cabet, puerile.
870   Subsist no law of life outside of life;
No perfect manners, without Christian souls:
The Christ Himself had been no Lawgiver
Unless He had given the life, too, with the law.'

I echoed thoughtfully—'The man, most man,
875   Works best for men, and, if most men indeed,
He gets his manhood plainest from his soul:
While, obviously, this stringent soul itself
Obeys our old rules of development;
The Spirit ever witnessing in ours,
880   And Love, the soul of soul, within the soul,
Evolving it sublimely. First, God's love.'

'And next,' he smiled, 'the love of wedded souls,
Which still presents that mystery's counterpart.
Sweet shadow-rose, upon the water of life,

885   Of such a mystic substance, Sharon gave
       A name to! human, vital, fructuous rose,
       Whose calyx holds the multitude of leaves,—
       Loves filial, loves fraternal, neighbour-loves,
       And civic, . . all fair petals, all good scents,
890   All reddened, sweetened from one central Heart!'

       'Alas,' I cried, 'it was not long ago
       You swore this very social rose smelt ill.'

       'Alas,' he answered, 'is it a rose at all?
       The filial's thankless, the fraternal's hard,
895   The rest is lost. I do but stand and think,
       Across dim waters of a troubled life
       The Flower of Heaven so vainly overhangs,—
       What perfect counterpart would be in sight
       If tanks were clearer. Let us clean the tubes,
900   And wait for rains. O poet, O my love,
       Since *I* was too ambitious in my deed,
       And thought to distance all men in success,
       Till God came on me, marked the place, and said,
       'Ill-doer, henceforth keep within this line,
905   Attempting less than others,'—and I stand
       And work among Christ's little ones, content,—
       Come thou, my compensation, my dear sight,
       My morning-star, my morning! rise and shine,
       And touch my hills with radiance not their own;
910   Shine out for two, Aurora, and fulfil
       My falling-short that must be! work for two,
       As I, though thus restrained, for two, shall love!
       Gaze on, with inscient vision toward the sun,
       And, from his visceral heat, pluck out the roots
915   Of light beyond him. Art's a service,—mark:
       A silver key is given to thy clasp,
       And thou shalt stand unwearied, night and day,
       And fix it in the hard, slow-turning wards,
       To open, so, that intermediate door
920   Betwixt the different planes of sensuous form
       And form insensuous, that inferior men

May learn to feel on still through these to those,
And bless thy ministration. The world waits
For help. Beloved, let us love so well,
925   Our work shall still be better for our love,
And still our love be sweeter for our work,
And both, commended, for the sake of each,
By all true workers and true lovers born.
Now press the clarion on thy women's lip
930   (Love's holy kiss shall still keep consecrate)
And breathe the fine keen breath along the brass,
And blow all class-walls level as Jericho's
Past Jordan; crying from the top of souls,
To souls, that they assemble on earth's flats,
935   To get them to some purer eminence
Than any hitherto beheld for clouds!
What height we know not,—but the way we know,
And how by mounting aye, we must attain,
And so climb on. It is the hour for souls;
940   That bodies, leavened by the will and love,
Be lightened to redemption. The world's old;
But the old world waits the hour to be renewed:
Toward which, new hearts in individual growth
Must quicken, and increase to multitude
945   In new dynasties of the race of men,—
Developed whence, shall grow spontaneously
New churches, new œconomies, new laws
Admitting freedom, new societies
Excluding falsehood. HE shall make all new.'

950   My Romney!—Lifting up my hand in his,
As wheeled by Seeing spirits toward the east,
He turned instinctively,—where, faint and fair,
Along the tingling desert of the sky,
Beyond the circle of the conscious hills,
955   Were laid in jasper-stone as clear as glass
The first foundations of that new, near Day
Which should be builded out of heaven, to God.

*

He stood a moment with erected brows,
In silence, as a creature might, who gazed:
960   Stood calm, and fed his blind, majestic eyes
Upon the thought of perfect noon. And when
I saw his soul saw,—'Jasper first,' I said,
'And second, sapphire; third, chalcedony;
The rest in order, . . last, an amethyst.'

FROM *ESSAY ON MIND, WITH OTHER POEMS* (1826)

Verses to My Brother

'For we were nurs'd upon the self-same hill.' LYCIDAS

I WILL write down thy name, and when 'tis writ,
Will turn me from the hum that mortals keep
In the wide world without, and gaze on it!
It telleth of the past—calling from sleep
5   Such dear, yet mournful thoughts, as make us smile, and
        weep.

Belov'd and best! what thousand feelings start,
As o'er the paper's course my fingers move—
My Brother! dearest, kindest as thou art!
How can these lips my heart's affection prove?
10 I could not speak the words, if words could speak my love.

Together have we past our infant hours,
Together sported Childhood's spring away,
Together cull'd young Hope's fast budding flowers,
To wreathe the forehead of each coming day!
15 Yes! for the present's sun makes e'en the future gay.

And when the laughing mood was nearly o'er,
Together, many a minute did we wile
On Horace' page, or Maro's sweeter lore;
While one young critic, on the classic style,
20 Would sagely try to frown, and make the other smile.

But now alone thou con'st the ancient tome—
And sometimes thy dear studies, it may be,
Are cross'd by dearer dreams of me and home!
Alone I muse on Homer—thoughts are free—
25 And if mine often stray, they go in search of thee!

I may not praise thee *here*—I will not bless!
Yet all thy goodness doth my memory bear,
Cherish'd by more than Friendship's tenderness—
And, in the silence of my evening prayer,
30   Thou shalt not be forgot—thy dear name shall be there!

Stanzas on the Death of Lord Byron [*1824*]

'——λέγε πᾶσιν ἀπώλετο.' BION

                —'I am not now
That which I have been.' CHILDE HAROLD

HE *was*, and *is* not! Græcia's trembling shore,
Sighing through all her palmy groves, shall tell
That Harold's pilgrimage at last is o'er—
Mute the impassioned tongue, and tuneful shell,
5   That erst was wont in noblest strains to swell—
Hush'd the proud shouts that rode Ægæa's wave!
For lo! the great Deliv'rer breathes farewell!
Gives to the world his mem'ry and a grave—
Expiring in the land he only lived to save!

10   Mourn, Hellas, mourn! and o'er thy widow'd brow,
For aye, the cypress wreath of sorrow twine;
And in thy new-formed beauty, desolate, throw
The fresh-cull'd flowers on *his* sepulchral shrine.
Yes! let that heart whose fervour was all thine,
15   In consecrated urn lamented be!
That generous heart where genius thrill'd divine,
Hath spent its last most glorious throb for thee—
Then sank amid the storm that made thy children free!

Britannia's Poet! Græcia's hero, sleeps!
20   And Freedom, bending o'er the breathless clay,
Lifts up her voice, and in her anguish weeps!
For *us*, a night hath clouded o'er our day,

And hush'd the lips that breath'd our fairest lay.
Alas! and must the British lyre resound
25   A requiem, while the spirit wings away
Of him who on its strings such music found,
And taught its startling chords to give so sweet a sound!

The theme grows sadder—but my soul shall find
30   A language in these tears! No more—no more!
Soon, 'midst the shriekings of the tossing wind,
The 'dark blue depths' he sang of, shall have bore
Our *all* of Byron to his native shore!
His grave is thick with voices—to the ear
35   Murm'ring an awful tale of greatness o'er;
But Memory strives with Death, and lingering near,
Shall consecrate the dust of Harold's lonely bier!

Lines on the Portrait of the Widow of Riego
PLACED IN THE EXHIBITION

DAUGHTER of Spain! a passer by
May mark the cheek serenely pale—
The sorrow in the calm dark eye,
Which gleams beneath thy mourning veil.

5   Calm! for it bears no deeper trace
Of feelings it disdained to show!
We look upon the Widow's face,
And only read the Patriot's woe!

Spouse of the dead! the widow's sighs
10   Should n'er her hero's glory dim;
Nor would'st thou give to vulgar eyes
The sacred tear which fell for *him*:

Thou would'st not hold to the world's view
Thy ruined joys, thy broken heart—
15   The jeering world—it only knew
Of all thine anguish—that thou WERT;

While o'er *his* grave thy steps would go
With a firm tread,—stilling thy love,—
As if the dust would blush below
20   To feel one faltering foot above.

For Spain, *he* dared the noble strife—
For Spain, he gave his latest breath;
And he who lived the Patriot's life,
Was dragged to die the felon's death!

25   And the recreant shout around him came,
As he stood the felon's block beside;
But his dying lips spoke Freedom's name—
Let the foe weep!—THY brow hath *pride*!—

Yet haply in the midnight air,
30   When none might part thy God and thee,
The lengthened sob, the passionate prayer,
Hath spoke thy full soul's agony!

But silent else thou past away—
The plaint unbreath'd, the anguish hid—
35   More voiceless than the echoing clay
Which idly knocked thy coffin's lid.

Peace be to thee! while Britons seek
This place, if British souls they bear,
'Twill start the crimson in the cheek
40   To see Riego's *widow* THERE!

FROM *PROMETHEUS BOUND, AND MISCELLANEOUS POEMS* (1833)

The Death-Bed of Teresa del Riego

—Si fia muta ogni altra cosa, al fine
    Parlerà il mio morire,
E ti dirà la morte il mio martire.
                                        GUARINI

The room was darken'd; but a wan lamp shed
Its light upon a half-uncurtain'd bed,
Whereon the widow'd sate. Blackly as death
Her veiling hair hung round her, and no breath
5 Came from her lips to motion it. Between
Its parted clouds, the calm fair face was seen
In a snow paleness and snow silentness,
With eyes unquenchable, whereon did press
A little, their white lids, so taught to lie,
10 By weights of frequent tears wept secretly.
Her hands were clasp'd and raised—the lamp did fling
A glory on her brow's meek suffering.

Beautiful form of woman! seeming made
Alone to shine in mirrors, there to braid
15 The hair and zone the waist—to garland flowers—
To walk like sunshine through the orange bowers—
To strike her land's guitar—and often see
In other eyes how lovely hers must be—
Grew she acquaint with anguish? Did she sever
20 For ever from the one she loved for ever,
To dwell among the strangers? Ay! and she,
Who shone most brightly in that festive glee,
Sate down in this despair most patiently.

Some hearts are Niobes! In grief's down-sweeping,
25 They turn to very stone from over-weeping,
And after, feel no more. Hers did remain
In life, which is the power of feeling pain,
Till pain consumed the life so call'd below.
She heard that he was dead!—she ask'd not how—
30 For *he* was dead! She wail'd not o'er his urn,
For *he* was dead—and in *her* hands, should burn
His vestal flame of honour radiantly.
Sighing would dim its light—she did not sigh.

She only died. They laid her in the ground,
35 Whereon th' unloving tread, and accents sound
Which are not of her Spain. She left behind,
For those among the strangers who were kind
Unto the poor heart-broken, her dark hair.
It once was gauded out with jewels rare;
40 It swept her dying pillow—it doth lie
Beside me, (thank the giver) droopingly,
And very long and bright! Its tale doth go
Half to the dumb grave, half to life-time woe,
Making the heart of man, if manly, ring
45 Like Dodonæan brass, with echoing.

THE CRY OF THE CHILDREN (1843, 1844)

'φεῦ, φεῦ, τί προσδέρκεσθέ μ᾽ὄμμασιν, τέκνα.' MEDEA

Do ye hear the children weeping, O my brothers,
    Ere the sorrow comes with years?
They are leaning their young heads against their mothers,—
    And *that* cannot stop their tears.
5 The young lambs are bleating in the meadows;
  The young birds are chirping in the nest;
The young fawns are playing with the shadows;
  The young flowers are blowing toward the west—
But the young, young children, O my brothers,
10   They are weeping bitterly!—
They are weeping in the playtime of the others,
    In the country of the free.

Do you question the young children in the sorrow,
    Why their tears are falling so?—
15 The old man may weep for his to-morrow
    Which is lost in Long Ago—
The old tree is leafless in the forest—
  The old year is ending in the frost—
The old wound, if stricken, is the sorest—
20   The old hope is hardest to be lost:
But the young, young children, O my brothers,
    Do you ask them why they stand
Weeping sore before the bosoms of their mothers,
    In our happy Fatherland?

25 They look up with their pale and sunken faces,
    And their looks are sad to see,
For the man's grief abhorrent, draws and presses
    Down the cheeks of infancy—

'Your old earth,' they say, 'is very dreary;'
30   'Our young feet,' they say, 'are very weak!
Few paces have we taken, yet are weary—
   Our grave-rest is very far to seek.
Ask the old why they weep, and not the children,
      For the outside earth is cold,—
35   And we young ones stand without, in our bewildering,
      And the graves are for the old.

'True,' say the young children, 'it may happen
      That we die before our time!
Little Alice died last year—the grave is shapen
40   Like a snowball, in the rime.
We looked into the pit prepared to take her—
   Was no room for any work in the close clay:
From the sleep wherein she lieth none will wake her,
   Crying, 'Get up, little Alice! it is day'.
45   If you listen by that grave, in sun and shower,
   With your ear down, little Alice never cries!—
Could we see her face, be sure we should not know her,
   For the smile has time for growing in her eyes,—
And merry go her moments, lulled and stilled in
50   The shroud, by the kirk-chime!
It is good when it happens,' say the children,
      'That we die before our time.'

Alas, the wretched children! they are seeking
      Death in life, as best to have!
55   They are binding up their hearts away from breaking,
      With a cerement from the grave.
Go out, children, from the mine and from the city—
   Sing out, children, as the little thrushes do—
Pluck your handfuls of the meadow-cowslips pretty—
60   Laugh aloud, to feel your fingers let them through!
But they answer, 'Are your cowslips of the meadows
      Like our weeds anear the mine?
Leave us quiet in the dark of the coal-shadows,
      From your pleasures fair and fine!

65 'For oh,' say the children, 'we are weary,
       And we cannot run or leap—
If we cared for any meadows, it were merely
       To drop down in them and sleep.
Our knees tremble sorely in the stooping—
70 We fall upon our faces, trying to go;
And, underneath our heavy eyelids drooping,
    The reddest flower would look as pale as snow.
For, all day, we drag our burden tiring,
       Through the coal-dark, underground—
75 Or, all day, we drive the wheels of iron
       In the factories, round and round.

'For, all day, the wheels are droning, turning,—
       Their wind comes in our faces,—
Till our hearts turn,—our head, with pulses burning,
80   And the walls turn in their places—
Turns the sky in the high window blank and reeling—
    Turns the long light that droppeth down the wall—
Turn the black flies that crawl along the ceiling—
    All are turning, all the day, and we with all!—
85 And all day, the iron wheels are droning;
       And sometimes we could pray,
'O ye wheels,' (breaking out in a mad moaning)
       'Stop! be silent for to-day!''

Ay, be silent! Let them hear each other breathing
90   For a moment, mouth to mouth—
Let them touch each other's hands, in a fresh wreathing
       Of their tender human youth!
Let them feel that this cold metallic motion
    Is not all the life God fashions or reveals—
95 Let them prove their inward souls against the notion
    That they live in you, or under you, O wheels!—
Still, all day, the iron wheels go onward,
       As if Fate in each were stark;
And the children's souls, which God is calling sunward,
100   Spin on blindly in the dark.

Now tell the poor young children, O my brothers,
    That they look to Him and pray—
So the blessed One, who blesseth all the others,
    Will bless them another day.
105 They answer, 'Who is God that He should hear us,
   While the rushing of the iron wheels is stirred?
When we sob aloud, the human creatures near us
   Pass by, hearing not, or answer not a word!
And *we* hear not (for the wheels in their resounding)
110   Strangers speaking at the door:
Is it likely God, with angels singing round Him,
    Hears our weeping any more?

'Two words, indeed, of praying we remember;
    And at midnight's hour of harm,—
115, 'Our Father,' looking upward in the chamber,
    We say softly for a charm.*
We know no other words, except 'Our Father,'
   And we think that, in some pause of angels' song,
God may pluck them with the silence sweet to gather,
120   And hold both within His right hand which is strong.
'Our Father!' If He heard us, He would surely
    (For they call Him good and mild)
Answer, smiling down the steep world very purely,
    'Come and rest with me, my child.''

125 'But, no!' say the children, weeping faster,
    'He is speechless as a stone;
And they tell us, of His image is the master
    Who commands us to work on.

---

*A fact rendered pathetically historical by Mr. Horne's report of his commission. The name of the poet of 'Orion' and 'Cosimo de' Medici' has, however, a change of associations; and comes in time to remind me (with other noble instances) that we have some brave poetic heat of literature still,—though open to the reproach, on certain points, of being somewhat gelid in our humanity.

Go to!' say the children,—'Up in Heaven,
130   Dark, wheel-like, turning clouds are all we find.
Do not mock us; grief has made us unbelieving—
    We look up for God, but tears have made us blind.'
Do you hear the children weeping and disproving,
    O my brothers, what ye preach?
135   For God's possible is taught by His world's loving—
    And the children doubt of each.

And well may the children weep before you;
    They are weary ere they run;
They have never seen the sunshine, nor the glory
140   Which is brighter than the sun:
They know the grief of man, but not the wisdom;
    They sink in the despair, without the calm—
Are slaves, without the liberty in Christdom,—
    Are martyrs, by the pang without the palm,—
145   Are worn, as if with age, yet unretrievingly
    No dear remembrance keep,—
Are orphans of the earthly love and heavenly:
    Let them weep! let them weep!

They look up, with their pale and sunken faces,
150   And their look is dread to see,
For you think you see their angels in their places,
    With eyes meant for Deity;—
'How long,' they say, 'how long, O cruel nation,
    Will you stand, to move the world, on a child's heart,—
155   Stifle down with a mailed heel its palpitation,
    And tread onward to your throne amid the mart?
Our blood splashes upward, O our tyrants,
    And your purple shows your path;
But the child's sob curseth deeper in the silence
160   Than the strong man in his wrath!'

FROM *POEMS* (1844)

Past and Future

My future will not copy fair my past
On any leaf but Heaven's. Be fully done,
Supernal Will! I would not fain be one
Who, satisfying thirst and breaking fast,
5 Upon the fulness of the heart at last
Says no grace after meat. My wine has run
Indeed out of my cup, and there is none
To gather up the bread of my repast
Scattered and trampled; yet I find some good
10 In earth's green herbs, and streams that bubble up
Clear from the darkling ground,—content until
I sit with angels before better food:
Dear Christ! when Thy new vintage fills my cup,
This hand shall shake no more, nor that wine spill.

To George Sand. A Desire

Thou large-brained woman and large-hearted man,
Self-called George Sand! whose soul, amid the lions
Of thy tumultuous senses, moans defiance,
And answers roar for roar, as spirits can:
5 I would some mild miraculous thunder ran
Above the applauded circus, in appliance
Of thine own nobler nature's strength and science,—
Drawing two pinions, white as wings of swan,
From thy strong shoulders, to amaze the place
10 With holier light! That thou to woman's claim,
And man's, might join beside the angel's grace
Of a pure genius sanctified from blame;
Till child and maiden pressed to thine embrace,
To kiss upon thy lips a stainless fame.

Lady Geraldine's Courtship:

A ROMANCE OF THE AGE

A poet writes to his friend. Place—A room in Wycombe Hall.
Time—Late in the evening.

Dear my friend and fellow-student, I would lean my spirit
o'er you;
Down the purple of this chamber, tears should scarcely run
at will!
I am humbled who was humble! Friend,—I bow my head
before you!
You should lead me to my peasants:—but their faces are
too still.

5   There's a lady—an earl's daughter; she is proud and
she is noble,
And she treads the crimson carpet, and she breathes the
perfumed air;
And a kingly blood sends glances up her princely eye to
trouble,
And the shadow of a monarch's crown, is softened in her
hair.

She has halls and she has castles, and the resonant steam-
eagles
10   Follow far on the directing of her floating dove-like
hand—
With a thundrous vapour trailing, underneath the starry
vigils,
So to mark upon the blasted heaven, the measure of her
land.

There be none of England's daughters, who can show a
prouder presence;
Upon princely suitors suing, she has looked in her disdain:

15   She was sprung of English nobles, I was born of English
        peasants;
     What was *I* that I should love her—save for feeling of the
        pain?

     I was only a poor poet, made for singing at her casement,
     As the finches or the thrushes, while she thought of other
        things.
     Oh, she walked so high above me, she appeared to my
        abasement,
20   In her lovely silken murmur, like an angel clad in wings!

     Many vassals bow before her, as her chariot sweeps their
        door-ways;
     She hath blest their little children,—as a priest or queen
        were she!
     Oh, too tender, or too cruel far, her smile upon the poor
        was,
     For I thought it was the same smile, which she used, to
        smile on *me*.

25   She has voters in the commons, she has lovers in the
        palace—
     And of all the fair court-ladies, few have jewels half as fine:
     Even the prince has named her beauty, 'twixt the red wine
        and the chalice:
     Oh, and what was *I* to love her? my beloved, my
        Geraldine!

     Yet I could not choose but love her—I was born to poet
        uses—
30   To love all things set above me, all of good and all of fair.
     Nymphs of old Parnassus, we are wont to call the Muses—
     And in silver-footed climbing, poets pass from mount to
        star.

And because I was a poet, and because the public praised me,
With their critical deductions for the modern writer's fault;
35   I could sit at rich men's tables,—though the courtesies
        that raised me,
Still suggested clear between us, the pale spectrum of the salt.

And they praised me in her presence;—'Will your book
        appear this summer?'
Then returning to each other—'Yes, our plans are for the
        moors;'
Then with whisper dropped behind me—'There he is! the
        latest comer!'
40   Oh, she only likes his verses! what is over, she endures.

'Quite low-born! self-educated! somewhat gifted though by
        nature,—
And we make a point of asking him,—of being very kind:
You may speak, he does not hear you; and besides, he
        writes no satire,—
These new charmers who keep serpents with the antique
        sting resigned.'

45   I grew colder, I grew colder, as I stood up there among
        them,—
Till as frost intense will burn you, the cold scorning
        scorched my brow;
When a sudden silver speaking, gravely cadenced, over-
        rung them,
And a sudden silken stirring touched my inner nature
        through.

I looked upward and beheld her! With a calm and regnant
        spirit,
50   Slowly round she swept her eyelids, and said clear before
        them all—
'Have you such superfluous honour, sir, that, able to
        confer it,
You will come down, Mr. Bertram, as my guest to
        Wycombe Hall?'

Here she paused,—she had been paler at the first word of
    her speaking;
But because a silence followed it, blushed scarlet, as for shame;
55   Then, as scorning her own feeling, resumed·calmly—'I am
    seeking
More distinction than these gentlemen think worthy of my
    claim.

'Ne'ertheless, you see, I seek it—not because I am a
    woman,'—
(Here her smile sprang like a fountain, and, so, overflowed
    her mouth)
'But because my woods in Sussex have some purple shades
    at gloaming,
60   Which are worthy of a king in state, or poet in his youth.

'I invite you, Mr. Bertram, to no hive for worldly
    speeches—
Sir, I scarce should dare—but only where God asked the
    thrushes first—
And if *you* will sing beside them, in the covert of my
    beeches,
I will thank you for the woodlands, . . . for the human
    world, at worst.'

65   Then, she smiled around right childly, then, she gazed
    around right queenly;
And I bowed—I could not answer! Alternated light and
    gloom—
While as one who quells the lions, with a steady eye
    serenely,
She, with level fronting eyelids, passed out stately from the
    room.

Oh, the blessed woods of Sussex, I can hear them still
    around me,
70   With their leafy tide of greenery still rippling up the wind!
Oh, the cursed woods of Sussex! Oh, the cruel love that
    bound me

Up against the boles of cedars, to be shaméd where I pined!
Oh, the cursed woods of Sussex! where the hunter's dart
    has found me,
When a fair face and a tender voice had made me mad and
    blind!

75   In that ancient hall of Wycombe, thronged the numerous
    guests invited,
And the lovely London ladies trod the floors with gliding
    feet;
And their voices low with fashion, not with feeling, softly
    freighted
All the air about the windows, with elastic laughters sweet.

For at eve, the open windows flung their light out on the
    terrace,
80   Which the floating orbs of curtains, did with gradual
    shadow sweep;
While the swans upon the river, fed at morning by the
    heiress,
Trembled downward through their snowy wings, at music
    in their sleep.

And there evermore was music, both of instrument and
    singing,
Till the finches of the shrubberies, grew restless in the
    dark;
85   But the cedars stood up motionless, each in a moonlight
    ringing,
And the deer, half in the glimmer, strewed the hollows of
    the park.

And though sometimes she would bind me with her silver-
    corded speeches,
To commix my words and laughter with the converse and
    the jest,—
Oft I sate apart, and gazing on the river, through the
    beeches,
90   Heard, as pure the swans swam down it, her pure voice
    o'erfloat the rest.

In the morning, horn of huntsman, hoof of steed, and
    laugh of rider,
Spread out cheery from the court-yard, till we lost them in
    the hills;
While herself and other ladies, and her suitors left beside
    her,
Went a-wandering up the gardens, through the laurels and
    abeles.

95   Thus, her foot upon the new-mown grasses—
    bareheaded—with the flowings
Of the virginal white vesture, gathered closely to her
    throat;
With the golden ringlets in her neck, just quickened by her
    going,
And appearing to breathe sun for air, and doubting if to
    float,—

With a branch of dewy maple, which her right hand held
    above her,
100 And which trembled a green shadow in betwixt her and the
    skies,—
As she turned her face in going, thus, she drew me on to
    love her,
And to study the deep meaning of the smile hid in her
    eyes.

For her eyes alone smiled constantly: her lips had serious
    sweetness,
And her front was calm—the dimple rarely rippled on her
    cheek:
105 But her deep blue eyes smiled constantly,—as if they had
    by fitness
Won the secret of a happy dream, she did not care to
    speak.

Thus she drew me the first morning, out across into the
    garden:
And I walked among her noble friends, and could not keep
    behind;

Spake she unto all and unto me—'Behold, I am the
  warden,
110 Of the birds within these lindens, which are cages to their
  mind.

'But here, in this swarded circle, into which the lime-walk
  brings us—
Whence the beeches rounded greenly, stand away in
  reverent fear,—
I will let no music enter, saving what the fountain sings us,
Which the lilies round the basin, may seem pure enough to
  hear.

115 'And the air that waves the lilies, waves this slender jet of
  water,
Like a holy thought sent feebly up from soul of fasting saint!
Whereby lies a marble Silence, sleeping! (Lough the
  sculptor wrought her)
So asleep, she is forgetting to say Hush!—a fancy quaint.

'Mark how heavy white her eyelids! not a dream between
  them lingers!
120 And the left hand's index droppeth from the lips upon the
  cheek:
And the right hand,—with the symbol rose held slack
  within the fingers,—
Has fallen backward in the basin—yet this Silence will not
  speak!

'That the essential meaning growing, may exceed the special
  symbol,
Is the thought, as I conceive it: it applies more high and low,—
125 Your true noblemen will often, through right nobleness,
  grow humble,
And assert an inward honour, by denying outward show.'

'Yes, your Silence,' said I, 'truly, holds her symbol rose
  but slackly,
Yet she holds it—or would scarcely be a Silence to our ken!

And your nobles wear their ermine on the outside, or walk
    blackly
130   In the presence of the social law, as most ignoble men.

'Let the poets dream such dreaming! Madam, in these
    British islands,
'Tis the substance that wanes ever, 'tis the symbol that
    exceeds:
Soon we shall have nought but symbol! and for statues like
    this Silence
Shall accept the rose's marble—in another case, the
    weed's.'

135   'I let *you* dream,' she retorted, 'and I grant where'er you
    go, you
Find for things, names—shows for actions, and pure gold
    for honour clear;
But when all is run to symbol in the Social, I will throw
    you
The world's book, which now reads drily, and sit down
    with Silence here.'

Half in playfulness she spoke, I thought, and half in
    indignation;
140   Her friends turned her words to laughter, while her lovers
    deemed her fair,—
A fair woman, flushed with feeling, in her noble-lighted
    station,
Near the statue's white reposing—and both bathed in
    sunny air!—

With the trees round, not so distant, but you heard their
    vernal murmur,
And beheld in light and shadow the leaves in and outward
    move;
145   And the little fountain leaping toward the sun-heart to be
    warmer,
And recoiling backward, trembling with too much light
    above—

'Tis a picture for remembrance! and thus, morning after
    morning,
Did I follow as she drew me, by the spirit, to her feet—
Why her greyhound followed also! dogs—we both were
    dogs for scorning—
150 To be sent back when she pleased it, and her path lay
    through the wheat.

And thus, morning after morning, spite of oath, and spite
    of sorrow,
Did I follow at her drawing, while the week-days passed
    along;
Just to feed the swans this noontide, or to see the fawns to-
    morrow,
Or to teach the hill-side echo, some sweet Tuscan in a
    song.

155 Ay, and sometimes on the hill-side, while we sate down in
    the gowans,
With the forest green behind us, and its shadow cast
    before;
And the river running under; and across it, from the
    rowans,
A brown partridge whirring near us, till we felt the air it
    bore,—

There, obedient to her praying, did I read aloud the poems
160 Made by Tuscan flutes, or instruments more various, of
    our own;
Read the pastoral parts of Spenser—or the subtle
    interflowings
Found in Petrarch's sonnets—here's the book—the leaf is
    folded down!—

Or at times a modern volume,—Wordsworth's solemn-
    thoughted idyl,
Howitt's ballad-dew, or Tennyson's enchanted reverie,—

165 Or from Browning some 'Pomegranate,' which, if cut deep
      down the middle,
  Shows a heart within blood-tinctured, of a veined
      humanity!—

  Or I read there sometimes, hoarsely, some new poem of
      my making—
  Oh, your poets never read their own best verses to their
      worth,—
  For the echo, in you, breaks upon the words which you are
      speaking,
170 And the chariot-wheels jar in the gate, through which you
      drive them forth.

  After, when we were grown tired of books, the silence
      round us flinging
  A slow arm of sweet compression, felt with beatings at the
      breast,—
  She would break out, on a sudden, in a gush of woodland
      singing,
  Like a child's emotion in a god—a naiad tired of rest.

175 Oh, to see or hear her singing! scarce I know which is
      divinest—
  For her looks sing too—she modulates her gestures on the
      tune;
  And her mouth stirs with the song, like song; and when the
      notes are finest,
  'Tis the eyes that shoot out vocal light, and seem to swell
      them on.

  Then we talked—oh, how we talked! her voice, so cadenced
      in the talking,
180 Made another singing—of the soul! a music without
      bars—
  While the leafy sounds of woodlands, humming round
      where we were walking,
  Brought interposition worthy-sweet,—as skies about the
      stars.

And she spake such good thoughts natural, as if she always
    thought them—
And had sympathies so ready, open, free as bird on branch,
185 Just as ready to fly east as west, whichever way besought
    them,
In the birchen wood a chirrup, or a cock-crow in the
    grange.

In her utmost lightness there is truth—and often she
    speaks lightly;
And she has a grace in being gay, which mourners even
    approve;
For the root of some grave earnest thought is understruck
    so rightly,
190 As to justify the foliage and the waving flowers above.

And she talked on—*we* talked truly! upon all things
    —substance—shadow—
Of the sheep that browsed the grasses—of the reapers in
    the corn—
Of the little children from the schools, seen winding
    through the meadow—
Of the poor rich world beyond them, still kept poorer by
    its scorn!

195 So of men, and so, of letters—books are men of higher
    stature,
And the only men that speak aloud for future times to hear!
So, of mankind in the abstract, which grows slowly into
    nature,
Yet will lift the cry of 'progress,' as it trod from sphere to
    sphere.

And her custom was to praise me, when I said,—'The Age
    culls simples,
200 With a broad clown's back turned broadly, to the glory of
    the stars—

We are gods by our own reck'ning,—and may well shut up
　　the temples,
And wield on, amid the incense-steam, the thunder of our
　　cars.

'For we throw out acclamations of self-thanking, self-
　　admiring,
With, at every mile run faster,—'O the wondrous,
　　wondrous age,'
205　Little thinking if we work our SOULS as nobly as our
　　iron,—
Or if angels will commend us, at the goal of pilgrimage.

'Why, what *is* this patient entrance into nature's deep
　　resources,
But the child's most gradual learning to walk straightly
　　without bane—?
When we drive out, from the cloud of steam, majestical
　　white horses,
210　Are we greater than the first men, who led black ones by
　　the mane?

'If we sided with the eagles, if we struck the stars in rising,
If we wrapped the globe intensely, with one hot electric
　　breath
'Twere but power within our *tether*—no new spirit-power
　　conferring—
And in life we were not greater men, nor bolder men in
　　death.'

215　She was patient with my talking; and I loved her—loved
　　her certes,
As I loved all Heavenly objects, with uplifted eyes and
　　hands!
As I loved pure inspirations—loved the graces, loved the
　　virtues,—
In a Love content with writing his own name, on desert
　　sands.

Or at least I thought so, purely!—thought, no idiot Hope
was raising
220 Any crown to crown Love's silence—silent Love that sate
alone—
Out, alas! the stag is like me—he, that tries to go on
grazing
With the great deep gun-wound in his neck, then reels
with sudden moan.

It was thus I reeled! I told you that her hand had many
suitors—
But she rose above them, smiling down, as Venus down the
waves—
225 And with such a gracious coldness, that they could not
press their futures
On that present of her courtesy, which yieldingly enslaves.

And this morning, as I sat alone within the inner chamber
With the great saloon beyond it, lost in pleasant thought
serene—
For I had been reading Camoëns—that poem you
remember,
230 Which his lady's eyes are praised in, as the sweetest ever
seen.

And the book lay open, and my thought flew from it,
taking from it
A vibration and impulsion to an end beyond its own,—
As the branch of a green osier, when a child would
overcome it,
Springs up freely from his clasping, and goes swinging in
the sun.

235 As I mused I heard a murmur,—it grew deep as it grew
longer—
Speakers using earnest language—'Lady Geraldine, you
would!'

And I heard a voice that pleaded ever on, in accents
    stronger,
As a sense of reason gave it power to make its rhetoric
    good.

Well I knew that voice—it was an earl's, of soul that
    matched his station—
240 Of a soul complete in lordship—might and right read on
    his brow;
Very finely courteous—far too proud to doubt his
    domination
Of the common people,—he atones for grandeur by a bow.

High straight forehead, nose of eagle, cold blue eyes, of less
    expression
Than resistance,—coldly casting off the looks of other
    men,
245 As steel, arrows,—unelastic lips, which seem to taste
    possession,
And be cautious lest the common air should injure or
    distrain.

For the rest, accomplished, upright,—ay, and standing by
    his order
With a bearing not ungraceful; fond of arts, and letters too;
Just a good man, made a proud man,—as the sandy rocks
    that border
250 A wild coast, by circumstances, in a regnant ebb and flow.

Thus, I knew that voice—I heard it—and I could not help
    the hearkening:
In the room I stood up blindly, and my burning heart
    within
Seemed to seethe and fuse my senses, till they ran on all
    sides, darkening,
And scorched, weighed, like melted metal, round my feet
    that stood therein.

255 And that voice, I heard it pleading, for love's sake—for
      wealth, position, . .
For the sake of liberal uses, and great actions to be done—
And she answered, answered gently,—'Nay, my lord, the
      old tradition
Of your Normans, by some worthier hand than mine is,
      should be won.'

'Ah, that white hand!' he said quickly,—and in his he
      either drew it,
260 Or attempted—for which gravity and instance she
      replied—
'Nay, indeed, my lord, this talk is vain, and we had best
      eschew it,
And pass on, like friends, to other points, less easy to
      decide.'

What he said again, I know not. It is likely that his trouble
Worked his pride up to the surface, for she answered in
      slow scorn—
265 'And your lordship judges rightly. Whom I marry, shall be
      noble,
Ay, and wealthy. I shall never blush to think how he was
      born.'

There, I maddened! her words stung me! Life swept
      through me into fever,
And my soul sprang up astonished; sprang, full-statured in
      an hour.
Know you what it is when anguish, with apocalyptic
      NEVER,
270 To a Pythian height dilates you,—and despair sublimes to
      power?

From my brain, the soul-wings budded!—waved a flame
      about my body,
Whence conventions coiled to ashes. I felt self-drawn out,
      as man,

From amalgamate false natures; and I saw the skies grow
ruddy
With the deepening feet of angels, and I knew what spirits
can.
275   I was mad—inspired—say either! anguish worketh
inspiration!
Was a man, or beast—perhaps so; for the tiger roars, when
speared!
And I walked on, step by step, along the level of my
passion—
Oh my soul! and passed the doorway to her face, and never
feared.

He had left her,—peradventure, when my footstep proved
my coming—
280   But for *her*—she half arose, then sate—grew scarlet and
grew pale:
Oh, she trembled!—'tis so always with a worldly man or
woman,
In the presence of true spirits—what else *can* they do but
quail?

Oh, she fluttered like a tame bird, in among its forest-
brothers,
Far too strong for it! then drooping, bowed her face upon
her hands—
285   And I spake out wildly, fiercely, brutal truths of her and
others!
I, she planted in the desert, swathed her, windlike, with
my sands.

I plucked up her social fictions, bloody-rooted, though
leaf-verdant,—
Trod them down with words of shaming,—all the purples
and the gold,
And the 'landed stakes' and Lordships—all that spirits
pure and ardent
290   Are cast out of love and reverence, because chancing not to
hold.

'For myself I do not argue,' said I, 'though I love you, Madam,
But for better souls, that nearer to the height of yours have
            trod—
And this age shows, to my thinking, still more infidels to
            Adam,
Than directly, by profession, simple infidels to God.

295 'Yet, O God' (I said), 'O grave' (I said), 'O mother's heart
            and bosom,
With whom first and last are equal, saint and corpse and
            little child!
We are fools to your deductions, in these figments of heart-
            closing!
We are traitors to your causes, in these sympathies defiled!

'Learn more reverence, Madam, not for rank or
            wealth—*that* needs no learning;
300 *That* comes quickly—quick as sin does! ay, and often
            works to sin;
But for Adam's seed, MAN! Trust me, 'tis a clay above
            your scorning,
With God's image stamped upon it, and God's kindling
            breath within.

'What right have you, Madam, gazing in your shining
            mirror daily,
Getting so, by heart, your beauty, which all others must
            adore,—
305 While you draw the golden ringlets down your fingers, to
            vow gaily, . .
You will wed no man that's only good to God,—and
            nothing more?

'Why, what right have you, made fair by that same God
            —the sweetest woman
Of all women He has fashioned—with your lovely spirit-
            face,

Which would seem too near to vanish, if its smile were not
          so human,—
310   And your voice of holy sweetness, turning common words
          to grace:

'What right *can* you have, God's other works, to scorn,
          despise, . . . revile them
In the gross, as mere men, broadly—not as *noble* men,
          forsooth,—
But as Parias of the outer world, forbidden to assoil them,
In the hope of living,—dying,—near that sweetness of
          your mouth?

315   'Have you any answer, Madam? If my spirits were less
          earthy—
If its instruments were gifted with more vibrant silver
          strings—
I would kneel down where I stand, and say—'Behold me!
          I am worthy
Of thy loving, for I love thee! I am worthy as a king.'

'As it is—your ermined pride, I swear, shall feel this stain
          upon her—
320   That *I*, poor, weak, tost with passion, scorned by me and
          you again,
Love you, Madam—dare to love you—to my grief and
          your dishonour—
To my endless desolation, and your impotent disdain!'

More mad words like these—mere madness! friend, I need
          not write them fuller;
And I hear my hot soul dropping on the lines in showers of
          tears—
325   Oh, a woman! friend, a woman! Why, a beast had scarce
          been duller,
Than roar bestial loud complaints against the shining of
          the spheres.

But at last there came a pause. I stood all vibrating with
    thunder,
Which my soul had used. The silence drew her face up like
    a call.
Could you guess what word she uttered? She looked up, as
    if in wonder,
330 With tears beaded on her lashes, and said 'Bertram!' It was all.

If she had cursed me—and she might have—or if even,
    with queenly bearing,
Which at need is used by women, she had risen up and said,
'Sir, you are my guest, and therefore I have given you a full
    hearing—
Now, beseech you, choose a name exacting somewhat less,
    instead—'

335 I had borne it!—but that 'Bertram'—why it lies there on
    the paper
A mere word, without her accents,—and you cannot judge
    the weight
Of the calm that crushed my passion! I seemed swimming
    in a vapour,—
And her gentleness did shame me, whom her scorn made
    desolate.

So, struck backward, and exhausted with that inward flow
    of passion
340 Which had passed, in deadly rushing, into forms of abstract
    truth,—
With a logic agonising through unfit denunciation,—
And with youth's own anguish turning grimly grey the
    hairs of youth,—

With the sense accursed and instant, that if even I spake
    wisely,
I spake basely—using truth,—if what I spake, indeed was
    true—

345   To avenge wrong on a woman—*her*, who sate there
           weighing nicely
       A poor manhood's worth, found guilty of such deeds as I
           could do!—

       With such wrong and woe exhausted—what I suffered and
           occasioned,—
       As a wild horse, through a city, runs with lightning in his eyes,
       And then dashing at a church's cold and passive wall,
           impassioned,
350   Strikes the death into his burning brain, and blindly drops
           and dies—

       So I fell, struck down before her! Do you blame me, friend
           for weakness?
       'Twas my strength of passion slew me!—fell before her
           like a stone;
       Fast the dreadful world rolled from me, on its roaring
           wheels of blackness!
       When the light came I was lying in this chamber—and
           alone.

355   Oh, of course, she charged her lacqueys to bear out the
           sickly burden,
       And to cast it from her scornful sight—but not *beyond* the
           gate—
       She is too kind to be cruel, and too haughty not to pardon
       Such a man as I—'twere something to be level to her hate.

       But for *me*—you now are conscious why, my friend, I
           write this letter,—
360   How my life is read all backward, and the charm of life
           undone!
       I shall leave this house at dawn—I would to-night, if I
           were better—
       And I charge my soul to hold my body strengthened for
           the sun.

When the sun has dyed the oriel, I depart with no last
    gazes,
No weak moanings—one word only, left in writing for her
    hands,—
365 Out of reach of her derisions, and some unavailing praises,
To make front against this anguish in the far and foreign
    lands.

Blame me not, I would not squander life in grief—I am
    abstemious;
I but nurse my spirit's falcon, that its wing may soar again.
There's no room for tears of weakness, in the blind eyes of
    a Phemius:
370 Into work the poet kneads them,—and he does not die *till*
    then.

CONCLUSION

Bertram finished the last pages, while along the silence ever
Still in hot and heavy splashes, fell his tears on every leaf:
Having ended, he leans backward in his chair, with lips
    that quiver
From the deep unspoken, ay, and deep unwritten thoughts
    of grief.

375 Soh! how still the lady standeth! 'tis a dream—a dream of
    mercies!
'Twixt the purple-lattice curtains, how she standeth still
    and pale!
'Tis a vision, sure, of mercies, sent to soften his self-
    curses—
Sent to sweep a patient quiet, o'er the tossing of his wail.

'Eyes,' he said, 'now throbbing through me! are ye eyes
    that did undo me?
380 Shining eyes, like antique jewels set in Parian statue-stone!
Underneath that calm white forehead, are ye ever burning
    torrid,
O'er the desolate sand-desert of my heart and life undone?'

With a murmurous stir, uncertain, in the air, the purple
   curtain
Swelleth in and swelleth out around her motionless pale
   brows;
385 While the gliding of the river sends a rippling noise for
   ever,
Through the open casement whitened by the moonlight's
   slant repose.

Said he—'Vision of a lady! stand there silent, stand there
   steady!
Now I see it plainly, plainly; now I cannot hope or
   doubt—
There, the cheeks of calm expression—there, the lips of
   silent passion,
390 Curvéd like an archer's bow, to send the bitter arrows out.'

Ever, evermore the while in a slow silence she kept
   smiling,—
And approached him slowly, slowly, in a gliding measured
   pace;
With her two white hands extended, as if praying one
   offended,
And a look of supplication, gazing earnest in his face.

395 Said he—'Wake me by no gesture,—sound of breath, or
   stir of vesture;
Let the blessed apparition melt not yet to its divine!
No approaching—hush! no breathing! or my heart must
   swoon to death in
The too utter life thou bringest—O thou dream of
   Geraldine!'

Ever, evermore the while in a slow silence she kept
   smiling—
400 But the tears ran over lightly from her eyes, and tenderly;
'Dost thou, Bertram, truly love me? Is no woman far above
   me,
Found more worthy of thy poet-heart, than such a one as
   I?'

Said he—'I would dream so ever, like the flowing of that
    river,
Flowing ever in a shadow, greenly onward to the sea;
410   So, thou vision of all sweetness—princely to a full
    completeness,—
Would my heart and life flow onward—deathward—
    through this dream of THEE!'

Ever, evermore the while in a slow silence she kept
    smiling,—
While the shining tears ran faster down the blushing of her
    cheeks;
Then with both her hands enfolding both of his, she softly
    told him,
415   'Bertram, if I say I love thee, . . . 'tis the vision only
    speaks.'

Softened, quickened to adore her, on his knee he fell before
    her—
And she whispered low in triumph—'It shall be as I have
    sworn!
Very rich is he in virtues,—very noble,—noble, certes;
And I shall not blush in knowing, that men call him lowly
    born.'

Crowned and Wedded [1840]

When last before her people's face, her own fair face she
    bent,
Within the meek projection of that shade she was content
To erase the child-smile from her lips, which seemed as if
    it might
Be still kept holy from the world to childhood still in
    sight—

5   To erase it with a solemn vow,—a princely vow—to
        rule—
  A priestly vow—to rule by grace of God the pitiful,—
  A very godlike vow—to rule in right and righteousness,
  And with the law and for the land!—so God the vower bless!

  The minster was alight that day, but not with fire, I ween,
10   And long-drawn glitterings swept adown that mighty aisled
        scene.
  The priests stood stoled in their pomp, the sworded chiefs
        in theirs,
  And so, the collared knights,—and so, the civil
        ministers,—
  And so, the waiting lords and dames—and little pages best
  At holding trains—and legates so, from countries east and
        west—
15   So, alien princes, native peers, and high-born ladies bright,
  Along whose brows the Queen's, new crowned, flashed
        coronets to light!—
  And so, the people at the gates, with priestly hands on
        high,
  Which bring the first anointing to all legal majesty!
  And so the DEAD—who lie in rows beneath the minster
        floor,
20   There, verily an awful state maintaining evermore—
  The statesman, whose clean palm will kiss no bribe whate'er
        it be
  The courtier, who, for no fair queen, will rise up to his
        knee—
  The court-dame, who, for no court-tire, will leave her
        shroud behind—
  The laureate, who no courtlier rhyme than 'dust to dust'
        can find—
25   The kings and queens who having made that vow and
        worn that crown,
  Descended into lower thrones and darker, deep adown!
  Dieu et mon droit—what is't to them?—what meaning can
        it have?—
  The King of kings, the rights of death—God's judgment
        and the grave!

And when betwixt the quick and dead the young fair queen
　　had vowed,
30　The living shouted 'May she live! Victoria, live!' aloud—
And as the loyal shouts went up, true spirits prayed
　　between,
'The blessings happy monarchs have, be thine, O crowned
　　queen!'

But now before her people's face she bended her's anew,
And calls them, while she vows, to be her witness
　　thereunto.
35　She vowed to rule, and, in that oath, her childhood put
　　away—
She doth maintain her womanhood, in vowing love today.
O, lovely lady!—let her vow!—such lips become such
　　vows,
And fairer goeth bridal wreath than crown with vernal
　　brows.
O lovely lady!—let her vow!—yea, let her vow to love!—
40　And though she be no less a queen—with purples hung
　　above,
The pageant of a court behind, the royal kin around,
And woven gold to catch her looks turned maidenly to
　　ground,—
Yet may the bride-veil hide from her a little of that state,
While loving hopes, for retinues, about her sweetness wait.
45　SHE vows to love, who vowed to rule—the chosen at her
　　side;
Let none say, God preserve the queen!—but rather, Bless
　　the bride!
None blow the trump, none bend the knee, none violate
　　the dream
Wherein no monarch, but a wife, she to herself may seem.
Or if ye say, Preserve the queen!—oh, breathe it inward
　　low—
50　She is a *woman*, and *beloved!*—and 'tis enough but so.
Count it enough, thou noble prince, who tak'st her by the
　　hand,
And claimest for thy lady-love, our lady of the land!—

And since, Prince Albert, men have called thy spirit high
    and rare,
And true to truth and brave for truth, as some at Augsburg
    were,—
55 We charge thee by thy lofty thoughts, and by thy poet-
    mind
Which not by glory and degree takes measure of mankind,
Esteem that wedded hand less dear for sceptre than for ring,
And hold her uncrowned womanhood to be the royal thing!

And now, upon our queen's last vow, what blessings shall
    we pray?
60 None straitened to a shallow crown, will suit our lips
    today.
Behold, they must be free as love—they must be broad as
    free,
Even to the borders of heaven's light and earth's humanity.
Long live she!—send up loyal shouts—and true hearts
    pray between,—
'The blessings happy PEASANTS have, be thine, O crowned
    queen!'

Wine of Cyprus

GIVEN TO ME BY H. S. BOYD, ESQ., AUTHOR OF
'SELECT PASSAGES FROM THE GREEK FATHERS', ETC.,
TO WHOM THESE STANZAS ARE ADDRESSED.

If old Bacchus were the speaker
  He would tell you with a sigh,
Of the Cyprus in this beaker,
  I am sipping like a fly,—
5 Like a fly or gnat on Ida
  At the hour of goblet-pledge,
By queen Juno brushed aside, a
  Full white arm-sweep, from the edge!

Sooth, the drinking should be ampler,
10   When the drink is so divine;
And some deep-mouthed Greek exampler
   Would become your Cyprian wine!
Cyclop's mouth might plunge aright in,
   While his one eye over-leered—
15 Nor too large were mouth of Titan,
   Drinking rivers down his beard.

Pan might dip his head so deep in,
   That his ears alone pricked out;
Fauns around him, pressing, leaping,
20   Each one pointing to his throat!
While the Naiads like Bacchantes,
   Wild, with urns thrown out to waste,
Cry,—'O earth, that thou wouldst grant us
   Springs to keep, of such a taste!'

25 But for me, I am not worthy
   After gods and Greeks to drink;
And my lips are pale and earthy,
   To go bathing from this brink!
Since you heard them speak the last time,
30   They have faded from their blooms;
And the laughter of my pastime
   Has learnt silence at the tombs.

Ah, my friend! the antique drinkers
   Crowned the cup and crowned the brow!
35 Can I answer the old thinkers
   In the forms they thought of, now?
Who will fetch from garden-closes
   Some new garlands while I speak,
That the forehead, crowned with roses,
40   May strike scarlet down the cheek?

Do not mock me! with my mortal,
   Suits no wreath again, indeed!
I am sad-voiced as the turtle,
   Which Anacreon used to feed:

45 Yet as that same bird demurely
  Wet her beak in cup of his,—
 So, without a garland, surely
  I may touch the brim of this.

 Go!—let others praise the Chian!—
50   This is soft as Muses' string—
 This is tawny as Rhea's lion,
  This is rapid as its spring,—
 Bright as Paphia's eyes e'er met us,
  Light as ever trod her feet!
55 And the brown bees of Hymettus
  Make their honey, not so sweet.

 Very copious are my praises,
  Though I sip it like a fly!—
 Ah—but, sipping,—times and places
60   Change before me suddenly—
 As Ulysses' old libation
  Drew the ghosts from every part,
 So your Cyprus wine, dear Græcian,
  Stirs the Hades of my heart.

65 And I think of those long mornings
  Which my thought goes far to seek,
 When, betwixt the folio's turnings,
  Solemn flowed the rhythmic Greek.
 Past the pane, the mountain spreading,
70   Swept the sheep-bell's tinkling noise,
 While a girlish voice was reading,—
  Somewhat low for αι's and οι's!

 Then what golden hours were for us!—
  While we sate together there,
75 How the white vests of the chorus
  Seemed to wave up a live air!
 How the cothurns trod majestic
  Down the deep iambic lines!
 And the rolling anapæstic
80   Curled, like vapour over shrines!

Oh, our Æschylus, the thunderous!
  How he drove the bolted breath
Through the cloud, to wedge it ponderous
  In the gnarled oak beneath.
85 Oh, our Sophocles, the royal,
  Who was born to monarch's place—
And who made the whole world loyal,
  Less by kingly power than grace.

Our Euripides, the human—
90   With his droppings of warm tears;
And his touches of things common,
  Till they rose to touch the spheres!
Our Theocritus, our Bion,
  And our Pindar's shining goals!—
95 These were cup-bearers undying,
  Of the wine that's meant for souls.

And my Plato, the divine one,—
  If men know the gods aright
By their motions as they shine on
100   With a glorious trail of light!—
And your noble Christian bishops,
  Who mouthed grandly the last Greek:
Though the sponges of their hyssops
  Were distent with wine—too weak.

105 Yet, your Chrysostoms, you praised him,
  With his glorious mouth of gold;
And your Basil, you upraised him
  To the height of speakers old:
And we both praised Heliodorus
110   For his secret of pure lies;—
Who forged first his linked stories
  In the heat of lady's eyes.

And we both praised your Synesius,
  For the fire shot up his odes!
115 Though the Church was scarce propitious,
  As he whistled dogs and gods.—

And we both praised Nazianzen,
  For the fervid heart and speech!
Only I eschewed his glancing
120   At the lyre hung out of reach.

Do you mind that deed of Até,
  Which you bound me to, so fast,—
Reading 'De Virginitate,'
  From the first line to the last?
125 How I said at ending, solemn,
  As I turned and looked at you,
That St. Simeon on the column
  Had had somewhat less to do?

For we sometimes gently wrangled;
130   Very gently, be it said,—
For our thoughts were disentangled
  By no breaking of the thread!
And, I charged you with extortions
  On the nobler fames of old—
135 Ay, and sometimes thought your Porsons
  Stained the purple they would fold.

For the rest—a mystic moaning,
  Kept Cassandra at the gate!
With wild eyes the vision shone in—
140   And wide nostrils scenting fate!
And Prometheus, bound in passion
  By brute Force to the blind stone,
Showed us looks of invocation
  Turned to ocean and the sun.

145 And Medea we saw, burning
  At her nature's planted stake;
And proud Œdipus, fate-scorning,
  While the cloud came on to brake—
While the cloud came on slow—slower,
150   Till he stood discrowned, resigned!—
But the reader's voice dropped lower,
  When the poet called him BLIND!

Ah, my gossip! you were older,
   And more learned, and a man!—
155 Yet that shadow—the enfolder
   Of your quiet eyelids,—ran
Both our spirits to one level;
   And I turned from hill and lea
And the summer-sun's green revel,—
160 To your eyes that *could not see*.

Now Christ bless you with the one light
   Which goes shining night and day!
May the flowers which grow in sunlight
   Shed their fragrance in your way!
165 Is it not right to remember
   All your kindness, friend of mine,—
When we two sate in the chamber,
   And the poets poured us wine?

So, to come back to the drinking
170 Of this Cyprus:—it is well—
But those memories, to my thinking,
   Make a better œnomel:
And whoever be the speaker,
   None can murmur with a sigh—
175 That, in drinking from *that* beaker,
   I am sipping like a fly.

The Dead Pan

Gods of Hellas, gods of Hellas,
Can ye listen in your silence?
Can your mystic voices tell us
Where ye hide? In floating islands,
5 With a wind that evermore
Keeps you out of sight of shore?
      Pan, Pan is dead.

In what revels are ye sunken
In old Æthiopia?
10   Have the Pygmies made you drunken,
Bathing in mandragora
Your divine pale lips that shiver
Like the lotus in the river?
       Pan, Pan is dead.

15   Do ye sit there still in slumber,
In gigantic Alpine rows?
The black poppies out of number
Nodding, dripping from your brows
To the red lees of your wine,—
20   And so kept alive and fine?
       Pan, Pan is dead.

Or lie crushed your stagnant corses
Where the silver spheres roll on,
Stung to life by centric forces
25   Thrown like rays out from the sun?—
While the smoke of your old altars
Is the shroud that round you welters?
       Great Pan is dead.

'Gods of Hellas, gods of Hellas,'
30   Said the old Hellenic tongue!
Said the hero-oaths, as well as
Poets' songs the sweetest sung!
Have ye grown deaf in a day?
Can ye speak not yea or nay—
35   Since Pan is dead?

Do ye leave your rivers flowing
All alone, O Naiades,
While your drenched locks dry slow in
This cold feeble sun and breeze?—
40   Not a word the Naiads say,
Though the rivers run for aya.
       For Pan is dead.

From the gloaming of the oak-wood,
O ye Dryads, could ye flee?
45 At the rushing thunderstroke, would
No sob tremble through the tree?—
Not a word the Dryads say,
Though the forests wave for aye.
        For Pan is dead.

50 Have ye left the mountain places,
Oreads wild, for other tryst?
Shall we see no sudden faces
Strike a glory through the mist?
Not a sound the silence thrills,
55 Of the everlasting hills.
        Pan, Pan is dead.

O twelve gods of Plato's vision,
Crowned to starry wanderings,—
With your chariots in procession,
60 And your silver clash of wings!
Very pale ye seem to rise,
Ghosts of Grecian deities—
        Now Pan is dead!

Jove! that right hand is unloaded,
65 Whence the thunder did prevail:
While in idiocy of godhead,
Thou art staring the stars pale!
And thine eagle, blind and old,
Roughs his feathers in the cold.
70   Pan, Pan is dead.

Where, O Juno, is the glory
Of thy regal look and tread?
Will they lay, for evermore, thee,
On thy dim, straight, golden bed?
75 Will thy queendom all lie hid
Meekly under either lid?
        Pan, Pan is dead.

Ha, Apollo! Floats his golden
Hair, all mist-like where he stands;
80 While the Muses hang enfolding
Knee and foot with faint wild hands?
'Neath the clanging of thy bow,
Niobe looked lost as thou!
        Pan, Pan is dead.

85 Shall the casque with its brown iron,
Pallas' broad blue eyes, eclipse,—
And no hero take inspiring
From the God-Greek of her lips?
'Neath her olive dost thou sit,
90 Mars the mighty, cursing it?
        Pan, Pan is dead.

Bacchus, Bacchus! on the panther
He swoons,—bound with his own vines!
And his Mænads slowly saunter,
95 Head aside, among the pines,
While they murmur dreamingly,—
'Evohe—ah—evohe—!'
        Ah, Pan is dead.

Neptune lies beside the trident,
100 Dull and senseless as a stone:
And old Pluto deaf and silent
Is cast out into the sun.
Ceres smileth stern thereat,—
'We *all* now are desolate—'
105   Now Pan is dead.

Aphrodite! dead and driven
As thy native foam, thou art;
With the cestus long done heaving
On the white calm of thy heart!
110 *Ai Adonis!* At that shriek,
Not a tear runs down her cheek—
        Pan, Pan is dead.

And the Loves, we used to know from
One another,—huddled lie,
115 Frore as taken in a snow-storm,
Close beside her tenderly,—
As if each had weakly tried
Once to kiss her as he died.
     Pan, Pan is dead.

120 What, and Hermes? Time enthralleth
All thy cunning, Hermes, thus,—
And the ivy blindly crawleth
Round thy brave caduceus?
Hast thou no new message for us,
125 Full of thunder and Jove-glories?
     Nay! Pan is dead.

Crowned Cybele's great turret
Rocks and crumbles on her head:
Roar the lions of her chariot
130 Toward the wilderness, unfed:
Scornful children are not mute,—
'Mother, mother, walk a-foot—
     Since Pan is dead.'

In the fiery-hearted centre
135 Of the solemn universe,
Ancient Vesta,—who could enter
To consume thee with this curse?
Drop thy grey chin on thy knee,
O thou palsied Mystery!
140   For Pan is dead.

Gods! we vainly do adjure you,—
Ye return nor voice nor sign:
Not a votary could secure you
Even a grave for your Divine!
145 Not a grave, to show thereby,
Here these grey old gods do lie.
     Pan, Pan is dead.

Even that Greece who took your wages,
Calls the obolus outworn:
150 And the hoarse deep-throated ages
Laugh your godships into scorn—
And the poets do disclaim you,
Or grow colder if they name you—
        And Pan is dead.

155 Gods bereaved, gods belated,—
With your purples rent asunder!
Gods discrowned and desecrated,
Disinherited of thunder!
Now, the goats may climb and crop
160 The soft grass on Ida's top—
        Now, Pan is dead.

Calm, of old, the bark went onward,
When a cry more loud than wind,
Rose up, deepened, and swept sunward,
165 From the pilèd Dark behind:
And the sun shrank and grew pale,
Breathed against by the great wail—
        'Pan, Pan is dead,'

And the rowers from the benches
170 Fell,—each shuddering on his face—
While departing Influences
Struck a cold back through the place:
And the shadow of the ship
Reeled along the passive deep—
175   Pan, Pan is dead.

And that dismal cry rose slowly,
And sank slowly through the air;
Full of spirit's melancholy
And eternity's despair!
180 And they heard the words it said—
PAN IS DEAD—GREAT PAN IS DEAD—
        PAN, PAN IS DEAD.

'Twas the hour when One in Sion
Hung for love's sake on a cross—
185   When His brow was chill with dying,
And His soul was faint with loss;
When His priestly blood dropped downward,
And His kingly eyes looked throneward—
　　　　Then, Pan was dead.

190   By the love He stood alone in,
His sole Godhead rose complete:
And the false gods fell down moaning,
Each from off his golden seat—
All the false gods with a cry
195   Rendered up their deity—
　　　　Pan, Pan was dead.

Wailing wide across the islands,
They rent, vest-like, their Divine!
And a darkness and a silence
200   Quenched the light of every shrine:
And Dodona's oak swang lonely
Henceforth, to the tempest only.
　　　　Pan, Pan was dead.

Pythia staggered,—feeling o'er her,
205   Her lost god's forsaking look!
Straight her eyeballs filmed with horror,
And her crispy fillets shook—
And her lips gasped through their foam,
For a word that did not come.
210   　　　　Pan, Pan was dead.

O ye vain false gods of Hellas,
Ye are silent evermore!
And I dash down this old chalice,
Whence libations ran of yore.
215   See! the wine crawls in the dust
Wormlike—as your glories must!
　　　　Since Pan is dead.

Get to dust, as common mortals,
By a common doom and track!
220 Let no Schiller from the portals
Of that Hades, call you back,—
Or instruct us to weep all
At your antique funeral.
            Pan, Pan is dead.

225 By your beauty, which confesses
Some chief Beauty conquering you,—
By our grand heroic guesses,
Through your falsehood, at the True,—
We will weep *not* . . . ! earth shall roll
230 Heir to each god's aureole—
            And Pan is dead.

Earth outgrows the mythic fancies
Sung beside her in her youth:
And those debonaire romances
235 Sound but dull beside the truth.
Phœbus' chariot-course is run!
Look up, poets, to the sun!
            Pan, Pan is dead.

Christ hath sent us down the angels;
240 And the whole earth and the skies
Are illumed by altar-candles
Lit for blessed mysteries:
And a Priest's Hand, through creation,
Waveth calm and consecration—
245   And Pan is dead.

Truth is fair: should we forego it?
Can we sigh right for a wrong?
God Himself is the best Poet,
And the Real is His song.
250 Sing His truth out fair and full,
And secure His beautiful.
            Let Pan be dead.

Truth is large. Our aspiration
Scarce embraces half we be.
255 Shame! to stand in His creation
And doubt Truth's sufficiency!—
To think God's song unexcelling
The poor tales of our own telling—
      When Pan is dead.

260 What is true and just and honest,
What is lovely, what is pure—
All of praise that hath admonisht,—
All of virtue, shall endure,—
These are themes for poets' uses,
265 Stirring nobler than the Muses—
      Ere Pan was dead.

O brave poets, keep back nothing;
Nor mix falsehood with the whole!
Look up Godward! speak the truth in
270 Worthy song from earnest soul!
Hold, in high poetic duty,
Truest Truth the fairest Beauty!
      Pan, Pan is dead.

Caterina to Camoëns;
DYING IN HIS ABSENCE ABROAD, AND REFERRING
TO THE POEM IN WHICH HE RECORDED THE
SWEETNESS OF HER EYES.

On the door you will not enter,
   I have gazed too long—adieu!
Hope withdraws her peradventure—
   Death is near me,—and not *you!*
5   Come, O lover,
    Close and cover
These poor eyes, you called, I ween,
'Sweetest eyes, were ever seen.'

When I heard you sing that burden
10   In my vernal days and bowers,
Other praises disregarding,
    I but hearkened that of yours,—
        Only saying
        In heart-playing,
15   'Blessed eyes mine eyes have been,
If the sweetest, HIS have seen!'

But all changeth. At this vesper,
    Cold the sun shines down the door.
If you stood there, would you whisper
20   'Love, I love you,' as before,—
        Death pervading
        Now, and shading
Eyes you sang of, that yestreen,
As the sweetest, ever seen?

25   Yes! I think, were you beside them,
    Near the bed I die upon,—
Though their beauty you denied them,
    As you stood there, looking down,
        You would truly
30   Call them duly,
For the love's sake found therein,—
'Sweetest eyes, were ever seen.'

And if *you* looked down upon them,
    And if *they* looked up to *you*,
35   All the light which has forgone them
    Would be gathered back anew!
        They would truly
        Be as duly
Love-transformed to Beauty's sheen,—
40   'Sweetest eyes, were ever seen.'

But, ah me! you only see me
  In your thoughts of loving man,
Smiling soft perhaps and dreamy
  Through the wavings of my fan,—
45   And unweeting
      Go repeating,
In your reverie serene,
'Sweetest eyes, were ever seen.'

While my spirit leans and reaches
50 From my body still and pale,
Fain to hear what tender speech is
  In your love, to help my bale—
     O my poet,
      Come and show it!
55 Come, of latest love, to glean
'Sweetest eyes, were ever seen.'

O my poet, O my prophet,
  When you praised their sweetness so,
Did you think, in singing of it,
60 That it might be near to go?
     Had you fancies
     From their glances,
That the grave would quickly screen
'Sweetest eyes, were ever seen?'

65 No reply! The fountain's warble
  In the court-yard sounds alone.
As the water to the marble
  So my heart falls with a moan,
     From love-sighing
70   To this dying!
Death forerunneth Love, to win
'Sweetest eyes, were ever seen.'

Will you come? When I'm departed
　　Where all sweetnesses are hid—
75　When thy voice, my tender-hearted,
　　Will not lift up either lid.
　　　　Cry, O lover,
　　　　Love is over!
　Cry beneath the cypress green—
80　'Sweetest eyes were ever seen.'

When the angelus is ringing,
　　Near the convent will you walk,
And recall the choral singing
　　Which brought angels down our talk?
85　　　　Spirit-shriven
　　　　I viewed Heaven,
Till you smiled—'Is earth unclean,
'Sweetest eyes, were ever seen?'

When beneath the palace-lattice,
90　You ride slow as you have done,
And you see a face there—*that* is
　　Not the old familiar one,—
　　　　Will you oftly
　　　　Murmur softly,
95　'Here, ye watched me morn and e'en,
Sweetest eyes, were ever seen!'

When the palace ladies sitting
　　Round your gittern, shall have said,
'Poet, sing those verses written
100　For the lady who is dead,'—
　　　　Will you tremble,
　　　　Yet dissemble,—
Or sing hoarse, with tears between,
'Sweetest eyes, were ever seen?'

105 'Sweetest eyes!' How sweet in flowings,
    The repeated cadence is!
Though you sang a hundred poems,
    Still the best one would be this.
      I can hear it
110   'Twixt my spirit
And the earth-noise, intervene—
'Sweetest eyes, were ever seen!'

But the priest waits for the praying,
    And the choir are on their knees,—
115 And the soul must pass away in
    Strains more solemn high than these!
      Miserere
      For the weary—
Oh, no longer for Catrine,
120 'Sweetest eyes, were ever seen!'

Keep my riband: take and keep it,—
    I have loosed it from my hair;*
Feeling, while you overweep it,
    Not alone in your despair,—
125   Since with saintly
      Watch, unfaintly,
Out of Heaven shall o'er you lean
'Sweetest eyes, were ever seen.'

But—but *now*—yet unremoved
130   Up to Heaven, they glisten fast:
You may cast away, Beloved,
    In your future, all my past;
      Such old phrases
      May be praises
135 For some fairer bosom-queen—
'Sweetest eyes, were ever seen!'

---

*She left him the riband from her hair.

Eyes of mine, what are ye doing?
  Faithless, faithless,—praised amiss,
If a tear be of your showing,
140   Dropt for any hope of HIS!
        Death hath boldness
        Beside coldness,
If unworthy tears demean
'Sweetest eyes, were ever seen.'

145 I will look out to his future—
    I will bless it till it shine.
Should he ever be a suitor
  Unto sweeter eyes than mine,
        Sunshine gild them,
150   Angels shield them,
Whatsoever eyes terrene
Be the sweetest HIS have seen!

THE RUNAWAY SLAVE AT
PILGRIM'S POINT (1848, 1849, 1850)

[ADVERTISEMENT, The following verses were the contribution of
the Authoress to a volume entitled 'The Liberty Bell, by Friends
of Freedom,' printed in America last year for sale at the Boston
National Anti-Slavery Bazaar. It is for the use of a few 'friends of
freedom' and of the writer on this side of the Atlantic that the
verses are now reprinted. FLORENCE, 1849.]

I

I stand on the mark, beside the shore
  Of the first white pilgrim's bended knee,
Where exile changed to ancestor,
  And God was thanked for liberty.
5 I have run through the night—my skin is as dark—
I bend my knee down on this mark:—
  I look on the sky and the sea.

II

O, pilgrim-souls, I speak to you:
  I see you come out proud and slow
10 From the land of the spirits, pale as dew,
  And round me and round me ye go.
O pilgrims, I have gasped and run
All night long from the whips of one
  Who, in your names, works sin and woe.

III

15 And thus I thought that I would come
  And kneel here where ye knelt before,
And feel your souls around me hum
  In undertone to the ocean's roar;
And lift my black face, my black hand,
20 Here, in your names, to curse this land
  Ye blessed in Freedom's, evermore.

IV

I am black—I am black!
  And yet God made me, they say:
But *if* He did so, smiling, back
25   He must have cast His work away
Under the feet of His white creatures,
With a look of scorn, that the dusky features
  Might be trodden again to clay.

V

And yet He has made dark things
30   To be glad and merry as light:
There's a little dark bird sits and sings;
  There's a dark stream ripples out of sight;
And the dark frogs chant in the safe morass,
And the sweetest stars are made to pass
35   O'er the face of the darkest night.

VI

But *we* who are dark, we are dark!
  O God, we have no stars!
About our souls, in care and cark,
  Our blackness shuts like prison bars:
40 And crouch our souls so far behind,
That never a comfort can they find
  By reaching through the prison-bars.

[VII

Indeed we live beneath the sky, . .
  That great smooth Hand of God, stretched out
45 On all His children fatherly,
  To bless them from the fear and doubt,
Which would be, if, from this low place,
All opened straight up to His face
  Into the grand eternity.]

VIII

50 Howbeit God's sunshine and His frost,
   They make us hot, they make us cold,
As if we were not black and lost;
   And the beasts and birds, in wood and wold,
Do fear and take us for very men:—
55 Could the weep-poor-will or the cat of the glen
   Look into my eyes and be bold?

IX

I am black, I am black!
   And, once, I laughed in girlish glee;
For one of my colour stood in the track
60   Where the drivers drove, and looked at me—
And tender and full was the look he gave!
A Slave looked *so* at another Slave,—
   I look at the sky and the sea.

X

And from that hour our spirits grew
65   As free as if unsold, unbought:
We were strong enough, since we were two,
   To conquer the world, we thought!
The drivers drove us day by day;
We did not mind, we went one way
70   And no better a liberty sought.

XI

In the open ground, between the canes,
   He said 'I love you' as he passed;
Where the shingle-roof rang sharp with the rains,
   I heard how he vowed it fast.
75 While others trembled, he sate in the hut
And carved me a bowl of the cocoa-nut
   Through the roar of the hurricanes.

XII

I sang his name instead of a song;
  Over and over I sang his name;
80 Backward and forward I drew it along
  With my sweetest notes, it was still the same!
I sang it low, that the slave-girls near
Might never guess, from aught they could hear,
  That all the song was a name.

XIII

85 I look on the sky and the sea!
  We were two to love, and two to pray,—
Yes, two, O God, who cried on Thee,
  Though nothing didst Thou say.
Coldly Thou sat'st behind the sun:
90 And now I cry, who am but one,—
  Thou wilt not speak to-day!

XIV

We were black, we were black!
  We had no claim to love and bliss;
What marvel, ours was cast to wrack?
95   They wrung my cold hands out of his,—
They dragged him—where? I crawled to touch
His blood's mark in the dust—not much,
  Ye pilgrim-souls,—though plain as *this!*

XV

Wrong, followed by a greater wrong!
100   Grief seemed too good for such as I:
So the white men brought the shame ere long
  To stifle the sob in my throat thereby.
They would not leave me for my dull
Wet eyes!—it was too merciful
105   To let me weep pure tears, and die.

XVI
I am black, I am black!
  I wore a child upon my breast—
An amulet that hung too slack,
  And, in my unrest, could not rest:
110 Thus we went moaning, child and mother,
One to another, one to another,
  Until all ended for the best.

XVII
For hark! I will tell you low—low—
  I am black, you see,—
115 And the babe, who lay on my bosom so,
  Was far too white, too white for me;
As white as the ladies who scorned to pray
Beside me at church but yesterday,
  Though my tears had washed a place for my knee.

XVIII
120 And my own child! I could not bear
  To look in his face, it was so white;
I covered him up with a kerchief rare,
  I covered his face in, close and tight:
And he moaned and struggled, as well might be,
125 For the white child wanted his liberty—
  Ha, ha! he wanted the master's right.

XIX
He moaned and beat with his head and feet,
  His little feet that never grew;
He struck them out, as it was meet,
130 Against my heart to break it through.
  I might have sung like a mother—
But I dared not sing to the white-faced child
  The only song I knew.

XX

And yet I pulled the kerchief close:
135   He could not see the sun, I swear
More, then, alive, than now he does
    From between the roots of the mango—where?
I know where. Close! A child and mother
Do wrong to look at one another,
140   When one is black and one is fair.

XXI

Even in that single glance I had
  Of my child's face,—I tell you all,—
I saw a look that made me mad!—
  The *master's* look, that used to fall
145 On my soul like his lash . . or worse!—
Therefore, to save it from my curse
  I twisted it round in my shawl.

XXII

And he moaned and trembled from foot to head,
  He shivered from head to foot,—
150 Till, after a time, he lay, instead,
    Too suddenly still and mute.
And I felt, beside, a creeping cold—
I dared to lift up just a fold,
  As in lifting a leaf of the mango-fruit.

XXIII

155 But *my* fruit! ha, ha!—there had been
    (I laugh to think on't at this hour!)
Your fine white angels (who have seen
    God's secret nearest to His power)
And gathered my fruit to make them wine,
160 And sucked the soul of that child of mine,
  As the humming-bird sucks the soul of the flower.

XXIV

Ha, ha! for the trick of the angels white!
  They freed the white child's spirit so.
I said not a word, but day and night,
165   I carried the body to and fro;
And it lay on my heart like a stone—as chill;
The sun may shine out as much as he will:
  I am cold, though it happened a month ago.

XXV

From the white man's house, and the black man's hut,
170   I carried the little body on;
The forest's arms did round us shut,
  And silence through the trees did run!
They asked no questions as I went,—
They stood too high for astonishment,—
175   They could see God rise on his throne.

XXVI

My little body, kerchiefed fast,
  I bore it on through the forest—on—
And when I felt it was tired at last,
  I scooped a hole beneath the moon.
180 Through the forest-tops the angels far,
With a white fine finger in every star,
  Did point and mock at what was done.

XXVII

Yet when it was all done aright,
  Earth, 'twixt me and my baby strewed,—
185 All changed to black earth,—nothing white,—
  A dark child in the dark,—ensued
Some comfort, and my heart grew young;
I sate down smiling there, and sung
  The song I told you of, for good.

XXVIII

190 And thus we two were reconciled,
   The white child and black mother, thus;
For, as I sang it,—soft, slow and wild
   The same song, more melodious,
Rose from the grave whereon I sate!
195 It was the dead child singing that,
   To join the souls of both of us.

XXIX

I look on the sea and the sky!
   Where the Pilgrims' ships first anchored lay.
The great sun rideth gloriously!
200   But the Pilgrims' ghosts have slid away
Through the first faint streaks of the morn!
My face is black, but it glares a scorn
   Which they dare not meet by day.

XXX

Ah!—in their stead their hunter sons!
205   Ah, ah! they are on me! they form in a ring!
Keep off!—I brave you all at once!—
   I throw off your eyes like a noisome thing!
You have killed the black eagle at nest, I think:
Did you never stand still in your triumph, and shrink
210   From the stroke of her wounded wing?

XXXI

(Man, drop that stone you dared to lift!—)
   I wish you who stand there seven abreast,
Each for his own wife's joy and gift,
   A little corpse as safely at rest,
215 Hid in the mangos!—Yes, but *she*
May keep live babies on her knee
   And sing the song she liketh best.

XXXII

I am not mad: I am black!
　I see you staring in my face—
220　I know you staring, shrinking back! . .
　　Ye are born of the Washington race:
And this land is the Free America—
And this mark on my wrist, (I prove what I say)
　Ropes tied me up here to the flogging-place.

XXXIII

225　You think I shrieked then? Not a sound!
　　I hung as a gourd hangs in the sun:
I only cursed them all around,
　　As softly as I might have done
My own child after. From these sands
230　Up to the mountains, lift your hands,
　　O Slaves, and end what I began!

XXXIV

Whips, curses; these must answer those!
　For in this UNION, you have set
Two kinds of men in adverse rows,
235　Each loathing each! and all forget
The seven wounds in Christ's body fair;
While HE see gaping everywhere
　Our countless wounds that pay no debt.

XXXV

Our wounds are different. Your white men
240　Are, after all, not gods indeed,
Nor able to make Christ's again
　Do good with bleeding. *We* who bleed—
(Stand off)—*we* help not in our loss,—
We are too heavy for our cross,
245　And fall and crush you and your seed.

XXXVI

I fall, I swoon! I look at the sky.
  The clouds are breaking on my brain;
I am floated along, as if I should die
  Of Liberty's exquisite pain—
250 In the name of the white child waiting for me
In the deep black death where our kisses agree,—
White men, I leave you all curse-free
  In my broken heart's disdain!

FROM *POEMS* (1850)

Flush or Faunus

You see this dog. It was but yesterday
I mused forgetful of his presence here
Till thought on thought drew downward tear on tear;
When from the pillow, where wet-cheeked I lay,
5   A head as hairy as Faunus, thrust its way
Right sudden against my face,—two golden clear
Large eyes astonished mine,—a drooping ear
Did flap me on either cheek, to dry the spray!
I started first, as some Arcadian,
10   Amazed by goatly God in twilight grove:
But as my bearded vision closelier ran
My tears off, I knew Flush, and rose above
Surprise and sadness; thanking the true PAN,
Who, by low creatures, leads to heights of love.

Hiram Powers' Greek Slave

They say Ideal Beauty cannot enter
The house of anguish. On the threshold stands
An alien Image with the shackled hands,
Called the Greek Slave: as if the sculptor meant her,
5   (That passionless perfection which he lent her,
Shadowed, not darkened, where the sill expands)
To, so, confront men's crimes in different lands,
With man's ideal sense. Pierce to the centre,
Art's fiery finger!—and break up erelong
10   The serfdom of this world! Appeal, fair stone,
From God's pure heights of beauty, against man's wrong!
Catch up in thy divine face, not alone
East griefs but west,—and strike and shame the strong,
By thunders of white silence, overthrown!

Hugh Stuart Boyd: His Blindness

God would not let the spheric Light accost
This God-loved man, and bade the earth stand off
With all her beckoning hills, whose golden stuff
Under the feet of the royal sun is crossed.
5   Yet such things were, to him, not wholly lost,—
Permitted, with his wandering eyes light-proof,
To have fair visions rendered full enough
By many a ministrant accomplished ghost:
And seeing, to sounds of softly-turned book leaves.
10 Sappho's crown-rose, and Meleager's spring,
And Gregory's starlight, on Greek-burnished eves:
Till Sensual and Unsensual seemed one thing
Viewed from one level;—earth's reapers at the sheaves,
Not plainer than Heaven's angels marshalling!

Hugh Stuart Boyd: Legacies

Three gifts the Dying left me: Æschylus,
And Gregory Nazianzen, and a clock
Chiming the gradual hours out like a flock
Of stars, whose motion is melodious.
5   The books were those I used to read from, thus
Assisting my dear teacher's soul to unlock
The darkness of his eyes: now, mine they mock,
Blinded in turn, by tears: now, murmurous
Sad echoes of my young voice, years agone,
10 Entoning, from these leaves, the Græcian phrase,
Return and choke my utterance. Books, lie down
In silence on the shelf within my gaze!
And thou, clock, striking the hour's pulse on,
Chime in the day which ends these parting days!

Sonnets from the Portuguese [1846]

I

I thought once how Theocritus had sung
Of the sweet years, the dear and wished for years,
Who each one in a gracious hand appears
To bear a gift for mortals, old or young =
5 And, as I mused it in his antique tongue
I saw, in gradual vision through my tears,
The sweet, sad years, the melancholy years, . .
Those of my own life, who by turns had flung
A shadow across me. Straightway I was 'ware,
10 So weeping, how a mystic Shape did move
Behind me and drew me backward by the hair;
And a voice said in mastery while I strove,
'Guess now who holds thee!' '*Death*' I saidx = but, there,
The silver answer rang . . 'Not Death, but Love.'

II

But only three in all God's universe—
Have heard this word thou hast said! Himself, beside
Thee speaking & me listening = and replied
One of us . . *that* was God! . . and laid the curse
5 So darkly on my eyelids as to amerce
My sight from seeing thee, . . . that if I had died,
The deathweights, placed there, would have signified
Less absolute exclusion—'Nay' is worse
From God than from all others, O my friend!
10 Men could not part us with their worldly jars,—
Nor the seas, change us, nor the tempests, bend!
Our hands would touch, for all the mountain = bars;—
And heaven being rolled between us, at the end,
We should but vow the faster, for the stars.

III

Unlike are we, unlike, O princely Heart!
Unlike our uses, and our destinies!
Our ministering two angels look surprise
On one another, as they strike athwart
5   Their wings in passing. Thou, bethink thee, art
A guest for queens to social pageantries,
With gages from a hundred brighter eyes
Than tears, even, can make mine, to ply thy part
Of chief musician! What hast *thou* to do,
10 With looking from the lattice = lights at me,
A poor, tired, wandering singer? . . singing through
The dark, and leaning up a cypress tree?
The chrism is on thine head,—on mine, the dew, . .
And Death must dig the level where these agree!

IV

Thou hast thy calling to some palace floor,
Most gracious singer of high poems! . . where
The dancers will break footing from the care
Of watching up thy pregnant lips for more.
5   And dost thou lift this house's latch, too poor
For hand of thine?—and canst thou think & bear
To let thy music drop here unaware
In folds of golden fulness at my door?
Look up and see the casement broken in—
10 The bats and owlets builders in the roof =
My cricket chirps against thy mandolin!
Hush!—call no echo up in further proof
Of desolation!—there's a voice within
That weeps . . as thou must sing . . alone . . aloof!—

V

I lift my heavy heart up solemnly,
As once Electra her sepulchral urn,
And, looking in thine eyes, I overturn
The ashes at thy feet. Behold & see
5 What a great heap of grief lay hid in me,
And how the red wild sparkles dimly burn
Through the ashen greyness. If thy foot in scorn
Could tread them out to darkness utterly,
It might be well perhaps—But if instead
10 Thou wait beside me for the wind to blow
The grey dust up; . . . those laurels on thine head,
O my beloved, will not shield thee so,
That none of all the fires shall scorch & shred
The hair beneath! stand further off then! Go.

VI

Go from me. Yet I feel that I shall stand
Henceforward in thy shadow nevermore
Alone upon the threshold of my door
Of individual life, I shall command
5 The uses of my soul, nor lift my hand
Serenely in the sunshine as before,
Without the sense of that which I forbore, . . .
Thy touch upon the palm—The widest land
Doom takes to part us, leaves thy heart in mine
10 With pulses that beat double. What I do
And what I dream include thee, as the wine
Must taste of its own grapes. And when I sue
God for myself, He hears that name of thine,
And sees within my eyes, the tears of two—

VII

The face of all the world is changed I think
Since first I heard the footsteps of thy soul
Move still 'oh, still' beside me = as they stole
Betwixt me and the dreadful outer brink
5   Of obvious death, . . where I who thought to sink
Was caught up into love & taught the whole
Of life in a new rhythm. The cup of dole
God gave for baptism, I am fain to drink,
And praise its sweetness, sweet, with thee anear!—
10   The names of country, Heaven, are changed away
For where thou art or shalt be, there or here =
And this . . this lute and song . . loved yesterday, . .
(The singing angels know!) . . . are only dear,
Because thy name moves right in what they say.

VIII

What can I give thee back, o liberal
And princely giver, . . who hast brought the gold
And purple of thine heart, unstained . . untold . .
And laid them on the outside of the wall
5   For such as I to take or leave withal,
In unexpected largesse? Am I cold,
Ungrateful . . . that for these most manifold
High gifts, I render nothing back at all?
Not so—not cold!—but very poor instead!—
10   Ask God who knows!—for frequent tears have run
The colours from my life, and left so dead
And pale a stuff, it were not fitly done
To give the same as pillow to thy head—
Go farther!—Let it serve to trample on—

IX

Can it be right to give what I can give?—
To let thee sit beneath the fall of tears
As salt as mine, and hear the sighing years
Re-sighing on my lips renunciative,
5 Through those infrequent smiles which fail to live
For all thy adjurations? O my fears,
That this can scarce be right! We are not peers,
So to be lovers; and I own & grieve
That givers of such gifts as mine are, must
10 Be counted with the ungenerous—Out, alas!—
I will not soil thy purple with my dust,
Nor breathe my soul against thy Venice-glass,
Nor give thee any love . . . which were unjust!—
Beloved, I only *love thee!*—let it pass—

X

Yet, love, mere love, is beautiful indeed
And worthy of acceptation. Fire is bright,
Let temple burn, or flax!—an equal light
Leaps in the flame from cedar-plank or weed—
5 And love is fire!—and when I say at need
I *love thee* . . mark! . . *I love thee!* . . in thy sight
I stand transfigured, glorified aright
With conscience of the new rays that proceed
Out of my face to thine. There's nothing low
10 In love, when love the lowest,—meanest creatures
Who love God, God accepts while loving so—
And what I *feel*, across the inferior features
Of what I *am*, doth flash itself, and show
How that great work of Love enhances Nature's.

XI

And therefore if to love can be desert,
I am not all unworthy. Cheeks as pale
As these you see, and trembling knees that fail
To bear a burden of a heavy heart,
5   This weary minstrel = life that once was girt
To climb Aornus, and can scarce avail
To pipe now 'gainst the woodland nightingale
A melancholy music! . . . why advert
To these things? O beloved, it is plain
10   I am not of thy worth nor for thy place!—
And yet because I love thee I obtain
From that same love this vindicating grace . .
To live on still in love and yet in vain,
To bless thee yet renounce thee, to thy face.

XII

Indeed this very Love, which is my boast,
And which, when rising up from breast to brow,
Doth crown me with a ruby large enow
To draw men's eyes, and prove the inner cost, . .
5   This love even . . . all my worth . . . to the uttermost, . .
I should not love withal, . . unless that thou
Hadst set me an exemplar, . . shown me how,
When first thine earnest eyes with mine were crossed,
And love called love. And thus, I cannot speak
10   Of love even, as a good thing of my own!—
Thy soul hath snatched up mine all faint & weak,
And placed it by thee on a golden throne =
And that I love . . (O soul I must be meek!)
Is by thee only, whom I love alone—

XIII

And wilt thou have me fashion into speech
The love I bear thee, finding words enough,
And hold the torch out, where the words are rough,
Between our faces, to cast light on each? . .
5   I drop it at thy feet—I cannot teach
My hand to hold my spirit so far off
From myself . . me . . that I should bring thee proof
In words . . of love hid in me out of reach.
Nay,—let the silence of my womanhood
10 Commend my woman-love to thy belief,—
And that I stand unwon, however wooed,
Rending the garment of my life, in brief,
By a most dauntless, voiceless fortitude,
Lest one touch of this heart, convey its grief.

XIV

If thou must love me, let it be for nought
Except for love's sake only. Do not say
"I love her for her smile . . her look . . her way
Of speaking gently . . ; for a trick of thought
5   That falls in well with mine, and certes brought
A sense of pleasant ease on such a day—"
For these things in themselves, beloved, may
Be changed, or change for thee, . . and love so wrought,
May be unwrought so. Neither love me for
10 Thine own dear pity wiping my cheeks dry!—
For one might well forget to weep, who bore
Thy comfort long, and lose thy love thereby—
But love me for love's sake, that evermore
Thou may'st love on through love's eternity—

XV

Accuse me not, beseech thee, that I wear
Too calm and sad a face in front of thine,
For we two look two ways, and cannot shine
With the same sunlight on our brow & hair.
5   Thou lookest, sweet, on me, without a care,
As on a bee shut in a crystalline . .
For sorrow hath shut me safe in love's divine,
And to spread wing & fly in the outer air
Were most impossible failure, if I strove
10 To fail so—But I look on thee . . on thee . .
Beholding besides love, the end of love,
Hearing oblivion beyond memory . . .
As one who sits and gazes, from above,
Over the rivers to the bitter sea.

XVI

And yet . . because thou overcomest so, . .
Because thou art more princely and like a king,
Thou canst prevail against my fears & fling
Thy purple round me, till my heart shall grow
5   Too close against thine heart, to henceforth know
How it shook when alone. Why, conquering
May prove as noble and complete a thing
In lifting upward as in crushing low!
And, as a soldier, struck down by a sword,
10 May cry, 'My strife ends here,' and sinks to earth, . . .
Even so, beloved, I at last record,
    . . . Here ends my doubt!—If *thou* invite me forth,
I rise above abasement, at the word.
Make thy love larger to enlarge thy worth.

XVII

My poet, thou canst touch on all the notes
God set between His after and before,
And strike up and strike off the general roar
Of the rushing worlds, a melody that floats
5 In a serene air purely. Antidotes
Of medicated music answering for
Mankind's forlornest uses, thou canst pour
From thence into their ears. God's will devotes
Thine to such ends, and mine to wait on thine—
10 How, dearest, wilt thou have me for most use?—
A hope, to sing by gladly? . . or a fine
Sad memory, with thy songs to interfuse? . .
A shade, in which to sing . . of palm or pine?
A grave, on which to rest from singing? . . Choose.

XVIII

I never gave a lock of hair away
To a man, dearest, except this to thee,
Which now upon my fingers thoughtfuly
I ring out to the full brown length and say
5 'Take it.'—My day of youth went yesterday—
My hair no longer bounds to my foot's glee,
Nor plant I it from rose or myrtle tree,
As girls do, any more. It only may
Now shade on two pale cheeks, the mark of tears,
10 Taught drooping from the head that hangs aside
Through sorrow's trick. I thought the funeral shears
Would take this first; . . but Love is justified—
Take it, thou, . . finding pure, from all those years,
The kiss my mother left here when she died—

XIX

The soul's Rialto hath its merchandise;
I barter curl for curl upon that mart;
And from my poet's forehead to my heart
Receive this lock which outweighs argosies— . .
5   As purply black as erst to Pindar's eyes
The dim purpureal tresses gloomed athwart
The nine white Muse = brows. For this counterpart, . . .
Thy bay = crown's shade, beloved, I surmise
Still lingers on thy curl, it is so black!—
10   Thus with the fillet of smooth = kissing breath
I tie the shadow safe from gliding back,
And lay the gift where nothing hindereth—
Here on my heart as on thy brow, to lack
No natural heat till mine grows cold in death.

XX

Beloved, my beloved, when I think
That thou wast in the world a year ago
What time I sate alone here in the snow
And saw no footprint, heard the silence sink.
5   No moment at thy voice, . . . but link by link
Went counting all my chains as if that so
They never could fall off at any blow
Struck by thy possible hand . . . why thus I drink
Of life's great cup of wonder! Wonderful,
10   Never to feel thee thrill the day or night
With personal act or speech, . . nor ever cull
Some prescience of thee with the blossoms white
Thou sawest growing. Atheists are as dull,
Who cannot guess God's presence out of sight—

XXI

Beloved, say again and yet again
That thou dost love me—Though the word repeated
Should seem a cuckoo-song, as thou dost treat it,
Remember, never to the hill & plain,
5   Valley & wood, without her cuckoo-strain,
Comes the sweet Spring in all her green, completed!
Beloved!—I, amid the darkness greeted
By a doubtful spirit = voice, in the doubt's pain
Cry . . speak once more . . thou lovest! Who can fear
10   Too many stars, though each in heaven should roll . .
Too many flowers, though each should crown the year?—
Say thou dost love me, love me, love me—toll
The silver iterance!—only minding, dear,
To love me also in silence, with thy soul.

XXII

When our two souls stand up erect and strong,
Face to face, silent, drawing nigh & nigher,
Until their lengthening wings break into fire
At either curvèd point, ... what bitter wrong,
5   Can the earth do to us, that we should not long
Be here contented?—Think, . . in mounting higher,
The angels would press on us, and aspire
To drop some golden orb of perfect song
Into our deep, dear silence. Let us stay
10   Rather on earth, beloved,—. . where the unfit
Contrarious moods of men recoil away
And isolate pure spirits, and permit
A place to stand and love in, for a day,
With darkness and the death-hour rounding it.

XXIII

Is it indeed so?—If I lay here dead,
Would'st thou miss any life in losing mine, . .
And would the sun for thee more coldly shine,
Because of grave = damps falling round my head?
5 I marvelled, my beloved, when I read
Thy thought so in the letter. I am thine—
But . . . *so* much to thee? Can I pour thy wine,
While my hands tremble?—Then my soul, instead
Of dreams of death, resumes life's lower range!—
10 Then, . . love me, love!—look on me . . breathe on me!—
As brighter ladies do not count it strange,
For love, to give up lands and degree,
I yield the grave for thy sake, and exchange
My near sweet view of Heaven, . . for earth with *thee!*

XXIV

Let the world's sharpness like a clasping knife
Shut in upon itself, and do no harm
In this close hand of Love now soft & warm,—
And let us hear no sound of human strife,
5 After the click of the shutting. Life to life—
I lean upon thee, dear, without alarm,
And feel as safe as witches by a charm,
Against the stabs of worldlings, who are rife
But weak to attaint us. Very whitely, still,
10 The lilies of our lives may reassure
Their blossoms, from their roots = . . their cups, they fill,
From Heaven's amreeta fatal to the impure,
And grow straight, out of man's reach, on the hill!—
God only, who made us rich, can make us poor.

XXV

A heavy heart, beloved, have I borne
From year to year until I saw thy face;
And sorrow after sorrow took the place
Of all those natural joys, as lightly worn
5 As the stringed pearls . . each lifted in its turn,
By a beating heart at dance = time. Hopes apace
Were changed to long despairs, . . . till God's own grace
Could scarcely lift above the world forlorn,
My heavy heart. Then *thou* didst bid me bring
10 And let it drop adown thy calmly great
Deep being! Fast it sinketh, as a thing
Which its own nature doth precipitate,
While thine doth close above it, mediating
Betwixt the stars and the unaccomplished fate.

XXVI

I lived with visions for all my company
Instead of men & women, years ago,
And found them gentle mates, nor thought to know
A sweeter music than they played to me—
5 But soon their trailing purple was not free
Of this world's dust;—their lutes did silent grow,
And I myself grew faint & blind below
Their vanishing eyes. Then *thou* didst come . . to *be*,
Beloved, what they *seemed*. Their shining fronts,
10 Their songs, their splendours, . . . (better, yet the same, . .
As river = water hallowed into fonts . .)
Met in thee, and, from out thee, overcame
My soul with satisfaction of all wants—
Because God's gifts put man's best dreams to shame.

XXVII

My own belovd, who hast lifted me
From this drear flat of earth where I was thrown,—
And in betwixt the languid ringlets blown
A life-breath, till the forehead hopefully
5 Shines out again as all the angels see,
Against thy saving kiss! . . . My own, my own . .
Who camest to me when the world was gone,
And I who looked for only God, found *thee!*
I find thee!—I am safe, & strong, & glad!—
10 As one who stands in dewless asphodel
Looks backward on the tedious time he had
In the upper life . . so I, with bosom = swell,
Make witness here between the good & bad,
That Love, as strong as Death, retrieves as well.

XXVIII

My letters!—all dead paper, . . mute and white!—
And yet they seem alive and quivering
Against my tremulous hands which loose the string
And let them drop down on my knee tonight.
5 This said, . . he wished to have me in his sight
Once, as a friend = this fixed a day in spring
To come and touch my hand . . a simple thing, . .
Yet I wept for it!—This . . . the paper's light . . .
Said, *Dear, I love thee!*—and I sank & quailed
10 As if God's future thundered on my past =
This said, '*I am thine*'—and so, its ink has paled
With lying at my heart that beats too fast =
And this . . . . O love, thy words have ill availed,
If, what this said, I dared repeat at last!—

XXIX

I think of thee!—my thoughts do twine & bud
About thee, as wild vines about a tree,—
Put out broad leaves, . . and soon there's nought to see,
Except the straggling green which hides the wood.
5 Yet, O my palm-tree, be it understood
I will not have my thoughts instead of thee
Who art dearer, better!—Rather instantly
Renew thy presence!—As a strong tree should,
Rustle thy boughs, and set thy trunk all bare,
10 And let these bands of greenery which insphere thee,
Drop heavily down, . . burst, shattered, everywhere!—
Because, in this deep joy to see and hear thee
And breathe within thy shadow a new air,
I do not think of thee . . . I am too near thee.

XXX

I see thine image through my tears tonight,
And yet today I saw thee smiling—How,
Refer the cause?—Beloved, is it thou
Or I? . . Who makes me sad?—The acolyte
5 Amid the chanted joy & thankful rite,
May, so, fall flat, with pale insensate brow,
On the altar = stair. I hear thy voice & vow
Perplexed . , uncertain . , since thou'rt out of sight,
As he, in his swooning ears, the choir's amen!—
10 Beloved, dost thou love? . . or did I see all
The glory as I dreamed, and fainted when
Too vehement light dilated my Ideal
For my soul's eyes?—Will that light come again,
As now these tears come, ... falling hot and real?—

XXXI

Thou comest!—all is said without a word!—
I sit beneath thy looks, as children do
In the noon = sun, with souls that tremble through
Their happy eyelids, from an unaverred
5   Yet prodigal inward joy. Behold, I erred
In that last doubt!—and yet I cannot rue
The sin most, but the occasion . . . . that we two
Should for a moment stand unministerred
By a mutual presence. Ah, keep near & close,
10 Thou dovelike help!—and, when my fears would rise,
With thy broad heart serenely interpose!—
Brood down with thy divine sufficiencies
These thoughts which tremble when bereft of those,
Like callow birds left desert to the skies.

XXXII

The first time that the sun rose on thine oath
To love me, I looked foward to the moon
To slacken all those bonds which seemed too soon
And quickly tied to make a lasting troth.
5   Quick-loving hearts, I thought, may quickly loathe—
And, looking on myself, I seemed not one
For such man's love!—more like an out of tune
Worn viol, a good singer would be wroth
To spoil his song with; and which, snatched in haste,
10 Is laid down at the first ill-sounding note.
I did not wrong myself so, but I placed
A wrong on *thee*. For perfect strains may float,
'Neath master = hands, from instruments defaced,—
And great souls, at one stroke, may do & doat.

XXXIII

Yes, call me by my pet-name: let me hear
The name I used to run at, when a child,
From innocent play, & leave the cowslips piled,
To look up in some face that proved me dear,
5 With the look of its eyes—I miss some clear
Fond voices, which, being drawn & reconciled
Into the music of Heaven's Undefiled,
Call *me* no longer. Silence on the bier,
While I call God . . call God!—So let thy mouth
10 Be heir to those who are now exanimate:—
Gather the north = flowers to complete the south,
And catch the early love up in the late!—
Yes, call me by that name,—and I, in truth,
With the same heart, will answer & not wait.

XXXIV

With the same heart, I said, I'll answer thee
As those, when thou shalt call me by my name!—
Lo, the vain promise! Is the same, the same,
Perplexed and ruffled by Life's strategy?
5 When called before, I told how certainly
I dropped my flowers, or brake off from a game,
To run and answer with the smile that came
At play last moment, and went on with me
Through my obedience. When I answer now,
10 I drop a sad thought:—break from solitude—
Yet still my heart goes to thee . . . ponder how . .
Not as to a single good, but as to all my good!—
Lay thy hand on it, best One! . . and allow
That no child's foot could run fast as this blood.

XXXV

If I leave all for *thee*, wilt thou exchange
And *be* all to me?—Shall I never miss
Home-talk and blessing and the common kiss
Which comes to each in turn? nor count it strange,
5   When I look up, to drop on a new range
Of walls and floors . . another home than this?—
Nay, wilt thou fill that place by me which is
Filled by dead eyes too tender to know change?—
That's hardest!—If to conquer Love has tried . .
10 To conquer grief, tries more; as all things prove!—
For Grief indeed is Love . . . and grief beside!—
Alas!—I have grieved so, I am hard to love—
Yet love me—wilt thou? open thine heart wide,
And fold within, the wet wings of thy dove,—

XXXVI

When we met first and loved, I did not build
Upon the event with marble. Could it mean
To last, a love set pendulous between
Sorrow and sorrow?—Nay, I rather thrilled,
5   Distrusting every light that seemed to gild
The onward path, & feared to overlean
A finger even. And though I have grown serene
And strong since then, I think that God has willed
A still renewable fear . . o love, o troth . .
10 Lest these enclasped hands should never hold,
This mutual kiss drop down between us both . .
As an unowned thing, once the lips being cold!—
And, Love, be false!—if *he*, to keep one oath,
Must lose one joy by his star of life foretold.

XXXVII

Pardon, oh, pardon, that my soul should make
Of all that strong divineness which I know
For thine and thee, an image only so
Formed of the sand, & fit to shift & break.
5   It is, that distant years which did not take
Thy sovranty, recoiling with a blow,
Have forced my swimming brain to undergo
Their doubt and dread, and blindly to forsake
Thy purity of likeness and distort
10   Thy worthiest love with worthless counterfeit!—
As if a shipwrecked pagan, safe in port,
His guardian seagod to commemorate,
Should set a sculptured porpoise . . . gills a-snort,
And vibrant tail . . . within the temple = gate—

XXXVIII

First time he kissed me, he but only kissed
The fingers of this hand wherewith I write,
And ever since it grew more clean and white . .
Slow to world-greetings . . . quick with its "oh, list"
5   When the angels speake. A ring of amethyst,
I could not wear here plainer to my sight,
Than that first kiss!—The second passed in height
The first, & sought the forehead, & half missed,
Half falling on the hair . . O beyond meed!—
10   That was the chrism of Love, which Love's own crown,
With sanctifying sweetness, did precede!—
The third, upon my lips,—was folded down
In perfect, purple state!—since when, indeed,
I have been proud and said, 'My Love, my own'.

XXXIX

Because thou hast the power & own'st the grace
To look through & behind this mask of me,
(Against which, years have beat thus blanchingly
With their ruins!—) and behold my soul's true face . .
5 The dim and weary witness of Life's race!—
Because thou hast the faith and love to see,
Through that same soul's distracting lethargy,
The patient angel waiting for his place
In the new Heavens—because nor sin, nor woe,
10 Nor God's infliction, nor death's neighbourhood,
Nor all which, others viewing, turn to go, . .
Nor all which makes me tired of all, self-viewed, . .
. . Nothing repels thee, . . Dearest, teach me so
To pour out gratitude, as thou dost, good.

XL

Oh, yes!—they love through all this world of ours!—
I will not gainsay love, called love forsooth!—
I have heard love talked in my dawning youth,
And since, not so long back but that the flowers
5 Then gathered, smell still!—Mussulmans and Giaours
Throw kerchiefs at a smile, & have no ruth
For any weeping!—Polypheme's white tooth
Slips on the nut, if after frequent showers
The shell is oversmooth, and not so much
10 Will turn the thing called love, aside to hate,
Or else to oblivion!—*But thou* art not such
A lover, my beloved!—*thou* canst wait
Through sorrow and sickness, to bring souls to touch,
And think it soon when others cry 'Too late.'

XLI

I thank all who have loved me in their hearts,
With thanks and love from mine. Deep thanks to all
Who paused a little near the prison = wall,
To hear my music in its louder parts,
5   Ere they went onward, each one, to the mart's
Or temple's occupation, beyond call.
But *thou*, who, in my voice's sink and fall,
When the sob caught it, . . thy divinest Art's
Own instrument, didst drop down at thy foot,
10 To hearken what I said between my tears, . .
Instruct me how to thank *thee*!—Oh, to shoot
My soul's full meaning into future years,—
That *they* should lend it utterance, and salute
Love that endures, with Life that disappears!—

XLII

"*My future will not copy fair my past* . ."
I wrote that once; and thinking at my side
My ministering life-angel justified
My words by his appealing look upcast
5   To the white throne of God, I turned at last,
And saw thee here instead o thou allied
To angels in thy soul! Then I, long tried
By natural ills, received the comfort fast;
While budding at thy sight, my pilgrim's staff
10 Gave out green leaves with morning dews impearled!—
—I seek no copy now of life's first half . .
Leave here the pages with long musing curled!—
And write me new my future's epigraph,
New angel mine, unhoped for in the world!

XLIII

How do I love thee? Let me count the ways!—
I love thee to the depth & breadth & height
My soul can reach, when feeling out of sight
For the ends of Being and Ideal Grace.
5 I love thee to the level of everyday's
Most quiet need, by sun & candlelight—
I love thee freely, as men strive for Right,—
I love thee purely, as they turn from Praise;
I love thee with the passion, put to use
10 In my old griefs, . . and with my childhood's faith:
I love thee with the love I seemed to lose
With my lost Saints,—I love thee with the breath,
Smiles, tears, of all my life!—and, if God choose,
I shall but love thee better after my death.

XLIV

Beloved, thou hast brought me many flowers
Plucked in the garden all the summer through,
And winter, and it seemed as if they grew
In this close room, nor missed the sun & showers.
5 So, in the like name of that love of ours,
Take back these thoughts, which here, unfolded, too,
And which on warm & cold days I withdrew
From my heart's ground. (Indeed, those beds and bowers
Be overgrown with bitter weeds & rue,
10 And wait thy weeding; yet here's eglantine,
Here's ivy!)—take them, as I used to do
Thy flowers, and keep them where they shall not pine!
Instruct thine eyes to keep their colours true,
And tell thy soul, their roots are left in mine.

50 Wimpole Street
1846, Sept
Married—September 12th, 1846.

CASA GUIDI WINDOWS (1851)

Part One [1848]

I

I heard last night a little child go singing
  'Neath Casa Guidi windows, by the church,
'*O bella libertà, O bella!*' stringing
  The same words still on notes he went in search
5 So high for, you concluded the upspringing
  Of such a nimble bird to sky from perch
Must leave the whole bush in a tremble green;
  And that the heart of Italy must beat,
While such a voice had leave to rise serene
10 'Twixt church and palace of a Florence street!
A little child, too, who not long had been
  By mother's finger steadied on his feet;
And still *O bella libertà* he sang.

II

Then I thought, musing, of the innumerous
15 Sweet songs which still for Italy outrang
From older singers' lips, who sang not thus
  Exultingly and purely, yet, with pang
Sheathed into music, touched the heart of us
  So finely, that the pity scarcely pained!
20 I thought how Filicaja led on others,
  Bewailers for their Italy enchained,
And how they called her childless among mothers,
  Widow of empires, ay, and scarce refrained
Cursing her beauty to her face, as brothers
25 Might a shamed sister's,—'Had she been less fair
She were less wretched,'—how, evoking so
  From congregated wrong and heaped despair
Of men and women writhing under blow,

Harrowed and hideous in their filthy lair,
30   A personating Image, wherein woe
Was wrapt in beauty from offending much,
They called it Cybele, or Niobe,
Or laid it corpse-like on a bier for such,
Where the whole world might drop for Italy
35   Those cadenced tears which burn not where they
            touch,—
'Juliet of nations, canst thou die as we?
And was the violet crown that crowned thy head
So over-large, though new buds made it rough,
It slipped down and across thine eyelids dead,
40   O sweet, fair Juliet?' Of such songs enough;
Too many of such complaints! Behold, instead,
Void at Verona, Juliet's marble trough!
As void as that is, are all images
Men set between themselves and actual wrong,
45   To catch the weight of pity, meet the stress
Of conscience, though 'tis easier to gaze long
On personations, masks, and effigies,
Than to see live weak creatures crushed by strong.

III
For me who stand in Italy to-day,
50   Where worthier poets stood and sang before,
I kiss their footsteps, yet their words gainsay.
I can but muse in hope upon this shore
Of golden Arno as it shoots away
Straight through the heart of Florence, 'neath the four
55   Bent bridges, seeming to strain off like bows,
And tremble, while the arrowy undertide
Shoots on and cleaves the marble as it goes,
And strikes up palace-walls on either side,
And froths the cornice out in glittering rows,
60   With doors and windows quaintly multiplied,
And terrace-sweeps, and gazers upon all,
By whom if flower or kerchief were thrown out
From any lattice there, the same would fall
Into the river underneath no doubt,

65   It runs so close and fast 'twixt wall and wall.
How beautiful! The mountains from without
        In silence listen for the word said next,
(What word will men say?) here where Giotto planted
        His campanile, like an unperplexed
70 Question to Heaven, concerning the things granted
        To a great people who, being greatly vexed
In act, in aspiration keep undaunted!
        What word says God? The sculptor's Night and Day
And Dawn and Twilight, wait in marble scorn,
75   Like dogs upon a dunghill, on the clay
From whence the Medicean stamp's outworn,—
        The final putting off of all such sway
By all such hands, and freeing of the unborn
        In Florence and the great world outside his Florence.
80 That's Michel Angelo! his statucs wait
        In the small chapel of the dim St. Lawrence!
Day's eyes are breaking bold and passionate
        Over his shoulder, and will flash abhorrence
On darkness, and with level looks meet fate,
85   When once loose from that marble film of theirs:
The Night has wild dreams in her sleep, the Dawn
        Is haggard as the sleepless: Twilight wears
A sort of horror: as the veil withdrawn
        'Twixt the artist's soul and works had left them heirs
90 Of the deep thoughts which would not quail nor fawn,
        Of angers and contempts, of hope and love;
For not without a meaning did he place
        The princely Urbino on the seat above
With everlasting shadow on his face;
95   While the slow dawns and twilights disapprove
The ashes of his long-extinguished race,
        Which never more shall clog the feet of men.

IV
I do believe, divinest Angelo,
        That winter-hour, in Via Larga, when
100 Thou wert commanded to build up in snow
        Some marvel of thine art, which straight again

Dissolved beneath the sun's Italian glow,
　　While thine eyes, still broad with the plastic passion,
Thawed too, in drops of wounded manhood, . . since,
105　　Mocking alike thine art and indignation,
Laughed at the palace-window the new prince, . .
　　('Aha! this genius needs for exaltation,
When all's said, and howe'er the proud may wince,
　　A little marble from our princely mines!')
110 I do believe that hour thou laughedst too,
　　For the whole sad world and for thy Florentines,
After those few tears—which were only few!
　　That as, beneath the sun, the grand white lines
Of thy snow-statue trembled and withdrew,—
115　　The head, erect as Jove's, being palsied first,
The eyelids flattened, the full brow turned blank,—
　　When the right hand, upraised as if it cursed,
Dropped, a mere snowball, and the people sank
　　Their voices, though a louder laughter burst
120 From the window. Michel, then thy soul could thank
　　God and the prince, for promise and presage,
And laugh the laugh back, I think, verily,
　　Thine eyes being purged by tears of righteous rage,
To read a wrong into a prophecy,
125　　And measure a true great man's heritage
Against a mere Grand-duke's posterity.
　　I think thy soul said then, 'I do not need
A princedom and its quarries, after all;
　　For if I write, paint, carve a word, indeed,
130 On book or board or dust, on floor or wall,
　　The same is kept of God who taketh heed
That not a letter of the meaning fall,
　　Or ere it touch and teach His world's deep heart,
Outlasting, therefore, all your lordships, Sir!
135　　So keep your stone, beseech you, for your part,
To cover up your grave-place and refer
　　The proper titles; *I* live by my art!
The thought I threw into this snow shall stir
　　This gazing people when their gaze is done;
140 And the tradition of your act and mine,

When all the snow is melted in the sun,
Shall gather up, for unborn men, a sign
Of what is the true princedom! ay, and none
Shall laugh that day, except the drunk with wine.'

V

145   Amen, great Angelo! the day is come.
And, if we laugh not on it, shall we weep?
Much more we shall not. Though the mournful hum
Of poets sonneteering in their sleep,
And archaists mumbling dry bones up the land,
150 And sketchers lauding ruined towns a-heap,—
Through all that drowsy hum of voices smooth,
The hopeful bird mounts carolling from brake,
The hopeful child, with leaps to catch his growth,
Sings open-eyed for liberty's sweet sake;
155   And I, who am a singer too, forsooth,
Prefer to sing with these who are awake,
With birds, with babes, with men who will not fear
The baptism of the holy morning dew,
(And many of such workers now are here,
160 Complete in their anointed manhood, who
Will greatly dare and greatlier persevere!)
Than join those old thin voices with my new,
And sigh for Italy with some safe sigh
Cooped up in music 'twixt an oh and ah,—
165   Nay, hand in hand with that young child, will I
Rather go singing, '*Bella libertà*,'
Than, with those poets, croon the dead or cry
'*Se tu men bella fossi, Italia!*'

VI

    'Less wretched if less fair.' Perhaps a truth
170 Is so far plain in this—that Italy,
Long trammelled with the purple of her youth
Against her age's due activity,
Sate still upon her graves, without the ruth
Of death, but also without life's energy.

175   And hope of life. 'What's Italy?' men ask:
And others answer, 'Virgil, Cicero,
       Catullus, Cæsar.' What beside? to task
The memory closer—'Why, Boccaccio,
       Dante, Petrarca,'—and if still the flask
180 Appears to yield its wine by drops too slow,—
       'Angelo, Raffael, Pergolese,'—all
Whose strong hearts beat through stone, or charged again,
       Cloth-threads with fire of souls electrical,
Or broke up heaven for music. What more then?
185   Why, then, no more. The chaplet's last beads fall
In naming the last saintship within ken,
       And, after that, none prayeth in the land.
Alas, this Italy has too long swept
       Heroic ashes up for hour-glass sand;
190 Of her own past, impassioned nympholept!
       Consenting to be nailed here by the hand
To the very bay-tree under which she stepped
       A queen of old, and plucked a leafy branch.
And, licensing the world too long indeed
195   To use her broad phylacteries to staunch
And stop her bloody lips, she takes no heed
       How one clear word would draw an avalanche
Of living sons around her, to succeed
       The vanished generations. Could she count
200 These oil-eaters, with large, live, mobile mouths
       Agape for maccaroni, in the amount
Of consecrated heroes of her south's
       Bright rosary? The pitcher at the fount,
The gift of gods, being broken,—why one loathes
205   To let the ground-leaves of the place confer
A natural bowl. And thus she chose to seem
       No nation, but the poet's pensioner,
With alms from every land of song and dream,
       While her own pipers sweetly pipe of her,
210 Until their proper breaths, in that extreme
       Of sighing, split the reed on which they played!
Of which, no more. But never say 'no more'

To Italy! Her memories undismayed
Say rather 'evermore',—her graves implore
215   Her future to be strong and not afraid—
Her very statues send their looks before.

VII
      We do not serve the dead—the past is past!
God lives, and lifts his glorious mornings up
      Before the eyes of men, who wake at last,
220 Who put away the meats they used to sup,
      And on the dry dust of earth outcast
The dregs remaining of the ancient cup,
      And turn to wakeful prayer and worthy act.
The dead, upon their awful 'vantage ground,—
225   The sun not in their faces,—shall abstract
No more our strength: we will not be discrowned
      Through treasuring their crowns; nor deign transact
A barter of the present, for a sound
      For what was counted good in foregone days.
230 O Dead, ye shall no longer cling to us
      With your stiff hands of dessicating praise,
And drag us backward by the garment thus,
      To stand and laud you in long virelays!
Still, no! We will not be oblivious
235   Of our own lives, because ye lived before,
Nor of our acts, because ye acted well,—
      We thank you that ye first unlatched the door—
We will not make it inaccessible
      By thankings on the threshold any more,
240 But will go onward to extinguish hell
      With our fresh souls, our younger hope, and God's
Maturity of purpose. Soon shall we
      Be the dead too! and, that our periods
Of life may round themselves to memory,
245   As smoothly as on our graves the funeral-sods,
We now must look to it to excel as ye,
      And bear our age as far, unlimited
By the last sea-mark! so, to be invoked
      By future generations, as the Dead.

VIII

250 'Tis true that when the dust of death has choked
    A great man's voice, the common words he said
Turn oracles,—the meanings which he yoked
    Like horses, draw like griffins!—this is true
And acceptable. Also I desire,
255   When men make record, with the flowers they strew,
'Savonarola's soul went out in fire
    Upon our Grand-duke's piazza, and burned through
A moment first, or ere he did expire,
    The veil betwixt the right and wrong, and showed
260 How near God sate and judged the judges there,—'
    Desire, upon the pavement overstrewed,
To cast my violets with as reverent care,
    And prove that all the winters which have snowed
Cannot snow out the scent from stones and air,
265   Of a sincere man's virtues. This was he,
Savonarola, who, while Peter sank
    With his whole boat-load, called courageously
'Wake Christ, wake Christ!'—who, having tried the tank
    Of old church-waters used for baptistry
270 Ere Luther came to spill them, said they stank!
    Who also, by a princely deathbed, cried,
'Loose Florence, or God will not loose thy soul!'
    While the Magnificent fell back and died
Beneath the star-looks, shooting from the cowl,
275   Which turned to wormwood bitterness the wide
Deep sea of his ambitions. It were foul
    To grudge the Savonarola and the rest
Their violets! rather pay them quick and fresh!
    The emphasis of death makes manifest
280 The eloquence of action in our flesh;
    And men who, living, were but dimly guessed,
When once free from their life's entangled mesh,
    Show their full length in graves, or even indeed
Exaggerate their stature, in the flat,
285   To noble admirations which exceed
Nobly, nor sin in such excess. For that

Is wise and righteous. We, who are the seed
Of buried creatures, if we turned and spate
Upon our antecedents, we were vile.
290 Bring violets rather! If these had not walked
Their furlong, could we hope to walk our mile?
Therefore bring violets. Yet if we, self-baulked,
Stand still a-strewing violets all the while,
These had as well not moved, ourselves not talked
295 Of these. So rise up with a cheerful smile,
And, having strewn the violets, reap the corn,
And, having reaped and garnered, bring the plough
And draw new furrows 'neath the healthy morn,
And plant the great Hereafter in this Now.

IX

300 Of old 'twas so. How step by step was worn,
As each man gained on each, securely!—how
Each by his own strength sought his own ideal,—
The ultimate Perfection leaning bright
From out the sun and stars, to bless the leal
305 And earnest search of all for Fair and Right,
Through the dim forms, by earth accounted real!
Because old Jubal blew into delight
The souls of men, with clear-piped melodies,
What if young Asaph were content at most
310 To draw from Jubal's grave, with listening eyes,
Traditionary music's floating ghost
Into the grass-grown silence? were it wise?
Is it not wiser, Jubal's breath being lost,
That Miriam clashed her cymbals to surprise
315 The sun between her white arms flung apart,
With new, glad, golden sounds? that David's strings
O'erflowed his hand with music from his heart?
So harmony grows full from many springs,
And happy accident turns holy art.

X

320   Or enter, in your Florence wanderings,
          The church of St. Maria Novella. You pass
      The left stair, where, at plague-time, Macchiavel
          Saw one with set fair face as in a glass,
      Dressed out against the fear of death and hell,
325   Rustling her silks in pauses of the mass,
      To keep the thought off how her husband fell,
          When she left home, stark dead across her feet,—
      The stair leads up to what Orgagna gave
          Of Dante's dæmons; but you, passing it,
330   Ascend the right stair from the farther nave,
          To muse in a small chapel scarcely lit
      By Cimabue's Virgin. Bright and brave,
          That picture was accounted, mark, of old.
      A king stood bare before its sovran grace;
335   A reverent people shouted to behold
      The picture, not the king, and even the place
          Containing such a miracle, grew bold,
      Named the Glad Borgo from that beauteous face,
          Which thrilled the artist, after work, to think
340   His own ideal Mary-smile should stand
          So very near him,—he, within the brink
      Of all that glory, let in by his hand
          With too divine a rashness! Yet none shrink
      Who come to gaze here now—albeit is planned
345   Sublimely in the thought's simplicity.
      The Lady, throned in empyreal state,
          Minds only the young babe upon her knee,
      While, each side, angels bear the royal weight
          Prostrated meekly, smiling tenderly
350   Oblivion of their wings; the Child thereat
          Stretching its hand like God. If any should,
      Because of some stiff draperies and loose joints,
          Gaze scorn down from the heights of Raffaelhood,
      On Cimabue's picture,—Heaven anoints
355   The head of no such critic, and his blood
      The poet's curse strikes full on and appoints

To ague and cold spasms for evermore.
A noble picture! worthy of the shout
　　Wherewith along the streets the people bore
360　Its cherub faces, which the sun threw out
　　　　Until they stooped and entered the church door!—
Yet rightly was young Giotto talked about,
　　Whom Cimabue found among the sheep,
And knew, as gods know gods, and carried home
365　　To paint the things he had painted, with a deep
And fuller insight, and so overcome
　　His chapel-Virgin with a heavenlier sweep
Of light. For thus we mount into the sum
　　　　Of great things known or acted. I hold, too,
370　That Cimabue smiled upon the lad,
　　　　At the first stroke which passed what he could do,—
Or else his Virgin's smile had never had
　　Such sweetness in't. All great men who foreknew
Their heirs in art, for art's sake have been glad,
375　　And bent their old white heads as if uncrowned,
Fanatics of their pure ideals still
　　Far more than of their laurels, which were found
With some less stalwart struggle of the will.
　　If old Margheritone trembled, swooned,
380　And died despairing at the open sill
　　　　Of other men's achievements, (who achieved,
By loving art beyond the master!) he
　　Was old Margheritone, and conceived
Never, at youngest and most ecstasy,
385　　A Virgin like that dream of one, which heaved
The death-sigh from his heart. If wistfully
　　Margheritone sickened at the smell
Of Cimabue's laurel, let him go!—
　　　　For Cimabue stood up very well
390　In spite of Giotto's—and Angelico,
　　　　The artist-saint, kept smiling in his cell
The smile with which he welcomed the sweet slow
　　Inbreak of angels, (whitening through the dim
That he might paint them!) while the sudden sense
395　　Of Raffael's future was revealed to him

By force of his own fair works' competence.
    The same blue waters where the dolphins swim
Suggest the Tritons. Through the blue Immense,
    Strike out, all swimmers! cling not in the way
400 Of one another, so to sink; but learn
    The strong man's impulse, catch the fresh'ning spray
He throws up in his motions, and discern
    By his clear, westering eye, the time of day.
O God, thou hast set us worthy gifts to earn,
405   Besides thy heaven and Thee! and when I say
'Tis worth while for the weakest man alive
    To live and die,—there's room too, I repeat,
For all the strongest to live well, and strive
    Their own way, by their individual heat,—
410 Like some new bee-swarm leaving the old hive,
    Despite the wax which tempteth violet-sweet.
So let the living live, the dead retain
    Flowers on cold graves!—though honour's best
        supplied,
When we bring actions, to prove their's not vain.

XI

415   Cold graves, we say? It shall be testified
That living men who throb in heart and brain,
    Without the dead were colder. If we tried
To sink the past beneath our feet, be sure
    The future would not stand. Precipitate
420 This old roof from the shrine—and, insecure,
    The nesting swallows fly off, mate from mate.
Scant were the gardens, if the graves were fewer!
    And the green poplars grew no longer straight,
Whose tops not looked to Troy. Why, who would fight
425   For Athens, and not swear by Marathon?
Who would dare build temples, without tombs in sight?
    Or live, without some dead man's benison?
Or seek truth, hope for good, or strive for right,
    If, looking up, he saw not in the sun
430 Some angel of the martyrs, all day long
    Standing and waiting? your last rhythms will need

The earliest key-note. Could I sing this song,
    If my dead masters had not taken heed
To help the heavens and earth to make me strong,
435   As the wind ever will find out some reed,
And touch it to such issues as belong
      To such a frail thing? None may grudge the dead,
Libations from full cups. Unless we choose
      To look back to the hills behind us spread,
440 The plains before us, sadden and confuse;
      If orphaned, we are disinherited.

XII

I would but turn these lachrymals to use,
     Fill them with fresh oil from the olive grove,
To feed the new lamps fuller. Shall I say
445   What made my heart beat with exulting love,
A few weeks back?—

XIII

        . . . . The day was such a day
      As Florence owes the sun. The sky above,
Its weight upon the mountains seemed to lay,
      And palpitate in glory, like a dove
450 Who has flown too fast, full-hearted! Take away
      The image! for the heart of man beat higher
That day in Florence, flooding all her streets
      And piazzas with a tumult and desire.
The people, with accumulated heats,
455   And faces turned one way, as if one fire
Did drew and flush them, leaving their old beats,
      Went upward to the palace-Pitti wall,
To thank their Grand-duke, who, not quite of course,
      Had graciously permitted, at their call,
460 The citizens to use their civic force
      To guard the civic homes. So, one and all,
The Tuscan cities streamed up to the source
      Of this new good, at Florence; taking it
As good so far, presageful of more good,—
465   The first torch of Italian freedom, lit

To toss in the next tiger's face who should
    Approach too near them in a cruel fit,—
The first pulse of an even flow of blood,
    To prove the level of Italian veins
470 Toward rights perceived and granted. How we gazed
    From Casa Guidi windows, while, in trains
Of orderly procession—banners raised,
    And intermittent burst of martial strains
Which died upon the shout, as if amazed
475   By gladness beyond music—they passed on!
The magistrates, with their insignia, passed;
    And all the people shouted in the sun,
And all the thousand windows which had cast
    A ripple of silks, in blue and scarlet, down
480 As if the houses overflowed at last,
    Seemed growing larger with fair heads and eyes.
The lawyers passed,—and still arose the shout,
    And hands broke from the windows to surprise
Those grave calm brows with bay-tree leaves thrown out.
485   The priesthood passed,—the friars, with worldly-wise
Keen sidelong glances from their beards, about
    The street to see who shouted! many a monk
Who takes a long rope in the waist, was there!
    Whereat the popular exultation drunk
490 With indrawn 'vivas' the whole sunny air,
    While through the murmuring windows rose and sunk
A cloud of kerchiefed hands,—'the church makes fair
    Her welcome in the new Pope's name.' Ensued
The black sign of the 'Martyrs!' name no name,
495   But count the graves in silence. Next, were viewed
The Artists; next, the Trades; and after came
    The populace, with flag and rights as good,—
And very loud the shout was for that same
    Motto, 'Il popolo.' IL POPOLO,—
500 The word meant dukedom, empire, majesty,
    And kings in such an hour might read it so.
And next, with banners, each in his degree,
    Deputed representatives a-row,
Of every separate state of Tuscany.

505   Siena's she-wolf, bristling on the fold
Of the first flag, preceded Pisa's hare,
            And Massa's lion floated calm in gold,
Pienza's following with his silver stare;
            Arezzo's steed pranced clear from bridle-hold,—
510 And well might shout our Florence, greeting there
            These, and more brethren. Last, the world had sent
The various children of her teeming flanks—
            Greeks, English, French—as to some parliament
Of lovers of her Italy in ranks,
515   Each bearing its land's symbol reverent.
At which the stones seemed breaking into thanks
            And rattling up the sky, such sounds in proof
Arose! the very house-walls seemed to bend,
            The very windows, up from door to roof,
520 Flashed out a rapture of bright heads, to mend
            With passionate looks, the gesture's whirling off
A hurricane of leaves! Three hours did end
            While all these passed; and ever in the crowd,
Rude men, unconscious of the tears that kept
525   Their beards moist, shouted; and some laughed aloud,
And none asked any why they laughed and wept:
            Friends kissed each other's cheeks, and foes long
                        vowed
Did it more warmly;—two-months' babies leapt
            Right upward in their mother's arms, whose black,
530 Wide, glittering eyes looked elsewhere; lovers pressed
            Each before either, neither glancing back;
And peasant maidens, smoothly 'tired and tressed,
            Forgot to finger on their throats the slack
Great pearl-strings; while old blind men would not rest,
535   But pattered with their staves and slid their shoes
Along the stones, and smiled as if they saw.
            O Heaven, I think that day had noble use
Among God's days. So near stood Right and Law,
            Both mutually forborne! Law would not bruise,
540 Nor Right deny, and each in reverent awe
            Honoured the other. And if, ne'ertheless,
The sun did, that day, leave upon the vines

No charta, and the liberal Duke's excess
Did scarce exceed a Guelf's or Ghibelline's
545   In any special actual righteousness
Of what that day he granted;* still the signs
      Are good and full of promise, we must say,
When multitudes thank kings for granting prayers,
      And kings concede their people's right to pray,
550 Both in the sunshine. Griefs are not despairs,
      So uttered, nor can royal claims dismay,
When men from humble homes and ducal chairs,
      Hate wrong together. It was well to view
Those banners ruffled in a Grand-duke's face
555   Inscribed, 'Live freedom, union, and all true
Brave patriots who are aided by God's grace!'
      Nor was it ill, when Leopoldo drew
His little children to the window-place
      He stood in at the Pitti, to suggest
560 *They*, too, should govern as the people willed.
      What a cry rose then! some, who saw the best,
Sware that his eyes filled up, and overfilled
      With good warm human tears, which unrepressed
Ran down. I like his face: the forehead's build
565   Has no capacious genius, yet perhaps
Sufficient comprehension,—mild and sad,
      And careful nobly,—not with care that wraps
Self-loving hearts, to stifle and make mad,
      But careful with the care that shuns a lapse
570 Of faith and duty, studious not to add
      A burthen in the gathering of a gain.
And so, God save the Duke, I say with those
      Who that day shouted it, and while dukes reign,
May all wear in the visible overflows
575   Of spirit, such a look of careful pain!
For God loves it better than repose.

---

*Since when the constitutional concessions have been complete in Tuscany, as all the world knows. The event breaks in upon the meditation, and is too fast for prophecy in these strange times.

XIV
And all the people who went up to let ,
  Their hearts out to that Duke, as has been told—
Where guess ye that the living people met,
580   Kept tryst, formed ranks, chose leaders, first unrolled
Their banners?
      In the Loggia? where is set
  Cellini's godlike Perseus, bronze—or gold—
(How name the metal, when the statue flings
  Its soul so in your eyes?) with brow and sword
585 Superbly calm, as all opposing things,
  Slain with the Gorgon, were no more abhorred
Since ended?
     No the people sought no wings
  From Perseus in the Loggia, nor implored
An inspiration in the place beside,
590   From that dim bust of Brutus, jagged and grand,
Where Buonarroti passionately tried
  Out of the clenched marble to demand
The head of Rome's sublimest homicide,
  Then dropt the quivering mallet from his hand,
595 Despairing he could find no model stuff
  Of Brutus, in all Florence, where he found
The gods and gladiators thick enough.
  Nor there! the people chose still holier ground!
The people, who are simple, blind, and rough,
600   Know their own angels, after looking round.
Whom chose they then? where met they?

XV
        On the stone
  Called Dante's,—a plain flat stone, scarce discerned
From others in the pavement,—whereupon
  He used to bring his quiet chair out, turned
605 To Brunelleschi's church, and pour alone
  The lava of his spirit when it burned—
It is not cold to-day. O passionate
  Poor Dante, who, a banished Florentine,
Didst sit austere at banquets of the great,

610   And muse upon this far-off stone of thine,
      And think how oft the passers used to wait
          A moment, in the golden day's decline,
      With 'good night, dearest Dante!'—well, good night!
          I muse now, Dante, and think, verily,
615 Though chapelled in Ravenna's byeway, might,
          Thy buried bones be thrilled to ecstasy,
      Could'st know thy favourite stone's elected right
          As tryst-place for thy Tuscans to foresee
      Their earliest chartas from! good night, good morn,
620   Henceforward, Dante! now my soul is sure
      That thine is better comforted of scorn,
          And looks down from the stars in fuller cure,
      Than when, in Santa Croce church, forlorn
          Of any corpse, the architect and hewer
625 Did pile the empty marbles as thy tomb.
          For now thou art no longer exiled, now
      Best honoured!—we salute thee who art come
          Back to the old stone with a softer brow
      Than Giotto drew upon the wall, for some
630   Good lovers of our age to track and plough
      Their way to, through Time's ordures stratified,
          And startle broad awake into the dull
      Bargello chamber! now, thou'rt milder eyed,
          And Beatrix may leap up glad to cull
635 Thy first smile, even in heaven and at her side,
          Like that which, nine years old, looked beautiful
      At Tuscan May-game. Foolish words! I meant
          Only that Dante loved his Florence well,
      While Florence, now, to love him is content!
640   I meant too, certes, that the sweetest smell
      Of love's dear incense by the living sent
          To find the dead, is not accessible
      To your low livers! no narcotic,—not
          Swung in a censer to a sleepy tune,—
645 But trod out in the morning air, by hot
          Quick spirits, who tread firm to ends foreshown,
      And use the name of greatness unforgot,
          To meditate what greatness may be done.

XVI

For Dante sits in heaven, and ye stand here,
650   And more remains for doing, all must feel,
Than trysting on his stone from year to year
      To shift processions, civic heel to heel,
The town's thanks to the Pitti. Are ye freer
      For what was felt that day? A chariot-wheel
655 May spin fast, yet the chariot never roll.
      But if that day suggested something good,
And bettered, with one purpose, soul by soul,—
      Better means freer. A land's brotherhood
Is most puissant! Men, upon the whole,
660   Are what they can be,—nations, what they would.

XVII

Will, therefore, to be strong, thou Italy!
      Will to be noble! Austrian Metternich
Can fix no yoke unless the neck agree;
      And thine is like the lion's when the thick
665 Dews shudder from it, and no man would be
      The stroker of his mane, much less would prick
His nostril with a reed. When nations roar
      Like lions, who shall tame them, and defraud
Of the due pasture by the river-shore?
670   Roar, therefore! shake your dew-laps dry abroad.
The ampitheatre with open door
      Leads back upon the benchers, who applaud
The last spear-thruster.

XVIII

                  Yet the Heavens forbid
      That we should call on passion to confront
675 The brutal with the brutal, and, amid
      This ripening world, suggest a lion-hunt
And lion-vengeance for the wrongs men did
      And do now, though the spears are getting blunt.
We only call, because the sight and proof
680   Of lion-strength hurts nothing; and to show
A lion-heart, and measure paw with hoof,

Helps something, even, and will instruct a foe
As well as the onslaught, how to stand aloof!
Or else the world gets past the mere brute blow
685   Given or taken. Children use the fist
Until they are of age to use the brain:
And so we needed Cæsars to assist
Man's justice, and Napoleons to explain
God's counsel, when a point was nearly missed,
690   Until our generations should attain
Christ's stature nearer. Not that we, alas!
Attain already; but a single inch
Will raise to look down on the sworsdman's pass,
As Roland on a coward who could flinch;
695   And, after chloroform and ether-gas,
We find out slowly what the bee and finch
Have already found, through Nature's lamp in each,—
How to our races we may justify
Our individual claims, and, as we reach
700   Our own grapes, bend the top vines to supply
The children's uses: how to fill the breach
With olive branches; how to quench a lie
With truth, and smite a foe upon the cheek
With Christ's most conquering kiss! why, these are
things
705   Worth a great nation's finding, to prove weak
The 'glorious arms' of military kings!
And so with wide embrace, my England, seek
To stifle the bad heat and flickerings
Of this world's false and nearly expended fire!
710   Draw palpitating arrows to the wood,
And send abroad thy high hopes, and thy higher
Resolves, from that most virtuous altitude!
Till nations shall unconsciously aspire
By looking up to thee, and learn that good
715   And glory are not different. Announce law
By freedom; exalt chivalry by peace;
Instruct how clear calm eyes can overawe,
And how pure hands, stretched simply to release

A bond-slave, will not need a sword to draw
720   To be held dreadful. O my England, crease
Thy purple with no alien agonies
      Which reach thee through the net of war!
Disband thy captains, change thy victories,
      Be henceforth prosperous as the angels are—
725 Helping, not humbling.

XIX
                              Drums and battle cries
      Go out in music of the morning star—
And soon we shall have thinkers in the place
      Of fighters, each found able as a man
To strike electric influence through a race,
730   Unstayed by city-wall and barbican.
The poet shall look grander in the face
      Than ever he looked of old, when he began
To sing that 'Achillean wrath which slew
      So many heroes',—seeing he shall treat
735 The deeds of souls heroic toward the true—
      The oracles of life—previsions sweet
And awful, like divine swans gliding through
      White arms of Ledas, which will leave the heat
Of their escaping godship to endue
740   The human medium with a heavenly flush.
Meanwhile, in this same Italy we want
      Not popular passion, to arise and crush,
But popular conscience, which may covenant
      For what it knows. Concede without a blush—
745 To grant the 'civic guard' is not to grant
      The civic spirit, living and awake.
Those lappets on your shoulders, citizens,
      Your eyes strain after sideways till they ache,
While still, in admirations and amens,
750   The crowd comes up on festa-days, to take
The great sight in—are not intelligence,
      Not courage even—alas, if not the sign
Of something very noble, they are nought;

For every day ye dress your sallow kine
755   With fringes down their cheeks, though unbesought
They loll their heavy heads and drag the wine,
And bear the wooden yoke as they were taught
The first day. What ye want is light—indeed
Not sunlight—(ye may well look up surprised
760   To those unfathomable heavens that feed
Your purple hills!)—but God's light organised
In some high soul, crowned capable to lead
The conscious people, conscious and advised,—
For if we lift a people like mere clay,
765   It falls the same. We want thee, O unfound
And sovran teacher!—if thy beard be grey
Or black, we bid thee rise up from the ground
And speak the word God giveth thee to say,
Inspiring into all this people round,
770   Instead of passion, thought, which pioneers
All generous passion, purifies from sin,
And strikes the hour for. Rise thou, teacher! here's
A crowd to make a nation!—best begin
By making each a man, till all be peers
775   Of earth's true patriots and pure martyrs in
Knowing and daring. Best unbar the doors
Which Peter's heirs keep locked so overclose
They only let the mice across the floors,
While every churchman dangles as he goes
780   The great key at his girdle, and abhors
In Christ's name, meekly. Open wide the house—
Concede the entrance with Christ's liberal mind,
And set the tables with His wine and bread.
What! commune 'in both kinds?' In every kind—
785   Wine, wafer, love, hope, truth, unlimited,
Nothing kept back. For, when a man is blind
To starlight, will he see the rose is red?
A bondsman shivering at a Jesuit's foot—
'Væ! meâ culpâ!' is not like to stand
790   A freedman at a despot's, and dispute
His titles by the balance in his hand,

Weighing them 'suo jure.' Tend the root,
If careful of the branches; and expand
The inner souls of men before you strive
795   For civic heroes.

XX

But the teacher, where?
From all these crowded faces, all alive,—
Eyes, of their own lids flashing themselves bare,—
And brows that with a mobile life contrive
A deeper shadow,—may we in no wise dare
800   To put a finger out, and touch a man,
And cry 'this is the leader'. What, all these!—
Broad heads, black eyes,—yet not a soul that ran
From God down with a message? All, to please
The donna waving measures with her fan,
805   And not the judgment-angel on his knees,
The trumpet just an inch off from his lips—
Who when he breathes next, will put out the sun?
Yet mankind's self were foundered in eclipse,
If lacking, with a great work to be done,
810   A doer. No, the earth already dips
Back into light—a better day's begun—
And soon this doer, teacher, will stand plain,
And build the golden pipes and synthesise
This people-organ for a holy strain.
815   And we who hope, thus still in all these eyes,
Go sounding for the deep look which shall drain
Suffused thought into channelled enterprise.
Where is the teacher? What now may he do,
Who shall do greatly? Doth he gird his waist
820   With a monk's rope, like Luther? or pursue
The goat, like Tell? or dry his nets in haste,
Like Masaniello when the sky was blue?
Keep house, like any peasant, with inlaced,
Bare, brawny arms about his favourite child,
825   And meditative looks beyond the door,—
(But not to mark the kidling's teeth have filed
The green shoots of his vine which last year bore

Full twenty bunches;) or, on triple-piled
Throne-velvets, shall we see him bless the poor,
830   Like any Pontiff, in the Poorest's name?
While the tiara holds itself aslope
Upon his steady brows, which, all the same,
Bend mildly to permit the people's hope?

XXI
Whatever hand shall grasp this oriflamme,
835   Whatever man (last peasant or first Pope
Seeking to free his country!) shall appear,
Teach, lead, strike fire into the masses, fill
These empty bladders with fine air, insphere
These wills into a unity of will,
840   And make of Italy a nation—dear
And blessed be that man! the Heavens shall kill
No leaf the earth lets grow for him; and Death
Shall cast him back upon the lap of Life
To live more surely, in a clarion-breath
845   Of hero-music! Brutus, with the knife,
Rienzi, with the fasces, throb beneath
Rome's stones, and more, who threw away joy's fife
Like Pallas, that the beauty of their souls
Might ever shine untroubled and entire!
850   But if it can be true that he who rolls
The Church's thunders will reserve her fire
For only light, from eucharistic bowls
Will pour new life for nations that expire,
And rend the scarlet of his Papal vest
855   To gird the weak loins of his countrymen—
I hold that he surpasses all the rest
Of Romans, heroes, patriots,—and that when
He sat down on the throne, he dispossessed
The first graves of some glory. See again,
860   This country-saving is a glorious thing!
Why say a common man achieved it? Well!
Say, a rich man did? Excellent. A king?
That grows sublime. A priest? Improbable.

A Pope? Ah, there we stop, and cannot bring
865 Our faith up to the leap, with history's bell
     So heavy round the neck of it—albeit
We fain would grant the possibility,
     For *thy* sake, Pio Nono!

XXII

                 Stretch thy feet
In that case—I will kiss them reverently
870   As any pilgrim to the Papal seat!
And, such proved possible, thy throne to me
     Shall seem as holy a place as Pellico's
Venetian dungeon, or as Spielberg's grate,
     Where the Lombard woman hung the rose
875 Of her sweet soul, by its own dewy weight,
     (Because her sun shone *inside* to the close!
And pining so, died early, yet too late
     For what she suffered! Yea, I will not choose
Betwixt thy throne, Pope Pius, and the spot
880   Marked red for ever spite of rains or dews,
Where two fell riddled by the Austrian's shot—
     The brothers Bandiera, who accuse,
With one same mother-voice and face (that what
     They speak may be invincible), the sins
885 Of earth's tormentors before God, the just,
     Until the unconscious thunder-bolt begins
To loosen in His grasp.

XXIII

                And yet we must
     Beware, and mark the natural kiths and kins
Of circumstance and office, and distrust
890   A rich man reasoning in a poor man's hut,
The poet who neglects pure truth to prove
     Statistic fact; the child who leaves a rut
For the smooth road, a priest who vows his glove
     Exhales no grace; a prince who walks a-foot;
895 A woman who has sworn she will not love;

Ninth Pius sitting in Seventh Gregory's chair,
With Andrea Doria's forehead!

XXIV

                                    Count what goes
        To making up a Pope, before he wear
That triple crown. We pass the world-wide throes
900   Which went to make the Popedom,—the despair
Of free men, good men, wise men; the dread shows
        Of women's faces, by the faggot's flash,
Tossed out, to the minutest stir and throb
        Of the white lips, least tremble of a lash,
905 To glut the red stare of the licensed mob!
        The short mad cries down oubliettes,—the plash
So horribly far off! priests, trained to rob,
        And kings that, like encouraged nightmares, sate
On nations' hearts most heavily distressed
910   With monstrous sights and apophthegms of fate.
We pass these things,—because 'the times' are prest
        With necessary charges of the weight
Of all the sin, and 'Calvin, for the rest,
        Made bold to burn Servetus—Ah, men err!'—
915 And, so do *Churches!* which is all we mean
        To bring to proof in any register
Of theological fat kine and lean—
        So drive them back into the pens! refer
Old sins with long beards and 'I wis and ween,'
920   Entirely to the times—the times!
Nor ever ask why this preponderant,
        Infallible, pure Church could set her chimes
Most loudly then, just then; most jubilant,
        Precisely then—when mankind stood in crimes
925 Full heart-deep, and Heaven's judgments were not scant.
        Inquire still less, what signifies a church
Of perfect inspiration and pure laws,
        Who burns the first man with a brimstone-torch,
And grinds the second, bone by bone, because
930   The times, forsooth, are used to rack and scorch!
What *is* a holy Church, unless she awes

The times down from their sins? Did Christ select
Such amiable times, to come and teach
    Love to, and mercy? Why, the world were wrecked,
935 If every mere great man, who lives to reach
      A little leaf of popular respect,
Attained not simply by some special breach
    In his land's customs,—by some precedence
In thought and act, which, having proved him higher
940   Than his own times, proved his competence
Of helping them to wonder and aspire.

XXV
    My words are guiltless of the bigot's sense!
My soul has fire to mingle with the fire
    Of all these souls, within or out of doors
945 Of Rome's Church or another. I believe
      In one priest, and one temple, with its floors
Of shining jasper, gloom'd at morn and eve
    By countless knees of earnest auditors;
And crystal walls, too lucid to perceive,—
950   That none may take the measure of the place
And say, 'So far the porphyry, then, the flint—
    To this mark, mercy goes, and there, ends grace,'
While still the permeable crystals hint
    At some white starry distance, bathed in space!
955 I feel how nature's ice-crusts keep the dint
      Of undersprings of silent Deity.
I hold the articulated gospels, which
    Show Christ among us, crucified on tree;
I love all who love truth, if poor or rich
960   In what they have won of truth possessively!
No altars and no hands defiled with pitch
    Shall scare me off, but I will pray and eat
With all these—taking leave to choose my ewers
    And say at last, 'Your visible Churches cheat
965 Their inward types,—and, if a Church assures
      Of standing without failure and defeat,
The same both fails and lies.'

XXVI

                                    To leave which lures
        Of wider subject through past years,—behold,
    We come back from the Popedom to the Pope,
970   To ponder what he *must* be, ere we are bold
    For what he *may* be, with our heavy hope
        To trust upon his soul. So, fold by fold,
    Explore this mummy in the priestly cope,
        Transmitted through the darks of time, to catch
975 The man within the wrappage, and discern
        How he, an honest man, upon the watch
    Full fifty years, for what a man may learn,
        Contrived to get just there; with what a snatch
    Of old-world oboli he had to earn
980   The passage through; with what a drowsy sop,
    To drench the busy barkings of his brain;
        What ghosts of pale tradition, wreathed with hop
    'Gainst wakeful thought, he had to entertain
        For heavenly visions; and consent to stop
985 The clock at noon, and let the hour remain
        (Without vain windings up) inviolate,
    Against all chimings from the belfry. Lo!
        From every given pope you must abate,
    Albeit you love him, some things—good, you know—
990   Which every given heretic you hate,
    Claims for his own, as being plainly so.
        A pope must hold by popes a little,—yes,
    By councils,—from Nicæa up to Trent,—
        By hierocratic empire, more or less
995 Irresponsible to men,—he must resent
        Each man's particular conscience, and repress
    Inquiry, meditation, argument,
        As tyrants faction. Also, he must not
    Love truth too dangerously, but prefer
1000   'The interests of the Church', (because a blot
    Is better than a rent in miniver)
        Submit to see the people swallow hot
    Husk-porridge which his chartered churchmen stir

        Quoting the only true God's epigraph,
1005   'Feed my lambs, Peter!'—must consent to sit
        Attesting with his pastoral ring and staff,
To such a picture of our Lady, hit
        Off well by artist angels, though not half
As fair as Giotto would have painted it;
1010   To such a vial, where a dead man's blood
Runs yearly warm beneath a churchman's finger;
        To such a holy house of stone and wood,
Whereof a cloud of angels was the bringer
        From Bethlehem to Loreto!—Were it good
1015 For any pope on earth to be a flinger
        Of stones against these high-niched counterfeits?
Apostates only are iconoclasts.
        He dares not say, while this false thing abets
That true thing, 'this is false'. He keepeth fasts
1020   And prayers, as prayer and fast were silver frets
To change a note upon a string that lasts,
        And make a lie a virtue. Now, if he
Did more than this,—higher hoped, and braver dared,—
        I think he were a pope in jeopardy,
1025 Or no pope rather! for his soul had barred
        The vaulting of his life. And certainly,
If he do only this, mankind's regard
        Moves on from him at once, to seek some new
Teacher and leader! He is good and great
1030   According to the deeds a pope can do;
Most liberal, save those bonds; affectionate,
        As princes may be; and as priests are, true—
But only the ninth Pius after eight,
        When all's praised most. At best and hopefullest,
1035 He's pope—we want a man! his heart beats warm,
        But, like the prince enchanted to the waist,
He sits in stone, and hardens by a charm
        Into the marble of his throne high-placed!
Mild benediction, waves his saintly arm—
1040   So good! but what we want's a perfect man,
Complete and all alive: half travertine
        Half suits our need, and ill subserves our plan.

Feet, knees, nerves, sinews, energies divine
    Were never yet too much for men who ran
1045 In such exalted ways as this of thine,
    Deliverer whom we seek, whoe'er thou art,
Pope, prince, or peasant! If, indeed, the first,
    The noblest, therefore! since the heroic heart
Within thee must be great enough to burst
1050   Those trammels buckling to the baser part
Thy saintly peers in Rome, who crossed and cursed
    With the same finger.

XXVII

                Come, appear, be found,
If pope or peasant, come! we hear the cock,
    The courtier of the mountains when first crowned
1055 With golden dawn; and orient glories flock
    To meet the sun upon the highest ground.
Take voice and work! we wait to hear thee knock
    At some of our Florentine nine gates,
On each of whch was imaged a sublime
1060   Face of a Tuscan genius, which, for hate's
And love's sake, both, our Florence in her prime
    Turned boldly on all comers to her states,
As heroes turned their shields in antique time,
    Emblazoned with honourable acts. And though
1065 The gates are blank now of such images,
    And Petrarch looks no more from Nicolo
Toward dear Arezzo, 'twixt the acacia trees,
    Nor Dante, from gate Gallo—still we know,
Despite the razing of the blazonries,
1070   Remains the consecration of the shield,—
The dead heroic faces will start out
    On all these gates, if foes should take the field,
And blend sublimely, at the earliest shout,
    With our live fighters, who will scorn to yield
1075 A hair's-breadth ev'n, when, gazing round about,
    They find in what a glorious company
They fight the foes of Florence. Who will grudge
    His one poor life, when that great man we see

Has given five hundred years, the world being judge,
1080   To help the glory of his Italy?
Who, born the fair side of the Alps, will budge,
        When Dante stays, when Ariosto stays,
When Petrarch stays for ever? Ye bring swords,
        My Tuscans? Why, if wanted in this haze,
1085 Bring swords, but first bring souls!—bring thoughts and
                words
        Unrusted by a tear of yesterday's,
Yet awful by its wrong,—and cut these cords,
        And mow this green lush falseness to the roots,
And shut the mouth of hell below the swathe!
1090   And, if ye can bring songs too, let the lute's
Recoverable music softly bathe
        Some poet's hand, that, through all bursts and bruits
Of popular passion—all unripe and rather
        Convictions of the popular intellect,
1095 Ye may not lack a finger up the air,
        Annunciative, reproving, pure, erect,
To show which way your first Ideal bare
        The whiteness of its wings, when, sorely pecked
By falcons on your wrists, it unaware
1100   Arose up overhead, and out of sight.

XXVIII
Meanwhile, let all the far ends of the world
        Breathe back the deep breath of their old delight,
To swell the Italian banner just unfurled.
        Help, lands of Europe! for, if Austria fight,
1105 The drums will bar your slumber. Who had curled
        The laurel for your thousand artists' brows,
If these Italian hands had planted none?
        Can any sit down idle in the house,
Nor hear appeals from Buonarroti's stone
1110   And Raffael's canvas, rousing and to rouse?
Where's Poussin's master? Gallic Avignon
        Bred Laura, and Vaucluse's fount has stirred
The heart of France too strongly,—as it lets
        Its little stream out, like a wizard's bird

1115 Which bounds upon its emerald wing, and wets
  The rocks on each side that she should not gird
Her loins with Charlemagne's sword, when foes beset
  The country of her Petrarch. Spain may well
Be minded how from Italy she caught,
1120   To mingle with her tinkling Moorish bell,
A fuller cadence and a subtler thought;
  And even the New World, the receptacle
Of freemen, may send glad men, as it ought,
  To greet Vespucci Amerigo's door;
1125 While England claims, by trump of poetry,
  Verona, Venice, the Ravenna-shore,
And dearer holds her Milton's Fiesole
  Than Langlande's Malvern with the stars in flower.

XXIX
And Vallombrosa, we two went to see
1130   Last June, beloved companion,—where sublime
The mountains live in holy families,
  And the slow pinewoods ever climb and climb
Half up their breasts, just stagger as they seize
  Some grey crag—drop back with it many a time,
1135 And straggle blindly down the precipice!
  The Vallombrosan brooks were strewn as thick
That June-day, knee-deep, with dead beechen leaves,
  As Milton saw them ere his heart grew sick,
And his eyes blind. I think the monks and beeves
1140   Are all the same too: scarce they have changed the
    wick
On good St. Gualbert's altar, which receives
  The convent's pilgrims; and the pool in front
Wherein the hill-stream trout are cast, to wait
  The beatific vision, and the grunt
1145 Used at refectory, keeps its weedy state,
  To baffle saintly abbots, who would count
The fish across their breviary, nor 'bate
  The measure of their steps. O waterfalls
And forests! sound and silence! mountains bare,
1150   That leap up peak by peak, and catch the palls

Of purple and silver mist to rend and share
    With one another, at electric calls
Of life in the sunbeams,—till we cannot dare
    Fix your shapes, learn your number! we must think
1155 Your beauty and your glory helped to fill
    The cup of Milton's soul so to the brink,
That he no more was thirsty when God's will
    Had shattered to his sense the last chain-link
By which he had drawn from Nature's visible
1160   The fresh well-water. Satisfied by this,
He sang of Adam's paradise and smiled,
    Remembering Vallombrosa. Therefore is
The place divine to English man and child—
    We all love Italy.

XXX

                Our Italy's
1165 The darling of the earth—the treasury piled
    With reveries of gentle ladies, flung
Aside, like ravelled silk, from life's worn stuff;
    With coins of scholars' fancy, which, being rung
On work-day counter, still sound silver-proof,—
1170   In short, with all the dreams of dreamers young,
Before their heads have time for slipping off
    Hope's pillow to the ground. How oft, indeed,
We all have sent our souls out from the north,
    On bare white feet which would not print nor bleed,
1175 To climb the Alpine passes and look forth,
    Where the low murmuring Lombard rivers lead
Their bee-like way to gardens almost worth
    The sights which thou and I see afterward
From Tuscan Bellosguardo, wide awake,
1180   When standing on the actual, blessed sward
Where Galileo stood at nights to take
    The vision of the stars, we find it hard,
Gazing upon the earth and heaven, to make
    A choice of beauty. Therefore let us all
1185 In England, or in any other land,
    Refreshed once by the fountain-rise and fall,

Of dreams of this fair south,—who understand
    A little how the Tuscan musical
Vowels do round themselves, as if they plann'd
1190   Eternities of separate sweetness,—we ·
Who loved Sorrento vines in picture-book,
    Or ere in wine-cup we pledged faith or glee—
Who loved Rome's wolf, with demi-gods at suck,
    Or ere we loved truth's own divinity,—
1195 Who loved, in brief, the classic hill and brook,
    And Ovid's dreaming tales, and Petrarch's song,
Or ere we loved Love's self!—why, let us give
    The blessing of our souls, and wish them strong
To bear it to the height where prayers arrive,
1200   When faithful spirits pray against a wrong;
To this great cause of southern men, who strive
    In God's name for man's rights, and shall not fail!

XXXI
Behold, they shall not fail. The shouts ascend
    Above the shrieks, in Naples, and prevail.
1205 Rows of shot corpses, waiting for the end
    Of burial, seem to smile up straight and pale
Into the azure air and apprehend
    That final gun-flash from Palermo's coast,
Which lightens their apocalypse of death.
1210   So let them die! The world shows nothing lost;
Therefore, not blood Above or underneath,
    What matter, brothers, if we keep our post
On truth's and duty's side? As sword to sheath,
    Dust turns to grave, but souls find place in Heaven.
1215 O friends, heroic daring is success,
    The eucharistic bread requires no leaven;
And though your ends were hopeless, we should bless
    Your cause as holy! Strive—and, having striven,
Take, for God's recompense, that righteousness!

Part Two

I

I wrote a meditation and a dream,
　　Hearing a little child sing in the street.
I leant upon his music as a theme,
　　Till it gave way beneath my heart's full beat,
5　Which tried at an exultant prophecy
　　　But dropped before the measure was complete—
Alas, for songs and hearts! O Tuscany,
　　O Dante's Florence, is the type too plain?
Didst thou, too, only sing of liberty,
10　　As little children take up a high strain
With unintentioned voices, and break off
　　To sleep upon their mothers' knees again?
Could'st thou not watch one hour? then, sleep enough—
　　That sleep may hasten manhood, and sustain
15　The faint pale spirit with some muscular stuff.

II

　　But we, who cannot slumber as thou dost,
We thinkers, who have thought for thee and failed,
　　We hopers, who have hoped for thee and lost,
We poets, wandered round by dreams,* who hailed
20　　From this Atrides' roof (with lintel-post
Which still drips blood,—the worse part hath prevailed)
　　The fire-voice of the beacons, to declare
Troy taken, sorrow ended,—cozened through
　　A crimson sunset in a misty air,—
25　What now remains for such as we, to do?
　　God's judgments, peradventure, will He bare
To the roofs of thunder, if we kneel and sue?

---

*Referring to the well-known opening passage of the Agamemnon of
Æschylus.

III

From Casa Guidi windows I looked forth,
And saw ten thousand eyes of Florentines
30   Flash back the triumph of the Lombard north,—
Saw fifty banners, freighted with the signs
        And exultations of the awakened earth,
Float on above the multitude in lines,
        Straight to the Pitti. So, the vision went.
35 And so, between those populous rough hands
        Raised in the sun, Duke Leopold outleant,
And took the patriot's oath, which henceforth stands
        Among the oaths of perjurers, eminent
To catch the lightnings ripened for these lands.

IV

40   Why swear at all, thou false Duke Leopold?
What need to swear? What need to boast thy blood
        Unspoilt of Austria, and thy heart unsold
Away from Florence? It was understood
        God made thee not too vigorous or too bold,
45 And men had patience with thy quiet mood,
        And women, pity, as they saw thee pace
Their festive streets with premature grey hairs:
        We turned the mild dejection of thy face
To princely meanings, took thy wrinkling cares
50   For ruffling hopes, and called thee weak, not base.
Better to light the torches for more prayers
        And smoke the pale Madonnas at the shrine,
Being still 'our poor Grand-duke', 'our good Grand-duke',
        'Who cannot help the Austrian in his line,'
55 Than write an oath upon a nation's book
        For men to spit at with scorn's blurring brine!
Who dares forgive what none can overlook?

V

For me, I do repent me in this dust
Of towns and temples, which makes Italy,—
60   I sigh amid the sighs which breathe a gust
Of dying century to century,

Around us on the uneven crater-crust
Of the old worlds,—I bow my soul and knee,
And sigh and do repent me of my fault
65 That ever I believed the man was true.
These sceptered strangers shun the common salt,
And, therefore, when the general board's in view,
They standing up to carve for blind and halt,
We should suspect the viands which ensue.
70 And I repent that in this time and place,
Where all the corpse-lights of experience burn
From Cæsar's and Lorenzo's festering race,
To enlighten groping reasoners, I could learn
No better counsel for a simple case,
75 That to put faith in princes, in my turn.
Heavens! the death-piles of the ancient years
Flared up in vain before me? Knew I not
What stench arises from their purple gears,—
And how the sceptres witness whence they got
80 Their brier-wood, crackling through the atmosphere's
Foul smoke, by princely perjuries, kept hot?
Forgive me, ghost of patriots,—Brutus, thou,
Who trailest downhill into life again
Thy blood-weighed cloak, to indict me with thy slow
85 Reproachful eyes!—for being taught in vain
That, while the illegitimate Cæsars show
Of meaner stature than the first full strain,
(Confessed incompetent to conquer Gaul)
They swoon as feebly and cross Rubicons
90 As rashly as any Julius of them all.
Forgive, that I forgot the mind which runs
Through absolute races, too unsceptical!
I saw the man among his little sons,
His lips were warm with kisses while he swore,—
95 And I, because I am a woman, I
Who felt my own child's coming life before
The prescience of my soul, and held faith high,
I could not bear to think, whoever bore,
That lips, so warmed, could shape so cold a lie.

VI

100   From Casa Guidi windows I looked out,
Again looked, and beheld a different sight.
    The Duke had fled before the people's shout
'Long live the Duke!' A people, to speak right,
    Must speak as soft as courtiers, lest a doubt
105 Should turn sovereigns brows to curdled white.
    Moreover that same dangerous shouting meant
Some gratitude for future favours, which
    Were only promised;—the Constituent
Implied; the whole being subject to the hitch
110   In motu proprios, very incident
To all these Czars, from Paul to Paulovitch.
    Whereat the people rose up in the dust
Of the Duke's flying feet, and shouted still
    And loudly, only, this time, as was just,
115 Not 'Live the Duke,' who had fled, for good or ill,
    But 'Live the People,' who remained and must,
The unrenounced and unrenounceable.

VII

    Long life the people! How they lived! and boiled
And bubbled in the cauldron of the street!
120   How the young blustered, nor the old recoiled
And what a thunderous stir of tongues and feet
    Trod flat the palpitating bells, and foiled
The joy-guns of their echo, shattering it!
    How down they pulled the Duke's arms everywhere!
125 How up they set new café-signs, to show
    Where patriots might sip ices in pure air—
(Yet the fresh paint smelt somewhat). To and fro
    How marched the civic guard, and stopped to stare
When boys broke windows in a civic glow.
130   How rebel songs were sung to loyal tunes,
And the pope cursed, in ecclesiastic metres!
    How all the Circoli grew large as moons,
And all the speakers, moonstruck,—thankful greeters
    Of prospects which struck poor the ducal boons,
135 A mere free press, and chambers!—frank repeaters

Of great Guerrazzi's praises. . . . 'There's a man,
The father of the land!—who truly great,
 Takes off that national disgrace and ban,
The farthing tax upon our Florence-gate,
140 And saves Italia as he only can'.
How all the nobles fled, and would not wait,
 Because they were most noble! which being so,
How the mob vowed to burn their palaces,
 Because they were too to have leave to go.
145 How grown men raged at Austria's wickedness,
 And smoked,—while fifty striplings in a row
Marched straight to Piedmont for the wrong's redress!
 You say we failed in our duty, we who wore
Black velvet like Italian democrats,
150 Who slashed our sleeves like patriots, nor forswore
The true republic in the form of hats?
 We chased the archbishop from the duomo door—
We chalked the walls with bloody caveats
 Against all tyrants. If we did not fight
155 Exactly, we fired muskets up the void,
 To show that victory was ours of right.
We met, discussed in every place, self-buoyed
 (Except perhaps i' the chambers), day and night:
We proved that all the poor should be employed,
160 And yet the rich not worked for anywise,—
Pay certified, yet payers abrogated,
 Full work secured, yet liabilities
To over-work excluded,—not one bated
 Of all our holidays, that still, at twice
165 Or thrice a-week, are moderately rated.
 We proved that Austria was dislodged, or would
Or should be, and that Tuscany in arms
 Should, would, dislodge her, in high hardihood!
And yet, to leave our piazzas, shops and farms,
170 For the bare sake of fighting, was not good—
We proved that also—'Did we carry charms
 Against being killed ourselves, that we should rush
On killing others? What! desert herewith
 Our wives and mothers?—was that duty? Tush!'

175 At which we shook the sword within the sheath,
         Like heroes—only louder! and the flush
    Ran up our cheek to meet the victor's wreath.
         Nay, what we proved, we shouted—how we shouted,
    (Especially the boys did) planting
180   That tree of liberty, whose fruit is doubted
    Because the roots are not of nature's granting—
         A tree of good and evil!—none, without it,
    Grow gods!—alas, and, with, men are wanting!

    VIII
         O holy knowledge, holy liberty,
185 O holy rights of nations! If I speak
         These bitter things against the jugglery
    Of days that in your names proved blind and weak,
         It is that tears are bitter. When we see
    The brown skulls grin at death in churchyards bleak,
190   We do not cry, 'This Yorick is too light,'
    For death grows deathlier with that mouth he makes.
         So with my mocking. Bitter things I write,
    Because my soul is bitter for your sakes,
         O freedom! O my Florence!

    IX
                              Men who might
195 Do greatly in a universe that breaks
         And burns, must ever *know* before they do.
    Courage and patience are but sacrifice;
         And sacrifice is offered for and to
    Something conceived of. Each man pays a price
200   For what he himself counts precious, whether true
    Or false the appreciation it implies.
         Here, was no knowledge, no conception, nought!
    Desire was absent, that provides great deeds
         From out the greatness of prevenient thought;
205 And action, action, like a flame that needs
         A steady breath and fuel, being caught
    Up, like a burning reed from other reeds,

Flashed in the empty and uncertain air,
Then wavered, then went out. Behold, who blames
210   A crooked course, when not a goal is there,
To round the fervid striving of the games?
     An ignorance of means may minister
To greatness, but an ignorance of aims
     Makes it impossible to be great at all.
215 So, with our Tuscans! Let none dare to say,
     Here virtue never can be national.
Here fortitude can never cut a way
     Between the Austrian muskets, out of thrall.
I tell you rather, that, whoever may
220   Discern true ends here, shall grow pure enough
To love them, brave enough to strive for them,
     And strong enough to reach them, though the roads be
          rough:
That having learnt—by no mere apophthegm—
     Not the mere draping of a graceful stuff
225 About a statue, broidered at the hem,—
     Not the mere thrilling on an opera stage,
Of 'libertà' to bravos—(a fair word,
     Yet too allied to inarticulate rage
And breathless sobs, for singing, though the chord
230   Were deeper than they struck it!)—but the gauge
Of civil wants sustained, and wrongs abhorred,—
     The serious, sacred meaning and full use
Of freedom for a nation,—then, indeed,
     Our Tuscans, underneath the bloody dews
235 Of a new morning, rising up agreed
     And bold, will want no Saxon souls or thews,
To sweep their piazzas clear of Austria's breed.

X

     Alas, alas! it was not so this time.
Conviction was not, courage failed, and truth
240   Was something to be doubted of. The mime
Changed masks, because a mime; the tide as smooth
     In running in as out, no sense of crime
Because no sense of virtue. Sudden ruth

         Seized on the people . . . they would have again
245 Their good Grand-duke, and leave Guerrazzi, though
         He took that tax from Florence:—'Much in vain
He takes it from the market-carts, we trow,
         While urgent that no market-men remain,
But all march off, and leave the spade and plough,
250   To die among the Lombards. Was it thus
The dear paternal Duke did? Live the Duke!'
         At which the joy-bells multitudinous
Swept by an opposite wind, as loudly shook.
         Re call the mild Archbishop to his house,
255 To bless the people with his frightened look,
         He shall not be hanged yet, we intend.
Seize on Guerrazzi; guard him in full view,
         Or else we stab him in the back, to end.
Rub out those chalked devices! Set up new!
260   The Duke's arms; doff your Phrygian caps; and mend
The pavement of the piazzas broke into
         By barren poles of freedom! Smooth the way
For the Ducal carriage, lest his highness sigh
         'Here trees of liberty grew yesterday'.
265 'Long live the Duke!'—How roared the cannonry,
         How rocked the bell-towers, and through a spray
Of nosegays, wreaths, and kerchiefs, tossed on high,
         How marched the civic guard, the people still
Shouting,—especially the little boys.
270   Alas, poor people, of an unfledged will
Most fitly expressed by such a callow voice!
         Alas, still poorer Duke, incapable
Of being worthy even of so much noise!

XI

         You think he came back instantly, with thanks
275 And tears in his faint eyes, and hands extended
         To stretch the franchise through their utmost ranks?
That having, like a father, apprehended,
         He came to pardon fatherly those pranks
Played out, and now in filial service ended?—

280   That some love-token, like a prince, he threw,
        To meet the people's love-call, in return?
            Well, how he came I will relate to you;
        And if your hearts should burn, why, hearts *must* burn,
            To make the ashes which things old and new
285   Shall be washed clean in—as this Duke will learn.

XII
            From Casa Guidi windows, gazing, then,
        I saw and witness how the Duke came back.
            The regular tramp of horse and tread of men
        Did smite the silence like an anvil black
290   And sparkless. With her wide eyes at full strain,
        Our Tuscan nurse exclaimed, 'Alack, alack,
            Signora! these shall be the Austrians'. 'Nay,
        Hush, hush,' I answered, 'do not wake the child!'
            —For so, my two-months' baby sleeping lay
295   In milky dreams upon the bed and smiled,
            And I thought, 'he shall sleep on, while he may,
        Through the world's baseness. Not being yet defiled,
            Why should he be disturbed by what is done?'
        Then, gazing, I beheld the long-drawn street
300   Live out, from end to end, full in the sun,
        With Austria's thousands. Sword and bayonet,
            Horse, foot, artillery,—cannons rolling on,
        Like blind slow storm-clouds gestant with the heat
            Of undeveloped lightnings, each bestrode
305   By a single man, dust-white from head to heel,
            Indifferent as the dreadful thing he rode,
        Calm as a sculptured Fate, and terrible.
            As some smooth river which hath overflowed,
        Both slow and silent down its current wheel
310   A loosened forest, all the pines erect,—
        So, swept, in mute significance of storm,
            The marshalled thousands,—not an eye deflect
        To left or right, to catch a novel form
            Of the famed city adorned by architect
315   And carver, nor of Beauties live and warm

Scared at the casements!—all, straightforward eyes
And faces, held as steadfast as their swords,
    And cognisant of acts, not imageries.
The key, O Tuscans, too well fits the wards!
320   Ye asked for mimes; these bring you tragedies—
For purple; these shall wear it as your lords,
    Ye played like children: die like innocents!
Ye mimicked lightnings with a torch: the crack
    Of the actual bolt, your pastime, circumvents.
325 Ye called up ghosts, believing they were slack
    To follow any voice from Gilboa's tents, . . .
Here's Samuel!—and, so, Grand-dukes come back!

XIII

And yet, they are no prophets though they come.
That awful mantle they are drawing close,
330   Shall be searched, one day, by the shafts of Doom,
Through double folds now hoodwinking the brows.
    Resuscitated monarchs disentomb
Grave-reptiles with them, in their new life-throes.
    Let such beware. Behold, the people waits,
335 Like God. As He, in his serene of might,
    So they, in their endurance of long straits.
Ye stamp no nation out, though day and night
    Ye tread them with that absolute heel which grates
And grinds them flat from all attempted height.
340   You kill worms sooner with a garden-spade
Than you kill peoples: people will not die;
    The tail curls stronger when you lop the head;
They writhe at every wound and multiply,
    And shudder into a heap of life that's made
345 Thus vital from God's own vitality.
    'Tis hard to shrivel back a day of God's
Once fixed for judgment: 'tis as hard to change
    The people's, when they rise beneath their loads
And heave them from their back with violent wrench,
350   To crush the oppressor!—for that judgment rod's
The measure of this popular revenge.

XIV
    Meantime, from Casa Guidi windows we
Beheld the armament of Austria flow
    Into the drowning heart of Tuscany.
355 And yet none wept, none cursed, or, if 'twas so,
    They wept and cursed in silence. Silently
Our noisy Tuscans watched the invading foe;
    They had learnt silence. Pressed against the wall
And grouped upon the church-steps opposite,
360   A few pale men and women stared at all.
God knows what they were feeling, with their white
    Constrained faces! They, so prodigal
Of cry and gesture when the world goes right,
    Or wrong indeed. But here, was depth of wrong,
365 And here, still water: they were silent here:
    And through that sentient silence, struck along
That measured tramp from which it stood out clear,
    Distinct the sound and silence, like a gong
Tolled upon midnight,—each made awfuller;
370   While every soldier in his cap displayed
A leaf of olive. Dusty, bitter thing!
    Was such plucked at Novara, is it said?

XV
A cry is up in England, which doth ring
    The hollow world through, that for ends of trade
375 And virtue, and God's better worshipping,
    We henceforth should exalt the name of Peace,
And leave those rusty wars that eat the soul,—
    (Besides their clippings at our golden fleece.)
I, too, have loved peace, and from bole to bole
380   Of immemorial, undeciduous trees,
Would write, as lovers use, upon a scroll,
    The holy name of Peace, and set it high
Where none could pluck it down. On trees, I say,—
    Not upon gibbets!—With the greenery
385 Of dewy branches and the flowery May,
    Sweet meditation 'twixt earth and sky
Providing, for the shepherd's holiday!

Not upon gibbets!—though the vulture leaves
Some quiet the bones he first picked bare.
390   Not upon dungeons! though the wretch who grieves
And groans within, stirs not the outer air
As much as little field mice stir the sheaves.
Not upon chain-bolts! though the slave's despair
Has dulled his helpless, miserable brain,
395   And left him blank beneath the freeman's whip,
To sing and laugh out idiocies of pain.
Nor yet on starving homes! where many a lip
Has sobbed itself asleep through curses vain!
I love no peace which is not fellowship,
400   And which includes not mercy. I would have
Rather, the raking of the guns across
The world, and shrieks against Heaven's architrave.
Rather, the struggle in the slippery fosse
Of dying men and horses, and the wave
405   Blood-bubbling. . . . Enough said!—by Christ's own
cross,
And by the faint heart of my womanhood,
Such things are better than a Peace that sits
Beside a hearth in self-commended mood,
And takes not thought how wind and rain by fits
410   Are howling out of doors against the good
Of the poor wanderer. What! your peace admits
Of outside anguish while it sits at home?
I loathe to take its name upon my tongue—
It is no peace. 'Tis treason, stiff with doom,—
415   'Tis gagged despair, and inarticulate wrong,
Annihilated Poland, stifled Rome,
Dazed Naples, Hungary fainting 'neath the thong,
And Austria wearing a smooth olive-leaf
On her brute forehead, while her hoofs outpress
420   The life from these Italian souls, in brief.
O Lord of Peace, who art Lord of Righteousness,
Constrain the anguished worlds from sin and grief,
Pierce them with conscience, purge them with redress,
And give us peace which is no counterfeit!

XVI

425 But wherefore should we look out any more
  From Casa Guidi windows? Shut them straight,
And let us sit down by the folded door,
  And veil our saddened faces, and, so, wait
What next the judgment-heavens make ready for.
430   I have grown weary of these windows. Sights
Come thick enough and clear enough with thought,
  Without the sunshine; souls have inner lights.
And since the Grand-duke has come back and brought
  This army from the North which thus requites
435 His filial South, we leave him to be taught.
  His South, too, has learnt something certainly,
Whereof the practice will bring profit soon;
  And peradventure other eyes may see,
From Casa Guidi windows, what is done
440   Or undone. Whatsoever deeds they be,
Pope Pius will be glorified in none.

XVII

  Record that gain, Mazzini!—it shall top
Some heights of sorrow. Peter's rock, so named,
  Shall lure no vessel, any more, to drop
445 Among the breakers. Peter's chair is shamed
  Like any vulgar throne the nations lop
To pieces for their firewood unreclaimed;
  And, when it burns too, we shall see as well
In Italy as elsewhere. Let it burn.
450   The cross, accounted still adorable,
Is Christ's cross only!—if the thief's would earn
  Some stealthy genuflexions, we rebel;
And here the impenitent thief's has had its turn,
  As God knows; and the people on their knees
455 Scoff and toss back the croziers, stretched like yokes
  To press their heads down lower by degrees.
So Italy, by means of these last strokes,
  Escapes the danger which preceded these,
Of leaving captured hands in cloven oaks . . .

460   Of leaving very souls within the buckle
Whence bodies struggled outward . . . of supposing
        That freemen may, like bondsmen kneel and truckle,
And then stand up as usual, without losing
        An inch of stature.
                                Those whom she-wolves suckle
465   Will bite as wolves do in the grapple-closing
        Of adverse interests: this, at last, is known,
(Thank Pius for the lesson) that albeit,
        Among the Popedom's hundred heads of stone
Which blink down on you from the roof's retreat
470   In Siena's tiger-striped cathedral,—Joan
And Borgia 'mid their fellows you may greet,
        A harlot and a devil,—you will see
Not a man, still less angel, grandly set
        With open soul to render man more free.
475   The fishers are still thinking of the net,
        And if not thinking of the hook too, we
Are counted somewhat deeply in their debt;
        But that's a rare case—so, by hook and crook
They take the advantage, agonising Christ
480   By rustier nails than those of Cedron's brook,
I' the people's body very cheaply priced;
        Quoting high priesthood out of Holy book,
And buying death-fields with the sacrificed.

XVIII
        Priests, priests,—there's no such name!—God's own,
            except,
485   Ye take most vainly. Through Heaven's lifted gate
        The priestly ephod in sole glory swept,
When Christ ascended, entered in, and sate
        With victor face sublimely overwept,
At Deity's right hand, to mediate
490   He alone, He for ever. On his breast
The Urim and the Thummim, fed with fire
        From the full Godhead, flicker with the unrest
Of human, pitiful heartbeats. Come up higher,

All Christians! Levi's tribe is dispossest.
495 That solitary alb ye shall admire,
        But not cast lots for. The last chrism, poured right,
Was on that Head, and poured for burial,
        And not for domination in men's sight.
What are these churches? The old temple wall
500   Doth overlook them juggling with the sleight
Of surplice, candlestick, and altar-pall.
        East church and west church, ay, north church and
            south,
Rome's church and England's,—let them all repent,
        And make concordats 'twixt their soul and mouth,
505 Succeed St. Paul by working at the tent,
        Become infallible guides by speaking truth,
And excommunicate their own pride that bent
        And cramped the souls of men.
                                    Why, even here,
Priestcraft burns out, the twined linen blazes;
510   Not, like asbestos, to grow white and clear,
But all to perish!—while the fire-smell raises
        To life some swooning spirits, who, last year,
Lost breath and heart in these church-stifled places.
        Why, almost, through this Pius, we believed
515 The priesthood could be an honest thing, he smiled
        So saintly while our corn was being sheaved
For his own granaries. Showing now defiled
        His hireling hands, a better help's achieved
Than if he blessed us shepherd-like and mild.
520   False doctrine, strangled by its own amen,
Dies in the throat of all this nation. Who
        Will speak a pope's name, as they rise again?
What woman or what child will count him true?
        What dreamer praise him with the voice or pen?
525 What man fight for him?—Pius has his due.

XIX

        Record that gain, Mazzini!—Yes, but first
Set down thy people's faults;—set down the want
        Of soul-conviction; set down aims dispersed,

And incoherent means, and valour scant
530   Because of scanty faith, and schisms accursed,
That wrench these brother-hearts from covenant
    With freedom and each other. Set down this
And this, and see to overcome it when
    The seasons bring the fruits thou wilt not miss
535 If wary. Let no cry of patriot men
    Distract thee from the stern analysis
Of masses who cry only: keep thy ken
    Clear as thy soul is virtuous. Heroes' blood
Splashed up against thy noble brow in Rome,—
540   Let such not blind thee to an interlude
Which was not also holy, yet did come
    'Twixt sacramental actions:—brotherhood,
Despised even there—and something of the doom
    Of Remus, in the trenches. Listen now—
545 Rossi died silent near where Cæsar died.
    HE did not say, 'My Brutus, is it thou?'
Instead, rose Italy and testified,
    ''Twas *I*, and *I* am Brutus.—I avow.'
At which the whole world's laugh of scorn replied,
550   'A poor maimed copy of Brutus!'
                             Too much like,
Indeed, to be so unlike! Too unskilled
    At Philippi and the honest battle-pike,
To be so skilful where a man is killed
    Near Pompey's statue, and the daggers strike
555 At unawares i' the throat. Was thus fulfilled
    An omen once of Michel Angelo,—
When Marcus Brutus he conceived complete,
    And strove to hurl him out by blow on blow
Upon the marble, at Art's thunderheat,
560   Till haply some pre-shadow rising slow,
Of what his Italy would fancy meet
    To be called BRUTUS, straight his plastic hand
Fell back before his prophet soul, and left
    A fragment . . . a maimed Brutus,—but more grand
565 Than this, so named at Rome, was!
                           Let thy weft

Present one woof and warp, Mazzini!—stand
With no man of a spotless fame bereft—
     Not for Italia! Neither stand apart,
No, not for the republic!—from those pure
570   Brave men who hold the level of thy heart
In patriot truth, as lover and as doer,
     Albeit they will not follow where thou art
As extreme theorist. Trust and distrust fewer;
     And so bind strong and keep unstained the cause
575 Which are God's signal, war-trumps newly blown
     Shall yet annuntiate to the world's applause.

XX
Just now, the world is busy: it has grown
     A Fair-going world. Imperial England draws
The flowing ends of the earth, from Fez, Canton,
580   Delhi and Stockholm, Athens and Madrid,
The Russias and the vast Americas,
     As if a queen drew in her robes amid
Her golden cincture,—isles, peninsulas,
     Capes, continents, far inland countries hid
585 By jaspar-sands and hills of chrysopras,
     All trailing in their splendours through the door
Of the new Crystal Palace. Every nation,
     To every other nation, strange of yore,
Shall face to face give civic salutation,
590   And holds up in a proud right hand before
That congress, the best work which she could fashion
     By her best means.—'These corals, will you please
To match against your oaks? They grow as fast
     Within my wilderness of purple seas.'—
595 'This diamond stared upon me as I passed
     (As a live god's eye from a marble frieze)
Along a dark of diamonds. Is it classed?'—
     'I wove these stuffs so subtly that the gold
Swims to the surface of the silk like cream,
600   And curdles to fair patterns. Ye behold!'—
'These delicatest muslins rather seem

Than be, you think? Nay, touch them and be bold,
Though such veiled Chakhi's face in Hafiz' dream.'—
     'These carpets—you walk slow on them like kings,
605 Inaudible like spirits, while your foot
          Dips deep in velvet roses and such things.'—
'Even Apollonius might commend this flute.*
     The music, winding through the stops, upsprings
To make the player very rich! Compute.'—
610   'Here's goblet-glass, to take in with your wine
The very sun its grapes were ripened under!
          Drink light and juice together, and each fine.'—
'This model of a steam-ship moves your wonder?
     You should behold it crushing down the brine,
615 Like a blind Jove, who feels his way with thunder.'—
     'Here's sculpture! Ah, we live too! Why not throw
Our life into our marbles? Art has place
          For other artists after Angelo.'—
'I tried to paint out here a natural face—
620   For nature includes Raffael, as we know,
Not Raffael nature. Will it help my case?'—
     'Methinks you will not match this steel of ours!'—
'Nor you this porcelain! One might think the clay
          Retained in it the larvæ of flowers,
625 They bud so, round the cup, the old spring way.'—
     'Nor you these carven woods, where birds in bowers
With twisting snakes and climbing cupids, play.'

XXI
     O Magi of the east and of the west,
Your incense, gold, and myrrh are excellent.—
630   What gifts for Christ, then, bring ye with the rest?
Your hands have worked well. Is your courage spent
          In handwork only? Have you nothing best,
Which generous souls may perfect and present,

*Philostratus relates of Apollonius that he objected to the musical instru-
ment of Linus the Rhodian, its incompetence to enrich and beautify. The
history of music in our day, would, upon the former point, sufficiently
confute the philosopher.

And He shall thank the givers for? No light
635 Of teaching, liberal nations, for the poor,
Who sit in darkness when it is not night?
No cure for wicked children? Christ,—no cure!
No help for women, sobbing out of sight
Because men made the laws? No brothel-lure
640 Burnt out by popular lightnings?—Hast thou found
No remedy, my England, for such woes?
No outlet, Austria, for the scourged and bound,
No entrance for the exiled? no repose
Russia, for knouted Poles worked underground,
645 And gentle ladies bleached among the snows?—
No mercy for the slave, America?—
No hope for Rome, free France, chivalric France?—
Alas, great nations have great shames, I say.
No pity, O world, no tender utterance
650 Of benediction, and prayers stretched this way
For poor Italia, baffled by mischance?—
O gracious nations, give some ear to me!
You all go to your Fair, and I am one
Who at the roadside of humanity
655 Beseech your alms,—God's justice to be done.
So, prosper!

XXII

In the name of Italy,
Meantime, her patriot dead have benison!
They only have done well; and what they did
Being perfect, it shall triumph. Let them slumber.
660 No king of Egypt in a pyramid
Is safer from oblivion, though he number
Full seventy cerements for a coverlid.
These Dead be seeds of life, and shall encumber
The sad heart of the land until it loose
665 The clammy clods and let out the spring-growth
In beatific green through every bruise.
The tyrant should take heed to what he doth,
Since every victim-carrion turns to use,
And drives a chariot, like a god made wroth,

670   Against each piled injustice. Ay, the least,
Dead for Italia, not in vain has died,
      However vainly, ere life's struggle ceased,
To mad dissimilar ends have swerved aside.
      Each grave her nationality has pieced
675 By its own majestic breadth, and fortified,
      And pinned it deeper to the soil. Forlorn
Of thanks, be, therefore, no one of these graves!
      Not Hers,—who, at her husband's side, in scorn,
Outfaced the whistling shot and hissing waves,
680   Until she felt her little babe unborn
Recoil, within her, from the violent staves
      And bloodhounds of the world:—at which, her life
Dropt inwards from her eyes, and followed it
      Beyond the hunters. Garibaldi's wife
685 And child died so. And now, the sea-weeds fit
      Her body like a proper shroud and coif,
And murmurously the ebbing waters grit
      The little pebbles, while she lies interred
In the sea-sand. Perhaps, ere dying thus,
690   She looked up in his face which never stirred
From its clenched anguish, as to make excuse
      For leaving him for his, if so she erred.
Well he remembers that she could not choose.
      A memorable grave! Another is
695 At Genoa, where, a king may fitly lie,—
      Who, bursting that heroic heart of his
At lost Novara, that he could not die,
      Though thrice into the cannon's eyes for this
He plunged his shuddering steed, and felt the sky
700   Reel back between the fire-shocks;—stripped away
The ancestral ermine ere the smoke had cleared,
      And, naked to the soul, that none might say
His kingship covered what was base and bleared
      With treason, he went out an exile, yea,
705 An exiled patriot. Let him be revered.

XXIII

Yea, verily, Charles Albert has died well;
And if he lived not all so, as one spoke,
    The sin pass softly with the passing bell.
For he was shriven, I think, in cannon-smoke,
710   And taking off his crown, made visible
A hero's forehead. Shaking Austria's yoke
    He shattered his own hand and heart. 'So best,'
His last words were upon his lonely bed,—
    'I do not like popes and dukes at least—
715 Thank God for it.' And now that he is dead,
    Admitting it is proved and manifest
That he was worthy, with a discrowned head,
    To measure heights with patriots, let them stand
Beside the man in his Oporto shroud,
720   And each vouchsafe to take him by the hand,
And kiss him on the cheek, and say aloud,—
    'Thou, too, hast suffered for our native land!
My brother, thou art one of us! Be proud.'

XXIV

Still, graves, when Italy is talked upon!
725 Still, still, the patriot's tomb, the stranger's hate.
    Still Niobe! still fainting in the sun
By whose most dazzling arrows violate
    Her beauteous offspring perished! Has she won
Nothing but garlands for the graves, from Fate?
730   Nothing but death-songs?—Yes, be it understood,
Life throbs in noble Piedmont! while the feet
    Of Rome's clay image, dabbled soft in blood,
Grow flat with dissolution, and, as meet,
    Will soon be shovelled off, like other mud,
735 To leave the passage free in church and street.
    And I, who first took hope up in this song,
Because a child was singing one . . . behold,
    The hope and omen were not, haply, wrong!
Poets are soothsayers still, like those of old
740   Who studied flights of doves,—and creatures young
And tender, mighty meanings, may unfold.

XXV

The sun strikes, through the windows, up the floor:
Stand out in it, my own young Florentine,
    Not two years old, and let me see thee more!
745 It grows along thy amber curls, to shine
    Brighter than elsewhere. Now, look straight before,
And fix thy brave blue English eyes on mine,
    And from thy soul, which fronts the future so,
With unabashed and unabated gaze,
750   Teach me to hope for, what the Angels know
When they smile clear as thou dost. Down God's ways
    With just alighted feet between the snow
And snowdrops, where a little lamb may graze,
    Thou hast no fear, my lamb, about the road,
755 Albeit in our vain-glory we assume
    That, less than we have, thou hast learnt of God.
Stand out, my blue-eyed prophet!—thou, to whom
    The earliest world-day light that ever flowed,
Through Casa Guidi windows, chanced to come!
760   Now shake the glittering nimbus of thy hair,
And be God's witness;—that the elemental
    New springs of life are gushing everywhere,
To cleanse the water-courses, and prevent all
    Concrete obstructions which infest the air!
765 —That earth's alive, and gentle or ungentle
    Motions within her, signify but growth!—
The ground swells greenest o'er the labouring moles.
    Howe'er the uneasy world is vexed and wroth,
Young children, lifted high on parent souls,
770   Look round them with a smile upon the mouth,
And take for music every bell that tolls.
    WHO said we should be better if like these?
And *we* . . . despond we for the future, though
    Posterity is smiling on our knees,
775 Convicting us of folly? Let us go—
    We will trust God. The blank interstices
Men take for ruins, He will build into

With pillared marbles rare, or knit across
With generous arches, till the fane's complete.
780   This world has no perdition, if some loss.

XXVI

Such cheer I gather from thy smiling, Sweet!
    The self-same cherub-faces which emboss
The Vail, lean inward to the mercy-seat.

FROM *TWO POEMS BY ELIZABETH BARRETT AND ROBERT BROWNING* (1854)

A Plea for the Ragged Schools of London
WRITTEN IN ROME

I

I AM listening here in Rome.
'England's strong,' say many speakers,
'If she winks, the Czar must come,
'Prow and topsail, to the breakers.'

II

5 'England's rich in coal and oak,'
Adds a Roman, getting moody,
'If she shakes a travelling cloak,
'Down our Appian roll the scudi.'

III

'England's righteous,' they rejoin,
10 'Who shall grudge her exultations,
'When her wealth of golden coin
'Works the welfare of the nations?'

IV

I am listening here in Rome.
Over Alps a voice is sweeping—
15 'England's cruel! save us some
'Of these victims in her keeping!'

V

As the cry beneath the wheel
Of an old triumphal Roman
Cleft the people's shouts like steel,
20 While the show was spoilt for no man,

VI

Comes that voice. Let others shout,
Other poets praise my land here—
I am sadly sitting out,
Praying, 'God forgive her grandeur.'

VII

25 Shall we boast of empire, where
Time with ruin sits commissioned?
In God's liberal blue air
Peter's dome itself looks wizened;

VIII

And the mountains, in disdain,
30 Gather back their lights of opal
From the dumb, despondent plain,
Heaped with jawbones of a people.

IX

Lordly English, think it o'er,
Cæsar's doing is all undone!
35 You have cannons on your shore,
And free parliaments in London,

X

Princes' parks, and merchants' homes,
Tents for soldiers, ships for seamen,—
Ay, but ruins worse than Rome's
40 In your pauper men and women.

XI

Women leering through the gas,
Just such bosoms used to nurse you!
Men, turned wolves by famine—pass;
Those can speak themselves, and curse you.

XII

45   But these others—children small,
Spilt like blots about the city,
Quay and street, and palace-wall—
Take them up into your pity!

XIII

Ragged children with bare feet,
50   Whom the angels in white raiment
Know the names of, to repeat
When they come on you for payment.

XIV

Ragged children, hungry-eyed,
Huddled up out of the coldness
55   On your doorsteps, side by side,
Till your footman damns their boldness.

XV

In the alleys, in the squares,
Begging, lying little rebels;
In the noisy thoroughfares,
60   Struggling on with piteous trebles.

XVI

Patient children—think what pain
Makes a young child patient—ponder!
Wronged too commonly to strain
After right, or wish, or wonder.

XVII

65   Wicked children, with peaked chins,
And old foreheads! there are many
With no pleasures except sins,
Gambling with a stolen penny.

XVIII

Sickly children, that whine low
70   To themselves and not their mothers,
From mere habit,—never so
Hoping help or care from others.

XIX

Healthy children, with those blue
English eyes, fresh from their Maker,
75   Fierce and ravenous, staring through
At the brown loaves of the baker.

XX

I am listening here in Rome,
And the Romans are confessing,
'English children pass in bloom
80   'All the prettiest made for blessing.

XXI

'*Angli angeli!*' (resumed
From the mediæval story)
'Such rose angelhoods, emplumed
'In such ringlets of pure glory!'

XXII

85   Can we smooth down the bright hair,
O my sisters, calm, unthrilled in
Our heart's pulses? Can we bear
The sweet looks of our own children,

XXIII

While those others, lean and small,
90   Scurf and mildew of the city,
Spot our streets, convict us all
Till we take them into pity?

XXIV

'Is it our fault?' you reply,
'When, throughout civilisation,
95   'Every nation's empery
'Is asserted by starvation?'

XXV

'All these mouths we cannot feed,
'And we cannot clothe these bodies.'
Well, if man's so hard indeed,
100   Let them learn at least what God is!

XXVI

Little outcasts from life's fold,
The grave's hope they may be joined in,
By Christ's covenant consoled
For our social contract's grinding.

XXVII

105   If no better can be done,
Let us do but this,—endeavour
That the sun behind the sun
Shine upon them while they shiver!

XXVIII

On the dismal London flags,
110   Through the cruel social juggle,
Put a thought beneath their rags
To ennoble the heart's struggle.

XXIX

O my sisters, not so much
Are we asked for—not a blossom
115   From our children's nosegay, such
As we gave it from our bosom,—

XXX

Not the milk left in their cup,
Not the lamp while they are sleeping,
Not the little cloak hung up
120   While the coat's in daily keeping,—

XXXI

But a place in RAGGED SCHOOLS,
Where the outcasts may to-morrow
Learn by gentle words and rules
Just the uses of their sorrow.

XXXII

125   O my sisters! children small,
Blue-eyed, wailing through the city,
Our own babes cry in them all,
Let us take them into pity.

ELIZABETH BARRETT BROWNING
March 20th, 1854.

FROM *POEMS BEFORE CONGRESS* (1860)

Christmas Gifts

—'ὡς βασιλεῖ, ὡς θεῷ, ὡς νεκρῷ.' GREGORY NAZIANZEN

I

The Pope on Christmas Day
    Sits in St. Peter's chair;
But the people murmur and say,
    'Our souls are sick and forlorn,
5 And who will show us where
    Is the stable where Christ was born?'

II

The star is lost in the dark;
    The manger is lost in the straw;
The Christ cries faintly . . hark! . .
10   Through bands that swaddle and strangle—
But the Pope in the chair of awe
    Looks down the great quadrangle.

III

The magi kneel at his foot,
    Kings of the east and west,
15 But, instead of the angels, (mute
    Is the 'Peace on earth' of their song),
The peoples, perplexed and opprest,
    Are sighing, 'How long, how long?'

IV

And instead of the kine, bewilder in
20   Shadow of aisle and dome,
The bear who tore up the children,
    The fox who burnt up the corn,
And the wolf who suckled at Rome
    Brothers to slay and to scorn.

V

25 Cardinals left and right of him,
      Worshippers round and beneath,
The silver trumpets at sight of him
      Thrill with a musical blast:
But the people say through their teeth,
30   'Trumpets? we wait for the Last!'

VI

He sits in the place of the Lord,
      And asks for the gifts of the time;
Gold, for the haft of a sword,
      To win back Romagna averse,
35 Incense, to sweeten a crime,
      And myrrh, to embitter a curse.

VII

Then a king of the west said, 'Good!—
      I bring thee the gifts of the time;
Red, for the patriot's blood,
40   Green, for the martyr's crown,
White, for the dew and the rime,
      When the morning of God comes down.'

VIII

—O mystic tricolor bright!
      The Pope's heart quailed like a man's:
45 The cardinals froze at the sight,
      Bowing their tonsures hoary:
And the eyes in the peacock-fans
      Winked at the alien glory.

IX

But the peoples exclaimed in hope,
50   'Now blessed be he who has brought
These gifts of the time to the Pope,
      When our souls were sick and forlorn.
—And *here* is the star we sought,
      To show us where Christ was born!'

FROM *LAST POEMS* (1862)

The North and the South
ROME, MAY, 1861

I

'Now give us lands where the olives grow,'
    Cried the North to the South,
'Where the sun with a golden mouth can blow
Blue bubbles of grapes down a vineyard row!'
5   Cried the North to the South.

'Now give us men from the sunless plain,'
    Cried the South to the North,
'By need of work in the snow and the rain,
Made strong, and brave by familiar pain!'
10   Cried the South to the North.

II

'Give lucider hills and intenser seas,'
    Said the North to the South,
'Since ever by symbols and bright degrees
Art, childlike, climbs to the dear Lord's knees,'
15   Said the North to the South.

'Give strenuous souls for belief and prayer,'
    Said the South to the North,
'That stand in the dark on the lowest stair,
While affirming of God, 'He is certainly there','
20   Said the South to the North.

III

'Yet oh, for skies that are softer and higher!'
    Sighed the North to the South;
'For the flowers that blaze, and the trees that aspire,
And the insects made of a song or a fire!'
25   Sighed the North to the South.

'And oh, for a seer to discern the same!'
    Sighed the South to the North;
'For a poet's tongue of baptismal flame,
To call the tree or the flower by its name!'
30   Sighed the South to the North.

IV
The North sent therefore a man of men
    As a grace to the South;
And thus to Rome came Andersen.
—'*Alas, but must you take him again?*'
30   Said the South to the North.

Psyche Gazing on Cupid [1845]
FROM APULEIUS (*METAMORPHOSES*, IV)

Then Psyche, weak in body and soul, put on
    The cruelty of Fate, in place of strength:
She raised the lamp to see what should be done,
    And seized the steel, and was a man at length
5 In courage, though a woman! Yes, but when
    The light fell on the bed whereby she stood
To view the '*beast*' that lay there,—certes, then,
    She saw the gentlest, sweetest beast in wood—
Even Cupid's self, the beauteous god! more beauteous
10   For that sweet sleep across his eyelids dim!
The light, the lady carried as she viewed,
    Did blush for pleasure as it lighted him,
The dagger trembled from its aim unduteous;
    And *she* . . . oh, *she*—amazed and soul-distraught,
15 And faining in her whiteness like a veil,
    Slid down upon her knees, and, shuddering, thought
To hide—though in her heart—the dagger pale!
    She would have done it, but her hands did fail
To hold the guilty steel, they shivered so,—
20 And feeble, exhausted, unawares she took
    To gazing on the god,—till, by look,

Her eyes with larger life did fill and glow.
She saw his golden head alight with curls,—
　　　She might have guessed their brightness in the dark
25　　By that ambrosial smell of heavenly mark!
She saw the milky brow, more pure than pearls,
　　　The purple of the cheeks, divinely sundered
By the globed ringlets, as they glided free,
Some back, some forwards,—all so radiantly,
30　　That, as she watched them there, she never wondered
　　　To see the lamplight, where it touched them, tremble:
On the god's shoulders, too, she marked his wings
　　　Shine faintly at the edges and resemble
A flower that's near to blow. The poet sings
35　　And lover sighs, that Love is fugitive;
And certes, though these pinions lay reposing,
　　　The feathers on them seemed to stir and live
As if by instinct, closing and unclosing.
Meantime the god's fair body slumbered deep,
40　　All worthy of Venus, in his shining sleep;
　　　While at the bed's foot lay the quiver, bow,
And darts,—his arms of godhead. Psyche gazed
　　　With eyes that drank the wonders in,—said,—'Lo,
Be these my husband's arms?'—and straightway raised
45　　An arrow from the quiver-case, and tried
Its point against her finger,—trembling till
　　　She pushed it in too deeply (foolish bride!)
And made her blood some dewdrops small distil,
And learnt to love Love, of her own good-will.

NOTES

AURORA LEIGH (1856)

Aurora Leigh (hereafter referred to as *AL*) is a male epic and a woman's novel, written in nine books, echoing the nine books of the prophetic Cumaean Sibyl and the nine months of a woman's pregnancy. It quarries the Bible and the Classics, Homer, Aeschylus, Sophocles, Virgil, Apuleius, Dante, Langland, Shakespeare, Milton and Byron, while it also uses contemporary women's writings, Madame de Staël (1766–1817), George Sand (1804–76) and Charlotte Brontë (1816–55), and discusses Brook Farm's communism (1841–6), Ireland's Great Famine (1846–7), and the working conditions of women and children. EBB read the Bible's scriptures in Hebrew, Chaldean and Greek, the other texts in their original Greek, Latin, Italian, French and English; yet she filled her learning with life. Across *AL*'s pages we hear dialectic and reconciliation, the voices of women and men, of poor and rich, and in its epic similes genders are generally reversed. The poem contains remarkable ethical, religious and social phrases:

> There's not a crime
> But takes its proper change out still in crime,
> If once rung on the counter of this world;
> Let sinners look to it.   (III.869–72)

> Earth's crammed with heaven
> And every common bush afire with God: (VII.821–2)

> And blow all class-walls level as Jericho's.   (IX.932)

AL, besides containing libraries of books, is also a *roman à clef*, keyed to flesh-and-blood people, and is shot through with EBB's autobiography. Virginia Woolf observed that 'Aurora the fictitious seems to be throwing light upon Elizabeth the actual.' EBB's brother, Edward Barrett Moulton Barrett, the heir to the Cinnamon Hill slave plantation in Jamaica, had died by drowning (11 July 1840), which EBB felt was her fault, precipitating her tuberculosis to a crisis and deepening her opium dependency. *AL*'s two heroines are physically modelled on EBB herself (as the low-born Marian Erle) and on her surrogate self, the American

Margaret Fuller (fragmenting as the aristocratic heroine Aurora and the titled villainess Lady Waldemar). Margaret Fuller, called 'New England's Corinna' by the Transcendentalists after Madame de Staël's novel, had borne a child out of wedlock in the midst of the birth/death pangs of the Risorgimento's Roman Republic. She drowned at sea with her child and its father, the Marchese Ossoli, when crossing home to America on the ship *Elizabeth* (19 July 1850) after first establishing a great friendship with the initially disapproving EBB in Florence. Margaret's drowning in a namesake ship psychologically released Elizabeth to write this epic. Romney Leigh, the epic's anti-hero, likewise is a composite, of Robert Browning and of all EBB's previous loves, of the blind Greek scholar Hugh Stuart Boyd, of the social reformer and man of letters Richard Hengist Horne, and of EBB's cousin, the wealthy and most generous John Kenyon.

Critics observed that *AL* contained more lines than *Paradise Lost* or the *Odyssey*, yet they read to the end of it enthralled. John Ruskin repeatedly praised *AL*, associating it with Shakespeare; William Morris recommended it to his working-class audiences; Queen Victoria noted in her diary that it was 'a most extraordinary story and very strange for a woman to have written'. Virginia Woolf, in the *The Common Reader*, showed how *AL* 'rushed' into stuffy Victorian homes; for EBB wrote to RB (27 February 1845), saying her future epic was to be

[A] sort of novel-poem – a poem as completely modern as 'Geraldine's Courtship', running into the midst of our conventions and rushing into drawing rooms and the like, 'where angels fear to tread'; and so, meeting face to face and without mask the Humanity of the age, and speaking the truth as I conceive of it plainly. That is my intention.

Some of *AL* is written in the 'State of England' genre of the novels written by Elizabeth Gaskell (1810–65), Charlotte Brontë (1816–55), Benjamin Disraeli (1804–81) and Charles Dickens (1812–70). It is also a global work, its settings veering from Dante and Milton and de Staël's Italy to Langland, Shakespeare and Dickens's England, then to George Sand's France and back again to Italy. Between the lines, it even includes America's phalanstery of Brook Farm and Jamaica's slave plantation of Cinnamon Hill. *AL* should be read with Madame de Staël's *Corinne, ou Italie* (1807), RB's *The Ring and the Book* (1868–9) and Nathaniel Hawthorne's *The Marble Faun* (1860), as well as with an entire library of classic texts. It marries ancient and modern writing and includes its own literary theory, in the manner of Fielding, within its *Bildungsroman*. Its two heroines are modelled on Miriam of the Hebrew Scriptures and on Mary of the Greek Testament. Its Sibylline Aurora, the progeny of Madame de Staël's Sibylline Corinne, derives as well from Michelangelo's Medicean Tomb sculpture of Dawn and from his Sistine Chapel's Cumaean Sibyl, patroness of Virgil's Aeneas. *AL* is a woman's epic, earning Corinna's laurels.

EBB's prior publications were dedicated to her father. *AL* she dedicated (17 October 1856) to her dying benefactor, John Kenyon, with whom the Brownings were staying at 39 Devonshire Place, saying first that Kenyon as a cousin was far preferable to Romney, and then that 'I venture to leave in your hands this book, the most mature of my works, and the one into which my highest convictions upon Life and Art have entered.' The text given here follows that of the final revises for the first English edition, published by Chapman and Hall in London (21 October 1856), and which were corrected by RB for the first American edition set from it. Bound as a volume, with the American typesetters' pagination marks upon the pages, this transatlantic text is now in the Robert Taylor Collection, Princeton University, Robert Taylor having kindly given assent to its use. Later and more laboured corrected versions of the text of *AL*, culminating in the fourth edition issued in 1859, lose some of the dash and spontaneity of EBB's initial version, though these corrections are used in the editions by Charlotte Porter and Helen A. Clarke (1900) and by Margaret Reynolds (1992). Line numbers are given in bold type.

First Book

Aurora tells of her parents' courtship and of her birth in Florence: *My mother was a Florentine . . . My father was an austere Englishman* (lines 29, 65). She is closely modelled upon Madame de Staël's heroine in *Corinne, ou Italie*, likewise half Florentine, half English. (Anne Louise Germaine de Staël in real life was the daughter of Susanne Curchod, the historian Edward Gibbon's mistress.) Line 45 names the authorial heroine: *I, Aurora Leigh*, her first name evoking Michelangelo's sculpture of Aurora, Dawn, as well as being that of George Sand's true name, Aurore Dudevant, her last name being that of Byron's half-sister, Augusta Leigh. Aurora is first educated by her widowed father as if he were Prospero and she Miranda in Shakespeare's *The Tempest*. Next, orphaned, the grieving Florentine child is brought to England to be raised by a maiden aunt. This book discusses her education, the cultural wrench from Italy to England, and the beginning of her courtship with her cousin, Romney.

Proem

I.1 *OF writing many books there is no end*: Ecclesiastes 12.12; John 21.25. **2** *in prose and verse*: Milton, *Paradise Lost*, I.16, 'Things unattempted yet in Prose or Rhyme.' EBB begins *AL* by quoting the Bible and a Christian epic. **4–8**: a veiled dedication to RB.

Florence and Childhood

22 *Assunta*: Catholic Florentine maid named after Assumption of the Virgin into Heaven. EBB's Florentine maid actually named Annunziata, after Annunciation to the Virgin. **24** *scudi*: plural of scudo, obsolete Florentine coin. The blonde hair and blue eyes of Aurora Leigh are modelled upon those of Margaret Fuller, 'New England's Corinna'. **41–2** *lamb . . . fold*: Dante, *Paradiso*, XXV.4–9. **58** *Which burns and hurts not*: the burning bush, Exodus 3.2; see also *AL*, VII.821–3. **77** *Santissima*: square in front of church of the Florentine Order of the Servites of Mary, the Santissima Annunziata (Most Holy Annunciation); see also *AL*, VII.1278; date of the *festa* probably 25 March, Annunciation to the Virgin, shadowily making Aurora like Christ. **87** *A face flashed like a cymbal on his face*: Exodus 15.20–21:

Then the prophet Miriam, Aaron's sister, took a cymbal in her hand; and all the women went out after her with cymbals and with dancing. And Miriam sang to them:

> 'Sing to the Lord, for he has triumphed gloriously;
> horse and rider he has thrown into the sea.'

First of many allusions to Miriam in poem; see also *AL*, II.170–71, III.203, VIII.334–5, 1021–2; *Casa Guidi Windows*, I.314. **100–101** *make the stones Cry out*: Luke 19.40. **102** *Santa Croce*: Franciscan church, south east of Florence's Cathedral, with funerary monuments to Michelangelo and Dante. **111** *Pelago*: mountain village near the monastery of Vallombrosa. **114** *Pan's white goats, with udders warm*: for fresh milk during the voyage to America, Margaret Fuller's baby, Angelo Ossoli, nursed a goat on the ship *Elizabeth*. **127** *picture of my mother on the wall*: portrait painted by Joseph Wright of Derby (1734–97) of RB's Creole grandmother who holds a copy of James Thomson's *The Seasons* (1730); see also *AL*, III.973, VII.607; RB, when a child, saw her in her coffin. **130** *cameriera*: maid. **132** *Pitti*: grand ducal palace in Florence, almost opposite Casa Guidi; EBB attended a ball there. **155** *Muse . . . Fate*: female deities of art and death. **156** *Psyche*: (soul, butterfly) beloved of *Love*, Cupid, separated from him by jealous Venus, Apuleius, *Metamorphoses* (*The Golden Ass*) IV–VI. **157** *Medusa*: a Gorgon whose snake locks turned onlookers into stone. **160** *Our Lady of the Passion*: Mary, Christ's mother, told by Simeon that she would so mourn her son's life and death, Luke 2.35. **161** *Lamia*: the fatal snake woman of Keats's poem; see also *AL*, IV.990, VII.147, 170. **178** *Lazarus*: in Byzantine and Italian art shown in his shroud and bands as Christ restores him to life, John 11.44. **185–98, 710–28**: Shakespeare, *The Tempest*, Prospero and Miranda; also EBB and her father. **204** *nine*: Dante's *La Vita Nuova* number for Beatrice, 'blessedness'. See also *AL*, I.240, II.898.

England and Education

230–31: repetition used also by Dante to express grief, *Purgatorio*, XXX.56, 73. **235** *suppliants*: Homer, *Odyssey*, VI.142–7; Aeschylus, *Oresteia, Eumenides*, lines 34–45. **238** *pasture to the stars*: Dante, *Purgatorio*, XXXIII.142–5. **239–40**: English Milton used ten as symbolic of completion, nine of gestation, *Paradise Lost*, I.50, VI.194–5, VI.871; see also *AL*, VIII.45; Italian Dante, *La Vita Nuova*, had nine be sacred. See also *AL*, I.204, II.898. **342** *Tuscan*: region around Florence, people and language. **390** *lilies*: symbol of Annunciation to the Virgin and of Florence, here as Italian words, 'Bene', 'well', 'che ch'è', 'what is that?'. **394–5** *Articles... Tracts*: Established Church of England's controversial Oxford Movement publications; EBB and RB were both Dissenters, typical of West Indian Puritan stock; see also *AL*, VIII.900. **395** *Buonaventure's 'Prick of Love'*: Pre-Reformation devotional text. **420** *noisy Tophet*: Gehenna, furnaces for child sacrifices to Moloch, 2 Kings 23.10; Jeremiah 7.32. **424** *Cellarius*: a waltz. **454–5** *tortoise-shell*: Aeschylus' death caused by an eagle dropping a tortoise on his bald pate, which it mistook for a stone, killing him, Aelian, VIII.16; tortoise shells used for lyres by Greek epic and lyric poets. **467–9** *Brinvilliers ... water-torture*: tiny Marie Marguerite, Marquise de Brinvilliers, forced to drink three buckets of water, drowning her lungs, then beheaded (1676) for multiple murders in her family for the sake of her lover, St Croix; discussed by Madame de Sevigny. **527–8** *goats*: Matthew 25.32–3. **563** *visionary chariots*: 2 Kings 2.11; Ezekiel 1.4–28. **567–614**: description of EBB's Wimpole Street room, London, within Hope End landscape, Malvern. **612** *my Giotto's background*: Giotto's Byzantine and Gothic predecessors painted against a background of gold; Giotto broke from this convention. **616** *Vallombrosa*: monastery near Florence, which Milton (1638–9), and then the Brownings (1847), visited:

> Thick as Autumnal Leaves that strow the Brooks
> In Vallombrosa, where th'Etrurian shades
> High over-arch't embow'r; (Milton, *Paradise Lost*, I.302–4)

Milton and Browning played on organ there. See also *Casa Guidi Windows*, I.1129–64. **700–10** *books*: Milton, *Areopagitica; Paradise Regained*, IV.321, 330. **710–28**: *The Tempest*, Prospero teaching Caliban and Miranda; Daniel Defoe, *Robinson Crusoe*, teaching Man Friday. **712**

Theophrast: Theophrastus, friend and pupil of Aristotle, wrote *Characters*. **714** *Ælian*: wrote Aesopic fables and histories; EBB's reading with her brother at Hope End. **723–6** Achilles' mother hid him, disguised as a girl, at the court of King Lycomedes so he would not fight at Troy, Odysseus finding him. EBB's classical similes generally involve gender reversals: see also *AL*, I.454–5, 919–34, II.777–80, etc. **736–8** *Ah, babe i' the wood, without a brother-babe!*: reference to loss of EBB's brother, Edward. **739–844**: EBB here describes her father's library at Hope End, where she was allowed to read all the books except Edward Gibbon's *Decline and Fall of the Roman Empire* (1776–88) and a few others; library had to be stored in packing cases when Hope End was sold. **747** *Too long beside a fountain*: Narcissus and Echo, Ovid, *Metamorphoses*, III.339–510. **767** *Saul and Nahash*: 1 Samuel 11, 16.8–11; 2 Samuel 3. **792–800**: argument of Milton's *Areopagitica*. **797** *God*: Blenheim soldier prayed 'O God, if there be a God, save my soul, if I have a soul,' EBB to RB (15 January 1846). **826** *palimpsest*: a manuscript whose previous text has been scraped away and a new text added to the parchment; *holograph*: a manuscript in author's writing. **828** *The apocalypse, by a Longus!*: a medieval manuscript of the Apocalypse replaced with the erotic text of the Greek and Renaissance *Pastoral of Daphnis and Chloe*. **831** *alpha and omega*: Revelation 1.8, 17, first and last letters of Greek alphabet, inscribed on God's Book of the Apocalypse. **836–8**: early Victorians recognized the discovery of fossils, such as the *mastodon* and dinosaurs, while believing the world to be aged only the biblical six thousand years. **845–54**: Wordsworth, 'Composed upon Westminster Bridge' (1802). **855–80**: Sir Philip Sidney, *The Defense of Poesie* (1598); Percy Bysshe Shelley, *A Defence of Poetry* (1821), which relates the freeing of women and slaves and poetry; see EBB, 'A Vision of Poets' (1844). **865** *shadow on a charnel-wall*: Chaucer, *Canterbury Tales*, IV.1315, VII.9; Pisa, Campo Santo, Francesco Traini, *Triumph of Death*, the fresco John Ruskin was sketching when Brownings were in Pisa on their honeymoon. Anna Jameson, EBB's great friend, also discussed this fresco and sketched a similar work for her book *Sacred and Legendary Art*, II, pp. 757–9. **867–9** *measure*: Revelation 21.17. **896–915**: see EBB, *Seraphim, and Other Poems* (1838). **919–34** *My eagle*: Zeus in the form of an eagle seized the beautiful young Ganymede to be his cupbearer on Olympus; EBB/Aurora instead gives cup to Zeus' wife, Heré. **941** *Bourbon*: French royalty imprisoned during Revolution, slept on straw while awaiting death. **948–9**: Prodigal Son, Luke 15.11–32. **950** *sit down under their own vine*: 1 Kings 4.25; Jonah 4.5–11; Micah 4.4. **964** *the god Term*: Terminus, sacred boundary stones in Rome. **976–7** *'Touch not, do not taste'*: Colossians 2.21. **978** *phorminx*: seven-stringed harp or lyre in Homer, Apollo's instrument. **981** *purple-braided head*: Corinna won the laurel five times over Pindar, partly because of her great beauty, Pindar's description here being both of the Muses and of Corinna; see also AL, II.33–53, VIII.1220–22; 'Sonnets from the Portuguese', XX. **990–1002**: EBB is mocking her childhood poems, including the epic *The Battle of Marathon*, written in 1819, when she was twelve, and privately printed (6 March 1820) by her father, and her childhood lyrics as well. **1000–1002** *wine-skins*: Matthew 9.17; Mark 2.22; Luke 5.37–8. **1003–12** John *Keats*: see EBB, 'A Vision of Poets' (1844), lines 7–11. **1020–22**: Shelley, 'Ozymandias'. **1061–4**: EBB's anorexia nervosa over Bro's departure for Charterhouse. **1095–100** *Vincent Carrington*: EBB's painter friend was the suicide, Benjamin Haydon (1846); she especially treasured his portrait of Wordsworth on Helvellyn, which hung in her room at Wimpole Street; he also painted *Christ's Agony in the Garden, The Raising of Lazarus, Pharaoh Dismissing the Israelites, Achilles at the Court of Lycomedes Discovering His Sex, The Antislavery Convention*, etc. **1099** *Master*: God, Creator of the Soul. **1145** *Deliver us from evil*: Lord's Prayer, Matthew 6.13.

Second Book

In this book, on her twentieth birthday in June, Aurora crowns herself Poet Laureate with ivy, not bay, Romney Leigh's marriage proposal is rejected by her and, soon after, her maiden aunt dies, leaving her free and poor. This book is influenced by Genesis and Milton's *Paradise Lost*, IV, IX; by Mary Wollstonecraft's *A Vindication of the Rights of Women* (1792); by Madame de Staël's *Corinne, ou Italie* (1807); and by 'New England's Corinna', Margaret Fuller (1810–50); and her relationships with Emerson and Thoreau. EBB was proposed by the *Athenaeum* for Poet Laureate (1 June 1850).

II.33–53 *Dante's own*: laurel (bay) crown, *Paradiso*, XXV.7–9; Petrarch's coronation with laurel (Easter, 1341); Madame de Staël's heroine similarly crowned on the Capitoline; see also *AL*, I.981, VIII.1220–22; 'Sonnets from the Portuguese', XX (Aurora substitutes Bacchic ivy). **52** *thyrsus*: staff twined with ivy, surmounted with pine cone, sacred to Bacchus. **61–2** *caryatid*: Erectheum, on Athenian Acropolis, has stone maidens who hold up cornice on their heads. **66** *Aurora*: Dawn, figure upon Michelangelo's Medici Tomb, Florence. See also *Casa Guidi Windows*, I.73–4, which in the 1851 text, presented in this edition, begins 'The sculptor's . . .', but in the 1856 text has 'Michel's Night and Day/And Dawn and Twilight, wait in marble scorn,' using Strozzi's 'talking statues' epigram:

> The Night that here thou seest, in graceful guise
> Thus sleeping, by an Angel's hand was carved

> In this pure stone; but sleeping, still she lives.
> Awake her if thou doubtest, and she'll speak,

and Michelangelo's response in the face of Medicean tyranny:

> Happy am I to sleep, and still more blest
> To be of stone, while grief and shame endure;
> To see, nor feel, is now my utmost hope,
> Wherefore speak softly, and awake me not.

EBB adds that Florence is at last waking to a dawn of freedom, 'great Angelo! the day is come', *Casa Guidi Windows*, I.145. **66–71** *shipwrecked*: reminiscent of her brother's and Margaret Fuller's shipwrecks; of Shelley's drowning and Keats's epitaph, 'Here lies one whose name was writ in water.' **76–7** *lady's Greek/Without the accents*: 'naked' Greek. Bro and Ba studied the Charterhouse pronunciation together (1817–20), under their tutor, Daniel McSwiney, before Bro entered Charterhouse. EBB, when twenty, and Sir Uvedale Price (Wordsworth's friend) collaborated on a study of Greek metrics, which was published under his name (1827). The letters between Ba and Sir Uvedale Price, carefully discussing the Charterhouse accentuation of Greek, are in the Armstrong Browning Museum, Baylor University, Texas. **81–2**: Ophelia's garlanded drowning, 'There is a willow grows aslant a brook,' Shakespeare, *Hamlet*, IV.vii.166–83. **83** *Oread*: mountain nymph; *Naiad*: spring, river, lake nymph. **102** *God's Dead*: Revelation 7.9. **119–22**: falcon similes, Dante, *Inferno*, XVII.127–32; *Purgatorio*, XIX.61–7; *Paradiso*, XIX.34–6; Boccaccio, *Decameron*, V.IX; see also *AL*, VI.521–5, VIII.22. **167** *six thousand years*: believed from the Bible to be the world's age. **169** *sit upon a bank*: Shakespeare, *A Midsummer Night's Dream*, II.i.249–ii.32, III.i; *The Merchant of Venice*, V.i.53–88. **170–71** *Miriam*: her song, Exodus 15.19–21; see also *AL*, I.87–9, III.203, VIII.334–5, 1021–2; *Casa Guidi Windows*, I.314. **175–9** *sounding brass*: 1 Corinthians 13.1; Virgil, *Aeneid*, I.430–36; Dante, *Paradiso*, XXXI.7–9; Milton, *Paradise Lost*, I.690–776. **194–5** *Your father were a negro*: EBB's father partly was, from the Moulton side of the Barrett Moulton Barrett family; EBB published *The Cry of the Children* (1843), *The Runaway Slave at Pilgrim's Point* (1848). **202** *Tarsus*: noted for opulent merchandise, Acts 9.1–31. **210** *Cordelia*: Shakespeare, *King Lear*, IV.iii.11–24, vii.71–6. **269–70**: Roman triumph with chariots; Arch of Titus reliefs, Dante, *Purgatorio*, X.73–95; see also *AL*, II.975–6. **277–9** *Lazarus*: Luke 16.20–31. **412** *Hagar*: bondmaid, Genesis 16, 21. **415** *chief apostle*: Paul of Tarsus's Epistles. **482**: Charles François-Marie *Fourier* (1772–1837), French utopian who influenced European and American thought during the 'Hungry Forties', years of social breakdown and famine in the nineteenth century; see also *AL*,

III.108, 583–4, V.720–28, 782–93, IX.868–9. Brook Farm in America, where Nathaniel Hawthorne and Margaret Fuller stayed, was a phalanstery using Fourier's principles. EBB wrote to Mary Russell Mitford:

I love liberty so intensely that I hate Socialism. I hold it to be the most desecrating and dishonouring to Humanities, of all creeds. I would rather (for me) live under the absolutism of Nicholas of Russia, than in a Fourier-machine, with my individuality sucked out of me by a social air-pump.

536 *tribute*: Christ's Temptation, Matthew 4.1–11; Luke 4.1–13. **611** *entail*: restrictions governing inheritance of estate to oldest male heir. **622–41** *cousin*: such marriages were common in the Barrett Moulton Barrett family to ensure the entail of Jamaican slave plantations. **636** *fiefs and manors*: feudal rights and obligations of ownership. **678** *altar-horns*: Exodus 27.2, 38.1–2; Leviticus 4.25; Psalms 118.27; Revelation 9.13. **697–700** *brand*: mark of Cain, Genesis 4.15; Dante, *Purgatorio*, IX.112–13. **759**: EBB knows that swords have mouths in biblical, classical languages. **778–80** *Iphigenia*: her sacrifice at *Aulis* by her father to ensure success at Troy: Aeschylus, *Agamemnon*; Euripides, *Iphigenia at Aulis*. **792**: patient *Griseld*'s tale of spousal abuse: Boccaccio, *Decameron*, X; Petrarch, *De obedientia*; Chaucer, *Canterbury Tales*, XVIII; EBB's slave-owning West Indian ancestors. **794** *Ragged Schools*: schools for pauper children. EBB's sister, Arabella, established one for girls; see 'A Plea for the Ragged Schools of London'. **810–12** *dead love*: Pedro of Portugal crowned and enthroned the exhumed body of his dead wife, Inez, Camoëns, *The Lusiads*, III.118–35; Pedro of Spain followed suit. **813–15** *Olympian crowns*: Hellenic and scriptural: 1 Corinthians 9.25; 2 Timothy 2.5. **817** *Chaldean*: (Aramaic), a language EBB knew. Romney will speak of Aurora's Sanscrit, *AL*, VIII.477. **830** *Write woman's verses*: letter parallels RB's to EBB, written 15 August 1845, scorning George Sand's *Consuelo*: 'I shall tell you frankly that it strikes me as precisely what in conventional language with the customary silliness is styled a *woman's* book . . .' Here, in a George Sand-like *AL*, Romney scorns 'woman's verses' as he had earlier 'lady's Greek/Without the accents', *AL*, II.76–7. EBB kept the 'Sonnets from the Portuguese' (1846) secret from RB for three years because of a similar comment he had made to her about women sonneteers during the Wimpole Street courtship, finally giving the sonnets to him at Bagni di Lucca (1849). **834–5** *Chaldeans*: prophets, seers, like the Sibyls. **853, 973** '*Siste, viator*': 'Pause, traveller', tomb inscriptions on Appian Way. **863–5** *Cleopatra's breast*: Plutarch, *Lives*; Shakespeare, *Antony and Cleopatra*, V.ii; Dryden, *All for Love*. **898** *clock struck nine*: as with Milton's *Paradise Lost*, Dante's *La Vita Nuova*, nine is crucial to *AL*'s numerology; here it refers obliquely to the hour of Christ's death, at the ninth hour of daylight, Matthew 27.46. See also

AL, I.204, 240, IV.935. **960** *Babylon or Balbec*: Babylon was the name
in medieval and Renaissance texts for Old Cairo in the Egyptian desert,
with sands building up around the pyramids and Sphinx; Baalbek, also in
ruins, in Syria. **975-6** *Cæsar's chariot*: Dante, *Purgatorio*, X.73-95; see
also *AL*, II.269-70. Emily Dickinson influenced by this line in 'The soul
selects her own Society—' (1862). **990** *chronicle the pence*: Shakespeare,
Othello, II.i.157. **1068-9** *ship*: EBB's mother's family, the Graham
Clarkes of Newcastle-on-Tyne, were in such commerce, EBB herself
having shares in the ship *David Lyon*, which helped the Browning
household. **1133-5**: Shakespeare, *Twelfth Night*, II.v.94-8. **1148-52** *Solo-
mon ... his holy ring*: shown to Jerusalem pilgrims. **1165** *Valdarno*:
fallen-leaves simile in Virgil, *Aeneid*, VI.310-11; Dante, *Inferno* III.112-
17; Milton, *Paradise Lost*, I.301-4, in the last associated with Valdarno,
I.290, the valley of river Arno in which Florence is situated, as well as
Vallombrosa. **1170**: *Iliad*, III.2-6; Milton, *Paradise Lost*, I.775-92; Alex-
ander Pope, *The Rape of the Lock* (1714). **1237** *seven years*: biblical period
of apprenticeship, Genesis 29.20; Deuteronomy 15.1, 12-18. **1245** *divided
rocks*: Scylla and Charybdis, *Odyssey*, XII.234-59.

Third Book

Aurora, now twenty-seven, is living independently as a writer in a
London garret – like Harriet Martineau and Margaret Fuller. Titled
Lady Waldemar, this poem's Lamia/Medusa, tries to persuade Aurora to
prevent Romney's marriage to working-class Marian Erle (whose name,
however, suggests an aristocratic earlship). Aurora visits Marian, who
tells her of her abused childhood ('There's not a crime/But takes its
proper change out still in crime,/If once rung on the counter of this
world;' III. 869-71) and of Romney's rescue of her. Marian's account in
this book and the next, III–IV, followed by that in VI and VII, parallels
other tales within tales: Odysseus' narration to King Alcinous and Queen
Arete on Phaeacia, *Odyssey*, VII–XII; that of Cupid and Psyche the old
woman tells in the robbers' den prior to hanging herself, Apuleius,
Metamorphoses, IV–VI.

III.1-6 *thou girdest up thy loins*: Christ speaking to Peter, John 21.18-19,
with the expression frequently used in Hebrew Scriptures. **4-11**: Peter
asked to be crucified upside down at Rome. **25** *Susan*: this maid, from
Aurora's childhood house, *AL*, II.930, has followed her mistress into
London poverty. Elizabeth Wilson, EBB's maid, went with her to Italy,
purchased her laudanum. **42-4** *letters . . . with red seals*: Victorian letters
with penny red stamps on them, bearing the Queen's head and fastened
with red sealing wax. EBB's vivacious letters were sent in this manner

from her Wimpole Street sickroom. **48** *Ararat*: Armenian mountain where the Ark came to rest, Genesis 8.4. **53–60**: Kate Ward (perhaps Kate Field, the American) sees herself as disciple to Aurora Leigh, inheriting her cloak, as did *Elisha* from Elijah, 2 Kings 2.11–14; see also *AL*, I.563, VII.576–608. **61** *Rudgely*: perhaps Richard Hengist Horne, EBB's editor, *A New Spirit of the Age*. **80** *My critic Stokes*: RB used same name to designate inferior poets, 'Popularity' (1855). **88–90**: RB and EBB's friend, Seymour Kirkup, discovered Giotto's portrait of *Dante* in the Bargello Magdalen Chapel fresco (1850). **98–9** *A ninth seal*: Revelation 8.1, concerning the book with seven seals; EBB has altered number to harmonize with *AL*'s nine Sibylline books. **108** *phalansteries*: lodging houses on camel routes, here a utopia like Brook Farm, modelled upon the nineteenth-century writings of Charles Fourier, see also *AL*, II.482, III.583–4, V.720–28, 782–93, IX.868–9; EBB learned of these Franco-American projects from Margaret Fuller, Nathaniel Hawthorne; England's socialistic experiments were instead mainly fostered by Robert Owen. **110–11** *golden apple*: on Aphrodite's advice Hippomenes dropped three golden apples from the garden of the Hesperides in a foot race with Atalanta to win her in marriage; in tale of Paris and Helen, Paris awarded the golden apple of discord not to wise Athena but to strife-causing Aphrodite; Aurora is both Atalanta and Athena, Romney, Hippomenes and Paris. **113** *Lord Howe*: See note to *AL*, IV.709–44. **122** *Danae*: imprisoned in a brazen tower by her father, became mother of Perseus, who was sired by Jove in a golden shower; her father cast the mother and child adrift in a chest, Ovid, *Metamorphoses*, IV; analogue for EBB's relationship with her father, husband and child; cited again *AL*, VII.586. **164–5** *Sweat*: Genesis 3.19. **172–5** *fiery brass*: in which Druids burnt sacrificial victims to death; idols were actually of wicker, EBB combining them with brazen Phalerian Bull and other pagan sacrifices. **178–86**: Victorian London fog, due to coal smoke, now banned. **191** *Sinai*: Exodus 19.20, where Moses received the Hebraic Law; *Parnassus*: mountain of the Greek Muses. **197–203** *Pharoah's armaments*: Exodus 15.19–21; Milton, *Paradise Lost*, I.306–11. **203** *Miriam*: Exodus 15.20–21; see also *AL*, I.87, II.170–71, VIII.334–5, 1021–2; *Casa Guidi Windows*, I.314. **213–14**: *Emily* Dickinson, who read EBB, used *AL*, II.853 and 975–6. **218** *'Collegisse juvat'*: 'who delight to gather Olympic dust', Horace, *Odes*, I.i.3–4. **247–9**: EBB experienced several miscarriages, which her maid, Elizabeth Wilson, believed were due to her addiction to laudanum; with Wilson's help EBB stopped the intake long enough to bear the child Pen. **267–71** *yew*: necessary for the English longbow yet poisonous to cattle, they could only be safely planted in fenced-in graveyards, thus associated, though evergreen, with death. **274–8**: EBB's childhood tuberculosis, affecting her spine, compounded by anorexia nervosa, for which laudanum was prescribed. **324** *Nephelococcygia*:

'Cloud-cuckoo-land', Aristophanes' *The Birds*. **358** *Lady Waldemar*: 'Valley of the Sea', EBB's shadow self, associations with Vallombrosa, 'Valley of Shadows', Valdarno, 'Valley of the Arno River'. **363–4: the nine** *Muses* were daughters of Mnemosyne (Memory), celestial patrons of literature, music and art. The Cumaean *Sibyl* offered to sell nine books of prophetic oracles (*AL* similarly has nine books) in Greek hexameters to Tarquin the Superb. He refused to pay her price, so she burnt three, then again three more. The three last books he did acquire were kept in the Temple of Capitoline Jove, where Corinne (in de Staël's novel) was to utter her prophecies concerning Italy. **390–93** *Androcles*: pulled a thorn from a lion's paw, then was saved in gratitude by the lion in the arena, Aelian, VII.48. **414–21** *papist*: Roman Catholic; see Pope, *The Rape of the Lock* (1714), II.7–8. **459** *Blowsalinda*: implying pretty, but overblown, country girl, John Gay, *The Shepherd's Week* (1714). **471–3** *Wertherism*: Johann Wolfgang von Goethe's *Die Leiden des jungen Werthers, The Sorrows of Young Werther* (1774); *Champs Elysées*: Parisian boulevard named after Elysian Fields in Virgil, *Aeneid*, VI; *sighing like Dido: Aeneid*, VI.450–76. **484–8** *doves between the temple-columns*: classical augury partly carried out through watching bird flight patterns. **513** *Genius of the Vatican*: fragment by Apollonius; Michelangelo, when blind, would feel it with his hands. **516**: Praxiteles' *Drunken Fawn*. Nathaniel Hawthorne's family identified RB with this sculpture, which inspired Hawthorne's *The Marble Faun*. EBB misspells it. **518** *Buonarrotti's mask*: Michelangelo's sculpture of Night on the Medici Tomb rests on a grotesque swinish mask. EBB and RB, both fascinated by sculpture, had American sculptor friends in Italy, William Wetmore Story, Harriet Hosmer and Hiram Powers. **547** *Homer's ships*: epic catalogue, *Iliad*, II.493–760. **548**: William Lamb, Viscount *Melbourne's poor-bills*: against charity and pauperism, deliberately made workhouses uncongenial. Though Home Secretary, Melbourne actually had little to do with Poor Law Amendment Act of 1834; *Ashley's factory bills*: (1833–46), bills prohibiting labour by children under ten, limiting work day to eight hours for children under fourteen, providing for schooling, medical care, vigorously supported by Antony Ashley Cooper, Earl of Shaftesbury. EBB's *The Cry of the Children* instrumental in 1844 bill's passage. Richard Hengist Horne, who served on the Royal Commission for the Investigation of the Employment of Children in Mines and Manufactories (1842), is a model for Romney. **549** *Aspasia*: Pericles' learned and beautiful hetaera. Walter Savage Landor, friend of the Brownings, wrote 'Pericles and Aspasia' (1836). **555** *'stops bungholes'*: Lucian; *Hamlet*, V.i.199–212. **583–4**: Charles *Fourier*, originator of communistic phalansterianism; see also *AL*, II.482, III.108, V.720–28, 782–93, IX.868–9. Pierre-Joseph *Proudhon* (1809–65), stated 'All property is theft.' Victor *Considerant*

(1808–93), disciple of Fourier, editor of *La Phalange*. *Louis Blanc* (1811–82), considered man's labour should be for community rather than self. **595**: Eugène *Sue* wrote *The Mysteries of Paris* (1842), *The Wandering Jew* (1844–5), saw proletariats as Gauls, capitalists as conquering Franks. **600** *Ten Hours' movement*: Factory Act passed 1847 providing for ten-hour day for women and young people. **602** *Indian tortoise*: in Hindu myth the world rests on an elephant, which stands on a tortoise, which swims in primeval ocean; see *AL*, VIII.53. **613–14** EBB combines Greek Fathers' lives and martyrdoms she read with Hugh Boyd, *Book of Foxe's Martyrs* (1563, 1570) and King Charles Martyr's punning joke upon the axe's edge to behead him (1649). **680–81** *Hamlet*, V.ii.276–7; *Othello*, V.ii.342–4. **705** *Medicean Venus*: Greek copy, Praxiteles' *Venus of Cnido*, owned by Florentine Medici, in Uffizi Tribune, seen by EBB (1847). Elizabeth Wilson, EBB's maid, reacted in horror to the sculptured nudes in Florence. RB and EBB delighted in such sculpture.

Marian Erle's Childhood and Education

757–92: see Henry Mayhew, *London Labour and the London Poor* (1851); Dickens's novels. Margaret Street, Wimpole Street, Devonshire Place are close together in London, EBB learning of the poorer section, Margaret Court, from her quest to ransom Flush (5 September 1846). **805–8** *daughters*: *King Lear*, III.iv, IV.iv. **808–25**: Marian Erle, EBB's physical self-portrait. **830** *Malvern Hill*: EBB's childhood home and initial setting of Langland's *Piers Plowman*, fourteenth-century Wyclifite pilgrimage poem. **950–51** *fair scroll-finis of a wicked book*: Apocalypse, 5.1; Dante's metaphor of World as Book. EBB feared the sea, which drowned Percy Bysshe Shelley (1822), her brother, Edward Barrett Moulton Barrett (1840), and Margaret Fuller, Margaret being lost in the shipwreck of the *Elizabeth* (1850). **973**: RB's grandmother in portrait by Joseph Wright of Derby holds James *Thomson's Seasons*; see also *AL*, I.127, VII.607; *mulcted of the Spring*: EBB is to use word 'mulcted' of Romney's eyesight; see also *AL*, III.409, IX.564. Here EBB gives her other heroine's library. **978–9** *Ruth's/Small gleanings*: Ruth 2.3–4, paupers, such as widows and orphans, allowed by law to glean remaining wheat at harvests. **980** *Churchyard Elegies*: Gray, *Elegy Written in a Country Churchyard* (1751), notes unjust social conditions that depopulated the countryside; *Edens Lost*: Milton's *Paradise Lost* (1667). **981**: Robert *Burns* (1756–96), Scots poet, wrote of the common people; John *Bunyan* wrote *Pilgrim's Progress* in prison (1675); Alexander *Selkirk*, original for Daniel Defoe's *Robinson Crusoe* (1719); Henry Fielding, *Tom Jones* (1749), EBB's father forbade her to read it and Edward Gibbon's *Decline and Fall of the Roman Empire*. **996** *lecture at an institute*: Victorian popular education movement; William Morris was to recommend *AL* to working-class audiences attending such lectures. **1026–31** *pennyworth out of her*: Richard Hengist Horne's report (1842); see *The Cry of the Children*. **1173** *seraphs*: chronicling sun's making, order of angels, Isaiah 6.2–8; see EBB 'The Seraphim' (1838). **1202–5**: William Blake, 'The Little Black Boy', *Songs of Innocence* (1789). **1206–7** *where John was laid*: John 13.23–5; also echoes iconographically Mary Magdalen and Christ, Matthew 26.7–13; Luke 7.37–50; John 20.14–18. **1221–2** *ointment-box*: Luke 7.37–9; again Mary Magdalen and Christ. **1225**: Doubting Thomas so touched the *wounds of Christ*, John 20.24–9.

Fourth Book

Marian continues her narration to Aurora of her encounters with her saviour, Romney. Then Marian Erle's wedding at St James, Piccadilly, to Romney Leigh, attended by both lower- and upper-class guests, miscarries, amidst references to *Hamlet* and *King Lear*, and beneath the shadow of Christ's parables of wedding feasts to which sinners and paupers are ingathered while the wealthy and idle are excluded (Matthew 22, 25; Luke, 12, 14). Marian's letter to Romney names Lady Waldemar as agent in the bride's non-appearance.

IV.2: Lucy Gresham, the opposite of whoring Rose Bell, shares EBB's tuberculosis. **21**: Rose Bell? **27** *Lady Waldemar's new dress*: Oscar Wilde to borrow this motif, *The Happy Prince* (1888). **41–3** *drink*: Matthew 25.32–46. **46** *lamp of human love*: reflects Florence Nightingale, 'Lady with the Lamp' (1854–5), of whom EBB disapproved, believing women should be doctors, not nurses, though Margaret Fuller similarly worked with Cristina, Princess Belgioioso (Henry James's Princess Casamassima), in Roman hospitals (1849). **109–17**: Genesis 1.26, 2.7, 'Adam' in Hebrew meaning clay and Everyman; Lucian; *Hamlet*, V.i. **122–4**: Longinus the knight, in medieval legend, *pierced Christ's heart* with his lance, the one an aristocrat, the other a carpenter, an artisan. **146–7**: *hand* touching *ark*, 2 Samuel 6.6–7. **190** *Rialto-prices*: the Rialto, the commercial centre of Venice, favourite EBB image; see also 'Sonnets from the Portuguese', XX; *The Merchant of Venice*. **195–202**: Hindu *widows* immolated themselves on their husbands' pyres, committing suttee, Moslem widows went into purdah, Christian British authorities in India attempting to change such customs. **237** *flickering wild-fowl tails*: quills of wild goose feathers imported in barrels in the nineteenth century from Hudson Bay in Canada; also the calligraphic flourishes they write. **307–8** *obolus*: Greek silver coin, inscribed with owl and head of ruler, Matthew 22.19–21; Luke 20.20–26; also the legend of Belisarius, Justinian's general, blinded by him and begging in the streets of Constantinople for an obolus. **309-10** *Vandykes*: Anthony Van Dyck (1599-1641), painted England's nobility (especially Charles I, considered a martyr and saint); see also *AL*, VIII.949; and EBB's sonnet on 'The Picture Gallery at Penshurst' (1833). **334** *galley-couplings*: Vatican States flung political prisoners into dungeons, chaining them to benches until they died, as had been done in earlier times with criminal slaves on benches of galley ships. Such prisoners, called 'galeotti', were still mouldering in a living death in their chains in EBB's day, including several members of the Castellani family of patriot goldsmiths; RB, *The Ring and the Book*, I.1-4, XII.864-70. **370** *Austria's daughter to imperial France*: Emperor Napoleon took for his second wife the Habsbourg Emperor's daughter, Marie Louise, after divorcing Creole Josephine de Beauharnais. **373,** *Saint James's* fashionable church, built by Christopher Wren (1682). EBB's sister, Henrietta, married there (6 April 1850). **380-81** *cothurn*: thick-soled boot worn by Greek tragic actor. **383-4**: Aeschylus' *Eumenides* presented Furies in bloody garb on stage, frightening play's audience. **402**: François-Pierre *Guizot*, writer and statesman, twice disgraced (1830, 1848). **403-4**: EBB is emulating *Dickens*'s portrayal of social injustice. **405-6** *are potatoes to grow mythical/Like moly?*: potato blight in Ireland (1845-6), caused millions to die or emigrate in the Great Famine. **468** *Cain*: Genesis 4.1-25. **491** *bohea*: tea. **493** *Potiphar*: Genesis 39; Henry Fielding, *Joseph Andrews* (1742). **499** *Good critics*: the English bard, John Keats (1795-1821), according to Shelley, was killed by a cruel review (1818) in the *Quarterly Review*, founded in part by Sir Walter Scott, an idea Byron laughed at. Review journals in EBB's day were the *Edinburgh Review*, the *Athenaeum* (for which EBB wrote) and the *Westminster Review* (for which George Eliot wrote). **538-9** *St. Giles*: in poor section of London, inhabitants dressed in rough wool and shoddy (rewoven) cloth; *St. James*: aristocratic section of London, reference to Field of Cloth of Gold at Calais, where French and English nobility competed with display of opulence (1520); Shakespeare, *Henry VIII*, I.i.13-45; see also *AL*, VII.634. **561-3** *broidered hems*: recalls Lucy Gresham dying of tuberculosis while sewing such garments. **564-71** *snakes*: Virgil, *Aeneid*, II.203-33. **595** *Raffael's mild Madonna*: *Madonna of the Gold Finch*, Uffizi Tribune, Florence. EBB, with Anna Jameson, saw preparatory drawing for this painting in Samuel Rogers's collection (June 1846). **665** *Prince Albert's model lodging house*: Prince Consort addressed the Society for Improving the Condition of the Labouring Classes (18 May 1848) as their President; in 1851 he personally financed four model dwelling houses which, during the Exhibition, attracted over 250,000 visitors. **674-8**: Robert François *Damiens* attempted to assassinate Louis XV, was tortured and executed as a regicide (1757). **709-44** *Lord Howe*: composite of John Kenyon (1784-1856), EBB's Jamaican cousin to whom EBB dedicated *AL*, and whose dinner party she attended (28 May 1836), with William Wordsworth and Walter Savage Landor; James Scarlett, Lord Abinger (1769–1844), Jamaican opponent to slavery, guardian and friend of Edward Barrett Moulton Barrett; and Henry Fox, Lord Holland (1773–1840), whose second wife, the former Lady Webster (1770–1845), was Creole, the couple giving brilliant social gatherings at Holland House. EBB and RB, at the time *AL* was being written, attended gathering of Pre-Raphaelite Brotherhood, including Julia Margaret Cameron, the photographer, at Little Holland House, home of G. F. Watts. **747–68**: *Hamlet*, II.ii, III.ii. **769–91**: *King Lear*. **939–40**: Plato, 'Socrates to Agathon', lyric in *Greek Anthology*. **990** *Hydra-skin cast off*: tangential reference to Lady Waldemar as Lamia, the snake woman figure, projected here upon innocent Marian Erle; Hydra was the many-headed serpent overcome by Hercules, who then dipped his arrows in its gall, causing them to inflict incurable, mortal wounds. See also *AL*, I.157, 161–3. **1018–21**: journeying from Italy, EBB lost her box containing *AL*'s manuscript and Pen's fancy clothing, she was distressed about the latter and sent her brother to search for the box, who found it in a Marseilles customs house. **1118–23**: EBB and RB visited Vaucluse (1846), sacred to Petrarch and Laura de Sade, Flush baptizing himself in the fountain's waters, EBB said, in Petrarch's name; see also *AL*, I.446–55, where Aurora embroiders a shepherdess analogizing herself domestically to the tragedian Aeschylus. **1150–55** *gyres*: concepts from Giambattista Vico, *Scienza Nuova* (1725–30); Emanuel Swedenborg (1688–1772). **1183–4** *social Sphinx*: Sophocles, *Oedipus Rex*, lines 130–31, 391–8, 1525. **1185** *crystal heavens*: ancients and Milton (who knew Galileo) believed the heavens consisted of seven crystal spheres, one for each planet, the earth at the centre. **1218–21** *fly*: *King Lear*, IV.i.36–7; see also refrain of 'Wine of Cyprus'.

Fifth Book

This book begins with Aurora/EBB presenting a Defence of Poetry, arguing for her own modern epic and against Victorian medievalism. Her heroine attends a dinner party at Lord Howe's, writes to Romney concerning Lady Waldemar and Marian, then departs for Italy after packing up her father's books.

V.30 *theurgic*: God-stirred. **51** *saint's blood*: blood of St Januarius in Naples said to liquefy on his commemorative day. **75** '*Let no one be called happy till his death*': Aeschylus, *Agamemnon*, lines 928–30; Sophocles, *Oedipus Rex*, interpolated lines 1528–30. **105–12** *chrisms*: Lazarus and Mary Magdalen, John 11.1–44, 12.1–8. **113** *Panomphœan Joves*: all-oracle Jove. **139** *epics have died out*: EBB had herself written *The Battle of*

Marathon (1820) in the manner of Homer and Pope before she was twelve. She reviewed Richard Hengist Horne's epic poem *Orion* for the *Athenaeum* (24 June 1843); see her footnote to *The Cry of the Children*, line 116. **142–54**: Richard *Payne Knight* claimed the Elgin marbles were Roman, from Hadrian's era, and worthless; Benjamin Haydon, EBB's friend, argued in their favour as from Periclean Parthenon. **149**: *Iliad*, VI.466–502; see also *AL*, VIII.473–4. **190–212** *moat and drawbridge*: EBB speaks against Victorian medievalism in the writings of Sir Walter Scott (1771–1832), Alfred, Lord Tennyson (1809–92, appointed Poet Laureate, 1850) and even RB. **199–202** *poets . . . represent the age*: William Hazlitt's *Spirit of the Age* (1825), echoed in Richard Hengist Horne's *A New Spirit of the Age* (1844), for which EBB wrote and which included entries on Tennyson, RB and EBB. **212–21**: EBB knew that in Hebrew one name for God is 'El-Shaddai', 'אֵל שַׁדַּי', 'breasted one'. **228–34** *Five acts*: Shakespeare *The Winter's Tale*; versus Sir Philip Sidney, *The Defense of Poesie*. **239–41** *Jacob's white-peeled rods*: Genesis 30.37–42. **249** *wigless Hamlet*: when EBB heard Richard Hengist Horne was bald she was disenchanted, commenting that a bald Hamlet was unthinkable. **266–342**: EBB's *drama* criticism in connection with RB's plays and his attempts to have them be produced. **286–8** *King Saul's father's asses*: I Samuel 9.3–10, 14. **291–6**: *Aeschylus* and *tortoise*; see note to *AL*, I.454–5. **315** *Imogen and Juliet*: heroines in Shakespeare's *Cymbeline* and *Romeo and Juliet*. **318–24**: Greek drama originated in sacrifice of *goats* to *Bacchus*. **325** *Themis' son*: Prometheus of Aeschylus' play, which EBB translated (1833). Themis also mothered Seasons and Fates. **333–42** *stage the soul*: see EBB, 'The Seraphim' (1838), 'Drama of Exile' (1844), 'Psyche Apocalypté' (1877). **360–63** *St. Preux . . . Julie's drooping eyelid*: Saint Preux and Julie are the tutor and the pupil who become lovers in Jean Jacques Rousseau's epistolary romance, *La Nouvelle Héloïse* (1760), modelled on *The Letters of Abelard and Heloise* (1132–44). **387** *rhymes among the stars*: Dante, *Commedia*, terza rima, canticles' conclusions with word 'stelle', 'stars'; see also *AL*, VIII.314–15. **399–419**: EBB on RB criticizing women's books and women's sonnets; allusions are to Ovid, *Metamorphoses*, X, V; tales of *Pygmalion* in love with his sculpture; and of *Apollo*'s slaughter of Niobe's many children; EBB goes on to speak of fathers and children, obliquely discussing her own father's relation to his twelve children, of whom she was the eldest, ending with Dante's horrific tale of Ugolino. **446–55** *some page of ours*: 'Sonnets from the Portuguese'. **455–73** *your father*: EBB remembering her father's earlier kindnesses. **481–5** *heritage of many corn-fields*: Genesis 25.29–34. **492–6** *Ugolino*: Dante, *Inferno*, XXXII.125–XXXIII.78; EBB and RB in Pisa on their honeymoon saw the prison where Ugolino died from starvation after having eaten the bodies of his sons imprisoned with him. **504–7** *Graham*: Robert Browning. **508–10**, **517–23**: *Belmore* Alfred

Tennyson; *cedarn poems*: Tennyson's 'Oenone' (1833, 1842) translates Ovid's *Heroides'* tale of Paris cutting his ship from cedar to sail from the abandoned Oenone to attain Helen and commence the Trojan War; EBB also speaking of Tennyson's cedarn pencils that write the poem. She told Kenyon, and wrote in *A New Spirit of the Age*, of the excellence of Tennyson's 'Oenone'. EBB recalls here the 1833 edition; in the 1842 version Tennyson gives Ovid's cedars as pines. **510–15, 523–33**: *Mark Gage* John Ruskin? **533–8**: *Graham*'s wife and son, EBB herself and their child, Pen Browning. These sketches of poets are similar to those in EBB's 'A Vision of Poets' (1844), 'Lady Geraldine's Courtship', lines 160–67. **558–9** *Sparrows five*: Luke 12.6. **604** *Leeds mesmerist*: mesmerism and spiritualism, partly believed in by EBB, would become an obsession with her when scorned by RB. **605** *lecturer from 'the States'*: Margaret Fuller? **611** *One*: capitalization repeated *AL*, V.1108, yet Lady Waldemar is no Christ. **631–2**: *Sir Blaise* Delorme either Roman Catholic or, more likely, Anglo-Catholic; E. B. Pusey, John Keble, John Hurrell Froude and John Henry Newman's Oxford Movement Anglo-Catholic *Tracts for the Times* (1833–41) sought to return Church of England to Pre-Reformation *mediæval* foundations. **662–4** *neither sews nor spins*: Matthew 6.28; Shakespeare, Sonnet XCIV.14, 'Lilies that fester smell far worse than weeds'; see also *AL*, V. 790–93, which reflects Margaret Fuller, as in Hawthorne's Zenobia, *The Blithedale Romance* (1852). **676** *saintly Styrian monk*: plump Austrian monk combined with St Simon Stylites, an ascetic who lived on top of a column in Syria; later editions have cross be 'ebon', not *golden*. **682–3** *St. Lucy*: represented as holding her plucked-out eyes on a plate, to repel her would-be lover. **718**: pages 207–8 are transposed in Robert Taylor Collection, Princeton University Library, *AL* bound revises. **720–28**: Fourier preached Free Love; see also *AL*, II.482, III.108, 583–4, V.782–93, IX.868–9. **729** *Pisgah-hill*: Deuteronomy 3.24–7. **782–3**: *Leigh Hall* in *Shropshire*, on border of Wales, like EBB's Malvern. **782–93**: *famed phalanstery . . . christianised from Fourier's own*: Fourier's communities had orchards planted in phalanxes hence 'phalanstery' and practised Free Love. Lady Waldemar here enacts role of an English Margaret Fuller at an English Brook Farm; see also *AL*, II.482, III.108, 583–4, V.720–28, IX.868–9. **798** *A Pallas in the Vatican*: this statue has Athena stand with spear, helmeted, snake coiled at her feet; George Eliot similarly has Dorothea Brooke in *Middlemarch* (1871–2) gaze at a Cleopatra in the Vatican who is to kill herself with an asp – and in turn be gazed at by two men. **820**: Anna Jameson visited and wrote about the *Chipewa* in Canada. **822**: *Queen Pomare* IV (1813–77) of Tahiti; *Emperor* Faustin I *Soulouque* (c. 1782–1867), former slave, President (1847), then self-declared Emperor of Haiti (1849). **836** *transatlantic girl*: combines Margaret Fuller, correspondent to the New York *Tribune*, Kate Field, correspondent to the *Atlantic Monthly*, both EBB's friends in Italy. **897-908** *Ann Blyth, Pauline*: EBB here playfully alludes to RB's previous loves, RB having published *Pauline* anonymously at twenty (1833). **910-12**: the sacred bull of Egypt, *Apis*, represented the god Osiris who was consulted as an oracle in this form; for EBB a type of the false worshipping by the Israelites of the Golden Calf in Exodus. **916-17** *dropped star*: called 'Wormwood', Revelation 8.10-11. **923-5** *tare runs through . . . garnered sheaves*: scarlet poppy amidst golden ears of wheat, Matthew 13.25-30; Ruth 2. **939-42**: oracle at *Delphi*, dedicated to *Apollo*, had prophetess sit on *golden tripod*. **1001-4** *last book*: poems by the Brownings were so read at Brook Farm's phalanstery in the States. **1078-80**: *Hamlet*, V.ii. 276-343, union or *pearl* dissolved in wine. **1095** *woodland sister, sweet maid Marian*: Marian's name evokes legend of social justice, of Robin Hood and Maid Marian. **1099-104**: Emily Brontë, *Wuthering Heights* (1847), published pseudonymously as by Ellis Bell. **1108** *that Third*: when capitalized refers usually to Christ at Emmaus, Luke 24.13-35; here it is to the Lamia figure of the poem, Lady Waldemar; see also *AL*, V. 611. **1114-15** *Pan*: see 'The Dead Pan' and 'Flush or Faunus'. **1135** *drew my desk and wrote*: EBB had such a lap desk at Casa Guidi. **1217** *Elzevirs*: books published by Elzevir family in Amsterdam, Leyden (1583-1680), especially Greek classic texts. **1221-2** conferenda hæc cum his: 'this compared with that', scholar's Latin marginal notation to a Greek text; Corruptè citat: 'corruptly cited'; lege potiùs: 'better read'. EBB saw and used such notations in collections of Greek scholars, Sir Uvedale Price (1747-1829) and blind Hugh Stuart Boyd (1781-1848). **1227** *Proclus*: fifth-century Byzantine Neoplatonist who defended paganism against Christianity, wrote commentary on Euclid, another on Plato, seeking to prove world was eternal. **1245** *kissing Judas*: Luke 22.47-8; *Wolff*: Friedrich Wolf, professor at Halle, classical philologist, argued for multiple authorship of Homer, *Prolegomena in Homerum* (1795); EBB misspells his name. **1248** *house of Nobody*: *Odyssey*, IX. **1251**: Homer's *spondaic* hexameter, of six feet, fifth foot having two long spondaic syllables.

Sixth Book

On her way to Italy Aurora stops in the Paris of George Sand (whom EBB and RB met, 1852), where she finds Marian and her child. Aurora first objects unjustly to the child's illegitimacy, then listens again to Marian's unfolding Odyssean tale within a tale as the two women bend over a 'rosier flushed Pomegranate'. EBB here borrows the strategy used by Dante and other medieval poets who cast themselves as blameworthy scapegoats within their texts in order to convert their readers from the errors they themselves seem to enact.

VI.66-75 *democracy*: French plebiscite made Napoleon III Emperor with eight million votes (1852). **109-13** *Tuileries*: Empress Eugénie (1826–1920) was not descended from royalty, unlike previous queens reflected in palace's mirrors, but she was more beautiful. **128-30**: *Napoleon* I (1769–1821) first buried on St Helena (1821), then in mausoleum of Les Invalides, guarded by twelve allegorical Victories (1840, monument completed 1861); this veterans' hospital church has a clearly visible dome. **130-31** 'Shall/These dry bones live?': Ezekiel 37.3. **131** *Louis Philippe*: (1773–1850), deposed in 1848 Revolution, succeeded by Napoleon III (1808–73). **167** *Thessaly*: region of witches in Apuleius, *Metamorphoses*, I. **171-6** *osteologists*: consulted in EBB's case for her spinal deformity and pain from childhood tuberculosis. **213** *washing seven times*: 2 Kings 5.1–14. **231-41** *dead face*: EBB uses drowning imagery for the recognition scene with Marian, which recalls the deaths by drowning of Edward Barrett Moulton Barrett and Margaret Fuller. Manuscript draft here erratic and heavily revised. **263** *Institute*: the Institut de France, created by French Revolution, fostered by Napoleon I and III. **269** *button-hole with honourable red*: emblem of member of Légion d'Honneur. **272**: Alexandre *Dumas*, son of black author of *The Count of Monte Cristo* (1844), himself author of *La Dame aux camélias* (novel, 1848; play, 1852). **299-300** *too rough*: Shakespeare, Sonnet XVIII.3. **307-10** *floats up*: Hawthorne similarly wrote of Margaret Fuller's drowning with Zenobia, *The Blithedale Romance* (1852). **367** *arras*: *Hamlet*, III.iv. **514-17**: imagery of *goats* and *Bacchus*, associated with tragedy and with Margaret Fuller's baby, nursed by a goat on board the ship *Elizabeth*, then drowned with both his parents (1850). **521-5** *hawk*: falcon image, see also *AL*, II.119–22, VIII.22. **564-5** *rosier flushed Pomegranate*: EBB is speaking of her own child and RB's, and of his poems, *Bells and Pomegranates* (1841–6), and of her reference to them in 'Lady Geraldine's Courtship' (1844), which had prompted their courtship (1845), marriage (1846) and parenthood (1849). Pomegranate in the Persephone legend symbolized life and death; bells and pomegranates were embroidered on the High Priest Aaron's robe when he served in the Temple, Exodus 28, 39; RB was part Jewish. **585** *angelhood*: Margaret Fuller's child was named Angelo after his father, the Roman Marchese Angelo Ossoli, this baby in the poem being a composite of Margaret's child and of EBB's. **611-770**: Aurora's initial prejudice against Marian Erle portrays EBB's initial response to Margaret Fuller. EBB also disapproved of George Eliot for living out of wedlock and dismissed and never forgave Elizabeth Wilson for having two babies, Orestes and Pylades, when in her service, though Wilson was married. **620** *brazen altar-bars*: Jewish Temple's brass altar used for sacrificing lambs and doves in place of children, Exodus 38.30; Ezekiel 9.2. **712-14** *new Jerusalem*: Revelation 21.2. **719-20** *bids us go higher*: Luke 14.10. **1043-7**: *The Winter's Tale*, IV.iv.79–103. **1175** *swine's road*:

Christ cast out devils into a herd of Gadarene swine who rushed headlong over a precipice into the Sea of Galilee, Matthew 8.28–34; Mark 5.1–19; Luke 8.26–39. **1197, 1201** *stinks since Friday*: Lazarus, but not Christ, John 11.39. **1272–3** *stone upon my sepulchre*: stone on Christ's sepulchre rolled away by Angels before Mary Magdalen approached it, Matthew 28.2; Mark 16.3–4; Luke 24.1–5, 22–4, John 20.1.

Seventh Book

Marian's narration of her rape and resulting pregnancy continues. It is told in the manner of a George Sand novel, with a French setting. Aurora offers to take Marian and her child on to Italy and Marian accepts. Letters to and from England concerning Romney do not reach their destination. Aurora describes Florence.

VII.47–66: EBB herself did not realize she was pregnant until her miscarriage at Pisa, when she was writing *The Runaway Slave at Pilgrim's Point* (1847). **108–13**: early medieval iconography showed the Virgin spinning purple thread for the Temple's veil as her Child was woven in flesh within her womb. **147, 170** *Lamia*: Keats's 'Lamia'; see also *AL*, I.161. **224–7**: gender reversal of Cervantes, *Don Quixote*. George Eliot's heroine Dorothea, *Middlemarch* (1871–2), is such a Doña. **261–4**: an elm was hit by *lightning* at Hope End when EBB was a child, killing the young couple sheltering under it. **266–8**: Hermes, son of Zeus and Maia, a few hours after his birth, left his cradle and stole *Apollo's* oxen, disguising his feet, then found a tortoise shell from which he constructed the first lyre, which so charmed the angered Apollo that he gave Hermes the cattle. **307–9** *tares and wheat*: Matthew 13.25–30. **343** *poisonous porridge*: Genesis 25.28–34. **350** *ox and ass*: Deuteronomy 22.10. **418** *Dijon.Lyons*: describes the journey south along Rhone river that the Brownings themselves took several times from Italy. **470** *dull Odyssean ghosts*: Odyssey, XI.13–635. **485** EBB continues to describe her own journeyings; *Genoa*: associated with Shelley's drowning (1822) and with Byron, to be used by George Eliot for drowning of Gwendolen's husband, Grandcourt, *Daniel Deronda* (1874–6). **486** *Doria*: Genoa's princely dynasty. **515–41** *Bellosguardo*: 'beautiful view', landscape seen from it of Florence, the Arno river, Fiesole and Vallombrosa, is rich with associations from Dante and Milton, Milton visited there to look through Galileo's telescope, then described what he saw in a simile for Satan's epic shield, *Paradise Lost*, I.287–91; became home of Isa Blagden and Nathaniel Hawthorne, Hawthorne using it for *The Marble Faun's* Monte Beni. **566** *od-force*: Harriet Martineau (1802–76) introduced EBB to theories proposed by Baron Carl von Reichenbach (1788–1869) concerning light and electricity. **576–622** *Kate Ward*: is modelling herself upon Aurora, had asked her for the pattern of her cloak, *AL* III.53–60, to win Vincent Carrington. The canvases described here are less those of Benjamin Haydon than they are of Richard Rothwell, the Irish painter who died in Rome (1868), and who had painted Ovidian scenes and portraits, including Mary Shelley's in the National Portrait Gallery. **586** *Danaë*: Ovid, *Metamorphoses*, IV; see also *AL*, III.122. **607** *book folded in her . . . hands*: portrait of RB's grandmother with Thomson's *The Seasons* in her hands; see also *AL*, I.127, III.973; EBB's *last book*: *Casa Guidi Windows*, 1.73–4, spoke of Michelangelo's Medici Tomb sculpture of Aurora, as both Dawn and Spring, Italy's Risorgimento ('mulcted of the Spring'). **631** *voluble with lead*: old clocks had their chimes weighted with lead. **634**: *field* [of Cloth] *of gold*, see note to *AL*, IV.539. **666–7** *Love/And Psyche*: Apuleius, *Metamorphoses*, IV–VI; sculpture on exhibit in Uffizi's Tribune; see 'Psyche Gazing on Cupid'. **669** *vase of lilies*: used in Florentine art for the Annunciation to the Virgin. Margaret Fuller's son, Angelo Eugenio Filippo Ossoli, (born 5 September 1848) was close in age to EBB's own child by Robert, Pen, or, more fully, Robert Wiedemann Barrett Browning (born 9 March 1849). They were like Elizabeth's John the Baptist and Mary's Jesus (Luke 1–2). EBB endows the descriptions of Marian and her child in *AL* with Florentine Holy Family iconography; similarly Julia Margaret Cameron's photographs of her Victorian acquaintances can portray them as Pre-Raphaelite Madonnas and children. EBB's friend, Anna Jameson, like Ruskin, was a scholar of Italian iconography. **679** *nepenthe*: Helen gives this drug to her guests to remove their sorrows, *Odyssey*, IV. 220–32. **746**: Plato, *Phædon*, dialogue on the death of Socrates. **787** *Antinous*: Emperor Hadrian loved this beautiful androgynous youth who died young, sculpture of him and *Cupid and Psyche* in Uffizi Tribune. **809–10** *said a poet of our day*: RB, *Pippa Passes* (1841), lines 190–201. **822** *every common bush afire with God*: Exodus 3.2–6; see also *AL*, I.58. **887** *digamma*: obsolete Greek letter. **917** *Samminiato*: church and hill town, just above Florence, dedicated to San Miniato, an early martyr. **942**: the immortal gods had *ichor*, not blood, in their veins, *Iliad*, V.340. **942–57**: EBB's Pen waking up his mother, and Elizabeth Wilson, EBB's maid who followed her into exile from Malvern and London. **986** *Alaric*: Gothic conqueror of Rome, buried in river bed of Busentus, Edward Gibbon, *Decline and Fall of the Roman Empire* (1776–88). **1035** *the way, the truth, the life*: John 14.6. **1100–102** *gulph*: Dives and Lazarus, Luke 10.19–31, esp. 26. **1169** *Lucca*: the hill town Bagni di Lucca where the Brownings, Hawthornes and Walter Savage Landor often stayed, visited previously by Montaigne and Byron. **1255** *Benigna sis*: 'Be thou kind.' **1261** *young ravens when they cry*: Job 38.41; Psalms 147.9; Luke 12.24. **1278**: church of *Santissima* Annunziata, Florence; see also *AL*, I.77, where Aurora's father first sees her mother. **1302–4** *bells upon my robe*: High Priest Aaron's ephod worn in Temple, embroidered with pomegranates, hung about with bells, Exodus 39.24–6; RB's *Bells and Pomegranates* (1841–6); RB to EBB (18 October 1845), 'The Rabbis make Bells and Pomegranates symbolical of Pleasure and Profit, the gay and the grave, the Poetry and the Prose, Singing and Sermonizing.' **1308–10** *œnomel*: wine and honey, here obliquely also laudanum, or tincture of opium (which had been invented by Paracelsus, 1493–1541, of whom RB wrote in *Paracelsus*, 1835), and to which EBB was addicted from childhood; see also EBB, 'Wine of Cyprus', line 172.

Eighth Book

Aurora is reading Boccaccio's *Decameron* while Marian and her child are at play at Bellosguardo. Then Romney comes. She fails to realize he is now physically blind. Like Penelope and Odysseus they talk all night, discussing social issues and art. (*Odyssey*, XIII.344–9 has Athena at last rouse Dawn from Oceanus to end the night-long dialogue.) Romney tells Aurora that his phalanstery at Leigh Hall has gone up in flames and that he was injured by Marian's father as he carried out the picture of Aurora's ancestor, the Lady Maud. This book is influenced by Homer's *Odyssey*, Sophocles' *Oedipus at Colonus*, Dante's *Commedia*, Boccaccio's *Decameron*, Shakespeare's *The Merchant of Venice*, Milton and his *Samson Agonistes* and (though EBB did not consciously realize this) Charlotte Brontë's *Jane Eyre* (1847).

VIII.21–3 *Boccaccio's tales, The Falcon's*: of Sir Federigo, the ninth tale, fifth day, to be retold by Tennyson in the drama *The Falcon* (1884); EBB to RB, 20 March 1845, '*I am very fond of romances*; yes! . . . I am one who could have forgotten the plague, listening to Boccaccio's stories; and I am not ashamed of it,' while he was scornful of women's books. See also *AL*, II. 119–22, VI.521–5. **29** *sevenfold heavens*: Dante, *Paradiso*, medieval astronomy believing that seven spheres, one for each planet, one of which was the sun, another the moon, encircled the earth at the centre of the cosmos. **44** *duomo-bell*: massive bell of the Duomo, the Cathedral, Santa Maria del Fiore, which hangs in separate bell tower, built by Giotto, Florence. **45** *ten*: see note to I.239–40; *ten fathoms down*: echoes and deepens 'Full fathom five thy father lies,' *The Tempest* I.ii.397. **46–7** *fifty*: later editions corrected to twenty, but Florentine bells include not only those of public churches but also those of numerous convents. **50–58**: Dominican church of Santa *Maria Novella's Place*, spoken of as Michelangelo's *Bride*; its square has stone *obelisks* with *tortoises* as bases; see also *AL*, III.602; EBB later corrects to four tortoises on each base. Boccaccio's *Decameron* story-tellers first meet in this church in plague-tide; see also *Casa Guidi Windows*, I.321–73. **60–62** *sea-king*: sea imagery, through use of *The Tempest*, evokes EBB's father, brother and husband. In the Houghton Library, Harvard, *AL* manuscript, where these words originally ended the Seventh Book, RB noted 'Read this Book, this divine Book, Wednesday night July 9th '56. RB. 39 Devonshire Place,' where Brownings stayed while seeing *AL* through the press, RB only being privileged to read the poem in its penultimate version. **83–4**: EBB's *couch* upon which she wrote *AL*; it can be seen in the Mignaty painting of the Casa Guidi drawing room that RB commissioned at EBB's death, and in a later engraving of RB's study in London. **133–5** *eyes*: see 'Caterina to Camoëns'. **170–74** *Greek king . . . from a taken Troy*: Aeschylus, *Agamemnon*, lines 914–1033. **304–5**: Michelangelo's Medici Tomb sculptures of *morning and night*; Aurora is Morning, Dawn; Romney, with his not-yet-revealed blindness, Dusk, Evening, Night. **314–15** *stars*: so Dante ends each canticle of the Florentine *Commedia*; see also *AL*, V.387. **334–5** *Miriam*: Exodus 15.20–21; see also *AL*, I.87, II.170–71, III.203, VIII.1021–2; *Casa Guidi Windows*, I.314. **348**: Aurora Leigh is now thirty; they remember her birthday in Shropshire *ten* years earlier; her London apprenticeship was of seven years' duration; Marian's child, learning to talk, is about two, age of EBB's and Margaret Fuller's sons; in real life EBB and Margaret were in their forties when their children were born. **388** *Phalarian bull*: Sicilian tyrant had brazen bull made, used it first to torture its inventor, then his subjects revolted, torturing him with it. **395–418**: Romney speaks of the Hungry Forties, when crops failed throughout Europe, potato blight causing the Great Famine in Ireland. **429–30** *individualism . . . universal*: Dante wrote, 'Half way through the road of *our* life, I found *myself* again in a dark wood,' as Dante Alighieri the individual, and as universal Everyman, EBB translating these lines in Dante first as a child and later as an adult; see manuscripts at Baylor University's Armstrong Browning Library. **473–4** *hero's casque*: doomed Hector's plumed helm frightening his small son, Astyanax, *Iliad*, VI.466–502; see also *AL*, V.149. **477** *Sanscrit*: ancient, sacred Indian script, echoing *AL*, II.817, 834 references to Chaldean letters. **507–19**: EBB's spaniel, Flush, compared to Ulysses' dog, Argos, *Odyssey*, XVII.290–327. **568** *upon my forehead*: the High Priest wore a plate of gold, inscribed HOLINESS UNTO THE LORD, tied to his brow with a blue lace, Exodus 28.36–8; Zachariah 14.20–21. **631, 746** *Adam's corn*: wheat and other European grains, not Indian maize. **632** *Noah's wine*: Genesis 9.20–27. **645–55**: Papal elections in Sistine Chapel indicated by smoke rising from burnt ballots. **734–41**: Diderot's *Encyclopédie* published such manufacturing methods with text and engravings. **783** *softly*: Othello, V.ii.334. **789** *empty hand thrown impotently out*: Othello, V.ii.342–4; EBB remembers Shakespeare's plays but does not check their texts. **795–6** *prophet beats the ass*: Balaam and the ass, Numbers

22.21–34. 833–42; *statue*: Harriet Hosmer, sculptor, most famous for her *Clasped Hands* of the poets EBB and RB. 842–3 *cures the plague*: Jessie White Mario, doctor, friend and biographer of Garibaldi, impassioned about social issues and Italian Risorgimento. 844–5 *rights a land's finances*: Harriet Martineau (1802–76), wrote on political economy, explaining David Ricardo, which influenced Parliament; all three gifted women were EBB's acquaintances. 900 *'last tracts' but twelve*: Oxford Movement Tractarians, see also AL, I.394–5. 922 *as a baby drugged*: in Industrial Revolution factories hired women as they were cheaper than men, the women having to drug their babies with opiates to keep them from crying while they were gone; the use of drugs was also common among West Indian slave-owners, particularly women. 949 *Vandykes*: Anthony Van Dyck, Dutch artist, painted portraits of Charles I and cavalier aristocracy; see also *AL*, IV.309. 955 *Lady Maud*: Aurora Leigh has inherited her ancestress's features and therefore Romney saves the portrait; double reference to Wright of Derby's portrait of RB's grandmother, and Sir Thomas Lawrence's portrait (1795) of 'Pinkie', EBB's aunt (her father's sister), who was brought to England from Jamaica and who died young from tuberculosis. 1020 *burnt the viol*: inverse of Nero fiddling while Rome burnt. 1021–2 *dance . . . to cymbals*: Miriam danced so after the Israelites were freed from Egyptian slavery, Exodus 15.20–21; see also *AL*, I.87, II.170–71, III.203, VIII.334–5; *Casa Guidi Windows*, I.314. 1024 *sun is silent*: Dante, *Inferno*, I.60; EBB translated opening, *Inferno*, I, twice; manuscripts at Baylor University. 1063–6: Romney as Christ the Good Shepherd. 1113–7: *Casa Guidi Windows*, I.140–44; the sculpture here seems to be of the Uffizi Tribune's *Cupid and Psyche*. 1136–8 *cup at supper*: Last Supper, Crucifixion, Luke 22.11–20, 42; John 19.28–9. 1144–5 *Moses' bulrush-boat*: (actually papyrus) Exodus 2.3. 1220–22 *regent brows . . . garland*: coronation of Madame de Staël's Corinne on the Capitol; see also *AL*, I.981, II.33–53.

Ninth Book

Aurora reads Lady Waldemar's envy-filled letter, at last comes to learn of Romney's blindness (which EBB borrowed unconsciously from Rochester's blindness in Currer Bell/Charlotte Brontë, *Jane Eyre*, 1847). Romney proposes to Marian, who rejects his pseudo-paternity of her child. Aurora and Romney above Florence recite from the Apocalypse, concerning the heavenly Jerusalem. The epic *AL* begins and ends with the Bible, first with Ecclesiastes 12.12, and last with Revelation 21, while encompassing classical and modern literature, and England, America, France and Italy within its nine books.

IX.77–8 *to love . . . not wisely*: *Othello* V.ii.340. 103 *St. Sophia's dome*: of Byzantine Hagia Sophia in Istanbul, later made an Islamic mosque, but orginally dedicated to Holy Wisdom, the continuation in the Greek Christian world of the pagan Greek worship of Pallas Athena, goddess of wisdom. 119 *He'd wash his hands*: Matthew 27.24. 137 *To live and have his being*: Paul speaking on the Areopagus in Athens, quoting pagan philosophy, Acts 17.28. 150: Electra recognizes her brother, Orestes, from their matching hair and *footprint*, Aeschylus, *Choephoroi*, lines 167–211; see also 'Sonnets from the Portuguese', V.2; Elizabeth Wilson called her two sons Orestes and Pylades. 163 *droop of eyelid*: physical description of Margaret Fuller here given by Lady Waldemar to Aurora Leigh. 253–4 *blue as Aaron's priestly robe*: Exodus 39.22–31; Numbers 20.25–6; Jerome wrote an Epistle to the twice-wed Fabiola at her request on Aaron's garb, emphasizing the blue of the priestly robe. 277–8 *spaniel head/With all its . . . curls*: description of Marian Erle is of EBB, whom Flush resembled. 553–5 *boar . . . notched me with his tooth*: *Odyssey*, XIX.428–66; Apuleius, *Metamorphoses*, VIII.5; Shakespeare, *Venus and Adonis*, in which heroes are injured or killed by boars goring them with their tusks in the thigh, a euphemism for castration. 576–81 *Unspotted in their crystals*: Milton's blindness, *Paradise Lost* III.23–6; EBB's Greek tutor, Hugh Boyd, was blind; see 'Wine of Cyprus' and sonnets 'Hugh Stuart Boyd: His Blindness' and 'Hugh Stuart Boyd: Legacies'. EBB is also playing with Romney/Robert as Michelangelo's sculptures of Dusk to her Dawn as Aurora on the tomb of Lorenzo de' Medici, Dusk's features being similar to RB's. 651–2 *handful of the earth/To make God's image!*: Genesis 1.26, 2.7. 702–3 *Cloud . . . the wilderness*: Exodus 13.21. 813 *The morning and the evening made his day*: 'And there was evening and there was morning, the first day,' Genesis 1.5, EBB clearly recalling the Hebrew of that verse, 'וַיְהִי־עֶרֶב וַיְהִי־בֹקֶר יוֹם אֶחָד׃' and the Michelangelo Medici Tomb sculpture of Dawn and Dusk; see also *AL* V.148–60. 840 *audient circles*: music of the spheres, each planet emitting a musical note, all together playing the chord of the octave from Pythagoras, Milton. 845 *Selah*: EBB, 'Essay on Mind' (1826), line 1229; used seventy times in Psalms, twice in Habakkuk, to indicate a pause in the music. 847 *moon-bathed promontory*: Jessica and Lorenzo, *The Merchant of Venice*, V.i.1–126. 868–9 *Fourier's void,/And Comte is dwarfed,—and Cabet, puerile*: Comte (1798–1853) was a friend of Fourier. Cabet (1788–1856), influenced by the socialism of Robert Owen, wrote *Voyage en Icarie* and attempted to found an Icarian commune at Nauvoo on the Mississippi. For Fourier see also *AL*, II.482, III.108, 583–4, V.720–28, 782–93. 885 *Sharon*: Song of Solomon 2.1; rose image, Dante, *Paradiso*, XXXI. 932 *And blow all class-walls level as Jericho's*: Joshua 6.1–20. EBB, by giving aristocratic Romney Leigh gypsy names and suggesting a title with that for low-born Marian Erle, has shattered class

walls, as she also does those of gender with her classical similes' reversals.
962-4 *Jasper ... sapphire ... chalcedony ... amethyst*: as they look over
Florence from Galileo's and Milton's Bellosguardo they prophetically see
the city of the Apocalypse, the new Jerusalem, as a bride adorned for her
husband, where death, tears and night shall be no more, that city of the
soul sought by both poets and utopians, Revelation 21.1–20. The same
stones are also given as on Aaron's breastplate, Exodus 28.17–20, in the
chapter discussing the bells and pomegranates on his robe.

FROM *ESSAY ON MIND, WITH OTHER POEMS* (1826)

EBB had grown up, the first-born of twelve children, in the house near
Malvern her father had built from his Jamaican slave wealth, called Hope
End, and which he had architecturally resemble a Turkish palace with
crescents and minarets. Its library was excellently stocked with fine
books. Her earliest publication was *The Battle of Marathon* (London: W.
Lindsell, 1820) modelled on her reading of Homer in the Greek and on
Pope and Byron in English and written in 1819 before she was twelve. It
was dedicated to her father who paid its printing costs for fifty copies.
The epic poem, prominently featuring blue-eyed Athena, is preceded by
an excellent essay on classical literature.

EBB's second published volume was *Essay on Mind, with Other Poems*
(London: James Duncan, 1826), again published anonymously, this time its
printing costs being met by Mary Trepsack, the Barretts' Jamaican slave and
friend. 'Essay on Mind' is a learned philosophical treatise in verse, not given
here. With it are shorter poems, including the following three selections:

Verses to My Brother

EBB quoted Milton's *Lycidas*, line 23, prophetically; Milton's friend,
Edward King, drowned (1637), Milton writing the elegy of *Lycidas* in his
memory; so was EBB's brother, Edward Barrett Moulton Barrett, to die
by drowning (1840). Ba, and Bro read Horace and Virgil together (1817–
20), sharing his tutor, Daniel McSwiney; she read Homer alone after Bro
left for Charterhouse (1820).

18 *Maro*: Publius Vergilius Maro or Virgil.

Stanzas on the Death of Lord Byron [*1824*]

Byron died at thirty-six in 1824 when attempting to free Greece from Turkish oppression. The manuscript in the Armstrong Browning Collection at Baylor University is quite different, its quotation from *Childe Harold* being 'Ye who have traced the pilgrim to the scene/Which is his last –'. EBB's poem initially published at Byron's death in *Globe and Traveller* (30 June 1824).

Motto: 'λέγε πᾶσιν ἀπώλετο': Bion, *Lament for Adonis*, 'say to all that he is lost'; *Childe Harold's Pilgrimage* (1812, 1816, 1818), George Gordon, Lord Byron's quasi-autobiographical poem, to be followed by *Don Juan* (1819–24); 'Harold' alluding to the loss of England's freedom with the death of the last Saxon king in battle against the Norman William the Conqueror; these poems were to shape EBB's similarly part-autobiographical heroines in *AL*. 6 *Ægæa's wave*: Aegean Sea between Turkey and Greece. 10 *Hellas*: Greece, in 1827 struggling for freedom from Turkish conquest; see 'Hiram Powers's Greek Slave'.

Lines on the Portrait of the Widow of Riego

Transcribed from the manuscripts in the Baylor Armstrong Browning Collection, collated with their 1826 publication. We have used the manuscript title for this edition, although the poem was published as 'On a Picture of Riego's Widow'. With one manuscript of this poem is an envelope inscribed 'Ba told me years ago that the widow of Riego sent her a lock of hair as all the acknowledgement she could make of some verses of Ba upon Riego. This must be the hair. R. B. Alone, Casa Guidi, July 1861.' Within in blue tissue is a fine braid of strong black hair bound with silver. See also 'The Death-Bed of Teresa del Riego', lines 36–42, 'Sonnets from the Portuguese', XIX, XX. Riego was a leader in the 1820 Spanish Revolution, executed on 7 November 1823, despite his wife's attempts to save him through diplomatic intervention. She died in London in 1824.

FROM *PROMETHEUS BOUND, AND MISCELLANEOUS POEMS* (1833)

Another poem concerning Teresa del Riego appeared in *Prometheus Bound, and Miscellaneous Poems* (London: Saunders and Otley, 1833), which was published after the Barrett Moulton Barrett family, in relative penury after the freeing of the slaves in the West Indies, had sold Hope End.

The Death-Bed of Teresa del Riego

Motto: 'Si fia muta ogni altra cosa, al fine/Parlerà il mio morire/E ti dirà la morte il mio martire.': 'If all else changes, at the end my dying would still speak saying to you that my death was martyrdom.' Giambattista Guarini (1538–1612). **24** *Niobe*: she was turned to stone from grief, weeping for her children, slaughtered by Apollo; see also *Casa Guidi Windows*, I.32. **45** *Dodonæan brass*: brazen oracle in oak grove, sacred to Jupiter.

THE CRY OF THE CHILDREN (1843, 1844)

In 1838 EBB, seriously ill with tuberculosis, published *The Seraphim, and Other Poems*, none of which is included in the present selection. 'The Seraphim' is a verse drama of the angels' discourse at the Crucifixion. The remaining death-centred poems in the collection also reflect EBB's crippling illness – which afflicted her spine as well as her lungs – for which addicting opiates were prescribed. (The anonymous contributor wrote of EBB in *A New Spirit of the Age*, 'Miss Barrett often wanders amidst the supernatural darkness of Calvary sometimes with anguish and tears of blood, sometimes like one who echoes the songs of triumphal quires.') Then, in 1840, Bro drowned in Torbay while staying with the invalid EBB. In 1841, EBB published 'Queen Annelida and False Arcite' in a volume of translations from Chaucer, edited by Richard Hengist Horne.

The Cry of the Children, published in August 1843 in *Blackwood's Edinburgh Magazine* and again in August 1844 in the collected *Poems*, was written in response to Richard Hengist Horne's 'Report on the Employment of Children and Young Persons in Mines and Manufactories', at his request. With it, from her sickbed, EBB influenced legislation in Parliament. See note to *AL*, III.548. It was translated into Russian and published in Бремя, IV, St Petersburg, 1861, pp. 451–2, edited, М. Достоевскаго, as Елизабеть Барроть Броончнгь, 'Рпачъ Дьтен', its first line, 'О моч вратья!' Horne also had EBB edit and partially write *A New Spirit of the Age* (1844), which included anonymous essays on RB and EBB. At this time the Barretts, including the invalid EBB, came to live at 50 Wimpole Street. In 1846, in 'Sonnets from the Portuguese', EBB came to reject illness and death and chose life and love. She also chose RB over Hengist Horne as her literary agent.

Motto: 'φεῦ, φεῦ, τί προσδέρκεσθέ μ'ὅμμασιν, τέκνα.' 'Woe, woe, why do you look upon me with your eyes, my children?' said by Medea in Euripides' play of that name, line 1048, as she is about to murder her children. 116: EBB's footnote; see also *AL*, V.95-129, 139-41, 151-65.

FROM *POEMS* (1844)

In 1844 EBB published *Poems* in two volumes (London: Edward Moxon), this time under her own name of Elizabeth Barrett Barrett (she never used the Moulton in the family name) and, as always until her elopement and estrangement, dedicated her verses to her father:

When your eyes fall upon this page of dedication, and you start to see to whom it is inscribed, your first thought will be of the time far off when I was a child and wrote verses, and when I dedicated them to you who were my public and my critic. Of all that such a recollection implies of saddest and sweetest to both of us, it would become neither of us to speak before the world: nor would it be possible for us to speak of it to one another, with voices that did not falter. Enough, that what was in my heart when I wrote this, will be fully known to you.

Besides shorter poems, the volumes included 'A Drama of Exile', like 'The Seraphim' (1838), a verse drama, this time centred on Adam and Eve, EBB carrying out Milton's intent of writing dramas on biblical subjects in the classic vein.

Past and Future

This sonnet will be referred to again in EBB's 'Sonnets from the Portuguese', XVII; its images are eucharistic.

To George Sand. A Desire

EBB much read and admired George Sand (Madame Aurore Dudevant), and, despite RB's avowed disapproval of Sand's life and art, the Brownings would meet her in Paris in 1852. Margaret Fuller likewise met her. In this sonnet EBB both lionizes her and angelicizes Sand, lines 2 and 11, making of her two of the Gospels' Tetramorphs, lion and angel; the image of the sprouting wings in lines 7-8 also learnedly evokes Plato, *Phaedrus*, lines 251-2.

Lady Geraldine's Courtship

This poem was written in haste to fill up one of the two volumes to the 1844 poems and at the request of EBB's publisher. RB read the volume, which had been given to his family by John Kenyon, on his return from the Continent and dashed off a letter of appreciation to its poetess, thus starting their courtship. EBB's friend, Anna Jameson, had written *The Loves of the Poets*, which included a chapter devoted to Henry Howard, Earl of Surrey, and his sonnet 'Description and praise of his love Geraldine' (1537). When EBB and RB eloped, following their courtship scripted by 'Lady Geraldine's Courtship', they met Anna Jameson in Paris, who was travelling with her niece, Gerardine, and who shepherded the two middle-aged lovers on to Pisa. Mrs Jameson was both delighted to see the outcome of her own and EBB's writings on Geraldine and alarmed as EBB was very ill.

28 *Geraldine*: evokes Surrey's sonnet. **52** *Bertram*: evokes the anti-hero in *All's Well that Ends Well*, who is wooed and won by Helena. **117**: John Graham *Lough* (1806–76), sculpting statues of Victoria and Albert at time of poem's writing. **164** *Howitt's ballad-dew*: William (1792–1879) and Mary Howitt (1799–1888), Quaker husband and wife, published joint literary volumes, Mary especially writing ballad verse. **165** *Pomegranate*: RB's *Bells and Pomegranates* series published, at his father's expense (1841–6). EBB hung engravings from Horne's *A New Spirit of the Age* of RB and Tennyson on her Wimpole Street sickroom wall, though had both of them removed when RB would come and visit her. **229–30** *Camoëns*: see 'Caterina to Camoëns', RB using this for title for 'Sonnets from the Portuguese'. EBB in 'A Vision of Poets' (1844), wrote

> And Camoëns, with that look he had,
> Compelling India's Genius sad
> From the wave through the Lusiad,—

> The murmurs of the storm-cape ocean
> Indrawn in vibrative emotion
> Along the verse.

270 *Pythian*: Apollo's priestess's prophetic frenzy, Delphi. **369** *Phemius*: *Odyssey* I, XVII and XXII, minstrel on Ithaca. **380** *Parian*: marble, used for Athenian Parthenon.

Crowned and Wedded [1840]

This poem was originally published under the title 'The Crowned and Wedded Queen' (15 February) in the *Athenaeum*, its title being changed for the 1844 *Poems* to accord with another poem on Napoleon, title 'Crowned and Buried'. Queen Victoria was crowned on 28 June 1838 and married to Prince Albert on 10 February 1840. The scene for both events is Westminster Abbey, which EBB would visit (31 July 1846), when strengthening herself for her elopement, writing to RB of the Poets' Corner,

How grand—how solemn! Time itself seemed turned to stone there! . . . we stood where the poets were laid—oh, it is very fine—it is better than Laureateships and pensions. Do you remember what is written on Spenser's monument—'Here lyeth, in expectation of the second coming of Jesus Christ, . . Edmond Spenser, having given proof of his divine spirit in his poems.'

54 *Augsburg*: scene of Protestant Reformation: 'Confession of Augsburg' (1527), written by Luther and Melancthon; Peace of Augsburg (1555), granting Germany religious freedom from Rome.

Wine of Cyprus

EBB studied Greek with blind Hugh Boyd, assisted his work on the Greek Fathers and translated Aeschylus' *Prometheus Bound* and other works under his guidance. When she married RB secretly at St Marylebone Church (12 September 1846), she stopped at Hugh Boyd's for a drink of Cyprus wine before returning to Wimpole Street in preparation for her flight abroad with RB.

Refrain: 4, 59, 176: Though 'I am sipping like a fly,' seems an insipid line, EBB is indulging a classic convention of writing poems upon absurd and insignificant creatures, such as fleas; see Spenser, *Virgil's Gnat* (1591); Donne, 'The Flea' (1633); see also *AL*, IV.1218–21. 21 *Naiads*: water nymphs. 44 *Anacreon*: lyric poet and drunkard. 49 *Chian*: wine from Homer's 'rocky Chios'. 51 *Rhea*: wife of Titan Chronos, lion enthroned. 53 *Paphia*: Venus. 61 *Ulysses' old libation*: to the dead so they would speak, of milk and honey, then water sprinkled with barley meal, and last sheep's blood, *Odyssey*, XI.23–635. 77 *cothurns*: high buskins worn by tragic actors. 93 *Theocritus, Bion*: authors of idyls. 94 *Pindar*: author of odes. 103 *sponges of their hyssops*: Hellenism cleansed Judaically. 105 *Chrysostoms*: 'golden mouthed', Greek Church Father. 107 *Basil*:

Greek Church Father. 109 *Heliodorus*: Greek bishop, wrote romance
Aethiopica. 113 *Synesius*: Greek Christian poet. 117: Gregory *Nazianzen*,
Greek Church Father. 121 *Até*: goddess of strife. 135: Richard *Porson*
(1759–1808), English classical scholar, editor. 172 *œnomel*: mixture of
wine, honey; see also *AL*, VII.1308.

The Dead Pan

EBB dedicated this poem to John Kenyon who had paraphrased Schiller
for her, citing as well 'Plutarch's *De Oraculorum Defectu*, according to
which, at the hour of the Saviour's agony, a cry of "Great Pan is dead!"
swept across the waves in the hearing of certain mariners, – and the
oracles ceased'. This theme is present in Milton's 'Ode on the Morning
of Christ's Nativity' (1629) and in Swinburne, 'Hymn to Proserpina'
(1866), 'Thou hast conquered, O pale Galilean,/The world has grown
grey from thy breath.'

37 *Naiades*: nymphs of flowing waters. 44 *Dryads*: nymphs of woods and
trees. 51 *Oreads*: nymphs of mountains and hills. 57 *Plato's* [Socrates']
vision: *Phaedrus*, line 247. 127 *Crowned Cybele*: goddess, daughter of
Sky and Earth, crowned with city walls, loved Atys whom her father
mutilated, her priests, the Corybantes, similarly mutilated. 136 *Vesta*:
goddess of sacred fire. 201 *Dodona's oak*: city built by Deucalion after
the Deluge, a black dove founding the oracle of Jupiter in an oak
grove, the Argo built from its wood. 204 *Pythia*: Apollo's oracular
priestess at Delphi.

Caterina to Camoëns

Luis de Camoëns (1524–80), Portugal's epic poet and a sonneteer, loved
Caterina de Atayde, the queen's maid of honour, and therefore was
exiled; seeking to gain honour abroad in Africa and Asia, he returned to
find her dead. One episode among many in his adventurous life was his
shipwreck off the Mekong Delta, from which he saved himself by
swimming to shore with only the manuscript of the epic, *Os Lusiados*
('The Portuguese'), which he had written in a grotto in Goa, India, as
well as in Macao, the Philippines. He died in poverty in Lisbon, having
been supported there by his Japanese slave begging in the streets. RB
suggested the title for 'Sonnets from the Portuguese' on the basis of this
poem of EBB's, the similar reference in 'Lady Geraldine's Courtship',
lines 229–30, and EBB's own Creole eyes, while EBB had wanted them
titled 'Sonnets from the Bosnian'.

17 *vesper*: evening, Vespers being the evening Office sung by monks and nuns. **81** *angelus*: rung at dawn, noon and sunset while the 'Hail, Mary, Full of Grace' is said. **117** Miserere: David's Penitential Psalm, 51, said at Lauds and Vespers.

THE RUNAWAY SLAVE AT PILGRIM'S POINT (1848, 1849, 1850)

First published in the *Liberty Bell*, Boston (1848), next two editions being London: Edward Moxon (1849) and London: Chapman and Hall (1850); the work is based on a story told to EBB by a part-black Jamaican Barrett cousin visiting in England. EBB wrote it when herself pregnant and eloping from her father, a former slave-owner. Though she never visited America, in this poem she melds her ancestral Jamaica, the Southern States and, improbably, the North of Plymouth Rock. Text collated with the manuscripts at Baylor University and the 1849, 1850 editions. The American publication was titled *The Runaway Slave at Hurst Point*.

22–8: Blake, 'The Little Black Boy'. **43–9**: omitted in Baylor manuscripts. **211** *Man, drop that stone*: John 8.7. **236** *seven wounds*: more accurately, five.

FROM *POEMS* (1850)

The 1850 edition of EBB's *Poems* was published by Chapman and Hall of London, RB's publishers for *Paracelsus* and *Bells and Pomegranates*, and, besides *The Runaway Slave at Pilgrim's Point*, included the following five selections:

Flush or Faunus

For an account of this spaniel, see Virginia Woolf, *Flush: A Biography* (1933). Flush, who had been given by Miss Mitford to EBB, was stolen and ransomed several times from Wimpole Street, then travelled to the Continent with EBB, RB and Elizabeth Wilson, where he was baptized in Petrarch's name at the Sorgue, eventually dying of old age at the Casa Guidi, Florence, after being Pen's pet as well.

5 *Faunus*: half goat (legs, ears), half man, satyr. **9** *Arcadia*: rural Greece, region of pastoral poetry which associated it with paradise.

Hiram Powers' Greek Slave

Collation of 1850 text with manuscript in Baylor University's Armstrong Browning Library. EBB relates poetry with sculpture here as elsewhere and speaks out against the slavery practised not only by Turks in Europe but also by Christians in the Americas, in the West Indies and the Southern States, such slave-owners as was even her own father. The statue addressed in the poem was exhibited in the Crystal Palace Exhibition of 1851. Queen Victoria both read this poem and saw the statue. Hiram Powers, influenced by Byron, sculpted out of white marble a naked Greek virgin, sold as a slave by Turks, who clutches a culturally incorrect Roman Catholic rosary with a cross, to indicate her as Christian in the possession of Moslems. From Vermont, Hiram Powers set up his studio in Florence, and was EBB's friend. Another exquisite statue he sculpted is *The Last of Her Tribe*, of an American Indian maiden fleeing her white pursuers. EBB thought Hiram Powers was himself part American Indian. Powers's colossal statue of President John C. Calhoun in the cargo hold of the ship *Elizabeth*, with much other Carrara marble, old paintings, almonds and olive oil, largely caused the ship's breakup off Fire Island and the death of Margaret Fuller in 1850.

10 *serfdom*: the use of this word extends the sonnet's vision of liberation to Russia, as well as to Greece and America.

Hugh Stuart Boyd: His Blindness

This sonnet has for its model Milton's 'On his Blindness'. EBB gave the following footnote:

To whom was inscribed, in grateful affection, my poem of 'Cyprus Wine'. There comes a moment in life when even gratitude and affection turns to pain, as they do now to me. This excellent and learned man, enthusiastic for the good and the beautiful, and one of the most simple and upright of human beings, passed out of his long darkness through death in the summer of 1848.

EBB's Romney Leigh can be seen as a composite of Richard Hengist Horne, for his socialist views, Hugh Boyd, for his blindness, RB, with whom EBB shared Florence, and EBB herself, for her social concerns. The opening of the sonnet evokes Sophocles, *Oedipus at Colonus*.

10 *Sappho's crown-rose, and Meleager's spring:* Meleager made the first-known anthology, included in it a poem praising Sappho, saying he

culled rose blossoms from her. 11 *Gregory's starlight*: Gregory Nazianzen, Bishop of Constantinople, Greek Church Father, theologian and poet, whom Hugh Stuart Boyd and EBB translated, and who wrote Christian poems when the Emperor forbade Christians access to pagan poetry; see also 'Hugh Stuart Boyd: Legacies', line 2.

Sonnets from the Portuguese [*1846*]

During their courtship RB spoke out against women novelists and women sonnet writers – so EBB kept these sonnets she wrote a secret until after the birth of her child, Pen, shyly presenting them to RB one morning at Bagni di Lucca in 1849, where the family had gone to stay. RB insisted on their publication as translations in the 1850 *Poems*. Later, RB told Isa Blagden 'that was a strange heavy crown, that wreath of sonnets, put on me one morning unawares, three years after it had been twined. ... The publishing them was through me'. He told Edmund Gosse 'I dared not reserve to myself the finest sonnets written in any language since Shakespeare's'. (The forger T. J. Wise published the sonnets with the false date of 1847, Graham Pollard in 1934 proving the edition was published on paper manufactured after 1874, some of the type after 1880.) EBB suggested they be titled 'Sonnets from the Bosnian'. RB decided on 'Sonnets from the Portuguese' in honour of her poem 'Caterina to Camoëns'. Already, in 'Lady Geraldine's Courtship' (lines 162-3) she had borrowed from Surrey's sonnet cycle, under the influence of Anna Jameson's *The Loves of the Poets*, other major sonnet cycles influencing her being those of Petrarch, Wyatt, Sidney, Spenser and Shakespeare; but EBB has reversed their genders and modernized their courtships. Further on in the British Library manuscript note-book, which EBB gave RB in Bagni di Lucca, are unpublished poems which doubt their love, in one of which EBB speaks of her finger as too little and frail to wear a wedding ring, p. 63. But the two poets did marry, with Elizabeth Wilson as witness, at St Marylebone Church (12 September 1846) EBB dressed in nun-like black, only relieved by the gold ring, which she then took off and hid (after first meeting with Hugh Boyd for a glass of Cyprus wine), when returning home to Wimpole Street, before the elopement to France and Italy with Elizabeth Wilson and Flush (19 September). Alongside these sonnets one should also read the magnificently learned and witty love letters written between EBB and RB during their courtship (1845-6), first published by their son, Pen, in 1899.

The much-published and republished 'Sonnets from the Portuguese' text is based on the Houghton manuscript, now at Baylor University's Armstrong Browning Library, which was prepared for its 1850 publication. The text presented here instead is based on the British Library manuscript notebook, which EBB wrote out at 50 Wimpole Street in 1846, then gave to RB three years after their writing, in 1849. We preserve its numbering and her idiosyncrasies: EBB often uses equal signs for dashes; her exclamation marks lack the point (which cannot be replicated typographically); she often, as in the letters, uses two dots only instead of the conventional three; and she employs ampersands.

I.1 *Theocritus*: Greek writer of bucolic idyls, from Syracuse, Sicily. III.3 *ministering . . . angels*: *Hamlet*, I.iv.39, V.i.237, thus EBB casts herself as Ophelia. 9: Asaph, David's *Chief musician*, composer of Psalms 50, 73–83; see also *Casa Guidi Windows*, I.309. V.2 *Electra*: Aeschylus' *Choephoroi*, Orestes' sister, believing her brother dead, finds him alive; see also *AL*, IX.150. IX.12: Houghton manuscript variant reads, 'Nor breathe my poison on thy Venice-glass,' such goblets said to shatter when filled with poisoned wine. X.3 *temple burn, or flax*: in Jerusalem Temple, soiled priestly linen garments were not washed but used as wicks for lamps; see also *Casa Guidi Windows*, II.509. XI.6 *Aornus:* lofty rock in India, taken by Alexander, Hercules could not storm it. XVIII.1, XIX.2, 4: Victorians would treasure *a lock of hair* from the living and the dead. XIX.1–4 *The soul's Rialto*: mercantile region of rich sea port, Venice; *argosies*: merchant fleets. 5–9: *Pindar's* first Pythian ode speaks of the Muses as having purply-black hair; see also *AL*, I.981. EBB's hair was very dark. 8 *bay = crown*: EBB speaks of RB as wearing the crown of laurel awarded to poets. Corinna, said to have been Pindar's teacher, won the laurel against him five times for her odes. EBB herself was to be seriously proposed for England's Poet Laureate by the *Athenaeum* on Wordsworth's death (1850), not RB; see also *AL*, II.33–58. XXIV.12 *amreeta*: Sanskrit, immortal, ambrosial drink; published variant 'Alone to heavenly dews that drop not fewer'. XXVIII.1 *My letters!*: EBB and RB both kept their collection of letters, which were sold at auction of contents of Casa Guidi at Pen Browning's death. XXXIII.1: on her *pet-name*, Ba, her brother's as Bro. XXXVI.2 *marble*: echoing Shakespeare's 'Not marble nor the gilded monuments', Sonnet LV; Horace's 'exegi monumentum aere perennius' *Odes*, III.30.1. 10: prophetic of Harriet Hosmer's bronze of the poets' *enclasped hands*. XXXVII.13 *sculptured porpoise*: plays learnedly on Aldine emblem of dolphin and anchor, 'Ancora speme', of continuing hopefulness. XXXVIII.1–3: plays with the poetic convention 'I sent thee late a rosy wreath,/Not so much honouring thee,/As giving it a hope that there/It could not withered be' (Ben Jonson, 'To Celia', *Volpone*, 1607, translating Alexandrian lyric). XL.5 *Mussulmans*: Muslims; *Giaours*: term of contempt used by Turks of non-Muslims, Christians. 7 *Polypheme*: the Cyclops and cannibal, *Odyssey*, IX. XLII: originally published apart from the 'Sonnets from the Portuguese' first line quotes opening of 'Past and Future', and deserves comparison with that sonnet, particularly in its autobiographical aspects, the first being written just before the RB courtship, the latter during it. British Library manuscript version is heavily corrected. 9–10: rejuvenating pilgrim staff image (like Joseph's flowering rod and Joseph of Arimathea's Glastonbury Thorn) reverses Petrarch's Sonnet XVI, which had jokingly compared the young lover to an aged, impotent pilgrim, tottering to Rome. **XLIII.14**: *my* cancelled in original reading, *I shall but love thee better after my death* restored here. **XLIV**: *Hamlet*, IV.v.159–200, IV.vii.166–83, Ophelia imagery.

CASA GUIDI WINDOWS (1851)

This poem, a twice-told tale, is about Italy's struggle for freedom, first from the perspective of victory (1847), then of defeat (1849–50). In between these events, EBB and RB's child, Pen, was born at Casa Guidi (9 March 1849). EBB's Italy was not a unified nation, Tuscany being governed by the Austrian Grand Duke Leopold II of Habsburg-Lorraine; Venice and Milan ruled by the Austrians; the Vatican States by the Pope; Naples and Sicily being oppressed by the Spanish. The Risorgimento was an eventually successful liberation movement, though in 1849 it failed disastrously when the short-lived Roman Republic of Mazzini and Garibaldi fell to the French called in by the Pope. This poem in total is named for the Florentine home of the Brownings, their apartment in the Palazzo Guidi by the Church of San Felice and the Palazzo Pitti, and from whose windows the family witnessed history. Chapman and Hall published it in London (1851). *Casa Guidi Windows* was simultaneously published in an Italian translation in *Scritti Inglesi sulla Politica Contemporanea* in Florence (1851), despite censorship. Italians, to this day, revere EBB's work for the Risorgimento in her verse.

Part One [1848]

Part One centres on the Florentine celebration (12 September 1847), of the Grand Duke's restoration of the people's civic liberties; that day was also the Brownings' first wedding anniversary in Florence. Part One, originally titled 'A Hope in Italy' and 'A Meditation in Tuscany', was rejected by Blackwood, with the suggestion that EBB append explanatory notes to the poem's text. Her footnotes are given in the text; her endnotes are supplied here, signed with her initials: [EBB].

I.1–3: the opening with a child singing of freedom is influenced by RB's 1841 play, *Pippa Passes*, in which a girl worker in Asolo's silk factory, on her one day's holiday a year, sings beneath people's windows, affecting their thoughts and deeds. **3** 'O bella libertà': 'O sweet freedom'. **20, 25–6**: Vincenzo da *Filicaja* (1642–1707), poet, patriot and senator, his sonnet 'All'Italia' translated by Byron in *Childe Harold's Pilgrimage* (1817), IV.xlii

> Oh, God! that thou wert in thy nakedness
> Less lovely or more powerful, and couldst claim
> Thy right, and awe the robbers back, who press
> To shed thy blood, and drink the tears of thy distress;

32 *Cybele*: goddess mourning Atys; *Niobe*: weeping for her children, slaughtered by Apollo and Artemis, was turned into stone by Zeus; see also 'The Death-Bed of Teresa del Riego', line 24. **40–42** *Juliet*: 'They show at Verona an empty trough of stone as the tomb of Juliet' [EBB]. **53** *golden Arno*: river passing through Florence, the Ponte Vecchio, Old Bridge, spanning it houses the Florentine goldsmiths' quarter. **68–70**: *Giotto*'s bell tower, like an exclamation mark (which EBB wrote without the point). **73–97** *the sculptor's Night and Day and Dawn and Twilight . . . in marble scorn*: the 1856 text of *Casa Guidi Windows* gives this line as 'Michel's Night and Day . . .'; Michelangelo's answering epigram to one by Strozzi (Italians traditionally use 'talking statues' for politically dangerous statements) spoke bitterly of Florence's loss of liberty because of the tyrannical Medici, stating his Night had best not wake; he shows Dawn who has done so with an expression of agony; see also note to *AL*, II.66. *Aurora Leigh*'s title and its heroine's name are taken in part from this sculpture; 'In the Sagrestia Nuova, where the statues of Day and Night, Dawn and Twilight, recline on the tombs of Giuliano de' Medici, third son of Lorenzo the Magnificent, and Lorenzo of Urbino, his grandson. Strozzi's epigram on the Night, with Michel Angelo's rejoinder, is well known' [EBB]. **98–120**: 'This mocking task was set by Pietro, the unworthy successor of Lorenzo the Magnificent' [EBB]. **147–50**: text here supplied from later editions. **168** 'Se tu men bella fossi, Italia!': 'Had you been less fair, Italy!', Filicaja. **190** *nympholept*: Ruskin complained about EBB's use of word. See Frederic Kenyon, ed., The *Letters of Elizabeth Barrett Browning* (Florence, 2 June 1855), where she defined 'nympholepsy' as 'that mystical passion for an invisible nymph common to a certain class of visionaries', and quoted Byron's 'The nympholepsy of a fond despair.' She continued, in her letter to Ruskin, 'We are all nympholepts in running after our ideals – and none more than yourself, indeed!' **195** *phylacteries*: parchment inscribed with Exodus 13.1–6; Deuteronomy 6.4–9, 11.13–21, placed in leather boxes bound on the forehead and arm with thongs. **253** *griffins*: Dante, *Purgatorio*, XXIX.107. **255–99**: Girolama Savonarola forced Lorenzo de' Medici on his deathbed to restore the Florentine Republic, whose King was Christ. See George Eliot, *Romola* (1862–3). 'Savonarola was burnt in martyrdom for his testimony against Papal corruptions as early as March 1498: and, as late as our own day, it is a custom in Florence to strew violets on the pavement where he suffered, in grateful recognition of the anniversary' [EBB]. **266–7** *Peter sank*: Mark 4.37–41. **274** *star-looks*: St Dominic associated with a star, from his godmother at his baptism seeing a most bright star upon his brow, Dante, *Paradiso*, XII.61–3; Fra Angelico's frescoes of St Dominic, San Marco, show the star; by association Savonarola, a Dominican at the convent of San Marco, has a 'star-look'. **309** *Asaph*: chief musician to David. See also 'Sonnets from the Portuguese', III.9; Harvard A and Yale manuscripts have 'Timotheus', a Greek musician who introduced polyphony, corrupting the Spartans by his music. **314** *Miriam*: Exodus 15.20–21; see also *AL*, I.87, II.170–71, III.203, VIII.334–5, 1021–2. **320–73** *St. Maria Novella*: Boccaccio's *Decameron* (1351–3) begins here in plague-tide; see also *AL*, VIII.50–58. **322** *Macchiavel*: 'See his description of the plague in Florence' [EBB]; Nicolò Machiavelli, *Istorie Fiorentine* (1434), merely tells reader to see description Boccaccio gives. **328–9**: Andrea and Jacopo *Orcagna*'s fresco of Dante's *Inferno*, Strozzi Chapel, Santa Maria Novelle (1354–7). **332–4**: *Cimabue's* (1240–1301) *Virgin* in EBB's day was in Rucellai Chapel, Santa Maria Novelle, now in Uffizi; 'Charles of Anjou, whom, in his passage through Florence, Cimabue allowed to see this picture while yet in his "Bottega". The populace followed the royal visitor, and in the universal delight and admiration, the quarter of the city in which the artist lived was called "Borgo Allegri". The picture was carried in triumph to the church, and deposited there' [EBB]. **362–78** *Giotto . . . whom Cimabue found*: 'How Cimabue found Giotto [1266–1336], the shepherd-boy, sketching a ram of his flock upon a stone, is a pretty story told by Vasari, – who also relates that the elder artist Margheritone died "infastidito" of the successes of the new school' [EBB]. EBB's art criticism is exactly contemporary with the founding of the Pre-Raphaelite Brotherhood, early 1848; her friend was the art historian, Anna Jameson. **390**: Fra Giovanni da Fiesole *Angelico* (1387–1455), Dominican artist monk at San Marco. **425** *Marathon*: EBB's Homeric, Byronic poem (1820) on the battle of 490 BC, in which Athenians defeated Persians. **471–2** *Casa Guidi windows*: RB and EBB watched from the front windows of the Palazzo Guidi, which had the better view, rather than from those of their own apartment on the piano nobile. **493** *the new Pope*: Pius IX, 'Pio Nono', appeared to be a friend of Risorgimento, then proved to be tyrannical, calling in the French, fleeing to the repressive Kingdom of the Two Sicilies, dashing Italian hopes. **499** *'Il popolo'*:

'the people', motto of exiled Giuseppe Mazzini (1805–72); see also *Casa Guildi Windows*, II.442, 526. **546**: EBB's ecstatic footnote in text deleted in 1856 edition. **623** *Santa Croce church*: 'The Florentines, to whom the Ravennese denied the body of Dante which was asked of them in a "late remorse of love", have given a cenotaph to their divine poet in this church. Something less than a grave!' [EBB] **629** *Giotto drew*: 'In allusion to Mr. Kirkup's well-known discovery of Giotto's fresco-portrait of Dante' [EBB]. See EBB letter to Mrs Jameson (2 April 1850). **873–87** *Pellico's Venetian dungeon . . . Spielberg's grate . . . the brothers Bandiera*: references to Italian political prisoners in Austrian-controlled prisons. **1124** *Vespucci Amerigo*: (1451–1512) Florentine traveller to New World after whom America was named. **1127** *Milton's Fiesole*: Milton visited Florence and Galileo, described Fiesole and Valdarno (*Paradise Lost*, I.287–9):

> The Moon, whose Orb
> Through Optic Glass the Tuscan Artist views
> At Ev'ning from the top of Fesolè.

Today, one may look through that telescope in the Museo del'Istoria della Scienza in Florence. **1128** *Langlande's Malvern*: medieval poet, William Langland, from Malvern, where EBB grew up, wrote *Piers Plowman* concerning 1381 Peasants' Revolt. **1129** *Vallombrosa*: beautiful wooded region near Florence, mentioned by Milton, *Paradise Lost*, I.302–4; see also *AL*, I.616; Milton and RB played organ at abbey; EBB, because she was a woman, was ordered to leave after a three days' stay, successfully resisting for another two (14–19 July 1847). It is advisable to visit Vallombrosa Abbey on any Sunday when Florence becomes unbearably hot and hear the organ played at Mass, then picnic in the Pratomagno beneath the chestnut woods. **1179–82**: 'Galileo's villa near Florence is built on an eminence called Bellosguardo' [EEB]; this is setting for conclusion of *AL*; the Brownings' friend, Isa Blagden, had her villa there. **1203–10** *Naples . . . Palermo*: Kingdom of Two Sicilies, Palermo Revolt (two squares from 'Sicilian Vespers' of Easter Monday, 1282), on 12 January 1848, caused Neapolitans to demand a Constitution; these are Garibaldi's Risorgimento campaigns.

Part Two

Part Two was written and published, together with Part One, in 1851, after the birth of EBB's child, Pen Browning (9 March 1849), after the failure of the 1849 Roman Republic, and after first the visit and then the death of Margaret Fuller in 1850. EBB had watched both the celebration of Tuscan freedom (12 September 1847), of Part One and the arrival of the Austrian occupying forces (2–5 May 1849), of Part Two from the windows next to their apartments of the Palazzo Guidi. EBB, being republican in her sympathies, renamed the Palazzo simply 'Casa Guidi', and had their salon decorated in red, white and green, the colours of the illegal flag of the Italian Risorgimento (worn by Dante's Beatrice in *Purgatorio*, XXX.31–3). EBB was also to write *AL* in that room.

II.13 *Could'st thou not watch one hour?*: Christ to Peter at Gethsemane, Mark 14.37. **20** *Atrides' roof (with lintel-post which still drips blood*: combines Aeschylus' *Agamemnon* and Exodus' Passover, 12.7, where the lintel posts were marked by the blood of the Pascal Lamb. **36**: Grand Duke of Tuscany, *Leopold* II of Habsburg-Lorraine, was to use Austrian military might against the Italian people he ruled (May 1849); Medici line had died out. **110** *motu proprios*: papal document wielded by Pope in his own person; Pio Nono initially, under Gioberti's influence, in 1848 appeared to favour Italian sovereignty in such a document. **136**: Francesco Domenico *Guerrazzi* made Dictator of Tuscan Republic in March 1849, overthrown in May 1849. **190** *Yorick*: Hamlet addresses skull of court jester Yorick in graveyard scene, V.i.181. **226**: Giuseppe Verdi's *opera*, *The Sicilian Vespers* (1855), was applauded with cries of 'Viva Verdi!', the name spelling the initials of Vittorio Emanuele Re d'Italia, the people thus acclaiming 'Long live King Victor Emanuel, King of Italy!', despite censorship. At that time Victor Emanuel was only King of Sardinia and Piedmont, not becoming King of Italy until 1861. **372**: Battle of *Novara*, fought (March 23 1849) between the Austrians and the forces of King Charles Albert of Piedmont and Sardinia. **442, 526**: Giuseppe *Mazzini* (1805–72), Italian patriot and architect of the short-lived Roman Republic (1849), friend of Margaret Fuller and the Carlyles; see also *Casa Guidi Windows*, I.499. **480**: sacrificial blood from Jerusalem's Temple drained into *Cedron's brook* outside the city wall, Judas's potter's field being near by, John 18.1; Matthew 27.8–10; Acts 1.18–19. **486–91**, *ephod . . . Urim . . . Thummim*: High Priest Aaron's garb and breastplate with precious stones; bells and pomegranates adorn ephod, Exodus 28.6–39. **496** *last chrism*: poured by Mary Magdalen on Christ, anointing him 'Christ', Matthew 26.6–16; Mark 14.3–11, 16.1; Luke 7.36–8.3, 23.55–24.11; John 12.1–8, 19.40. **509** *twined linen*: see note to 'Sonnets from the Portuguese', X.3. **545**: Count Pellegrino *Rossi*, minister to Pope Pius IX (Pio Nono), assassinated (November 1848), in manner similar to Caesar's, on the stairs of the Palazzo della Cancelleria. **546** *Brutus*: Caesar's assassin. **556–65**: Michelangelo sculpted *Brutus*'s bust, implying Florentines should assassinate tyrants to restore Florentine Republic, then left the work unfinished. **587** *Crystal Palace*: Exhibition of 1851, encouraged by Prince Albert, heralded Industrial Age; see note to 'Hiram Powers' Greek

Slave'. **678–94** *Garibaldi's wife*: Anita was pregnant when her husband was fighting for the Roman Republic; they fled together at the defeat, she died in his arms in childbirth near Ravenna, was hastily buried in the sand, dogs dug up the body; Giuseppe Garibaldi, leader of the 'Red-shirts', in exile when EBB wrote these lines, was to return and fight for Italy's Risorgimento (1859–60), which would not succeed until 1870. **705** *exiled patriot*: King Charles Albert of Piedmont and Sardinia, was equivocal about Risorgimento, died four months after his defeat at Novara, repenting his treachery to Italy, having abdicated his throne to his son, King Victor Emanuel II. **743** *my own young Florentine*: Pen Browning, EBB's child, born when she was in her forties; he resembled her and even had his hair dressed in long spaniel-like ringlets as did she, but unlike her he was not crippled. **783** *The Vail, lean inward to the mercy-seat*: description of Exodus tabernacle has cherubim adorn it, Exodus 25.18–20; EBB says her child is such a cherub.

FROM *TWO POEMS BY ELIZABETH BARRETT AND ROBERT BROWNING* (1854)

A Plea for the Ragged Schools of London

Originally published, coupled with a poem by RB, for EBB's sister Arabella Barrett's Ragged School and sold for sixpence.

XXI.81 'Angli angeli!': Pope Gregory I, seeing blue-eyed, blond-haired slaves in Roman market, asked where they came from, was told they were Angles, said they were like angels, sent missionaries to pagan island to convert Angles to Christianity, Bede, *Ecclesiastical History of the English People*, II.1.

FROM *POEMS BEFORE CONGRESS* (1860)

AL, published in 1856, was EBB's greatest achievement. But EBB and RB, the most romantic couple of their age, after ten years of an idyllic marriage, grew apart during the last five. They quarrelled over the raising of Pen, especially his long hair, and over EBB's liberation politics and growing dependency on spiritualism. RB's opposition to her in-creased EBB's passionate convictions and diminished her desire to live.

EBB's poetry during their marriage supported the household while RB's, except for *Men and Women*, during this period lay dormant. He was her literary agent and also interested in sculpting, reading the papers in the male-only Vieusseux reading room, and meeting with a circle of friends.

The Hawthornes first met the Brownings on 8 June 1858, Sophia Amelia Hawthorne describing the visit:

[A]t eight we went to the illustrious Casa Guidi. We found a little boy in an upper hall . . . . In the dim light he looked like a waif of poetry, drifted up into the dark corner, with long, curling, brown hair, and buff silk tunic, embroidered with white. He took us through an anteroom, into the drawing room, and out upon the balcony. In a brighter light he was lovelier still, with brown eyes, fair skin, and a slender, graceful figure. In a moment Mr. Browning appeared, and welcomed us cordially. In a church near by, opposite the house, a melodious choir was chanting. . . . The music, the stars, the flowers, Mr. Browning and his child, all combined to entrance my wits. Then Mrs. Browning came out to us—very small, delicate, dark, and expressive. She looked like a spirit. A cloud of hair falls on each side of her face in curls, so as partly to veil her features. But out of the veil look sweet, sad eyes, musing and farseeing and weird. Her fairy fingers seem too airy to hold, and yet their pressure was very firm and strong. The smallest possible amount of substance encloses her soul, and every particle of it is infused with heart and intellect. I was never conscious of so little unredeemed perishable dust in any human being. . . . We soon returned to the drawing room—a lofty, spacious apartment, hung with gobelin tapestry and pictures, and filled with carved furniture and objects of vertu. Everything harmonized—poet, poetess, child, house, the rich air and the starry night. . . . Tea was brought and served on a long, narrow table, placed before a sofa, and Mrs. Browning presided. . . . Mr. Browning introduced the subject of spiritism, and there was an animated talk. Mr. Browning cannot believe, and Mrs. Browning cannot help believing.

The Prince of Wales, in March of 1859, at Victoria's request, met with RB in Rome, not with EBB (Frederic Kenyon, ed., *The Letters of Elizabeth Barrett Browning*, 27 March 1859). Shattered by the apparent failure of Italy's Risorgimento, EBB wrote from Siena in August of that year to Isa Blagden of her dreams in which she would follow a mystic woman down palatial corridors, a woman in white, with a white mask on her head the likeness of a crown, who was Italy. She was also disturbed by RB's infatuation with 'The Old Yellow Book', a collection of legal documents in connection with the murder of Pompilia by her husband, Guido Franceschini, in 1698, which RB found in the San Lorenzo market in Florence (June 1860). She sensed RB's identification of Pompilia with herself.

EBB's *Poems before Congress* (London: Chapman and Hall) of 1860 lack the persuasive subtlety of her earlier masterpieces. The volume was deemed a failure on both sides of the Atlantic. Tuberculosis, laudanum, anorexia and estrangement from RB were taking their toll. She lived only one more year.

Christmas Gifts

Italy's Risorgimento, when EBB wrote this poem and when she died, was not yet completed, the Papal States, supported by the French, resisting the unification of Italy until 1870. EBB was deeply Christian, but criticized the Papal States' political oppression.

Motto: 'ὡς βασιλεῖ, ὡς θεῷ, ὡς νεκρῷ.': 'As to a king, as to a god, as to a corpse.' **IV.21** *bear*: 2 Kings 2.23-4. **22** *fox*: Judges 14.4-5. **23** *wolf*: Romulus and Remus legend; similar to three beasts of Dante's *Inferno*, I.31-60. **VII.39-41** *Red . . . Green . . . White*: colours of Risorgimento, banned in Papal States, based by patriots on Beatrice's garb, *Purgatorio*, XXX.31-3, today Italy's flag. **VIII.47** *peacock-fans*: then used in papal pomps, emblematic of imperial pride.

FROM *LAST POEMS* (1862)

The North and the South [*1861*]

EBB was barely well enough to attend a party for Pen in Rome in May 1861, at which Hans Christian Andersen recited 'The Ugly Duckling' and RB led the children in 'The Pied Piper of Hamelin'. This poem, 'The North and the South', was written to commemorate that event and sent to Thackeray for the *Cornhill Magazine* (21 May 1861). EBB died in RB's arms as he was attempting to feed her at Casa Guidi in Florence (29 June 1861). RB published EBB's *Last Poems* (London: Chapman and Hall) after her death, and included this work as 'The Last Poem'.

Psyche Gazing on Cupid [*1845*]

RB also included her translations from the Greek and Latin, among them a series of poems from Apuleius' *Metamorphoses*, in the 1862 volume of *Last Poems*. This episode 'Psyche Gazing on Cupid' is from V.22-3, but RB incorrectly gave it as being from *Metamorphoses*, IV. EBB had written to John Kenyon in April 1845, during RB's Wimpole

Street courtship, speaking of her translations from Apuleius, noting that she is not sending Kenyon this one she has just finished, of 'Psyche contemplating Cupid'. In the autumn of 1860, EBB wrote in a letter that RB was sculpting two busts, one of young Augustus, the other of Psyche. A marble sculpture of this Apuleian scene is in the Florentine Uffizi Tribune, that Medicean collection of art she knew and loved and which is the repository of so much of EBB's imagery. See also *AL*, I.156, VIII.666-7, 1113-17, *Casa Guidi Windows*, I.140-44.

Once RB gave his wife a ring carved with Florence's lilies by the Castellani brothers. The Castellani were Roman patriots, some of whom were imprisoned in the Castel Sant'Angelo for their politics. They showed Harriet Beecher Stowe an onyx statue of an Egyptian slave and said to her, 'Italy also is a slave.' She stood in their shop in tears. At EBB's death, Florence, now capital of liberated Italy (except for the Papal States), placed a tablet on the Casa Guidi honouring EBB's poetic service to the newly freed nation, its words written in Italian by the poet Niccoló Tommaseo (1802-74):

> HERE WROTE AND DIED
> ELIZABETH BARRETT BROWNING
> WHO IN A WOMAN'S HEART HARMONIZED THE
> LEARNING OF A SCHOLAR AND THE INSPIRATION OF A POET
> AND MADE OF HER VERSE A GOLDEN RING
> WEDDING ITALY AND ENGLAND.
> THIS TABLET IS PLACED BY
> GRATEFUL FLORENCE
> 1861

It was from these lines and from 'The Old Yellow Book' of documents of a murder trial he found one day in San Lorenzo's market in Florence that RB forged his ring for his book, *The Ring and the Book*.

> Do you see this Ring?
>   'Tis Rome-work, made to match
> (By Castellani's imitative craft)
> Etrurian circlets . . .

opens that work;

> Thy rare gold ring of verse (the poet praised)
> Linking our England to his Italy!

closes it.

Years later, RB told Katherine Bronson of the tiny Castellani ring and the Venetian coin he always wore on his watch chain: 'This was hers . . . Can you believe that a woman could wear such a circlet as this? It is a child's.' (She said herself she was 'five feet one high', though her spinal condition would have further contracted that height, and 'Sonnets from the Portuguese', XIX.10–11 notes that her 'head . . . hangs aside/Through sorrow's trick'.) The coin was struck with the date 1848 to record the freedom of Venice from Austrian domination. RB continued, 'I love this coin as she would have loved it. You know what she felt and wrote about United Italy.'

The poets' son, Robert Wiedemann, Pen, Browning, failed Classics at Balliol, Benjamin Jowett saying he was not the scholar his mother was, and then became an artist, studying, like Camille Claudel, under Rodin. His model, Ginevra, from Brittany, was likely his illegitimate daughter, thus EBB's grandchild. He called a bronze bust he cast of her *Pompilia*, after the heroine of *The Ring and the Book*. *AL* and *The Ring and the Book* are spousal poems – but in *AL* EBB blinds Romney and in *The Ring and the Book* RB murders Pompilia. Today, RB's bones lie in pomp in Westminster Abbey's Poets' Corner, while EBB's remains, though she was proposed as Queen Victoria's Poet Laureate, are in exile, entombed in the Protestant Cemetery of Florence.

INDEX OF TITLES

INDEX OF FIRST LINES

READ MORE IN PENGUIN

In every corner of the world, on every subject under the sun, Penguin represents quality and variety – the very best in publishing today.

For complete information about books available from Penguin – including Puffins, Penguin Classics and Arkana – and how to order them, write to us at the appropriate address below. Please note that for copyright reasons the selection of books varies from country to country.

In the United Kingdom: Please write to *Dept. JC, Penguin Books Ltd, FREEPOST, West Drayton, Middlesex UB7 OBR.*

If you have any difficulty in obtaining a title, please send your order with the correct money, plus ten per cent for postage and packaging, to *PO Box No. 11, West Drayton, Middlesex UB7 OBR*

In the United States: Please write to *Consumer Sales, Penguin USA, P.O. Box 999, Dept. 17109, Bergenfield, New Jersey 07621-0120.* VISA and MasterCard holders call 1-800-253-6476 to order all Penguin titles

In Canada: Please write to *Penguin Books Canada Ltd, 10 Alcorn Avenue, Suite 300, Toronto, Ontario M4V 3B2*

In Australia: Please write to *Penguin Books Australia Ltd, P.O. Box 257, Ringwood, Victoria 3134*

In New Zealand: Please write to *Penguin Books (NZ) Ltd, Private Bag 102902, North Shore Mail Centre, Auckland 10*

In India: Please write to *Penguin Books India Pvt Ltd, 706 Eros Apartments, 56 Nehru Place, New Delhi 110 019*

In the Netherlands: Please write to *Penguin Books Netherlands bv, Postbus 3507, NL-1001 AH Amsterdam*

In Germany: Please write to *Penguin Books Deutschland GmbH, Metzlerstrasse 26, 60594 Frankfurt am Main*

In Spain: Please write to *Penguin Books S. A., Bravo Murillo 19, 1° B, 28015 Madrid*

In Italy: Please write to *Penguin Italia s.r.l., Via Felice Casati 20, I–20124 Milano*

In France: Please write to *Penguin France S. A., 17 rue Lejeune, F–31000 Toulouse*

In Japan: Please write to *Penguin Books Japan, Ishikiribashi Building, 2–5–4, Suido, Bunkyo-ku, Tokyo 112*

In Greece: Please write to *Penguin Hellas Ltd, Dimocritou 3, GR–106 71 Athens*

In South Africa: Please write to *Longman Penguin Southern Africa (Pty) Ltd, Private Bag X08, Bertsham 2013*

READ MORE IN PENGUIN

A CHOICE OF CLASSICS

Matthew Arnold	**Selected Prose**
Jane Austen	**Emma**
	Lady Susan/The Watsons/Sanditon
	Mansfield Park
	Northanger Abbey
	Persuasion
	Pride and Prejudice
	Sense and Sensibility
William Barnes	**Selected Poems**
Anne Brontë	**Agnes Grey**
	The Tenant of Wildfell Hall
Charlotte Brontë	**Jane Eyre**
	Shirley
	Villette
Emily Brontë	**Wuthering Heights**
Samuel Butler	**Erewhon**
	The Way of All Flesh
Thomas Carlyle	**Selected Writings**
Arthur Hugh Clough	**Selected Poems**
Wilkie Collins	**The Moonstone**
	The Woman in White
Charles Darwin	**The Origin of Species**
	The Voyage of the _Beagle_
Benjamin Disraeli	**Sybil**
George Eliot	**Adam Bede**
	Daniel Deronda
	Felix Holt
	Middlemarch
	The Mill on the Floss
	Romola
	Scenes of Clerical Life
	Silas Marner
Elizabeth Gaskell	**Cranford/Cousin Phillis**
	The Life of Charlotte Brontë
	Mary Barton
	North and South
	Wives and Daughters

READ MORE IN PENGUIN

A CHOICE OF CLASSICS

READ MORE IN PENGUIN

A CHOICE OF CLASSICS

Lord Macaulay	**The History of England**
Henry Mayhew	**London Labour and the London Poor**
John Stuart Mill	**The Autobiography**
	On Liberty
William Morris	**News from Nowhere and Selected Writings and Designs**
John Henry Newman	**Apologia Pro Vita Sua**
Robert Owen	**A New View of Society and Other Writings**
Walter Pater	**Marius the Epicurean**
John Ruskin	**'Unto This Last' and Other Writings**
Walter Scott	**Ivanhoe**
	Heart of Midlothian
Robert Louis Stevenson	**Kidnapped**
	Dr Jekyll and Mr Hyde and Other Stories
William Makepeace Thackeray	**The History of Henry Esmond**
	The History of Pendennis
	Vanity Fair
Anthony Trollope	**Barchester Towers**
	Can You Forgive Her?
	The Eustace Diamonds
	Framley Parsonage
	He Knew He Was Right
	The Last Chronicle of Barset
	Phineas Finn
	The Prime Minister
	The Small House at Allington
	The Warden
	The Way We Live Now
Oscar Wilde	**Complete Short Fiction**
Mary Wollstonecraft	**A Vindication of the Rights of Woman**
	Mary and Maria
	Matilda
Dorothy and William Wordsworth	**Home at Grasmere**